I0131386

LABOUR IN VIETNAM

The **Institute of Southeast Asian Studies (ISEAS)** was established as an autonomous organization in 1968. It is a regional centre dedicated to the study of socio-political, security and economic trends and developments in Southeast Asia and its wider geostrategic and economic environment. The Institute's research programmes are the Regional Economic Studies (RES, including ASEAN and APEC), Regional Strategic and Political Studies (RSPS), and Regional Social and Cultural Studies (RSCS).

ISEAS Publishing, an established academic press, has issued more than 2,000 books and journals. It is the largest scholarly publisher of research about Southeast Asia from within the region. ISEAS Publishing works with many other academic and trade publishers and distributors to disseminate important research and analyses from and about Southeast Asia to the rest of the world.

The **Vietnam Update** is a series of annual conferences that focus on recent economic, political and social conditions in Vietnam and provide in-depth analysis on a theme of particular relevance to Vietnam's socio-economic development. The first Vietnam Update was held at the Australian National University in 1990. In recent years, the series has been organized in conjunction with ISEAS.

VIETNAM UPDATE SERIES

LABOUR IN VIETNAM

EDITED BY
ANITA CHAN

ISEAS

Institute of Southeast Asian Studies
Singapore

First published in Singapore in 2011 by ISEAS Publishing
Institute of Southeast Asian Studies
30 Heng Mui Keng Terrace
Pasir Panjang
Singapore 119614

E-mail: publish@iseas.edu.sg
Website: http://bookshop.iseas.edu.sg

All rights reserved. No part of this publication may be reproduced, stored in a retrieval system, or transmitted in any form or by any means, electronic, mechanical, photocopying, recording or otherwise, without the prior permission of the Institute of Southeast Asian Studies.

© 2011 Institute of Southeast Asian Studies, Singapore

The responsibility for facts and opinions in this publication rests exclusively with the editor and contributors and their interpretations do not necessarily reflect the views or the policy of the Insititute or its supporters.

ISEAS Library Cataloguing-in-Publication Data

Chan, Anita.
    Labour in Vietnam.
    1.   Labour—Vietnam.
    I.   Title.
    II. Series: Vietnam update series.
HD8700.5 C45   2011

ISBN 978-981-4311-94-6 (soft cover)
ISBN 978-981-4311-95-3 (PDF)

Photo Credit
Cover photograph by Hong-zen Wang: Shop floor at a large foreign-owned factory in Vietnam

Typeset by International Typesetters Pte Ltd
Printed in Singapore by

CONTENTS

TABLES AND FIGURES

Tables

Figures

ABBREVIATIONS

ADB	Asian Development Bank
ACFTU	All-China Federation of Trade Unions
CBA	collective bargaining agreement
CEE	Compagnie des Eaux et d'Electricité
CFTC	French Confederation of Christian Workers
CGT	Confédération Générale du Travail
CIA	Central Intelligence Agency
COAM	Le Centre des Archives d'Outre-Mer
CIEM	Central Institute for Economic Management
CoC	code of conduct
Comecon	Council for Mutual Economic Assistance
CPV	Communist Party of Vietnam
CSR	Corporate Social Responsibility
CVT	Vietnamese Confederation of Labour
CVTC	Vietnamese Confederation of Christian Workers
DOLISA	Department of Labour, Invalids, and Social Affairs
DRV	Democratic Republic of Vietnam
EIU	Economist Intelligence Unit
EPZ	Export Processing Zone
EVTA	Employment and Vocational Training Administration
FDI	foreign direct investment
FLA	Fair Labour Association
GMMA	George Meany Memorial Archives
GTZ	Deutsche Gesellschaft für Technische Zusammenarbeit
HCMC	Ho Chi Minh City

HEPZA	HCMC Export-Processing Zones Authority
HDQT	Hoi Dong Quan Tri
IFC	International Finance Corporation
IFCTU	International Federation of Christian Trade Unions
ILO	International Labour Organization
ILSSA	Institute of Labour Science and Social Affairs
IOM	International Migration Organization
ITUV	Independent Trade Union of Vietnam
IWAY	IKEA Way
IZ	industrial zone
KMRT	Kaohsiung Mass Rapid Transit Company
MEC	Mountain Equipment Cooperative
MNC	multinational corporation
MOI	Ministry of the Interior
MOLISA	Ministry of Labour, Invalids, and Social Affairs
NA	National Archives, College Park, Maryland
NGO	non-governmental organization
NLF	National Liberation Front
OCP	Office of Civilian Personnel
PRA	participatory rural appraisal
PRO	Public Records Office
RLS	ratcheting labour system
RVN	Republic of Vietnam
SOE	state-owned enterprise
SRV	Socialist Republic of Vietnam
TCC	Tripartite Consultative Committee
USOM	United States Operations Mission
UWFA	United Workers–Farmers Association
VCA	Vietnamese Cooperatives Alliance
VCCI	Vietnam Chamber of Commerce and Industry
VFTU	Vietnam Federation of Trade Unions
VGCL	Vietnam Confederation of Labour
VITAS	Vietnam Textile and Garment Association
WRAP	Worldwide Responsible Apparel Foundation

ACKNOWLEDGEMENTS

This book originated from the annual Vietnam Update conference held in November 2008 at the Australian National University. Since 1990, each year the Vietnam Update conference focuses on one particular economic, political, or social issue in Vietnam and provides in-depth analyses of its particular relevance to Vietnam's socio-economic development.

Vietnam's economic development has been galloping at high speed for a decade, leading to a proliferation of factories and industrial zones. In view of this, the conference organizing committee decided that it was timely to devote a conference volume to the issue of labour in Vietnam.

Leading researchers from around the world were invited to write papers on this topic for publication, and the conference provided an opportunity to hear and discuss their papers. I subsequently arranged for eleven papers to be evaluated by external referees. On the basis of the conference discussions and the referees' and my own suggestions, eight of the authors have revised their contributions and have integrated their chapters into the overall book. The volume also includes a jointly authored chapter by Professor Hong-zen Wang and Danièle Bélanger.

Thanks are due to the main sponsors of the conference: the Australian National University, Singapore's Institute of Southeast Asian Studies, the Australian Agency for International Development (AusAID), and Taiwan's Chiang Ching-Kuo Foundation for International Scholarly Exchange.

I am indebted to Janelle Caiger for copyediting the first revised drafts and to Dayaneetha de Silva for editing, standardizing, and formatting the entire manuscript. I am also grateful to the Chiang Ching-Kuo Foundation for underwriting the cost of copyediting. Finally, I am indebted to the Vietnam Update organizing committee, and particularly Philip Taylor, who provided me with enormous help when organizing the conference.

THE CONTRIBUTORS

DANIÈLE BÉLANGER is Associate Professor of Sociology at the University of Western Ontario, London, Canada. She is the holder of the Canada Research Chair in Population, Gender and Development. Her current research focuses on labour and marriage migration from Vietnam to East Asian countries. She is the co-editor of Reconfiguring Families in Contemporary Vietnam (Stanford University Press, 2009).

ANITA CHAN is Research Professor at the China Research Centre of the University of Technology, Sydney and Visiting Fellow, Political and Social Change Department, Australian National University. She has published widely on Chinese labour issues, rural China, and Chinese youth. She recently published, as co-author *Chen Village: Revolution to Globalization* (University of California Press, 2009) and edited *Wal-Mart in China* (in press). She has launched a new research project on China's auto industry.

SUHONG CHAE is Associate Professor and Department Head, Department of Archaeology and Anthropology, Chonbuk National University. He was General Director, Korean Association of Southeast Asian Study (2007–2009). His research has included the changing politics of production in multinational factories in Vietnam; Vietnamese perspectives on the region; and Vietnamese transnational labour.

MICHAEL KARADJIS has recently completed a PhD in the Department of Political and Social Change, Research School of Pacific and Asian Studies,

The Australian National University on *The Vietnamese Communist Party Debate and the Leading Role of the State Sector: Ideological Straight-jacket, Vested Interests or Real Social Progress?* He is currently a teacher at the Royal Melbourne Institute of Technology in Hanoi, Vietnam.

BENEDICT J. TRIA KERKVLIET, Emeritus Professor at The Australian National University, is also an Affiliate Graduate Faculty member at the University of Hawai'i. His research emphasizes politics in the Philippines and Vietnam. His books include *Beyond Hanoi: Local Government in Vietna*m, co-edited with David G. Marr (Institute of Southeast Asian Studies, 2004), and *The Power of Everyday Politics: How Vietnamese Peasants Transformed National Policy* (Cornell University Press, 2005).

JEE YOUNG KIM is Assistant Professor of Sociology at The Chinese University of Hong Kong. She obtained her Ph.D. from Harvard University in 2008. Her research centres on various factors shaping labour conditions in Vietnam's factories. The main focus is on the effectiveness of transnational private regulation in shaping factory conditions.

NGUYEN PHUONG LE is a scholar of Agricultural Economics and Sustainable Development. She has been a lecturer on Policy and Rural Development in the Faculty of Economics and Rural Development, Hanoi University of Agriculture since 1994. She has conducted research related to rural livelihood, the gender division of labour and agrarian transformation in northern Vietnam.

ANGIE NGOC TRAN is Professor of Political Economy at California State University, Monterey Bay. Her research includes gender division of labour, labour resistance, labour codes of conduct in Vietnam, role of the Vietnamese state, labour unions and their press in labour-management relations. Ongoing projects include studies of Vietnamese migrant workers in Vietnam, East and Southeast Asia; the role of cultural identity, class and law in Vietnamese labour movements (dating back to colonial French); and comparison between Vietnamese and Cambodian migrant workers.

HONG-ZEN WANG is Professor of Sociology at the National Sun Yat-sen University, Kaohsiung, Taiwan. His current research focuses on marriage and labour migration between Vietnam and Taiwan. He is the co-editor of the recent published books *Cross-Border Marriages with Asian Characteristics* and *To Cross or Not to Cross: Transnational Taiwan, Taiwan's Transnationality* (both by CAPAS, Academia Sinica, 2009).

EDMUND F. WEHRLE is Associate Professor of History at Eastern Illinois University and the author of *Between a River and a Mountain: The AFL-CIO, the Vietnamese Confederation of Labor, and the Vietnam War* (University of Michigan Press, 2005), and *America and the World: Ideas, Trade and Warfare* (co-authored with Lawrence Peskin, forthcoming). He is currently at work on a study of Vietnamese civilians working for the U.S. military during the Second Indochinese War.

1

INTRODUCTION

Anita Chan

It has been three decades since Vietnam began to liberalize its planned economy and two-and-a-half decades since the policy of *Doi Moi* (renovation) was officially introduced. Today, alongside China, Vietnam is an "economic miracle" — a Communist Party-led state that has successfully transformed its economy and whose export industry is internationally competitive. With an average GDP growth rate of almost 7 per cent over this entire period of transformation, Vietnam is one of the fastest-growing economies in the world. It has become an attractive destination for foreign direct investment (FDI) in good part because Vietnamese labour is considered "cheap", at about half the wage level of China.

Rapid urbanization and industrialization could not take place in Vietnam without a growing industrial labour force, and it is this new "proletariat" under *Doi Moi* that is the subject of this volume. "Proletariat" is used here as a reminder that Vietnam still calls itself a socialist state, and it is within this context that this Introduction is situated. As will be seen, in the view of one of the contributors, Michael Karadjis, for the time being Vietnam's state-sector workers are still in a halfway house.

1

VIETNAM AND THE ASIAN MARKET-SOCIALISM DEVELOPMENT MODEL

In the early 1990s, shortly after the collapse of the communist one-party regimes of the Soviet Union and Eastern Europe, the question arose as to what would occur in the last two remaining socialist countries that counted — Vietnam and China. By then, both countries were embarking on the road to "market socialism". Where would their political, economic, and social transformation lead them? Would they be able to succeed in their "latecomer" development projects (see Woodside 1999)?

Twenty years on, these two states have jumped the hurdle of late development and have been able to catch up on lost time. Still using five-year plans, but minus the hitherto authoritarian and rigid top-down methods of implementation, they have succeeded in transforming themselves from the status of poor Third World countries into what are today known as newly emerging economies. They have proved to the world that economic development can be achieved under a one-party state, that they are in fact more efficient, better organized, and developing faster than almost all of the "democratic" states. Vietnam and China embody a new model of Asian development, termed the "Beijing Consensus" by some political economists, in place of the "Washington Consensus" (Lee and Mathews 2010, pp. 86–103). Well-planned industrial policies managed by the state, as had been practised in a few earlier developed Asian states — Japan, Korea and Taiwan—have proved to be more effective than neoliberal policies that profess to rely on the globalized free market. Refusing to transform themselves into democratic multi-party states, Vietnam and China have also shown themselves capable of integrating their economies with the global economy.

While making a transition to market-based operations, Vietnam has nonetheless retained a substantial state-managed and owned industrial sector. Michael Karadjis's chapter on state enterprise workers explores their circumstances. Though this sector shrank in the earlier *Doi Moi* period, as of 1996 state-owned enterprises (SOEs) still accounted for half of the industrial output, though their share declined to 34 per cent by 2004 (Beresford 2008, p. 228), since when the percentage has stabilized.

The party–state has continued to support and reform the state-owned sector, which influences the labour conditions of SOE employees. Using documentation and field research findings at two state enterprises, Karadjis convincingly argues in his chapter that "while Vietnamese workers were never absolute 'masters', their traditional participation in the workplace has continued to have a role in the state enterprises' decision-making and this has prevented them from becoming commodities in the post-*Doi Moi* period." The survival of socialist ideology in SOEs allows for the continued existence of workplace institutions such as the workers' congress, trade union, youth league, and the war veterans' groups, which have some participatory rights in management. Despite never having been able to fully exercise these rights, these bodies are avenues through which informal pressure can be exerted on management. Most tellingly, state enterprise workers earn more than workers who are employed in the FDI factories in Vietnam, even though the minimum wage set for the state sector is lower than for the FDI sector. When welfare benefits and shorter work hours are taken into consideration, state workers are much better off. As a result, state enterprise profits are lower than domestic non-state enterprises and FDI enterprises. This has aroused criticism from some quarters that state enterprises are inefficient and overstaffed, but from Karadjis's perspective, the evidence is that state workers are less exploited.

A different sector of the Vietnamese workforce is also not embedded in modern globalized capitalist relations. These are the craft industry workers in rural settings. Nguyen Phuong Le's study focuses on the re-division of labour and class formation in a Red River Delta village where there has been a lot of in-migration from other rural villages. Through her year-long study of the village, she observed that some in-migrants have resided in the village as labourers in the woodcarving craft industry for several years, while others are only casual day labourers. They are hired by the local owners of the woodcraft workshops, who are often themselves still part-farmers or who have fields tended by their family members. Since the workshop owners sometimes work alongside their employees while running their business, one could call them a "labourer-capitalist" class.[1] The owners' engagement in manual labour narrows the divide between employers and employees. Thus, the migrants, while hierarchically divided according to their specific allotted tasks, coexist peacefully with their employers. Nguyen argues that while the "patron–client relationship" in such rural settings often masks exploitative labour relations, the rural migrants-turned-industrial craft labourers did not transform themselves into a proletariat and they do not feel they are being exploited at all. Instead, they see their transition from farmhand to industrial labourer as a rung up the ladder of economic mobility.

ADVERSITIES OF EXPORT-ORIENTED INDUSTRIALIZATION

Far more Vietnamese workers, however, are part of a globalized foreign-invested industrial sector that generates most of Vietnam's manufactured exports, much as in China. This export economy unfortunately has entailed growing income disparities, low wages, precarious employment, harsh working and living conditions, and loss of dignity among those who have contributed their labour to generate the rapidly growing GNPs of Vietnam and China. In Vietnam, based on World Bank figures, the Gini coefficient has increased from 0.34 in 1993, to 0.35 in 1998 and 0.38 in 2009 (Bonschab and Klump 2004, p. 10; UNDP 2009).[2] (China's was 0.415 in 2009.)

The thrust of the private and FDI manufacturing economy has posed a danger to the state-owned industrial sector. Above all, like other socialist and post-socialist economies, Vietnam had to restructure and revamp inefficient SOEs. In the process, from 1985 to 1992 the number of SOE workers declined from 1.4 million to 1 million workers (Tran 1994, p. 146). Some of those who were able to keep their jobs live today under the threat of a decline in job security and social benefits and harsher shop floor labour regimes (except for those lucky enough to work in key SOEs like those described in Karadjis's chapter). By the turn of the millennium, to resolve SOE inefficiency, equitization (i.e., privatization) was permitted, followed by a further squeeze on workers in a labour regime geared to greater efficiency and increased productivity.

While the state sector shrank, the non-state sector composed of private and foreign enterprises grew and flourished. This new industrial sector is staffed mainly by domestic migrant workers, particularly in the Ho Chi Minh City region where foreign-invested enterprises are concentrated. These are the manufacturing plants that have been drawing the most media attention both outside and inside Vietnam. For one, they are seen as a driving force for change. They symbolize Vietnam's successful integration with the global economy, as almost all of these enterprises are suppliers for the global production chain. The very fact that some of these factories manufacture for internationally well-known brand-name companies brings Western media attention to the issue of exploited labour. Vietnam, alongside other Asian countries such as China, Indonesia, Cambodia, Bangladesh, and Thailand, are targeted by international labour NGOs as sites of female migrant labour exploitation. As just one example, low wages and physical abuse of migrant workers in Nike supplier factories were exposed by an NGO, Vietnam Labour Watch, in 1997 (Global Exchange 2007). A flurry of bad publicity ensued for a few years until Nike implemented a system to monitor its suppliers. The NGOs' attacks on the labour practices of international brands and their suppliers in Vietnam never totally subsided. These practices also became the subject of research by scholars such as Angie Tran (2001; 2007), whose latest research on Vietnam's FDI export-sector workers is included in this volume.

FROM PASSIVE WORKERS TO ACTIVE PROTESTERS

While few cases of physical abuse have surfaced since the spate of bad press in the 1990s, beginning in 2006 Vietnamese workers in the FDI sector once again became the focus of attention. But instead of being victims of management abuse, as they have been portrayed by sympathetic advocates and sections of the mass media, Vietnamese migrant workers have taken centre-stage as self-motivated actors taking collective strike actions to demand higher wages and better work conditions. The Vietnamese government has kept a record of the number of strikes and has allowed the media to report the strike statistics, which show a steady increase in strikes starting in the 1990s. By 2008, the number had climbed to 762. When the world recession hit, the number dropped to 216 strikes in 2009, nearly a 70 per cent drop,[3] but in 2010, when the economy picked up again, the number of strikes climbed again. At the time of writing, strikes up to June 2010 stood at more than 200 (Investment in Vietnam 2010). They are concentrated disproportionately in the foreign-managed export factories. According to Ben Kerkvliet's chapter, while workers at foreign-invested factories in the industrial zones and export processing zones make up less than 8 per cent of the 20.4 million Vietnamese industrial workforce, 70 per cent of the strikes between 1995 and mid-2007 took place in these sites. Almost 60 per cent of these strikes were in Taiwanese and Korean owned or managed factories — a hugely disproportionate figure.

Several chapters in this volume — those by Wehrle, Kerkvliet, Chan, Chae, and Kim — focus partially or fully on this phenomenon of strikes. It will be seen that many of the strikes involve migrant workers, and that a majority of the strike actions have taken place in the export-oriented Asian-

invested FDI factories in southern Vietnam. These chapters provide some
answers to the following questions: What factors underlie the strike waves
in Vietnam? Are Vietnamese workers experiencing harsher work conditions
on the shop floor, which instigates resistance? Are strikes principally due to
wages not keeping up with inflation? Are the strikes premised on a belief
that sectors of the Vietnamese state will support the striking workers? Are
Vietnamese workers ideologically anti-foreign capital?

LEGACY OF THE PAST

The first chapter, by Edmund Wehrle, focuses on the labour movement in
Vietnam from 1947 to 1975, and addresses the nature of the strikes from a
historical perspective. Vietnamese workers had a militant labour history up
till 1975. According to Wehrle's extensive research, there were thousands
of strikes, especially in the south (not dissimilar to today), including
wildcat strikes, sympathy strikes, and even a few general strikes. More
than that, there were independent trade unions, and often the strikes were
led by the unions. Wehrle documents the several decades of struggles of
the biggest union in the south, the Vietnamese Confederation of Workers
and its predecessor, the Vietnamese Confederation of Christian Workers.
In the 1960s a new generation of workers emerged who waged strikes
against American employers. At one time the union movement was so
strong that it could even be considered as a "third force". In short, up
to the mid-1970s there was a militant history of organized labour in the
south that is still in living memory. The legacy of this militancy has not
been entirely snuffed out by a Communist Party-controlled official union
that is bureaucratized to the point of impotence.

TO STRIKE OR NOT TO STRIKE

Angie Tran's chapter on corporate social responsibility (CSR) in Vietnam
focuses on the FDI enterprises via the global production chain. The
fundamental reason why some of the workers in these factories resort to
strikes to better their conditions is because the international brand name
clients, while recognizing they are responsible for overseeing that the
workers who make their goods are not being exploited, have not done
enough *vis-à-vis* wages and work conditions. They drew up "corporate
codes of conduct" and then sought compliance from their Asian-owned

supplier factories, but the fact that Vietnamese workers in these supplier factories go on strike is evidence that the initiative has failed to achieve its goals.

Apart from the brand name companies, Tran describes in some detail the perspectives of the other stakeholders who are involved in the CSR initiative in a variety of capacities. The International Labour Organization (ILO) has been actively helping the Vietnamese government to set up a tripartite structure to form a platform for dialogue between the state, employers, and labour. These efforts have yet been able to claim much success, as the employers' association is still weak and so is the Vietnamese trade union at the workplace level. These weaknesses prevent meaningful negotiations that might pre-empt workers from taking industrial action. However, Tran is not optimistic that CSR will lead to meaningful changes, because without significant workers' participation there can be no real collective bargaining, and without a means to settle their grievances, workers will continue to resort to industrial action.

My own chapter examines strikes in Taiwanese-owned factories in Vietnam, and similarly does not foresee that strikes will subside unless the FDI investors introduce meaningful changes. Instead of comparing strikes in the FDI sector with the other ownership sectors, this chapter compares strikes in Taiwanese-owned factories in both Vietnam and China. In part, the chapter argues that Vietnam's Labour Code, while legalizing collective action and laying out in detail the procedures, makes the procedures so difficult to implement effectively that the Code impedes workers from complying. The result is that they engage instead in wildcat strikes. Ironically, the Vietnamese government's attempt to establish procedures for orderly legal strikes has unintentionally encouraged illegal wildcat strikes.

Low wages and long work hours are generally seen as two of the main reasons for strikes. The authors of two chapters, Suhong Chae and Jee Young Kim, question this general perception. In addition, Kim questions whether foreign ownership is a factor positively correlated to strike actions. Chae offers a detailed case study of a Korean-managed FDI factory which he visited frequently for more than a decade, and Kim uses a survey of 101 workers from 52 FDI factories. Both authors uncover mechanisms at these workplaces that prevent simmering conflicts from escalating into collective resistance such as strikes. The reasons, they argue, are complex and can be found on the shop floor.

The factory that Suhong Chae studied was a Korean-managed joint venture established with a Vietnamese SOE. Many of the workers were initially inherited from the Vietnamese parent company. A year after it began operations in 1993, workers went on strike because the new management did not pay the normal bonus of a thirteenth month salary just before the Vietnamese New Year, *Tet*. Striking over a *Tet* bonus is one of the main reasons for strikes in Vietnam. But in my view, there was a more fundamental reason at this Korean-owned factory than not getting the bonus. Borrowing Karadjis's words, the workers felt their "master" status was being violated. One can call it a clash of national cultures, but it was really a clash of socialist versus capitalist values at a time when workers still believed they had a right to a share of the profits, and not just a wage as compensation for their labour. Management partially conceded and a union was allowed to be elected.

But the Korean management subsequently was able to use what Chae calls Vietnamese "middlemen" — i.e., staff at middle management rank (including the trade union officials who had initially replaced the elected ones soon forced out by management), interpreters, and higher level office staff — to serve a mediating role between management and workers. This helped to diffuse serious discontent in the workforce for more than a decade. Industrial peace led Chae to note that "the central concern of this chapter is to understand why the workers at SIL did not show any signs of conspicuous resistance in the face of deteriorating work conditions". Both management hegemony and industrial peace were attained through a complex mix of three realms of politics: management and workers; the use of middlemen; and, lastly, gender politics. To Chae, understanding "class passivity" is just as important as studying workers' struggles.

In the same vein, Jee Young Kim found in her survey that two factors are salient in causing workers to strike or not: the presence or absence of grievance procedures and management's responsiveness to such grievances. When comparing state-owned firms, Vietnamese private firms, FDI firms, and shadow-foreign firms (i.e., FDI firms registered as domestic firms), what stands out is whether the union can represent workers' grievances to management and thus assuage workers' dissatisfaction. Other factors such as the presence or absence of a union, whether there are entertainment programmes, whether wages are low or work hours are long, are not as relevant. In addition, Kim finds that management's responsiveness to workers' complaints is critical. Of the four ownership types in the survey,

SOE management followed by domestic enterprises are perceived by workers to be the most responsive. Kim concludes the internal "buffering mechanism can lower the chance of workers' discontent developing into collective resistance."

Using two very different approaches to collect information but asking quite similar questions, Chae and Kim arrived at the same conclusion — that a mediating institution at the workplace can let off steam and allay workers' strike intentions. The authors are sceptical that low wages, long work hours, and poor work conditions *per se* are adequate causes for strike actions. At first glance, it appears that their findings contradict the conclusions of other chapters that wages and work hours are important factors in instigating strikes. Yet the approaches used by Kim and Chae do not contradict but complement the other authors' findings. Kim's survey contains statistics showing that strikes are uncommon in SOEs because these have unions that act as mediators (see Karadjis's chapter) and that in domestic enterprises a patron–client culture has a mediating effect (as in Nguyen's study of a rural craft industry). One can in fact argue that given the high incidence of strikes in FDI enterprises, the mediating efforts of state enterprise unions and the patron–client relationships in domestic enterprises have been extremely effective in diffusing strike intentions. Indeed, it is a conscious policy of the Vietnamese government to allow the official union enough space to act as a mediator at the workplace, but not enough power to act independently from the state to represent workers' interests.

Finally, Hong-zen Wang and Daniéle Bèlanger's chapter on how Vietnamese migrant workers in Taiwan are allowed to be exploited in a foreign land provides supporting evidence about the ambivalent attitude of the Vietnamese government. The central government must be aware of the vulnerability of these Vietnamese workers abroad in conditions that are tantamount to indentured labour. The Taiwanese laws regulating imported labour are designed to keep wages low and work hours long. The Vietnamese workers have no recourse to escape mistreatment except to flee from their bosses. But the moment they leave their employers, to whom they are legally bonded, they are branded as "illegal" persons to be repatriated, penniless and in debt. Wang and Belanger suggest it is possible for the Vietnamese government to intervene in this situation, but it is obvious that the export labour industry is too lucrative to prohibit. The programme provides employment, and workers remit money to their families in Vietnam. Weighing the economic gains versus labour rights, the former override the latter. Taiwan's strategy to enable its remaining manufacturing facilities to compete in the global market is to import labour at the cheapest rate possible. Hence, no solution seems to be in sight unless the Vietnamese government intervenes, as it has shown itself more willing to do in FDI firms within Vietnam.

PROGNOSIS

A conclusion that we can draw from the studies in this book is that Vietnam's labour policies are mired in contradictions. While allowing the Vietnamese General Confederation of Labour (VGCL) some space to help workers, the state does not entirely loosen its corporatist constraints. Nor does it increase the legal minimum wage enough for it to keep abreast of inflation, a policy which would have decreased the number of strikes. Caught in a global economy that relentlessly drives down wages, the Vietnamese government does not want to raise the minimum wage for fear that its labour might be priced out of the international labour market.

But labour peace is also a precondition for attracting FDI. In the face of the large number of strikes, the VGCL and local governments have played a mediating role. The strikes are orderly, and once management and the outside union officials/local government officials come to an agreement approved by the strikers, workers are willing to resume work immediately. While strikes are often portrayed as disruptive and confrontational, in Vietnam all of the stakeholders have learned how to play the game and accept it as "normal". Investors always warn that strikes will drive away FDI, but FDI in Vietnam has been increasing in recent years despite the strikes. FDI in billions of dong has climbed from 41,342 in 2004 to 51,102 in 2005, to 65,604 in 2006, 129,399 in 2007, and 192,360 in 2008 (General Office of Statistics of Vietnam website).

The government realizes that more has to be done for the workers. For the time being, though, the reforms have been incremental. The government is more inclined to let the Ministry of Labour, Invalids, and Social Affairs (MOLISA) work closely with the ILO and foreign companies, foreign unions, and the VGCL to conduct CSR training programmes, as discussed in Tran's chapter. But as she concludes, this is not a long-term solution to the problems. Workplace collective bargaining and trade union democracy are more viable alternatives.

Notes

[1]   This is my expression, not Nguyen Phuong Le's.

[2]   The Gini coefficient figures vary. For instance, based on Euromonitor International, it was 0.345 in 1990 and rose to 0.432 in 2006 <http://www.euromonitor.com/Vietnams_income_distribution> (accessed 1 July 2010).

[3]   "Vietnam Workers Strike over Salary Increase", Deutsche Presse-Agentur, 22 January 2010. <http://www.Monstersandcritics.com/news/business/news/article_1527543.php/> (accessed 23 January 2010).

References

Beresford, Melanie. "*Doi Moi* in Review: The Challenges of Building Market Socialism in Vietnam". *Journal of Contemporary Asia* 38, no. 2 (May 2008): 221–43.

Birchall, Jonathan. "World: Asia-Pacific: Nike Slams Vietnam Labour Critics", BBC News Online Network, 21 January, 1999 <http://news.bbc.co.uk/2/hi/asia-pacific/259426.stm> (accessed 2 July 2010).

Bonschab, Thomas and Rainer Klump. "Operationalising Pro-Poor Growth: A Country Case Study on Vietnam" <http://siteresources.worldbank.org/INTPGI/Resources/342674-1115051237044/oppgvietnam.pdf> (accessed 1 July 2010).

Chan, Anita and Irene Norlund. "Vietnamese and Chinese Labour Regimes: On the Road to Divergence". In *Transforming Socialism: China and Vietnam Compared*, edited by Anita Chan, Benedict J. Tris Kerkvliet, and Jonathan Unger, pp. 204–28. St. Leonard's: Allen & Unwin and Boulder: Rowman & Littlefield, 1999.

Chan, Anita and Wang Hongzen. "The Impact of the State on Workers' Conditions: Comparing Taiwanese Factories in China and Vietnam". *Pacific Affairs* 77, no. 4 (Winter 2004): 629–46.

General Office of Statistics of Vietnam. <http://www.gso.gov.vn/default_en.aspx?tabid=491> (accessed 13 August 2010).

Global Exchange. "Sweatfree Communities" <http://www.globalexchange.org/campaigns/sweatshops/nike/vietnam.html#girls>.

Investment in Vietnam. "Vietnam Records 200 Strikes in Jan–Jun: Ministry (18/07/2010)" <http://www.investinvietnam.vn/Default.aspx?ctl=Article&tID=0&pID=120&aID=1931> (accessed 24 July 2010).

Lee, Kuen and John A. Mathews. "From Washington Consensus to Best Consensus for World Development". *Asian-Pacific Economic Literature* 24, no. 1 (May 2010): 86–103.

Tran, Angie Ngoc. "Global Subcontracting and Women Workers in Comparative Perspective". In *Globalization and Third World Socialism: Cuba and Vietnam*, edited by Claes Brundenius and John Weeks, pp. 217–36. Houndmills: Palgrave Macmillan, 2001.

————. "Gender Expectations of Vietnamese Garment Workers: Viet Nam's Re-Integration into the World Economy". In *Gender, Household, State: Doi Moi in Vietnam*, edited by Jayne Werner and Daniele Belanger, pp. 49–71. Ithaca: Southeast Asia Program Publications, Cornell University, 2002.

————. "The Third Sleeve: Emerging Labour Newspapers and the Response of Labour Unions and the State to Workers' Resistance in Vietnam". *Labour Studies Journal* 32, no. 3 (2007): 257–79.

Tran Hoang Kim. *Economy of Vietnam: Review and Statistics*. Hanoi: Statistical Publishing House, 1994.

United Nations Development Program (UNDP). *2009 Human Development Report*. Available online at <http://hdr.undp.org/en/>.

Vietnam Labour Watch. "Nike Labour Practices in Vietnam" <http://www.viet.net/~nike/reports/report1.html> (accessed 2 July 2010).

Woodside, Alexander. "Exalting the Latecomer State: Intellectuals and the State During the Chinese and Vietnamese Reforms". In *Transforming Asian Socialism: China and Vietnam Compared,* edited by Anita Chan, Benedict J. Tria Kerkvliet, and Jonathan Unger, pp. 15–42. St. Leonard's: Allen & Unwin and Boulder: Rowman & Littlefield, 1999.

2

"AWAKENING THE CONSCIENCE OF THE MASSES"
The Vietnamese Confederation of Labour, 1947–75

Edmund Wehrle

In 1948, Gilbert Jouan, a French colonial customs officer with twenty years' experience in Indochina and an abiding faith that trade unions would form a bulwark against Communist intrusion, took the first tentative steps toward organizing Vietnamese workers. Working with the French Confederation of Christian Workers (CFTC), Jouan and other Catholic trade unionists in 1947 formed a "delegation" representing CFTC interests in Vietnam, and notified French authorities of his intention to organize "an authentic Christian trade union in Indochina ... for the Indochinese themselves".[1]

Strictly speaking, Jouan's actions violated the law. Trade unions, explained one colonial official in 1948, had "absolutely no legal standing; groups such as these are merely tolerated by public officials".[2] Still, the French invested great hope in Jouan's work. An official report on Christian trade union organizing described Jouan as "worthy of our esteem". The colonial government even arranged time off from the customs office for Jouan so that he could focus on the organizing work that officials obviously hoped would counterbalance the appeal of the Viet Minh.[3] "The consolidation of the support of the working class in Vietnam is mainly to be achieved by close collaboration with the Christian Trade Union", explained the Vietnamese Minister of Social Action.[4] The result was an awkward modus vivendi between the nascent, still-illegal labour organization and the colonial state.

Within a few years, Jouan's Christian labour movement grew in numbers and clout, and eventually took the name the Confédération Vietnamienne du Travail Chrétien (Vietnamese Confederation of Christian Workers, known best by its French acronym, CVTC). The organization had far-reaching ambitions — to be an activist and independent voice for the oppressed workers of Vietnam. Its survival for the next two-and-a-half decades remains a testament to the skill and commitment of its leadership and rank-and-file. Likewise, frequent strikes, workplace actions, and political activism sponsored by the confederation suggest a genuine militancy on the part of South Vietnam's unions and workers. Yet true autonomy and independence of action in South Vietnam proved virtually impossible to maintain. In order to survive, the CVTC entered into compromising alliances with the French (described above) and a succession of problematic Saigon governments. This awkward balancing act between serving the interests of the state and acting aggressively on behalf of workers plagued the CVTC throughout its existence — and in some ways represents the central paradox facing today's labour movement in Vietnam. In the case of the CVTC, this limitation proved an insurmountable handicap.

This chapter discusses at length the CVTC's ill-fated struggle to preserve its autonomy. It explores the history of the organization from its inception (depicted in the opening vignette) to its end in 1975 as Saigon fell to the North Vietnamese. Understandably, an organization dedicated to mobilizing workers and remaking society faced an uphill struggle during the colonial era. Obstacles impeding the CVTC, however, further increased under the repressive Diem regime, which sought to harness South Vietnamese labour for its own political purposes. Ngo Dinh Diem's death and the U.S. intervention portended better days. The CVT (Vietnamese Confederation of Labour; the term "Christian" was later dropped from the Western translation) made great advances in the mid-1960s, organizing throngs of workers and negotiating beneficial contracts, especially with U.S. employers. However, while it sought to avoid conflict with Saigon government officials, labour–state tensions simmered. Seeking tighter control as war ravaged the country, state officials grew increasingly suspicious of a movement with its own agenda of empowering the lower classes. Rumours swirled constantly that the National Liberation Front (NLF or Viet Cong) had infiltrated the labour organization. These tensions came to a head in 1968, when the government moved to break a strike initiated by CVT militants.

Despite the devastating strike and the equally challenging Tet Offensive of 1968, the CVT managed to recover. It remained an active force, entering politics in the late 1960s and contributing to major legislative reforms, including the 1971 Land-to-the-Tiller Act. Still, caution — a reluctance to push its government and its American allies too far — continued to characterize the organization to its demise in 1975.

For the most part, scholars have overlooked the struggles of the CVT — despite its impressive membership numbers and political successes.[5] This is partly due to a lack of sources. With most CVT records apparently destroyed in 1975, researchers are forced to tease out information from available sources, including a 1969 official history of the CVT, U.S. and French government documentation, and oral interviews with surviving members. The contested and politicized atmosphere surrounding the Vietnam War also presents challenges to telling the full story of an organization caught between historical currents. Indeed, despite a paucity of evidence, several scholars have dismissed the CVT as a pawn of the brutal Saigon government and the U.S. Central Intelligence Agency (CIA). As immediate memories of the divisive war fade, one hopes that balanced treatments, neither vilifying nor sanctifying the CVT, will emerge — providing the integrated treatment this fascinating movement deserves.

THE LABOUR QUESTION IN VIETNAM

While the tortuous history of organized labour in South Vietnam — the focus of this chapter — began in the waning days of French colonialism, the "labour question" in Vietnam had deep roots. From the earliest days of French rule, rapacious labour practices in Indochina, especially conditions on rubber plantations, where workers toiled often as little more than slaves, drew international rebukes and violent resistance from Vietnamese workers. The worldwide economic crisis of the 1930s — felt deeply in Vietnam — lent new urgency to the issue. Reformers and radicals alike focused on organizing workers as a defence against the ravages of capitalism and colonialism. Throughout the decade, strikes at rubber plantations, smaller industries, and Saigon's docks presented a constant challenge to the French, who often launched brutal counteroffensives.

As tensions smouldered, the Marxist-Leninist interpretation of colonialism, rooted in a blistering critique of labour exploitation, gained a growing following. In 1929, activists founded the Red Federation of General Unions and in 1930, the Indochinese Communist Party.[6] While earlier nationalist campaigns focused on the small, educated elite of Vietnam, Communists targeted the country's proletariat (numbering roughly 200,000, including small factory employees, shipyard workers, and coal miners) and the large masses of the peasants in their recruitment drive.[7] By the late 1930s, French authorities began to shift tactics somewhat. In 1936, a reform-minded "Popular Front" government under Prime Minister Leon Blum came to power in Paris. Blum introduced a broad program of reform legislation granting new rights to colonial workers. Labour unions, however, remained illegal.[8]

Blum's government fell quickly, but colonial leadership in Vietnam remained in transition. During Second World War, the Axis-allied Vichy government took over in Indochina, but its hold remained fragile. The Japanese presence grew, while anticolonial groups coalesced into the umbrella organization known as the Viet Minh in 1941, which opposed both the French and Japanese.

With the defeat of Japan in August of 1945, Viet Minh leader Ho Chi Minh seized on the power vacuum to declare an independent Vietnam. The labour question quickly emerged to play a central role in Ho's initiatives. Announcing the creation of the Democratic Republic of Vietnam (DRV) in September 1945, Ho Chi Minh set about organizing workers into what he foresaw as "one big union", the Vietnam Federation of Trade Unions (VFTU), modelled on the French Confédération Générale du Travail (CGT). After initial Viet Minh successes, the French moved to reassert authority, and by late 1946 the first Indochina War was under way. As a result, the VFTU made little headway either in the South or in Vietnam's cities still controlled by the French.[9] Even so, by 1949 the VFTU could boast some 258,000 members.[10]

BUU AND THE BIRTH OF THE CVTC UNDER
FRENCH COLONIALISM

As the French struggled against increasing Viet Minh resistance, Jouan began his work in the South with the welcome addition of an energetic nationalist named Tran Quoc Buu. From his teens, Buu, who hailed from Binh Dinh Province in central Vietnam, devoted himself to the nationalist cause. In 1940, French authorities sentenced him to a lengthy term at Poulo Condore island prison. Following his release in 1945, Buu fought alongside the Viet Minh. After a time, disillusioned by Viet Minh excesses, Buu met Jouan, who quickly became his mentor.[11]

In particular, Jouan taught the virtues of corporatist labour relations, stressing the utility of *chambres mixtes de métiers*, or trade councils, in which employers, employee representatives, and local and national government authorities would meet and jointly make management decisions — ideas strongly promoted in Christian trade union circles as alternatives to radical socialism.[12] Despite their interest in such tripartite arrangements, Buu and Jouan stressed that labour unions must be separate independent forces, acting solely in the interests of their membership. Buu believed that he had found a "third force" capable of unifying and reconstructing Vietnamese society non-violently. This ideology remained at the core of his movement until 1975 — although circumstances, especially a hostile state and employers, thwarted any real implementation of such corporate labour arrangements.

Disregarding legal prohibitions, Buu and Jouan launched an aggressive campaign to organize workers and recruited approximately 8,000 members by the end of 1950. The organization quickly grew to include at least ten 'illegal' unions, representing the employees of Citroen and the airline Air Vietnam, as well as shoemakers, typesetters, tailors, and barbers.[13]

French authorities, while tolerating the burgeoning labour movement, at times sought to circumscribe its activities. For instance, colonial officials denied Buu's petition to hold a public demonstration on 1 May 1950, in honour of May Day. Manifesting a determined militancy, Buu and his fellow budding unionists instead organized a "requiem mass" at the Cathedral of Saigon. Following services, union leaders directed members to the federation's headquarters where they approved a series of resolutions to be presented to the government. Demands included new labour codes decriminalizing labour unions, the closure of a Cholon gambling house, and an end to the subcontracting system at Saigon's port.[14]

In 1952, under pressure from Viet Minh gains, Bao Dai, the head of state installed in 1949 by the French to allow the Vietnamese limited self-government, finally issued a new series of labour regulations which at last permitted workers to organize.[15] The decrees generated strong opposition from Vietnam's bourgeoisie, both French and Vietnamese. Nonetheless, the Bao Dai government and French officials clung fatuously to hopes that the reforms might generate support among the working classes for Bao Dai's struggling government.[16]

Buu and Jouan, seizing on their newly legal status, officially named their organization the Vietnamese Confederation of Christian Workers.[17] Perhaps to appeal to non-Christian workers, the organization did not use the designation of "Christian" in the Vietnamese name (Tong Lien Doan Lao Cong Vietnam). From the start, the CVTC focused considerable energy on recruiting rural workers, especially plantation workers and tenant farmers; the organization's rural unions quickly became and would remain the confederation's largest constituency, since the population was overwhelmingly involved in rural activities. It was estimated a little over a year later that the CVTC's membership had grown to 38,990, including around 1,300 unionists in Hanoi.[18] Despite the organization's ties to the International Federation of Christian Trade Unions (IFCTU), Christians remained in the minority. Officially, the CVTC "was open to all workers" and set out to attract a diverse membership, inclusive of all religious and minority groups.[19]

While on the one hand seeking to maintain peace with French and Vietnamese authorities, on the other the CVTC strove to maintain an active militancy. In 1953, the CVTC initiated strikes by employees of Air France, 500 shoemakers in Cholon, and workers in the five largest printing houses in Saigon. That same year, when government officials in the north moved to curb CVTC operations, Buu and Jouan protested loudly, "unleashing a violent campaign in the press for trade union freedom".[20]

The awkward dance between labour and colonial state, however, would soon be over. French colonialism was on its last legs by 1953, and CVTC officials began preparing for its aftermath. The organization adamantly opposed the temporary division of Vietnam mandated by the Geneva Accords in July 1954. Banners strung across the confederation's headquarters denounced the Geneva Accords with slogans such as "To Divide Vietnam is to Open the Door of Southeast Asia to Communism".[21] In particular, Buu and Jouan feared for the fate of the CVTC's northern affiliates. CVTC-affiliated workers at the Cai-Da mines in northern Vietnam launched a successful work stoppage in early 1954. The strike enhanced Buu's reputation and fed hopes for further organization in the more industrialized north.[22] Within a year, however, as feared, distressing news began to pour in from the north of persecution and union-breaking, including reports that the DRV government in the north, apparently viewing the CVTC as subservient to Western colonialism, had sentenced trade unionists to forced labour on the Chinese border.[23] The CVTC was "living though a real nightmare", an unnerved Buu wrote to a supporter.[24]

As the CVTC struggled, the VFTU became the sole legal union for all workers in the north. While serving as a representative agency for workers, the VFTU also served the state, mobilizing, training, and disciplining workers. It has remained closely associated with the Communist Party to this day.[25]

COOPERATING WITH
NGO DINH DIEM

Seeking to accommodate itself to new circumstances, the CVTC underwent important changes. Jouan, perhaps recognizing that a labour organization headed by a former colonial official would send the wrong message, decided to return home to France and leave the movement in the hands of Vietnamese, in particular Buu. CVTC officials also began seeking the leverage of new alliances as life grew more dangerous and complicated — alliances that would prove enormously problematic. The organization made contact with the CIA, establishing a long-lasting, shadowy relationship.[26] Additionally, despite the organization's avowed commitment to independence, the CVTC cautiously embraced the rising ambitions of Ngo Dinh Diem and his politically ambitious family, after Diem was appointed prime minister by Bao Dai in June 1954. As early as 1954, the French CFTC described the Ngos as "already for a long time having exercised a useful and discreet influence" on the CVTC.[27] Buu joined the Ngo family in forming the Can Lao Party (Revolutionary Personalist Labour Party), which Diem envisioned as his chief vehicle for promoting both social reform and his own control over the country.[28] Yet relations between the CVTC and Diem always retained a certain tension. On several occasions Buu and other labour leaders publicly blasted Diem for the latter's efforts to co-opt the confederation.[29]

Still, the CVTC supported Diem during the pivotal Battle of Saigon in 1955. With Diem firmly in power, the ranks of labour grew, as did organizing campaigns. The Tenant Farmers' Federation expanded dramatically under the personal patronage of Ngo Dinh Nhu, Diem's brother and chief political advisor.[30] By late 1955, the CVTC publicly claimed half a million members, although privately it admitted to the still-substantial figure of around 350,000.[31] The confederation expanded membership services, opening several consumer cooperatives and ambitiously planning a "worker city" to provide low-cost housing and services for urban workers.[32] It moved to set up *chambres mixtes de métiers* arrangements and to open a series of "Raiffeisen Cooperatives", modelled on the rural savings and loans associations begun by Friedrich Raiffeisen in Germany in the 1860s.[33]

The clashing visions of the Ngo family and the CVTC, however, could not be suppressed. Diem clearly intended to control the organization, while the CVTC remained determined to preserve its autonomy. Buu told confidants he was "reluctant to become over-obligated" to the government by "accepting outright grants from it or any of the political parties".[34] In a meeting with the president in February 1956, Buu bluntly told Diem that "his idea of democracy was not [Diem's] hand-picked assembly".[35] The CVTC followed up by amplifying its attacks on local officials who harassed union members. Such brazen outspokenness stoked the fires of Diem's and Nhu's obsessive suspicions. The final straw, according to U.S. Embassy observers, came when the CVTC failed to pass a resolution pledging support to Diem's government.[36] By late autumn 1956, Nhu unleashed a hostile campaign against the CVTC, targeting in particular the Tenant Farmers' Union. Soon rumours swirled that authorities planned to arrest Buu himself.[37]

Over the next several years, relations worsened. Soon Diem had virtually rendered the CVTC an organization in name only, and its agenda had largely stalled. Increasingly, Buu relied on his CIA ties and other American friends to offset the threat of the Ngos. Buu complained bitterly to allies in the CIA of recent arrests of CVTC officials designed to "intimidate labour", and warned that workers were growing "restive", some being attracted to Buddhist calls for a general strike against Diem.[38] In early autumn of 1963, he went public with complaints about the Diem presidency, sharply criticizing the Ngos before a United Nations committee investigating Vietnam.[39]

Clearly, Buu had ties to those conspiring against Diem, but if the CVTC leadership hoped that labour–state relations would improve following the coup resulting in Diem's killing in November 1963, they were sorely disappointed. The new Saigon government took Buu into custody, apparently concerned over his previous ties to the Diem regime. Only the personal intercession of the U.S. embassy allowed for his release.[40]

TOWARD THE SECOND INDOCHINA WAR

For several months, the CVTC waited for the tumult sweeping South Vietnamese politics to settle. By early 1964, a new government had been formed under General Nguyen Khanh. Again the U.S. embassy aided organized labour's cause by pushing Khanh to meet directly with Buu, a meeting where the two worked out an agreement allowing the CVTC vital room to organize.[41] By the mid-1960s, key U.S. officials clearly had come to view the CVTC as prime evidence of emerging democracy in Vietnam — evidence they could use to support intervention, as the White House and Congress began pondering the future of South Vietnam.

Seizing the newly liberalized atmosphere, the CVTC embarked on a flurry of new organizational activity. The plantation and tenant farmers' unions, decimated by Diem, rebounded as tens of thousands of Vietnamese farmers and workers joined CVTC-affiliated unions.[42] Seeking to broaden international support, Buu's federation dropped the term "Christian" from the Western translations of the confederation's title and was known from then on as the CVT, although it retained its affiliation with the Christian International.[43] Buoyed by success, in mid-1964, a CVT cadre ecstatically declared at a Singapore labour conference: "The activities of our syndicate are not like a thatch fire, burning for a short time and often dying out. But on the contrary, her activities persist like a coal fire under a layer of ashes".[44]

In the summer of 1964, a protracted conflict with the American-born Chinese owner of Vimytex textile factory provided Buu with an opportunity to stoke some of the ashes. Typical of the Asian textile industry, Vimytex, purchased with a US$6 million loan from the U.S. Operations Mission (USOM), had a reputation for dismal labour conditions.[45] Foreign-owned and linked to the Americans, Vimytex offered a tempting target — an opportunity for the CVT to play on mounting anxieties about expanding outside influence in South Vietnam. The mill owner, however, showed no signs of acceding to workers' demands. Eventually he locked out three-quarters of his workers, roughly 120 employees, and transferred others to a military camp.[46]

As the CVT mobilized, General Khanh suddenly threatened the campaign. On 19 August 1964, amid growing political chaos, the general declared a state of emergency, partly in reaction to the Gulf of Tonkin incident, but also to quell mounting protests in the streets of Saigon. Assuming total authority, Khanh banned all strikes and mass meetings.[47] Once again the state was determined to threaten labour advances.

In response, Buu upped the ante by announcing a general strike to involve all labour unions in Saigon. A general strike would demonstrate to all of Vietnam the independence and potency of the CVT.[48] "We have arrived at a point where we must take chances. We are taking this one now with the conviction that for the world of labour we represent the only solution outside Communism," Buu explained to French journalist Jean Lacouture.[49]

On 21 September 1964, the CVT shut down Saigon. With the city's electrical workers joining the strike, South Vietnam's capital city sat in darkness for a full day, without water, electricity, phone services, or bus transportation. Sixty thousand CVT members joined in the work stoppage. Buu led a parade of several thousand strikers through Saigon to Khanh's offices where they presented their demands. With the general conveniently out-of-town, his aides negotiated with strike leaders.[50] Thousands of workers waited outside for news of the deliberations. Finally, to great fanfare, Buu appeared, announcing a tentative settlement easing labour restrictions.[51]

Impressed by the militancy of Saigon workers, Lacouture wondered if the one-day mobilization marked the emergence of a potential third force: "For the first time a force arose that could be either a possible replacement for the present regime or a link to the enemy regime or the first pillar of a regime to come."[52] Buu's organization, however, was badly overextended — especially with regard to its relations with Saigon officials. While dramatically asserting itself, the CVT created new enemies and infuriated old ones. Buddhists as well as Buu's foes within the labour movement now viewed the confederation as a surging threat. More seriously, the CVT moved to the top of General Khanh's enemy list. Then on 10 October, General Khanh included Buu's name on a list of thirteen military officers and seven civilians to be arrested on charges of conspiring against Khanh in a failed coup on 13 September.[53]

Fortunately for Buu, on 22 October a military court, no doubt responding to pressure from the U.S. embassy, found him innocent of all charges; loud cheers reverberated through the courtroom when his acquittal was announced.[54] Following his exoneration, Buu sidestepped any direct condemnation of Saigon officials, doubtless understanding that he still depended on the state for survival. He still expressed the hope that the verdict signalled a new openness to democratic governance, and that Khanh, at last, was "ready to show sincere comprehension and cooperation with a free and independent labour organization in the national struggle".[55]

While the CVT had made remarkable gains since the fall of Diem, it obviously remained subject to a number of pernicious forces. First and foremost was the Saigon government, but there were also divisions within the trade union movement. While it was the largest and most influential labour organization in South Vietnam, it was not the only one. Upstart organizations, such as a military-led effort to organize longshoremen on Saigon's piers, presented constant annoyances — always presenting a threat but never rising to a substantial challenge.[56] A former CVT officer, Bui Luong, who had had a severe falling-out with the organization and formed a rival group, constantly hurled accusations at Buu, at one point charging him with accepting US$200,000 from the North Vietnamese to build a house and simultaneously with pocketing US$45,000 from the U.S. embassy.[57] Meanwhile, in early 1965, the Buddhist Institute for Secular Affairs began organizing workers. Quickly, the institute attempted to launch general strikes in several cities, including Hue, Quang Tri, and Da Nang.[58]

Even greater trials followed in 1965. Khanh fell from power, eventually to be replaced by a government headed by Air Marshall Nguyen Cao Ky as prime minister. Buu and the CVT concluded that the new prime minister considered them an enemy. Ky, they feared, meant to "thwart, if not destroy, the CVT".[59] The full-scale U.S. military intervention in the summer of 1965, fully endorsed by the CVT, also presented challenges and opportunities. With ever-growing leverage over the South Vietnamese leadership, the Americans, very much aware of the need to make South Vietnam appear democratic, pushed Ky to work with organized labour. Thrown on the defensive, Ky soon was insisting that his government was both "pro-worker and pro-peasant".[60] Again, a temporary modus vivendi allowed the CVT to continue its work.

The CVT leadership gained new appreciation for Ky when the prime minister moved against Buddhist protesters in Da Nang.[61] The Buddhist

Institute's drive to organize workers, of course, helped persuade trade unionists of the need for Ky's hard line; the CVT hoped to organize all workers, and competition from the upstart Buddhists was not appreciated. In August 1966, following decisive anti-Buddhist raids in Da Nang and Hue, the CVT invited Ky to its headquarters as its honoured guest. There, 500 unionists greeted the prime minister as a hero, interrupting Ky's speech with applause ten times.[62]

Buu's improved relationship with the national government allowed the CVT yet another opportunity to expand. In particular, the Tenant Farmers' Federation, a key CVT affiliate, flourished, expanding to nearly 100,000 members. At times, the Tenant Farmers competed directly with the Viet Cong for the loyalty of farmers and farm labourers. In early 1965, Viet Cong guerrillas, relying heavily upon violence and intimidation, drove away the French management of South Vietnam's largest rubber plantation in Binh Duong Province. The Viet Cong, however, quickly proved unable to pay or feed workers. A "delegation of workers therefore made their way to Saigon", where the CVT tenant farmers took up their cause, and successfully negotiated a new contract with Michelin.[63]

CAUGHT BETWEEN UNION MILITANTS
AND THE STATE

Its entente with Ky, however, hardly made up for the myriad challenges facing the CVT. As U.S. soldiers swept into the country, so too did painful inflation. The meagre wages paid to South Vietnam's workers, especially its rural workers, lagged behind rising prices, soaring at an annual rate of 124 per cent in 1966.[64] The CVT also remained at the mercy of the police. Buu openly worried that General Nguyen Ngoc Loan, the near-psychotic head of the national police, would kill him and blame it on the Viet Cong.[65]

It was in fact a clash with General Loan that set off the next big challenge facing the CVT — an episode that almost shattered organized labour in South Vietnam. While the CVT had grown tremendously since 1963, especially organizing campaigns on behalf of Vietnamese employed by Americans, the confederation worked to avoid direct confrontations with government-owned operations and Republic of Vietnam officials, especially the Saigon police. CVT leaders fully understood the mercurial nature of their government, but the organization's reluctance to take on the state irked many younger members eager to press democratization and workers' rights.

The first sparks of labour–state conflict flared in the summer of 1967 when the French-owned Compagnie des Eaux et d'Electricité (CEE) agreed to transfer operation and control of a large power plant serving Saigon to the South Vietnamese government.[66] Plant employees anticipated job losses, and the CVT-affiliated Water and Electricity Workers Union demanded a fair severance package for those who became unemployed. For employees who would remain, the union demanded a 12 per cent pay hike. When concessions failed to materialize, workers threatened to strike. Vo Van Tai, leader of the CVT's militant "young Turks" and chief of Saigon's labour council, aggressively pushed the electrical workers to take a strong stand. Buu obviously preferred moderation but feared stifling the ambitions of militants in his ranks.[67]

Both the CVT and state officials briefly put the mounting conflict aside as national elections won by General Nguyen Van Thieu consumed the country, but almost immediately thereafter the smouldering conflict returned. Seeing no signs of concessions from the government, Tai and CVT radicals scheduled a strike for early in the new year. On 30 December 1967, General Loan issued a communiqué declaring that the National Police would "no longer refrain from intervention in the growing number of strikes".[68] Ignoring the general, on 11 January 1968 1,000 power plant employees walked off the job.[69]

A few hours after declaring the strike, the CVT Saigon Labour Council arrived at the Labour Ministry's offices to open negotiations. Suddenly Loan's men burst into the room, and arrested six labour leaders, including Vo Van Tai.[70] Word of the arrests spread rapidly, and sympathy strikes broke out across Saigon. Bus drivers quit their routes, and longshoremen abandoned the ports.[71] However, these protests only spurred Loan to take harsher action. He loaded five garbage trucks with police, directed the convoy to CVT headquarters, and personally delivered "requisitions", ordering workers back to their jobs immediately. Police ripped down strike banners and arrested any who dared resist. Loan's violent reputation persuaded enough workers to return to their jobs to allow the electrical plant to reopen at full capacity. In the wake of Loan's crackdown, sympathy strikes petered out, but bitterness remained.[72]

Never enthusiastic about the strikes, Buu privately blamed CVT militants and moved to negotiate a settlement with the government before the upcoming *Tet* holidays. On 16 January he ordered remaining strikers back to work. In return, the Saigon government agreed to a 12 per cent pay increase, and General Loan released the labour leaders still in his custody, including Vo Van Tai.[73]

An uneasy stillness settled across the Saigon labour scene, but the Viet Cong, who had been applauding the strikes through radio propaganda, warned that "[o]n the eve of Tet, the stormy fire of revolutionary struggle of our workers and labourers will kindle fiercely right in the cities".[74] Only days later, the Viet Cong launched its Tet Offensive. As the conflagration spread, swelling violence destroyed the homes of more than 1,000 trade unionists.

Militant CVT members argued that, in light of the government's recent suppression, the confederation should assume a stony silence, sending authorities a pointed message. Again the organization faced a tough decision, weighing activism against good relations with its government. Buu and the CVT leadership decided to focus on the immediate terrorist threat from the Viet Cong and support their government. The organization issued a sharp condemnation of the "criminal action of the enemy".[75]

If the CVT hoped to be rewarded for its loyalty, it was sorely disappointed. As the dust settled in Saigon, General Loan rearrested a key trade union leader. The police action mystified Buu, who could only speculate that Loan "must be insane".[76] Another round of interventions by Buu and his American allies finally effected the release of the jailed CVT official.

Despite the extreme setbacks of the first half of 1968, the roller coaster pattern that defined the CVT's existence persisted. Following the Tet Offensive, the CVT managed to expand its influence, defying all expectations. Surprisingly, the CVT also found its relations with Saigon authorities improving, especially with the retirement of General Loan, who had suffered a severe injury in a Viet Cong rocket attack.[77] Likewise, as the Viet Cong retreated following what was certainly a military defeat, confederation organizers expanded their rural activities. "The sky was bright again after several months of tempest", a CVT official explained.[78] The South Vietnamese economy entered into a brief period of economic expansion, especially in the countryside.[79]

The CVT also continued aggressively to organize Vietnamese employed by the U.S. military and associated contractors — a workforce that at its peak included several hundred thousand workers, who were among the best paid in South Vietnam. The American military, with its focus on nation-building and winning "hearts and minds", sought to avoid confrontation with its Vietnamese employees at all costs. Likewise, informed by a New Deal worldview, official U.S. policy encouraged unionization. To this end, the military established a single agency, the Office of Civilian Personnel (OCP), to oversee labour relations with all employees. From the start, the OCP faced a restless, often militant workforce. While American employees signed a no-strike pledge, Vietnamese workers showed little reluctance to walk off jobs. Hundreds of wildcat and CVT-sanctioned strikes plagued the U.S. military and associated contractors throughout the war. Most related to wage issues, as inflation swept across the South Vietnamese economy, but issues of safety, treatment of employees, and the hiring of so-called third country nationals (usually Koreans or Taiwanese) also caused worker protest. Seeking to avoid full-scale labour conflict, the OCP tolerated brief strikes and worked hard, increasingly in alliance with the CVT, to appease its workforce.[80]

"AWAKENING THE CONSCIENCE OF THE MASSES": TOWARD POLITICS

Even as CVT members relied upon the Americans for jobs in a labour-friendly environment, many in both the rank-and-file and leadership recognized that South Vietnam's heavy dependence on outsiders was a double-edged sword that delegitimized their country as much as it represented a necessary lifeline. They looked forward to the promise of Vietnamization. An American departure, Buu optimistically forecasted, would inspire an "awakening of the conscience of the masses".[81]

Recognizing that its chief vulnerability was its often-tense relationship with Republic of Vietnam government officials, the CVT, which long eschewed direct involvement in politics, began testing the political waters. In 1968, breaking with precedent, it joined in forming a coalition called Lien Minh Dan Toc Cach Mang Xa Hoi (National Alliance for Social Revolution), composed of several political and ethnic parties, including Catholics, the Hoa Hao religious sect, the CVT, and Senator Tran Van Don (a perennial political player and one of the plotters of the 1963 coup against Diem).[82] From behind the scenes, President Nguyen Van Thieu encouraged the development, arguing that the alliance would bring political stability and, presumably, political security for himself.[83] The alliance, however, fell apart quickly, largely due to diverging ambitions of all parties and Thieu's meddling efforts to control the political organization.[84]

Undaunted, the CVT leadership moved to organize the Cong-Nong Party (the Worker-Farmer Party), a political party to represent the confederation's interests. Established in November 1969, Cong-Nong was purported to be an entity independent from the CVT, yet its connection to the labour movement was obvious — essentially an open secret.[85] Borrowing the CVT's pluralistic aims of uniting farmers, labourers, urban workers, minority groups, and various religious sects, Buu proposed to include a diverse conglomeration of largely underrepresented groups, possibly including his old allies in the religious organization Cao Dai, in his new political party.[86]

The CVT's political venture did enjoy considerable success. Using CVT unions and social centres as a base, the Cong-Nong Party, which aimed to train a cadre corps of some 3,000 organizers, quickly spread to forty provinces and many cities. Voters elected Cong-Nong Party candidates to seats in the General Assembly and local offices.[87] From positions of influence, Cong-Nong pressed such measures as civilian military training (with the aim of mobilizing South Vietnamese against Communists) and the 1971 Land-to-the-Tiller Act, which proposed to transfer three million acres of prime farmland in the Mekong Delta and central lowlands from landlords to tenant families.[88] The CVT seemed on the verge of becoming a major political force with its populist, reformist agenda.

By the end of 1971, however, progress seemed to stall. Inflation became an ever-greater problem, and unemployment rose as refugees filled South Vietnam's cities. The U.S. drawdown of troops and investment in Southeast Asia worsened the situation, as thousands of Vietnamese employed by Americans lost their jobs.

Meanwhile, the CVT faced increasing opposition from its trade union rivals. Vo Van Tai, the militant who had been imprisoned by General Loan during the labour tumult of early 1968, left the CVT shortly thereafter and established the rival National Confederation of Labour (LCL) to challenge what he saw as lethargy in the CVT. Obviously committed to aggressive action (which Buu and other CVT leaders increasingly saw as needlessly dangerous), in the summer of 1971, along with the Federation of Railroad Workers, Tai attempted to launch a general strike to protest against rising income taxes. While the two-day strike had little impact short of closing some banks, Tai's militancy reminded some of the CVT's shortcomings.[89] Within the CVT, younger, more militant members complained of the organization's stagnation and charged Buu and the confederation leadership with corruption — accusations not without some merit. Indeed, while the CVT became increasingly involved in politics, contributing to some impressive developments, a tendency to seek compromise and shy away from militant trade union action increasingly plagued the organization. No doubt, part of this reticence stemmed from anxiety about confronting the Saigon government, both out of fear of a backlash and concerns that such a challenge would only aid the Communist enemy.

The dilemmas of coexistence with the Saigon government in fact grew more taxing as the war dragged on. In the wake of the 1972 Easter Offensive, during which the North Vietnamese made impressive gains before being repelled by American airpower, President Thieu declared martial law and banned all strikes. Since its founding, the CVT regarded the right to strike as an indispensable component of democracy. Nevertheless, Buu, who had resolutely resisted such incursions in the past, chose to acquiesce and support the ban. His action appeared to many a sad capitulation to a corrupt, authoritarian government. Buu insisted the CVT was now on the inside and needed to make sacrifices to maintain stability. "Now the situation — the danger — is different", he explained.[90] With the imminent departure of American troops, Buu now felt it necessary to stand with the Saigon government, even as the CVT's Cong-Nong Party continued to press for reforms.

With the announcement of the Paris Accords in January 1973, ending the United States' direct participation in the war, Thieu seemed even more determined to rein in labour — and all potential political opponents. Without American leverage, Thieu felt no obligation to continue fostering democracy. Reminiscent of Diem's Can Lao, Thieu announced the formation of the "Democracy (Dan Chu) Party" and made it clear that it would be the dominant force in South Vietnamese politics. Buu's refusal to join the "Democracy Party" prompted a spiteful Thieu to launch a labour wing of Dan Chu to compete directly with Cong Nong.[91] CVT officials recognized the threat, viewing the Democracy Party's labour wing as a first step toward creating a national labour union under Thieu's direct control.[92] Under the surface, resentment smouldered, but Buu and other CVT leaders (to the lasting bitterness of more militant members) resisted direct confrontation with Thieu. Again, labour bent.

Paradoxically, as South Vietnam crumbled, the CVT's political clout seemed to grow. Buu became an important ambassador/lobbyist to

Washington, able to gain meetings with antiwar Democrats. By the fall of 1974, he was using his leverage to criticize the government openly, charging that it was "inefficient and corrupt". Both Thieu and the North Vietnamese, Buu insisted, needed to dedicate themselves honestly to implementing the Paris Accords.[93]

In Saigon's final hours, Buu travelled to Washington in March 1975 for one last desperate round of lobbying, meeting with President Gerald Ford and Senator Edward Kennedy. "Give us sufficient aid to survive. Do not let us die slowly, agonizingly," he pleaded.[94]

Buu was wrong, of course; the death of South Vietnam would come quickly — in fact, within a few short weeks. Buu managed to find a space on the infamous American airlift, while key CVT leaders and their families escaped out into the South China Sea on a barge. Floating toward safety, the CVT refugees listened in grim silence as radio announcers read lists of those wanted by victorious North Vietnam authorities; some heard their own names crackle over the airwaves. In the vanquished city, an observer noted constant activity at CVT headquarters as the new government moved in, eager to use the compound for its own purposes. In the midst of the bustle, for several days no one thought to remove a portrait of Buu from the wall.[95]

CONCLUSION:
LINKING THE PAST TO THE PRESENT

From its inception, the CVT walked a fine — and dangerous — line. While extolling independence of action and autonomy from the state and all other forces, it was compelled by circumstances to engage in compromising alliances, especially with a succession of problematic Saigon governments. In the late 1940s, French authorities had allowed the formation of what became the CVT, in the hope that the organization might attract mass support for the struggling colonial regime. Meanwhile, confederation leaders sought to forge a militant and anticommunist labour movement without falling afoul of the colonial government. After the French departure and the division of Vietnam, the same treacherous pattern persisted. Buu and the CVT leadership sought to work with the repressive Diem government, while maintaining some level of independence. As a result, the organization was tainted by association with the Ngos, and suffered at the same time from government repression. Later, the CVT strove to work with the Americans and with the Thieu regime, going so far as to acquiesce in Thieu's ban on strikes in 1972. Such compromises allowed the confederation to navigate the dangerous shoals of South Vietnamese politics, yet tarnished the organization in the eyes of many. What was left was a public perception of dependence on outsiders — hardly the goal of an organization aiming to establish itself as an independent voice for Vietnam's workers.

This labour history, however, certainly makes Vietnam fertile soil for labour activism and agitation, to hibernate and re-emerge when the time comes. During its brief existence, South Vietnam saw a remarkable number of strikes, as hundreds of thousands threw in their lot with trade unions and activism. The tradition of anticolonialism and militancy seems to have lived on, to organize and challenge social and workplace injustices, though two-and-a-half decades separate the experience of the CVT and present-day labour upheavals in Vietnam. While the vast majority of strikes have occurred in the southern region, especially around Ho Chi Minh City, participants are very unlikely to have memories of the CVT. Older workers and union officials might have been activists in those tumultuous war years. For instance, VGCL President Dang Ngoc Tung was a construction worker in Saigon in the 1970s.[96] Between 1975 and 2008 came the experiences of war, collectivization, *Doi Moi*, globalization, and a population 60 per cent of which is under the age of 30, yet parallels between the earlier movement and current developments are evident. To paraphrase American humourist Mark Twain, while history does not repeat itself, it frequently rhymes.

As in the early 1970s, inflation combined with soaring energy costs have resulted in serious economic hardship and large-scale strikes. A massive migration of rural peasants into cities took place during the second Indochina War; similar migrations clearly contribute to challenges faced by workers today. Employee complaints about corruption and being given no time off for the *Tet* holidays are as familiar today as in the pre-1975 period.[97] Fiscal deficits and balance-of-payment concerns also plagued pre-1975 South Vietnam, much as similar factors worry Hanoi today. However, two intriguing commonalities standout: awkward labour–state relations, and workers targeting foreign-owned enterprises.

That strikes and workplace protest would focus on foreign direct investment (FDI) firms is no surprise. That is where the jobs are; since the early 1990s, FDI has dramatically outpaced the growth of state-owned enterprises (SOEs). As will be seen in several subsequent chapters, these foreign, mostly Asian investors are also notoriously exploitative. Hence, the vast majority of strikes in Vietnam are directed at such foreign-owned firms. Additionally, there is, as Irene Norlund has suggested, a certain "political correctness" about strikes in a socialist country aimed at intensively capitalistic firms.[98] Targeting foreigners, in a country with a history of exploitation at the hands of outsiders, may both play into this political correctness and reflect a continuing perception that SOEs are more responsive to workers' needs. Concurrently, government officials walk a fine line — seeking to continue attract foreign investment, while pacifying worker discontent.[99] In a similar fashion, workers and trade unions in the 1960s and 1970s targeted foreign employers and operations, especially American-owned firms and the U.S. military. Workers responded enthusiastically, launching several thousand strikes in a few years.

Conversely, in the past the CVT and organized workers generally avoided direct challenges or confrontations with the government. Trade union leaders fully understood the dangers inherent in challenging the state. The events of 1968, when several labour leaders found themselves gaoled, certainly reinforced the wisdom of focusing on outsiders rather than challenging one's own government. A working relationship with the state — particularly with the Labour Ministry and other government offices — was imperative. Beyond this, the CVT's philosophy from its earliest days stressed corporatist labour relations and systematic cooperation between unions, the state, and employers. The CVT strove to establish such a working relationship with a host of Saigon governments; the results, however, were decidedly mixed.

Today's Vietnamese General Confederation of Labour (VGCL) is obviously much more closely associated with the state and Communist Party.[100] Without question, the Vietnamese state has a great deal invested in a globalized economy; strikes and labour agitation already have made foreign firms wary of Vietnam. The VGCL finds itself uncomfortably between its government and an increasingly angry workforce.[101] The Party and police today have more capacity to infiltrate and neutralize illegal unions than was the case under Ngo Dinh Diem or Nguyen Van Thieu in South Vietnam.

Despite the legitimate discontent of some of its members, the VGCL, like the CVT before it, has not been ineffectual in pursuing workers' interests.[102] VGCL officials have not been silent as pressure builds. In autumn 2008 at a Hanoi conference on labour protection, confederation leaders blamed the recent wave of strikes on employers who flout labour laws and disregard commitments made to workers. Officials also acknowledged "some shortcomings in the State's management of the issue".[103] At the Hanoi conference, Truong Lam Danh, deputy chairman of the HCMC City Federation of Labour, bemoaned strikes prompted by employers' "broken promises".[104] Still, as with the case of the CVT a generation earlier, workers have ample reason to doubt the state-controlled VGCL's absolute dedication to their interests. Workers frequently call wildcat strikes, circumventing the confederation.

Tran Quoc Buu and other leaders of the pre-1975 South Vietnamese labour movement insisted that trade unions must be independent of the state (even as they habitually compromised their autonomy). Today, in some circles, critics of the VGCL have made tentative steps toward forming independent trade unions.[105] Such initiatives, however, have met with swift reprisals from the state. In 2006, authorities sentenced eight activists involved in organizing independent trade unions to prison terms.[106]

Given the long history of the socialist state in Vietnam and its persistence despite globalization, however, the VGCL is unlikely to be challenged by independent trade unions. While the state has an obvious stake in expanding and facilitating FDI, it remains rhetorically committed to creating a "civilised and equitable society".[107] Workers and the VGCL have played off that premise and, linking up with the lingering distrust of foreigners and capitalism, have made such gains as the recent increase of the minimum wage.

The militancy of today's Vietnamese workers would hardly surprise the leaders of the CVT, who witnessed the dramatic proliferation of strikes and worker action during the 1960s and 1970s. They would also certainly recognize and perhaps even sympathize with the VGCL as it struggles with limited success to give voice to worker discontent. A host of debilitating dilemmas burdened the confederation. Yet, in the words of Melanie Beresford, the "voice of the poor" may still "offset the growing influence of public–private business networks."[108]

Notes

1   Gilbert Jouan to M. Scherer, "le Consoler aux Affairs Sociales", 25 September 1948, "Travailleurs Chrétiens" folder, HCI, CS/109, Le Centre des Archives d'Outre-Mer, Aix-en-Provence, France (henceforth CAOM).
2   H. Guiriec to Haut Commissioner, 5 February 1948, HCI, CS/109, "Confédération des Syndicat Libre" folder, CAOM.

3   Le Chef du Service Central d'Action Sociale to M. le Gouverneur Général, 23 January 1951, "Travailleurs Chrétiens" folder, HCI CS/109, CAOM.

4   John G. Dean, "Memorandum for Files: Discussion with Nguyen Van Huyen, Minister of Social Action", 19 January 1954, box 3, Mission to Vietnam, Office of Director, Subject Files, 1950–54, Records of the U.S. Foreign Assistance Agencies, RG 469, National Archives, College Park, Maryland (henceforth NA).

5   "In one of the least well studied activities of the second Indochina war," noted Alexander Woodside, "representatives of world Catholic labor unions and the largest American labor unions (which strongly supported the American war machine in Vietnam) visited Saigon frequently and sponsored training classes for southern labor union cadres, after 1956." Alexander Woodside, Community *and Revolution in Modern Vietnam* (Boston: Houghton Mifflin, 1976), p. 287. Also see James L. Tyson, *Target America: The Influence of Communist Propaganda on U.S. Media* (Chicago: Regnery Gateway, 1981), pp. 145–54. Tyson charges the Western media of the time with deliberately dismissing the significance of the South Vietnamese labour movement as part of a "continuing world-wide Communist effort to destroy free labor unions by propaganda" (p. 149).

6   For general background on the Viet Minh's labour organizing and the history of the VGCL see Irene Norlund, "Trade Unions in Vietnam in Historical Perspective: The Transformation of Concepts", in *Labor in Southeast Asia: Local Processes in a Globalized World*, edited by Rebecca Elmhirst and Ratna Saptari (London: Routledge Curzon, 2004), pp. 111–12.

7   D. R. SarDesai, *Vietnam: The Struggle for National Identity* (Boulder: Westview Press, 1992), p. 49; Hue-Tam Ho Tai, *Radicalism and the Origins of the Vietnamese Revolution* (Cambridge, Mass.: Harvard University Press, 1992). The "idiom of class-based social analysis," Tai explains, "produced a drastic intellectual reorientation" toward recruitment of the working classes (ibid., p. 226).

8   Denis MacShane, *International Labour and the Origins of the Cold War* (New York: Oxford University Press, 1992), p. 248; Bernard Fall, *The Two Vietnams: A Political and Military Analysis* (New York: Praeger, 1963), p. 27; John Loss, "The Rise of the Labour Movement in South Vietnam" (M.A. thesis, University of Texas, Austin, 1975), pp. 3–10.

9   Bernard Fall, *The Viet Minh Regime* (Ithaca: Cornell University Press, 1954), p. 140; Alice Shurcliff, "The Trade Union Movement in Vietnam", *Monthly Labour Review* 72 (January 1951): 31.

10 Pip Nicholson, "Vietnam's Labor Market", in *Law and Labor Marketing in East Asia*, edited by Sean Cooney *et al.* (New York: Routledge, 2002), p. 124.

11 Edmund F. Wehrle, *Between a River and a Mountain: The AFL-CIO and the Vietnam War* (Ann Arbor: University of Michigan Press, 2006), pp. 35–37.

12   Joseph Zisman, "Labour in Indochina", October 1952, box 4, Office of Labour
     Affairs, Far East Country Files, 1948–1961, Records of the U.S. Foreign
     Assistance Agencies, RG 469, NA; Su Tri Nguyen, interview by author,
     Houston, Texas, 7 February 2003. Su Tri Nguyen, CVT Commissioner of
     Information, Research, and Propaganda in the late 1960s, also recalled the
     contribution of Father Alexis Parrel of the Société des Missions Étrangères
     to shaping the early CVT. Parrel remained in Indochina into the 1960s. On
     Catholic corporatist teaching regarding labour relations during this era, see
     Gary Gerstle, "Catholic Corporatism, French Canadian Workers, and Industrial
     Unions in Rhode Island", in *Labour Divided: Race and Ethnicity in United
     States Labour Struggles, 1835–1960*, edited by Robert Asher and Charles
     Stephenson (Albany: State University of New York Press, 1990), pp. 213–15;
     Woodside, *Community and Revolution*, pp. 286–87. Buu, according to Woodside,
     later advocated policies based on a "triangular principle" in which business,
     labour, and government representatives would gather to resolve problems. The
     "triangular principle" clearly evolved from Jouan's advocacy of *chambres
     mixtes de métiers*.

13   Trinh Quang Quy, *Phong Trao lao-dong Viet-Nam* [The labor movement in
     Vietnam] (Saigon: no publisher listed, 1970), pp. 32–33; Donald Heath to State
     Department, 15 December 1950, box 3, Office of Labour Affairs, Far East
     Country Files, 1948–1961, Records of the U.S. Foreign Assistance Agencies,
     RG 469, NA; "Confédération Générale des Travailleurs Chrétiens", 22 January
     1951, HCI CS/109, CAOM.

14   Quy, *Phong Trao lao-dong*, p. 37.

15   Ibid., p. 158; Douglas Dacy, *Foreign Aid, War, and Economic Development: South
     Vietnam, 1955–1975* (Cambridge: Cambridge University Press, 1986), pp. 1,
     10, 111. Alongside labour reforms, Bao Dai also initiated "a soft approach
     to agrarian reform based on land tenure". Economist Douglas Dacy describes
     the Vietnamese economy in the early 1950s as "top-heavy", with roughly
     80 per cent of the population involved in agricultural production, and circa
     150,000 Vietnamese civilians either serving in the French army or involved
     in military-type service. Industry was limited to a few factories, producing
     beer, soft drinks, and textiles. In addition to recruiting urban workers such as
     pedicab drivers and dock workers, the CVTC focused considerable attention
     on organizing rural workers.

16   Joseph Buttinger, *Vietnam: A Dragon Embattled* (New York: Praeger, 1967),
     pp. 780–81.

17   Quy, *Phong Trao lao-dong*, pp. 30–38.

18   Estimate by the French Sûreté Générale, "Tableau d'effectifs du Syndicats
     affileès à la CVTC", 22 February 1954, SPCE/77, CAOM Buttinger (1967,
     p. 1,066) estimated the number as 45,000.

[19] Jouan to Ministre de l'Outre Mer, 2 February 1956, 5H 37, Confédération française démocratique du travail (CFDT) Archives, Paris.

[20] "Note de Renseignements concernant la CVTC", July 1954, SPEC-77, CAOM.

[21] J.R. Deborde to M. Commissaire General, 4 May 1954, HCI SPEC/77, CAOM.

[22] "Notes pour M. le General D'Armee Commissaire General de France", 6 December 1954, HCI SPEC/77, CAOM; Alexis Parrel, "Le Syndicalism Chrétien au Vietnam", 5H 37, CFDT Archives.

[23] "Labour Report", 5 February 1955, box 15, Office of Labour Affairs, Labour Programs Division, Far East, Country Files, 1948–1961, Records of the U.S. Foreign Assistance Agencies, RG 469, NA. A rough total of some 900,000 refugees fled from the North to the South (Dacy 1986, p. 2).

[24] Buu to Lucien Tronchet, 22 July 1954, 31/3, Country files, International Affairs Department Papers, George Meany Memorial Archives, Silver Spring, MD (henceforth GMMA).

[25] Norlund, *Trade Unions in Vietnam*, pp. 110–12.

[26] "Briefing for the Ambassador and Charge d'Affaires", folder C2768, "Top Secret", Summer, 1954, box 1, Viet Nam, Saigon Embassy, Top Secret Subject Files, Records of the Foreign Service Posts, Department of State, RG 84, NA. The story of the CVT's tortuous relationship with American trade unionists, intelligence officers, and other U.S. government officials is told in detail in Wehrle, *Between a River and a Mountain*. It is unclear whether Buu or the CIA initiated the contact.

[27] "Note", June 1954, 5H 37, CFDT Archives; "Bulletin de Renseignement", 4 July 1954, HCI, SPEC/77, CAOM.

[28] CIA, "Current Intelligence Memorandum, Subject: Cast of Characters South Vietnam", 28 August 1963, box 128a, President's Office Files, Vietnam General, John F. Kennedy Presidential Library, Boston MA; Elbridge Durbrow to State Department, 2 March 1959; U.S. Department of State, *Foreign Relations of the United States, 1958–1960* (Washington, D.C., 1990) 1: 145–48 (hereafter *FRUS*, with year and volume number). The full name of the Can Lao was Can Lao Nhan Vi Cach Mang Dang [Personalist Labour Revolutionary Party]. According to Durbrow, Buu joined Nhu's organization as early as 1952. The NLF later excoriated the CVT for its ties to Diem: "Through yellow trade-unions, it [the Can Lao Party] took over the General Federation of Trade Unions, which had a Christian leadership, whose prestige it tried to raise by various means (giving trade-union cadres American-style training, providing relief for workers)", Ton Vy, "The U.S.-Diem Regime", *Vietnam Studies* 18–19 (1968): 35.

29   "Bulletin de Renseignments", 2 July 1954, "CVTC" folder, HCI, SPEC/77, CAOM.

30   Robert Shaplen, *The Lost Revolution: The U.S. in Vietnam, 1946–1966* (New York: Harper and Row, 1966), pp. 146–47.

31   Durbrow to State Department, 2 March 1959, *FRUS, 1958–1960*, 1: 145–48. Jodie Eggers to State Department, 12 December 1955, box 14, Office of Labour Affairs, Labour Programs Division, Far East, Country Files, 1948–1961, Records of the U.S. Foreign Assistance Agencies, RG 469, NA; "Rapport Moral Pronounce le 7 Mars 1954 par Tran Quoc Buu", SPEC/77, CAOM. Roughly two years before, French authorities estimated CVTC membership at 40,000. CVTC insistence on including non dues-paying "members" (or members who paid nominal dues) in membership estimates no doubt contributed to confusion over actual numbers.

32   Eggers to Leland Barrows, 8 May 1956, box 12, Office of Director, Classified Subject Files, Office of Director, Subject Files, RG 469, NA; McCarthy to Barrows, Director of USOM, "Activities of CVTC", 13 December 1954, box 12, Mission to Vietnam, Office of Director, Classified Subject Files, Records of U.S. Foreign Assistance Agencies, RG 469, NA.

33   Buu to Gaston Tessier, 22 November 1955, 5H 37, CFDT Archives.

34   Eggers to State Department, 12 December 1955, box 14, Office of Labour Affairs, Labour Programs Division, Far East, Country Files, 1948–1961, Records of the U.S. Foreign Assistance Agencies, RG 469, NA.

35   Eggers to Barrows, 14 February 1956, box 14, Office of Labour Affairs, Labour Programs Division, Far East, Country Files, 1948–1961, Records of the U.S. Foreign Assistance Agencies, RG 469, NA.

36   Eggers to Barrows, 15 October 1956, box 15, Office of Labour Affairs, Labour Programs Division, Far East, Country Files, 1948–1961, Records of the U.S. Foreign Assistance Agencies, RG 469, NA.

37   Shaplen, *The Lost Revolution*, pp. 146–47; Durbrow to State Department, 5 September 1960, *FRUS, 1958–1960*, 1: 560–61.

38   *Central Intelligence Bulletin*, 15 October 1963, CIA-RDP79T009-75A007 30014001-S [accessed through CIA Records Search Tool, Declassification Database].

39   Jose Maria Aguirre to Ernest Lee, 13 December 1963, 31/3, International Affairs Department, Country Files, GMMA.

40   Dean Rusk to Saigon Embassy, 3 November 1963; Saigon Embassy to State Department, 4 November 1963, *FRUS, January–August 1963, Vietnam, 1961–1963*, 4: 550–51, 560–61; Tran Van Don, *Our Endless War: Inside Vietnam* (San Rafael: Presidio Press, 1978), p. 110. In this autobiography, coup leader General Tran Van Don seems to admit that the new government had

arrested Buu and then released the labour leader at the request of Ambassador Lodge.

[41]   Henry Cabot Lodge Jr to State Department, 6 February 1964, box 1340, Central Foreign Policy Files, 1964–1966, Labour and Manpower, General Records of the Department of State, RG 59, NA. Khanh's charges against Buu appear to have no merit. Most likely Khanh saw Buu and the CVTC as a political threat.

[42]   Saigon Embassy to State Department, 5 May 1964, box 1340, Central Foreign Policy Files, Labour and Manpower, General Records of the Department of State, RG 59, NA. Reforms instituted by General Khanh included the ratification of International Labour Organization provisions against discrimination in employment, inspection of industry and commerce, and the abolition of the labour contracting system on the waterfront. In addition, Khanh appointed Nguyen Le Giang, a former vice president of the CVTC, as his labour minister.

[43]   *Le Croix*, 4 January 1964. IFCTU President August Vandistendael pronounced in early 1964 that the qualifier "Christian" in the CVTC name was not of "primordial importance".

[44]   To-Thanh-Tuyen, *Speech Delivered on the Occasion of the Seminar of the PSI Secretariats, Singapore, 1964, Subject: "Vietnamese Workers Movement"* (Singapore, no publisher, 1964).

[45]   On current conditions in the Asian textile and fashion industries see Jee Young Kim's chapter in this volume.

[46]   Lovestone to Dr Phan Quang Dan, 8 October 1964, box 707, Lovestone Papers, Hoover Institution, Stanford University, Palo Alto, California (henceforth Hoover). John Condon to State Department, 10 October 1964, box 1340, Central Foreign Policy Files, Labour and Manpower, General Records of the Department of State, RG 59, NA; *Saigon Post*, 23 September 1964.

[47]   Jean Lacouture, *Vietnam Between Two Truces* (New York: Vintage Books, 1966), p. 196; *New York Times*, 21 September 1964; Lovestone to Phan Quang Dan, 8 October 1964, box 707, Lovestone Papers, Hoover.

[48]   Tran Van Don, *Our Endless War*, p. 91. The Viet Cong, like the CVT, were mobilizing to take advantage of the weakness of the Khanh government.

[49]   Lacouture, *Vietnam between Two Truces,* pp. 196–98.

[50]   *New York Times*, 21 September 1964; *New York Times*, 22 September 1964.

[51]   *Saigon Post,* 23 September 1964.

[52]   Lacouture, *Vietnam between Two Truces,* p. 196; *Saigon Post*, 9 October 1964. The Vimytex strike ended roughly two weeks after the general strike. For the National Liberation Front (NLF, the Viet Cong) version of the 1964 general strike see Ton Vy, "The Workers' Struggle" in *Vietnamese Studies, No. 8: South Vietnam: 1954–1965* (Hanoi, 1966), pp. 104–6. Throughout its existence,

NLF propaganda pointed to South Vietnamese labour strife as evidence of widespread discontent with the ruling regime and U.S. presence. The NLF, however, largely ignored the organizing role of the CVT and dismissed its president as "the reactionary Tran Quoc Buu … camouflaged as a 'trade union militant'".

53   *New York Times*, 10 October 1964.

54   *New York Times*, 23 October 1964; *Saigon Post*, 24 October 1964.

55   Buu to George Meany, 26 October 1964, 31/3, International Affairs Department, Country Files, GMMA; Meany to Buu, 28 October 1964, micro 81, Office of the President, GMMA.

56   Victor Riesel, "Hungry Viet Workers", *New York Journal American*, 25 September 1964.

57   John Condon to State Department, 8 December 1964; Condon to State Department, 10 December 1964, box 1340, Central Foreign Policy Files, Labour and Manpower, General Records of the Department of State, RG 59, NA.

58   *New York Times*, 12 February 1965; Robert Topmiller, "The Lotus Unleashed: The Buddhist Struggle Movement in South Vietnam, 1964–66" (Ph.D. diss., University of Kentucky, 1998), pp. 40–45.

59   Condon to State Department, 30 September 1965, box 1340, Central Foreign Policy Files, General Records of the State Department, RG 59, NA; Su Tri Nguyen, interview by author.

60   Saigon Embassy to State Department, 2 November 1965, box 1340, Central Foreign Policy Files, 1963–1966, General Records of the Department of State, RG 59, NA.

61   *Free Trade Union News*, August 1966.

62   Lodge to State Department, 5 August 1966, box 1339, Central Foreign Policy Files, 1963–1966, General Records of the Department of State, RG 59, NA.

63   C.E. Pestill, 9 November 1965, Foreign Office 371/180600, Public Records Office, Kew Gardens, Richmond, London (henceforth PRO).

64   "Statement by the Vietnamese Plantation Workers", box 1300, Central Foreign Policy Files, 1967–1969, RG 59, NA; E.H. Peck, "The Economic Situation", 10 November 1965, FO 371/180600, PRO. The CVT's Federation of Plantation Workers issued a statement in the summer of 1967 detailing the problems of rural workers: "The cost of living has been increasing without respite, giving much trouble to the working class in general and to the plantation workers in particular. Workers in other fields of production have been granted wage increases or some form of allowances. Only the plantation workers have been forgotten." Also see Directorate of Intelligence Memorandum, "The Situation in Vietnam", 26 April 1967, CIA-RDP79T00826A001900010017-7 [accessed through CIA Records Search Tool, Declassification Database].

65   Lodge to State Department, 30 October 1966, box 1339, Central Foreign Policy Files, 1963–1966, General Records of the Department of State, RG 59, NA. Edward Lansdale to Lodge, 29 July 1966, box 2, Lansdale Materials, National Security Agency. Buu, hoping the Americans might intercede, also expressed fears of Loan to Lansdale aide and infamous CIA operative Lucien Conein.

66   Jacques Despuech, *Le Trafic des Piastres* (Paris: La Table Ronde, 1974), pp. 28–29. The CEE, founded by the French in 1900, actually encompassed three plants in the Saigon vicinity: in Cho Quan, Cau Kho, and Cholon. The Saigon government purchased the plants from the French in 1967 for close to one billion piasters. "Round-Up Letter", 29 November 1967, FCO 15/1012, PRO. British observers described the CEE sale as marking "a further stage in declining French economic influence in South Vietnam".

67   Ellsworth Bunker to State Department, 14 December 1967, box 1300, Central Foreign Policy Files, 1967–1969, General Records of the Department of State, RG 59, NA. "Activities Syndicales: Creation du syndicat de la Compagnie des Eaux et de l'Electricité installée à Saigon", 2 March 1954, SPEC/77, CAOM. Founded in March 1954, the CVT's Water and Electrical Workers Union dated from the waning days of French colonialism.

68   "Communiqué Issued by National Police", 30 December 1967, box 1301, Central Foreign Policy Files, 1967–1969, RG 59, NA.

69   Bunker to State Department, 11 January 1968, box 1300, Central Foreign Policy Files, 1967–1969, General Records of the Department of State, RG 59, NA; *Saigon Post*, 10 January 1968; "Round-Up Letter", 24 January 1968, FCO 15/482, PRO. The negotiations between the CVT and electrical company were complicated by a debate between South Vietnamese officials and the French former owners of the CEE as to who would pay the severance packages and raises.

70   Saigon Embassy to State Department, 11 January 1968, box 1300, Central Foreign Policy Files, 1967–1969, General Records of the Department of State, RG 59, NA; Quy, *Phong Trao lao-dong*, p. 102; "Round-Up Letter", 24 January 1968, FCO 15/482, PRO.

71   Saigon Embassy to State Department, 11 January 1968, box 1226; Bunker to State Department, 12 January 1968, box 1227, Central Foreign Policy Files, Viet S, General Records of Department of State, RG 59, NA; *Saigon Post*, 15 January 1968; *Saigon Daily News*, 13 January 1968.

72   *Saigon Post*, 15 January 1968; *Saigon Daily News*, 14 January 1968; *Le Monde*, 15 January 1968; Bunker to State Department, 15 January 1968, box 1227, Central Foreign Policy Files, Viet S, General Records of Department of State, RG 59, NA; Saigon Embassy to State Department, 19 January 1968, box 1300, Central Foreign Policy Files, Viet S, General Records of Department of State, RG 59, NA.

73   Arthur J. Goldberg, "The Electrical Workers Strike in Vietnam", 18 January 1968; Goldberg, "The Electrical Workers Strike in Vietnam", 29 January 1968; Goldberg, "Latest Report from Saigon Situation", 23 January 1968, 31/8, International Affairs Department, Country Files, GMMA; *Le Monde*, 17 January 1968. The events of the strike are also detailed in Quy, *Phong Trao lao-dong*, pp. 101–22.

74   Bunker to State Department, 24 January 1968, box 1301, Central Foreign Policy Files, 1967–1969, General Records of Department of State, RG 59, NA.

75   Bunker to State Department, 19 February 1968, box 1300, Central Foreign Policy Files, 1967–1969, General Records of Department of State, RG 59, NA.

76   Calvin Mehlert to Lansdale, 28 February 1968, box 106, NSC Files, Vietnam Files, Lyndon B. Johnson (LBJ) Library. The arrests of Tai and Quyen were part of a larger post-Tet Offensive police roundup, which included Truong Dinh Dzu, runner-up to Thieu in the recent presidential campaign who advocated recognition of the NLF.

77   *Saigon Post*, 4 June 1968; Minutes of Labour Advisory Committee on Foreign Assistance, 17 June 1968, and 12 November 1968, box 594, Secretary of Labour, Papers of Willard Wirtz, General Records of the Department of Labour, RG 174, NA; Bunker to Johnson, 29 May 1968, box 105, NSC, Country Files, Vietnam, LBJ Library. Thieu's appointment of Dam Sy Hien, a CVT official, as Labour Minister also helped ease tensions between the CVT and Saigon government.

78   "What the CVT has done for the Country during 1968", *Cong Nhan*, 8 February 1968. Dacy, *Foreign Aid*, p. 12. Improved security allowed the South Vietnamese economy briefly to enter the most productive period in its history. Between 1969 and 1971, rice production rapidly rose and the net domestic product increased 28 per cent.

79   Dacy, *Foreign Aid,* pp. 10–15, 71–72, 113; T. Louise Brown, *War and Aftermath in Vietnam* (New York: Routledge, 1991), pp. 234–35; Hiroshi Tsujii, "Rice Economy and Rice Policy in South Vietnam up to 1975", *Southeast Asian Studies* 15, no. 3 (December 1977): 265; Philip Taylor, *Fragments of the Present: Searching for Modernity in Vietnam's South* (Honolulu, Hawaii: University of Hawaii Press, 2001), pp. 79–80.

80   On the OCP and strikes against the U.S. military and contractors see Edmund Wehrle, "'The Nucleus of Craftsmen Needed to Build a Firm National Foundation': The Office of Civilian Personnel and Nation-building in Vietnam, 1965–1973", paper presented at the annual meeting of the Society of Historians of American Foreign Relations, Columbus, Ohio, 26–28 June 2008.

81   "Press Conference", 19 November 1969, box 429, Lovestone Papers, Hoover.

82   "For the President from Bunker", 4 July 1968, in *The Bunker Papers: Reports to the President from Vietnam, 1967–1973*, Vol. 2, edited by Douglas Pike (Berkeley: University of California Press, 1990), p. 494.

83 Berger to State Department, 13 August 1968, box 1300, Central Foreign Policy Files, 1967–1969, Records of the State Department, RG 59, NA.

84 Bunker to Secretary of State, 16 January 1969, box 6, Saigon Embassy, Files of Ambassador, Records of the Foreign Service Posts of Department of State, RG 84, NA; "Round-Up Letter", 10 July 1968, FCO 15/483, PRO; CIA Directorate of Intelligence, "The Situation in South Vietnam", 30 September 1968, box 68, NSC, Country Files, Vietnam, LBJ Library; Robert Shaplen, *The Road from War, 1965–1971* (New York: Harper and Row, 1971), p. 295.

85 Bunker to State Department, 7 November 1969, box 1301, Central Foreign Policy Files, 1967–1969, Records of the State Department, RG 59, NA. Shaplen, *The Road from War*, pp. 314, 346. Journalist Robert Shaplen noted that Buu might "finally be ready to come out in the open and lead the party personally. If he does, it could be an important development, he controls several hundred thousand workers and peasants" (ibid., p. 314).

86 "Press Conference", 19 November 1969, box 429, Lovestone Papers, Hoover; C.M. MacLehose, "Call on Mr Tran Quoc Buu, President of the CVT", 17 April 1969, FCO 15/1012, PRO.

87 Tran Quoc Buu, "Memorandum on the Political Party Situation in South Vietnam and the Position of the CVT", 31/10, International Affairs Department, Country Files, GMMA. On Cong Nong and political parties in South Vietnam see Theresa Tull, "Broadening the Base: South Vietnamese Elections, 1967–1971", in *Electoral Politics in South Vietnam*, edited by John C. Donnell and Charles A. Joiner (Lexington: Lexington Books, 1974), pp. 35–52.

88 Stuart Callison, *The Land-to-Tiller Program and Rural Resource Mobilization in the Mekong Delta of South Vietnam* (Athens: Ohio University, Center for International Studies, 1974), pp. 327–44; *Christian Science Monitor*, 31 March 1970; Dacy, *Foreign Aid*, pp. 15, 113; Stephen B. Young, "Power to the People: Local Development in Vietnam, 1968–1971", in *Electoral Politics in South Vietnam,* pp. 89–91. South Vietnam relied heavily on the United States Agency for International Development (USAID) promises of money to fund the Land to the Tiller program.

89 Bunker to State Department, 3 August 1971, box 1436, Subject Numeric Files, Records of Department of State, RG 59, NA.

90 Saigon Embassy to State Department, 18 July 1972, box 1436, Subject Numeric Files, 1970–73, Records of the Department of State, RG 59, NA. Buu issued his no-strike pledge on 15 July 1972.

91 *Washington Post*, 23 June 1973. On Thieu's Democracy Party, see Ta Van Tai and Jerry Mark Silverman, "Elections and Political Party Constraints Following the 1972 Offensive", in *Electoral Politics in South Vietnam*, pp. 125–49.

92 Saigon Embassy to State Department, 28 June 1973, box 1435, Subject Numeric Files, 1970–73, Records of the Department of State, RG 59, NA.

On 27 December 1972, Thieu issued a decree placing further constraints on party organization, ostensibly to quell the fragmentation and chaos so much a feature of South Vietnamese politics. The decree limited political participation to "broadly based and publicly known parties". Although Buu publicly approved of the changes, the new restrictions were so stringent that the CVT's Cong Nong Party proved unable to qualify for elections. In desperation, it joined with other parties to form the Democratic Socialist Alliance (Lien Minh Dan Chu Xa Hoi).

93 *New York Times*, 30 October 1974; Arnold Isaacs, *Without Honor: Defeat in Vietnam and Cambodia* (Baltimore: Johns Hopkins Press, 1983), pp. 322–23. In attacking Thieu, Buu aligned the CVT with Roman Catholics, veterans, and other Saigon interest groups protesting governmental corruption.

94 *Free Trade Union News*, March–April 1975.

95 *New York Times*, 3 May 1975; Tiziano Terzani, *Giai Phong! The Fall and Liberation of Saigon* (New York: St. Martin's Press, 1976), pp. 183–84.

96 While the CVT has little to no resonance with Vietnamese today, it is worth noting that VGCL President Dang Ngoc Tung grew up in Saigon and was a construction worker in the early 1970s (in his early twenties). Without doubt he would have been aware of the CVT.

97 On the problem of corruption in present-day Vietnam, see Mark A. Ashwill and Thai Ngoc Diep, *Vietnam Today: A Guide to a Nation at a Crossroads* (Yarmouth: Intercultural Press, 2005), pp. 58–60.

98 Norlund, *Trade Unions in Vietnam*, p. 126.

99 Long S. Le, "Labor vs. Market Vietnam", *Asia Times Online*, 5 April 2008.

100 Norlund, *Trade Unions in Vietnam*, p. 123. The VFTU changed its name in 1988 to Vietnamese Confederation of Labour.

101 On the many pressures facing the VGCL, see Quynh Chi Do, "The Challenge from Below: Wildcat Strikes and the Pressure for Union Reform in Vietnam", paper presented at the Vietnam Update, 6–7 November 2008, The Australian National University, Canberra.

102 See Do, "Challenge from Below".

103 "Vietnamese Trade Union said Failing to Protect Workers, Prevent Strikes", BBC Worldwide Monitoring, 8 September 2008.

104 Ibid.

105 Tran, *Our Endless War*, p. 444. Long S. Le, "Labor vs. Market Vietnam", *Asia Times Online*, 5 April 2008.

106 "Vietnam: End Crackdown on Labor Activists", Human Rights Watch New Release, 4 May 2009.

107 Melanie Beresford, "Doi Moi in Review: The Challenges of Building Market Socialism in Vietnam", *Journal of Contemporary Asia* 38 (May 2008): 226.

108 Ibid., p. 241.

References

Asher, Robert and Charles Stephenson, eds. *Labour Divided: Race and Ethnicity in United States Labour Struggles, 1835–1960*. Albany: State University of New York Press, 1990, pp. 213–15.

Ashwill, Mark A. and Thai Ngoc Diep. *Vietnam Today: A Guide to a Nation at a Crossroads*. Yarmouth: Intercultural Press, 2005.

Beresford, Melanie. "Doi Moi in Review: The Challenges of Building Market Socialism in Vietnam". *Journal of Contemporary Asia 38* (May 2008): 221–43.

Brown, Louise T. *War and Aftermath in Vietnam*. New York: Routledge, 1991.

Buttinger, Joseph. *Vietnam: A Dragon Embattled*. New York: Praeger, 1967.

Callison, Stuart. *The Land-to-Tiller Program and Rural Resource Mobilization in the Mekong Delta of South Vietnam*. Athens: Ohio University, Center for International Studies, 1974.

Dacy, Douglas. *Foreign Aid, War, and Economic Development: South Vietnam, 1955–1975*. Cambridge: Cambridge University Press, 1986.

Despuech, Jacques. *Le Trafic des Piastres*. Paris: La Table Ronde, 1974.

Donnell, John C. and Charles A. Joiner, eds. *Electoral Politics in South Vietnam*. Lexington: Lexington Books, 1974.

Fall, Bernard. *The Two Vietnams: A Political and Military Analysis*. New York: Praeger, 1963.

————. *The Viet Minh Regime*. Ithaca: Cornell University Press, 1954.

Gerstle, Gary. "Catholic Corporatism, French Canadian Workers, and Industrial Unions in Rhode Island". In *Labour Divided: Race and Ethnicity in United States Labour Struggles, 1835–1960*, edited by Robert Asher and Charles Stephenson, pp. 213–15. Albany: State University of New York Press, 1990.

Hue-Tam Ho Tai. *Radicalism and the Origins of the Vietnamese Revolution*. Cambridge, Mass.: Harvard University Press, 1992.

Isaacs, Arnold. *Without Honor: Defeat in Vietnam and Cambodia*. Baltimore: Johns Hopkins Press, 1983.

Lacouture, Jean. *Vietnam Between Two Truces*. New York: Vintage Books, 1966.

Long S. Le. "Labor vs. Market Vietnam". *Asia Times Online*, 5 April 2008.

Loss, John. "The Rise of the Labour Movement in South Vietnam". M.A. thesis, University of Texas, 1975.

MacShane, Denis. *International Labour and the Origins of the Cold War*. New York: Oxford University Press, 1992.

Nicholson, Pip. "Vietnam's Labor Market". In *Law and Labor Marketing in East Asia*, edited by Sean Cooney *et al.*, pp. 122–56. New York: Routledge, 2002.

Norlund, Irene. "Trade Unions in Vietnam in Historical Perspective: The Transformation of Concepts". In *Labor in Southeast Asia: Local Processes in a Globalized World*, edited by Rebecca Elmhirst and Ratna Saptari, 107–28. London: RoutledgeCurzon, 2004.

Pike, Douglas, ed. *The Bunker Papers: Reports to the President from Vietnam, 1967–1973*, vol. 2. Berkeley: University of California Press, 1990.

Riesel, Victor. "Hungry Viet Workers". *New York Journal American*, 25 September 1964.

SarDesai, D.R. *Vietnam: The Struggle for National Identity*. Boulder: Westview Press, 1992.

Shaplen, Robert. *The Lost Revolution: The U.S. in Vietnam, 1946–1966*. New York: Harper and Row, 1966.

———. *The Road from War, 1965–1971*. New York: Harper and Row, 1971.

Shurcliff, Alice. "The Trade Union Movement in Vietnam". *Monthly Labour Review 72* (January 1951): 30–33.

Ta Van Tai and Jerry Mark Silverman. "Elections and Political Party Constraints Following the 1972 Offensive". In *Electoral Politics in South Vietnam*, edited by John C. Donnell and Charles A. Joiner, pp. 125–49. *Electoral Politics in South Vietnam*. Lexington: Lexington Books, 1974.

Taylor, Philip. *Fragments of the Present: Searching for Modernity in Vietnam's South*. Honolulu: University of Hawaii Press, 2001.

Terzani, Tiziano. *Giai Phong! The Fall and Liberation of Saigon*. New York: St. Martin's Press, 1976.

Ton Vy. "The Workers' Struggle". *Vietnamese Studies* 8 (1966): 78–111.

———. "The U.S.-Diem Regime". *Vietnamese Studies* 18–19 (1968).

Topmiller, Robert. "The Lotus Unleashed: The Buddhist Struggle Movement in South Vietnam, 1964–66". Ph.D. dissertation, University of Kentucky, 1998.

Tull, Theresa. "Broadening the Base: South Vietnamese Elections, 1967–1971". In *Electoral Politics in South Vietnam*, edited by John C. Donnell and Charles A. Joiner, pp. 35–52. Lexington: Lexington Books, 1974.

Tran Van Don. *Our Endless War: Inside Vietnam*. San Rafael: Presidio Press, 1978.

Trinh Quang Quy. *Phong Trao lao-dong Viet-Nam* [The labor movement in Vietnam]. Saigon: no publisher listed, 1970.

Tsujii, Hiroshi. "Rice Economy and Rice Policy in South Vietnam up to 1975". *Southeast Asian Studies* 15, no. 3 (December 1977): pp. 263–94.

Tyson, James L. *Target America: The Influence of Communist Propaganda on U.S. Media*. Chicago: Regnery Gateway, 1981.

Wehrle, Edmund F. *Between a River and a Mountain: The AFL-CIO and the Vietnam War*. Ann Arbor: University of Michigan Press, 2006.

Woodside, Alexander. *Community and Revolution in Modern Vietnam*. Boston: Houghton Mifflin, 1976.

Young, Stephen B. "Power to the People: Local Development in Vietnam, 1968–1971". In *Electoral Politics in South Vietnam*, edited by John C. Donnell, and Charles A. Joiner, pp. 89–91. Lexington: Lexington Books, 1974.

3

STATE ENTERPRISE WORKERS
"Masters" or "Commodities"?

Michael Karadjis

The Communist Party of Vietnam (CPV) claims to be still running a socialist-oriented political system, and continues to cite the state economy as a key sector in the country's development. There has been an ongoing debate between the more socialist-oriented wing of the party, which advocates retaining significant state ownership throughout the economy, and the more market-oriented wing, which wants majority state ownership only in areas such finance and infrastructure while leaving the rest to the private sector. By examining one aspect of the state sector that can be considered an essential element of the CPV's "socialist orientation" — worker participation in management — this chapters seeks to interpret this debate.

In line with Leninist ideology, the CPV officially claims that workers must become "masters in social production".[1] However, as in other communist regimes that have diverged from their democratic ideals, making Vietnamese workers complete "masters" seems to be an impossible goal. In the pre-reform era, one may be led to assume that, like the Soviet and Chinese models it outwardly resembles, the Vietnamese state was totalitarian and thus had complete control over society, state enterprises, and workers alike. It could also be argued that workers have lost more ground since *Doi Moi* because of the autonomy granted to state-owned enterprises (SOEs), which has lent itself to greater control by management, i.e., the enterprise level of the party–state. According to this argument, as participants in a market economy, SOE management would tend to exploit workers in the same vein as capitalists; in the process, workers have become "commodities" (see, for instance, Greenfield 1994, pp. 207–8).

However, I argue here that Vietnamese workers were never totally controlled before the reform era, nor have they now been turned into commodities. While the party and state retain extensive powers of repression, their legitimacy partly rests on some degree of accommodation to popular pressure from workers and peasants, an inheritance of their revolutionary origins (see Beresford and Dang 1998, p. 12; Ngo Vin Long in Tsang 2002, p. 460).[2] I argue instead that while Vietnamese workers were never absolute "masters", their traditional participation in the workplace has continued through to having a role in SOE decision-making and this prevents them from becoming commodities in the post-*Doi Moi* period.

The first section of the chapter briefly discusses the pre-*Doi Moi* status of workers, followed by an overview of the formal changes put in place since the reforms and the debate over this within the CPV as the power nexus changed between the state, SOE management, and workers. The rest of the chapter describes the current conditions and status of SOE workers, beginning with case studies of two large state enterprises where I conducted interviews. These case studies suggest that there is still a significant level of workers' benefits and participation in SOEs despite the commercialization of the state economy. The final section describes how the official trade union, the Vietnam General Confederation of Labour (VGCL), together with its media outlet, the daily newspaper, *Lao Dong,* has helped workers to resist the onslaught of equitization which assails the remnants of socialism.

While the findings in the two case studies do not necessarily apply to all SOEs, they may be common to enterprises in the heavy industrial sector, which the CPV has decided should remain state-dominated. Both plants are also part of a great number of similar SOEs traditionally located in the provincial north outside major cities, where they play an important role in local society, and hence are subject to specific social concerns. The conditions in such plants also differ from both bankrupt SOEs and the generally highly profit-driven SOEs that are more exposed to the world market.

I believe that the existence of socialist legacies, even if only in certain parts of the state sector, allows for a better understanding of the orientation of Vietnamese politics. The stereotypical view is that those with pro-state sector views are either rigid conservatives, or party cadres profiteering from the existence of semi-socialist elements amidst growing capitalism. While such descriptions may be apt for some, focusing on them ignores the fact that many workers, communities, and ordinary officials continue to have a real interest in maintaining the state sector. My argument here is that socialist-oriented aspirations in Vietnamese society have a broad and genuine social base.

Viewing the debate this way also necessitates a non-monolithic understanding of the "party–state". Sections of the party and party-led mass organizations react differently to pressures from workers and peasants. The debate within the party can be interpreted as a reflection of the party feeling the necessity to respond to such pressures from below. This phenomenon will be demonstrated in the section documenting the struggle by the CPV-led trade union leadership of the VGCL and its newspaper, *Lao Dong,* against the anti-worker dynamics of equitization, and how this struggle has helped to empower workers to take direct action.

WORKERS AND SOES PRE-*DOI MOI*

The pre-*Doi Moi* management structure in a typical SOE conferred much formal power to workers. As described by Nguyen Xuan Con, a former head of the Vinatex (Vietnam Textile Corporation) trade union, the leading management body in each SOE was the enterprise council (*hoi dong xi nghiep*), officially called the *ban thuong truc dai hoi cong nhan vien chuc* (standing board of the workers' congress), signifying the fact that it was elected by workers at their annual congress.[3] Then there was the annual workers' congress (*dai hoi cong nhan vien chuc*) — distinct from the trade union congress — attended by all workers. Through the workers' congress, shop floor employees can participate in decisions about company plans and draw up collective labour agreements. Con further described the workers' congress as "the highest authority in an enterprise" that drew up business plans.[4] In addition to the workers' congress, there was also an unofficial leading body called the "group of four",[5] consisting of the state-appointed director of the enterprise (neither before nor after *Doi Moi* was the director elected); the head of the CPV branch; and representatives of the trade union and youth union. The trade union committee was (and still is) elected at a trade union congress, attended by all workers, which takes place every two to five years.[6]

It is beyond the scope of this study to judge the extent to which these official structures gave real power to workers. Nevertheless, most Vietnamese respondents I interviewed saw the role of workers as having been stronger pre-*Doi Moi*. For instance, long-time unionist Nguyen Phuong Hoa claimed that "directors have more power post-*Doi Moi*, so unionists have to be very firm and knowledgeable to stand up for the workers",[7] echoing many Western analysts. Gareth Porter, discussing profiteering by managers in the 1980s, writes that the SOEs "generated profits for cadres and workers ... everyone in the enterprise usually got a share" (1993, pp. 130–32). Adam Fforde and Stephen de Vylder (1996, pp. 256–57) include trade unions as being involved in SOE management in their discussion of the "multiplicity of agencies", seeing the pre-1986 polity as more a "bargaining" than a "command" economy.[8] Even Gerard Greenfield, who believes there was never any workers' power, sees *Doi Moi* as a strategy for the same elite to exploit their workers more brutally than before (Greenfield 2000, pp. 8–9, 29–32, 35–36). While none of these writers give much credence to official structures, their comments suggest that the pro-worker nature of these earlier structures was not entirely divorced from reality.

Doi Moi: **New Power of Directors and Reduced Power of Workers**

The greater role given to the market and to SOE autonomy at the Sixth CPV Congress in 1986 necessitated strengthening the role of the director *vis-à-vis* the state, the party, the workers, and the "group of four". The market economy required an SOE director to make fast business decisions without "political interference". New legislation in the next two years clarified that the director "represents the enterprise with full power in all production and business ... has the right to decide on the organizational apparatus ... (and) carries out the work of planning, choosing, arranging and using cadres".[9]

This took place, however, before the collapse of the USSR when the new CPV General Secretary, Nguyen Van Linh, still believed that the role of the market was to renovate socialism, not undermine it. Linh's heyday included introducing a quasi-democratic opening. He empowered unions, mass organizations, and the media to check "from below" those among the elite who would use the market to enrich themselves and to develop capitalism (Stern 1993, p. 43). He also appealed to workers and unions "to be active and dynamic" in "protecting working people's interests and in participating in managing, controlling and supervising state management organs" and in "struggling against the negative forces of management" (ibid.). SOE autonomy gives "greater powers to the chief", but this "cannot be separated from collective mastery" of "labour collectives" which the CPV must "foster and give full play to" (Nguyen Van Linh 1988, pp. 16, 21, 76).

In addition, the new legislation mandated the director to take the "necessary steps to implement the decisions of the workers congress", giving him/her "the power to decide on any operation of the enterprise in compliance with state plans, policies and laws and decisions of the workers' congress".[10] Further legislation reasserted the role of the workers' congress in business and production plans and policies, electing the enterprise council as its standing board between congresses, electing a workers' inspection board, and having a vote of confidence for the director. If the director wanted to change something between congresses, he/she had to consult the enterprise council. If agreement was not reached, the director could decide on matters related to business, but should submit to the enterprise council matters related to workers' interests.[11]

In practice, however, the growth of the market, the private sector, and foreign investment made it easier to empower autonomous managers than workers. New state enterprises were rapidly set up with little regulatory constraints, leading to a depletion of state capital and the emergence of SOEs that often differed little in their management practices from privately-owned businesses. In other words, the new legislative clauses which attempted to reserve some power for workers often had little effect on actual business and management practices.

Meanwhile, the economic crisis of the 1980s, followed by the collapse of the Soviet Union and the Council for Mutual Economic Assistance (Comecon) trading bloc to which Vietnam's economy was tied, led to the virtual collapse of the state system around 1989–91.[12] The bankruptcy of the state economy meant that Vietnamese workers' high official status as "masters" was fiercely eroded by retrenchment and pauperization. The rise of an unregulated private economy meanwhile impacted negatively on SOE workers as managers subcontracted production to private firms to counteract intense competition for market share.[13] The party leadership's aim to use the "workers as masters" ideology and institutions to serve as a check on market-driven managers met with little success.

The state's response was to try to reassert some control over the SOE directors and enterprises. In 1990, a new decree replaced the enterprise council with a management board. While half its members were still elected by the workers' congress, the other half (including the chairperson) was appointed by the government (the board then appointed the director).[14] Though the aim was to regain control over the director, this new set up also reduced workers' power and in fact, further strengthened the power of the director over the workers. The workers' congress still met, but under this arrangement it could merely "contribute" opinions and discuss and propose how to implement the production and business plan. The timing of the new decree coincided with the move to undermine Linh's early democratic impulses because of the collapse of the Soviet bloc and the Tiananmen Square events in China. The official consensus was that political reform had to wait for economic reform.

Further Changes in Management Structure and Reassertion of State Control

Under the 1990 legislation, the state-appointed members who made up 50 per cent of an SOE board were chosen by a variety of ministries and departments which had overlapping or contradictory interests. This confused the lines of responsibility between government departments and SOE authorities, leading to chaotic management. The state saw it necessary to regain control over important SOEs by diminishing the role of the line ministries. In 1994, eighty-two state corporations were created out of two thousand SOEs,[15] accounting for 80 per cent of the sector's production capacity. This also helped the state consolidate its finances to improve its competitiveness in the global economy.

The management structure of these new state corporations was defined in the 1995 Law on State Enterprises.[16] After 1995, SOEs were run by management boards (*hoi dong quan tri*, HDQT), whose members were appointed by a relevant ministry, thus ending the election of half the HDQT by the workers' congress. There was no longer an elected council nor officially a "group of four", though trade union heads and party units still retained an unofficial role and virtually all correspondents claimed an unofficial group of four continues to exist.[17] This structure curbed the power of directors, government departments, and worker-elected bodies alike. The director was appointed by the prime minister based on the HDQT's recommendations and held "supreme managerial power". If there was a disagreement, however, the director could "ask the competent state body to settle it", though the ultimate decision had to comply with the HDQT recommendations.[18]

The Law on State Enterprises identified the workers' congress as "a direct forum for SOE workers to take part in management". Under the law, however, the workers' congress was now limited to "discussing and making suggestions" about plans, business, and management, and to "adopting" decisions about "the use of funds directly related to the interests of the workers". Workers' representatives signed a collective labour agreement at their congress.[19]

The changes in 1990 and 1994–95 made in the name of business efficiency increased state control at the expense of both the director and the workers' congress to prevent management from becoming too independent of state control and social concerns or siphoning away state capital. Yet the reduction of the power of the workers' congress also increased the power of directors at the expense of workers.

An interesting issue here is how the trade unions reacted to these changes. Nguyen Xuan Con argued that while management and unions had had common goals before *Doi Moi*, the SOEs' new involvement in the market economy made it difficult for workers to make decisions, because their goals as both managers and employees were contradictory, causing many trade unions to become tools of management.[20] He claims that the VGCL took part in formulating these changes which reduced workers' and enterprise unions' direct role in management. Ton Thien Chieu from the Institute of Sociology asserts that this partial separation of unions from management *increased* their standing among workers by making the enterprise unions' role of protecting workers clearer.[21]

After 1992, however, as Vietnam emerged from economic disaster, workers were able to regain some bargaining power in SOEs that performed well. Workers were able to share in the enterprise profits in the form of bonus and welfare funds which grew in size as productivity rose, reinforcing the ethos of collective ownership (Beresford 2001, pp. 226–27). According to Fforde and de Vylder (1996, pp. 256–57), the SOE trade unions "formed alliances with local government to protect employment", at the expense of profitability.

Grassroots Democracy Decree for SOEs of 1999

A few years later, however, when the crisis of Asia's capitalist economies in 1997 spread to Vietnam, workers' bargaining power again weakened. The crisis drove profit-oriented SOE managers to employ anti-worker strategies.[22] This instigated some members of the CPV to lash out at dictatorial and corrupt SOE managers. An article in the CPV's top theoretical journal *Tap Chi Cong San* asserted that after *Doi Moi* "the role, position and power of the director became very large and brought about absolutism" (Tien Hai 1998, pp. 27). Another article said that before 1999,

> though many regulations existed enterprises did not follow them regularly; the legal and compulsory requirements ... were not very high ... employees did not have enough legal bases to know, discuss and inspect the leadership and the direction taken by the directors' board ... many directors became bureaucratic and became separated from the masses, made arbitrary and thoughtless decisions, and abused their authority, doing harm to the interests of the enterprise, the state and the workers. These leaders tried by all means to squeeze money and property from the state budget ... while workers' work and living conditions were unstable ... and those who dared struggle for justice were pushed aside. Therefore, there were many petitions ... letters of complaint and exposure increased rapidly. (Nguyen M. T. 2004, p. 45)

These strong views corresponded to those of the new party leadership after 1997. Alongside the Asian crisis, that year also witnessed a huge peasant uprising in the northern province of Thai Binh. The new leadership ultimately came out in support of the peasants' grievances, and some 2,000 cadres were disciplined (Kerkvliet 2001, p. 267). The new CPV general secretary Le Kha Phieu blamed the problem on a "lack of democracy", and criticized some Party members for:

> continuing to be prejudiced and imperious and clipped the wings of the people who criticized them, aggravating a strained social atmosphere. ... No longer able to stand their rising feeling of hidden anger, many people went to complain to the top, but those at the top avoided the problem, passed the buck, or offered solutions too late and unsatisfactorily. (Le 1998, pp. 6–7)

Phieu used this opportunity to introduce a partial return to "mobilization" tactics and initiated a grassroots democracy decree for the communes, introduced in May 1998,[23] followed by another for SOE workers in 1999.

The "Regulations on Exercising Democracy in State Enterprises" detailed the rights of SOE workers in a complete reversal of the spirit of the 1990 and 1995 legislation.[24] It was introduced partly to stem "from below" arbitrary and corrupt managerial power, encouraging workers to "combat waste and corruption and violations of democracy" (Nguyen M. T. 2004, p. 46).[25]

The decree specifies that the things to be *decided* by workers at congresses include voting on the collective labour agreement, the establishment and use of the welfare fund, and election of the people's inspection board. The trade union can only sign the agreement after approval by the congress. Congress can only comment on production and business plans, which are ultimately decided on by management, but to give the workers some means to check managerial power, they also "must" comment on personnel issues, which *will serve as references* for management, party organizations and mass organizations before their decisions".[26] These recommendations include running opinion polls on candidates for the director, the deputy director, the chief accountant, the chair of the HDQT, and unionists who would sit on the board.

The decree also mandates all production plans, laws and policies, regulations on workers' rights and benefits, financial reports, complaints and denunciations to be publicized. Workers can question the director or the board, inspect and supervise all such public information and monitor the implementation of the decisions made at the congress. The avenues for communicating grievances available to workers include the workers' congress, holding meetings in their sections and production teams, making complaints when the party committee and the union collect workers' opinions, participating in union activities, the union participating in management, electing the people's inspection board, meetings with top management "as scheduled or at urgent request", and filing written complaints in boxes placed around the enterprise.[27]

The fundamental changes of 1990 and 1995 that replaced the congress-elected council with a state-appointed board remained. The new provisions, however, greatly enhanced the formal position of workers *vis-à-vis* management, and theoretically gave the former some influence and oversight over state decisions.

Wages and Conditions in SOEs Better than in non-SOEs

Thus far we have laid out the legal regulatory changes over state enterprises since *Doi Moi*. We turn now to reviewing the real conditions in state enterprises. In general it shall be seen that they are significantly better than those in domestic private and most foreign-invested enterprises.

According to the International Monetary Fund, Vietnamese SOE profits average 3 per cent, well below that of the private sector (Painter 2003, p. 27). A major audit of the sector conducted by various consulting companies for the Ministry of Finance, henceforth collectively referred to as the Miyazawa audit,[28] showed an average return on equity of major SOEs to be 7.6 per cent, compared to 12 per cent for Chinese and 24 per cent for Indian SOEs (Packard and VICA Consultants 2004, p. 15). These figures are commonly cited to demonstrate SOE inefficiency in Vietnam. Lower profit margins may have many causes, but the idea that *one* of these causes may be less exploitative working conditions is rarely highlighted.

The fact that exploitation is less serious in Vietnamese SOEs is evidenced by relative wages and benefits. One study found public sector workers compared to workers in non-state sectors were "overpaid" by 20 per cent compared to those in the private sector, without taking into account the better benefits, job security, and lower-intensity work pace in SOEs (Mekong Economics 2002, p. 12).[29] From 2006 to 2008 average SOE wages were double private sector wages and 20 per cent higher than wages in foreign firms, and the rate of increase in SOE wages was double that of private and foreign firms in 2006 (Vo 2008, citing data from Nguyen 2008). According to a report in *Than Nien* on a survey by the Ministry of Labour, Invalids, and Social Affairs (MOLISA), "the rate of wage increase in SOEs was much higher than that of labour productivity: 16.9 per cent compared with 8.2 per cent" respectively (Quang Duan 2006). In contrast, while foreign-invested enterprises (FIEs) increased profits and productivity by 41.2 per cent and 13.8 per cent respectively, salaries only increased 12.6 per cent. The head of the Institute for Labour and Social Science, Nguyen Huu Dung, explained that this difference was due to the fact that SOEs tended "to pay salaries close to the top wage level". So while both the official minimum wage and the highest wages paid to workers in FIEs are higher than in SOEs, FIEs "pay much closer to the minimum wage" (ibid.).

The evidence presented above contradicts the common belief that SOE wages are lower than in private, especially foreign, firms. This belief stems from the fact that managerial personnel get higher salaries in private firms than in SOEs. The Miyazawa audit found that SOEs follow "a non-market system of fixing salaries", with the result that "non-skilled people get better salaries in SOEs than in the private sector and skilled people and management get lower salaries" (Ernst & Young and A & C Sandwell 2004a, p. 12). This is well illustrated in the Miyazawa audit's report on Hoang Thach Cement Company (which is also the subject of the second case study in this chapter). While the report claims — presenting no evidence — that private and foreign firms pay much higher salaries, it shows in fact that the average wage at Hoang Thach was VND2.7 million per month (in 2002), which was much higher than at any comparable private or foreign firm, and a high wage for shop floor workers, especially in a provincial town.[30] However, there was a very low compensation range, of VND2.2 to 5.2 million (US$147–347). The Miyazawa audit consultants disapproved of this relative equality, claiming that "those in middle and upper management can earn several times more" in foreign or private firms (Ernst & Young 2004a, pp. 60, 99–100, 121). In other words, the high salaries of *management* in the non-SOE sector give the illusion that the average shop floor workers' wages are also high, whereas in fact they are lower than SOE shop floor workers' wages.

Another difference is that SOEs adhere to legal benefits and work conditions better than do private firms. A 2002 study found that 90 per cent of workers in SOEs had contracts, as compared to only 40 per cent in the private sector.[31] An inspection of thirty-four private firms in 2005 found that most were in violation of the Labour Law.[32] All enterprises employing at least ten workers must pay social and health insurance for them, but one study showed 92 per cent of workers with health insurance were state employees.[33] Enterprises with ten or more workers must also have unions, but of 63,874 grassroots unions, 51,000 were in the state sector. These unions had 3,400,000 members constituting almost the entire state sector workforce, but those in the private sector had only 1,200,000 members, which was a fraction of the private workforce.[34] According to one worker who had worked in an SOE for nineteen years:

> Before equitization, most policies were very good to workers, such as health care, training, education ... we had holidays, our children got rewards if they studied well; the trade union built compassionate houses for poor workers; female workers were sent to courses at the women's union ... the fee was paid by the company, we even had funds for funerals and weddings. ...[35]

SOEs also have a less profit-driven attitude to job security and employment. One report claims "as many as half the workers would be redundant if SOEs were to operate fully" like private firms do (Mekong Economics 2002, p. 7). A World Bank report indicates the stark difference between such conventional economic definitions of "redundant" labour, and that of the SOEs. While SOE directors thought there was almost zero redundant labour in the textiles and garments, plastic products, iron and steel, coal and minerals, 3 per cent in glass and ceramics, and 7 per cent in machinery and equipment industries, respectively, the Bank's estimate of redundancies in these industries was between 15 and 82 per cent (Truong and Bui 2004, citing Rama and Belser 2001). The Bank's estimate also derives from the leaner workforce and faster pace required by private firms' striving to maximize their profits, which helps to explain why the Bank recommends mass retrenchment at the time of equitization. On the other hand, the SOEs' contrasting interpretation of "redundant" labour, which is taken as a sign of their lower "efficiency", indicates their concern for providing employment; it may also explain why the SOE work environment is generally regarded as more humane.

These trade-offs should be taken into account when discussing "low" SOE profits. Superior conditions in SOEs stem not only from their partly non-profit nature and the fact that workers have some say in how the factory should be run, but that some 30–50 per cent of SOEs' after-tax profit additionally goes to the welfare and bonus funds managed by the union and the workers' congress.[36]

Admittedly, not all SOEs treat workers that well. One study of workers' conditions and attitudes in SOEs and private firms in the 1990s, for example, showed that workers in a state textile mill had much higher levels of job satisfaction over a number of issues than workers in state mechanical and rubber factories (Ton 1996).[37] This could be explained by the fact that the textile firm performed better in the market economy while the mechanical and rubber factories had old and outmoded equipment which prevented them from adapting to the new economic conditions (see Trinh 1997, p. 32).[38]

Compared with the commercially successful private firms in the same study, however, the workers in the state textile firm also showed a much higher satisfaction level with *all* issues, including income; and even in the two poorer SOEs, workers were more satisfied than in the private firms with most issues, except for income (Ton 1996). Thus, while this study indicates that successful SOEs were able to treat their workers better than ailing SOEs, the former were also regarded as providing better worker benefits than successful, profit-driven private firms. Similarly, other studies have shown that workers in state garment companies enjoy far superior conditions than those in private and foreign firms and their average wages are one-third higher (Navdi and De Armas 2002).[39] Of course, SOEs are increasingly exposed to pressures from global market competition, which may drive their work conditions down to that of the private sector (Kabeer 2002).

Having provided an overview of the structural changes in organizational arrangements in the SOEs and their general work conditions and compensation rates, I will now present case studies of two important SOEs in the provincial north to illustrate workers' participation in such enterprises. Following these will be a third case study of how workers struggled against the anti-worker actions of an SOE management, and a final section provides an overview of workers' struggles to retain these rights when equitization begins to take these benefits away.

Workers' Participation in SOE Management

It is not easy for a foreign scholar to go into large state enterprises to interview workers. Admittedly, this could also imply that there were some constraints in the responses provided, but generally I was impressed with the workers' openness.

In 2005, I visited two large, important SOEs: the Bai Bang Pulp and Paper Company in Phu Tho, a major subsidiary of the Vietnam National Paper Corporation (Vinapimex); and the Hoang Thach Cement Company in Hai Duong, the major subsidiary of the Vietnam National Cement Corporation (VNCC). Both companies are established leaders in their fields. Neither is highly profitable nor heading towards bankruptcy. But Bai Bang is under threat from further international trade liberalization. While certainly not representing all state enterprises, both Bai Bang and Hoang Thach may typify many companies in the large state-owned heavy industrial sector. Vinacoal, the third enterprise analysed here, is also in the same sector, yet the management and workers acted quite differently when it underwent a serious crisis in 1999 following increased world market exposure.

To check on the information acquired from within the factories, I conducted some interviews outside the two plants; the differences between the two sets of information obtained are minor. On topics such as workers' benefits and the workers' congress, which were discussed seriously, there is essentially no difference between information obtained from on-site interviews and those conducted elsewhere. Workers interviewed outside the plant were much more likely to complain, however, about the heavy-handed attitudes or behaviour of supervisors and middle-level bosses but they did not see top management as a source of such problems.

Case I: The Bai Bang Paper Co. Plant

Bai Bang Paper Company was built between 1974 and 1982 with Swedish aid. Inaugurated in 1982, the plant operated for eight years under the guidance of Swedish consultants until 1990 when it came under full Vietnamese management. Today Bai Bang is the largest of the seven pulp and paper plants owned by Vinapimex. In 2001 Vinapimex's annual turnover was VND2,426,822 million, with an after-tax profit of VND44,846 million (Ernst & Young/A & C Sandwell 2004a). Until recently it was the sole producer of pulp in Vietnam. In 2003, equipment was upgraded and annual capacity rose by quite a large margin. Bai Bang's Phase 2 expansion began in 2007, raising its pulp production to 250,000 tonnes, making it self-sufficient in pulp "and enabling it to supply pulp for much of the rest of the paper industry".[40]

As the sole producer of printing and writing paper, however, Vinapimex requires huge investment as demand continues to rise much faster than production. Though importing bulk timber was cheaper than paying farmers state-set minimum prices, Bai Bang's expansion had a social purpose. Bai Bang had been buying timber from farmers who had been provided subsidies as part of re-greening and poverty alleviation programs. According to Pham Van Tu from the Vinapimex management board, in 2002–03 the price paid to farmers was VND320,000 for one tonne of timber, while imports cost US$22 (VND308,000), but the government obligated Vinapimex to buy farmers' timber.[41] Bai Bang also had to buy all the farmers' timber despite lack of pulping capacity.[42] Additionally, instead of buying from supply areas nearby, out of "political consideration" Bai Bang buys from distant provinces, increasing costs and complicating planning and delivery time (Ernst & Young/A & C Sandwell 2004b, p. 76). Trade protection measures against imports and higher prices for urban consumers should be seen in this social context. When protection levels dropped after 2003, Bai Bang had to improve its paper quality.

My Bai Bang visit included a plant tour and discussions with Mr. Dai Van Hoi and Mr. Nguyen Xinh, the Chairman and Deputy Chairman of the Bai Bang trade union, with groups of workers from the maintenance section who had been working there for periods ranging from 18 to 27 years,[43] and from the paper mill, all working there at least twenty years and also with workers around town informally outside of work time.[44] Bai Bang has some 3,500 workers,[45] with an average monthly wage in 2005 of VND1.8–2 million (US$120–140), which is a significant sum in semi-rural areas. Workers claimed only two or three companies in the region paid such wages. This figure was corroborated not only in formal and informal discussions with workers, but also by the Miyazawa audit, which found an average wage of VND1.8 million already in 2001 (US$120). Salaries range between VND1.2 to VND5.4 million a month, reflecting the restriction in SOEs on high managerial salaries (Ernst & Young and A & C Sandwell 2004a, p. 21).[46] This may have doubled, according to workers on my subsequent visit in April 2007, when the average income at Bai Bang was reported as VND3.5 to 4 million.[47]

In general, workers agreed that shop floor conditions, benefits, and environmental and living standards were rather good. The company emphasizes safety standards, equipment, clothing, and the like, though in informal discussions some expressed some concerns about safety. But Bai Bang's work conditions were not as good as Hoang Thach's, the plant in the second case study. Many workers were wearing only Vietnamese sandals.[48] The noise level was high but workers were not wearing any ear protection. In fact, we were told there had been a recent dispute over safety issues. On the positive side, however, workers' houses next to Bai Bang looked rather magnificent and beautiful.

The workers' congress was seen by the workers as an important avenue via which they had some means to have some say in the running of the enterprise, for instance, when a draft production plan was first outlined by management and union leaders and submitted to the workers for discussion. Before the congress meets, small meetings are held during each shift and in each unit to discuss the proposed plan and suggest amendments. Workers told us that they "contribute to the production plan", "discuss solutions to problems", "discuss salaries and benefits", "decide how to spend the welfare and bonus funds", "discuss improvements to the Labour Code", "sign a collective labour agreement", "elect the workers' inspection board", and "vote for the management at the congress" without fear of reprisal at the workers' congress. One even claimed that "in SOEs, the workers congress determines almost all issues, from the production plan to the collective labour agreement". When we asked what happened when there is a disagreement, most said that this was very rare, and when conflicts did occur, they were related to workers' benefits, most often over safety standards. The most negative point made by some workers was that "they didn't have the information" regarding certain issues, particularly in strategic planning. Workers can make a real contribution in these pre-congress meetings and vote for or against the amended plan as a group. Therefore, there was little reason to vote against the final plan at the congress itself.

Workers have a confidence vote for the board of directors and chief accountant at the congress. If a candidate gets a low rating from workers, the union takes this to management for reconsideration. While the director makes the final decision, most thought a strong opinion from workers would be taken into account.

A 'people's inspection board' (*ban thanh tra*, BTT) is elected at the congress every two years. Workers say its roles include "dealing with questions, problems and complaints from workers", "investigating claims by workers about problems in the company and solving them", "investigating any suspicions workers have" (workers submit letters about concerns to the BTT), and "supervising management's compliance with the Labour Code and the collective labour agreement".

Seven hundred workers, a third of the workforce, are CPV members.[49] The CPV cell is not officially part of management but, like the trade union and sometimes the youth union, it plays an unofficial role as part of the "group of four", which is virtually always consulted about important decisions.

It is the congress that decides how the welfare fund is spent. The fund is spent on three main things: holidays for workers and their families; sports, cultural and leisure activities, and facilities; and solidarity funds and poverty alleviation programs. The size of these funds depends on company profit.[50] The trade union is entrusted to handle the fund between congresses.

Workers were very keen when the conversation turned to the topic of vacationing. They go everywhere in the country, and sometimes even overseas, to countries such as China, Thailand, Malaysia, Singapore, and Sweden. Workers have twelve days of paid annual leave, and an increase of one day for each five work years (for those working in toxic areas, two days). The work week is 40 hours, but when there is a sudden demand for rush orders or when a machine breaks down, they do overtime, but not more than 4 hours per day or 200 hours per year ("as in the Labour Code and the collective agreement signed at congress").

The plant also has impressive sports and entertainment facilities paid for and maintained by the welfare fund. The facilities include a stadium, sports complex, and sports grounds with a gymnasium, aerobics area, swimming pool, and three tennis courts; a dance hall, museum, library, and outdoor seating. There are also three kindergartens, and a primary and a secondary school funded by Bai Bang and run by the Ministry of Education and Training. In terms of health care, on top of medical benefits, the company runs three free clinics.

While workers are appreciative of these excellent work and living conditions, they are not seen in a positive light by others who tried to discredit them by showing the enormous cost this imposes on Bai Bang. The Miyazawa audit estimated Bai Bang's man-hours per production unit were 88 in 2002, compared to only 9 in an average Asian paper mill, and when converted to dollar terms, the cost was US$75 and US$26 respectively. The report therefore claimed that there was a serious overstaffing problem of 2,100 excess workers out of a total of 3,867. However, it lamented there was "no immediate solution" in "the current Vietnamese legal and social environment" (Ernst & Young and A & C Sandwell 2004a, pp. 120, 122) implying that social responsibility prevails over budget concerns. The latest information is that despite the report, there has been little retrenchment, suggesting that social concern for employment prevails.[51]

Case 2: The Hoang Thach Cement Plant

Hoang Thach Cement Company, the VNCC's largest subsidiary, was established in 1980.[52] The VNCC consists of fifteen enterprises, which includes nine cement companies and six trading, investment or materials companies; it also has a 35 per cent stake in two joint-ventures with foreign capital. In 2002, VNCC's domestic market share was 45 per cent (55 per cent if its joint ventures were included). Its main competitors are joint-stock companies, other SOEs, and joint ventures. All in all, the cement industry is state-dominated and VNCC aims to become the leading cement producer in Southeast Asia.

The factory premises look clean, uncluttered, and well organized. Work appears to be at a steady but relaxed and human pace. All workers were wearing hard hats. Signs for safety and safe use of equipment can be seen next to literally *every* machine. There was an ample supply of filtered drinking water. Meals are good and clean (we ate with the workers). Each worker is given a VND15,000 (US$1) allowance per meal, an amount that was more than adequate, since a decent meal cost only VND6,000.

At Hoang Thach we had extensive discussions with Mr. Tinh, the deputy chairman of the Hoang Thach trade union[53] and we met two groups of workers, one from the mechanical section and the other from the mechanical repair team.[54] In addition, we also had informal discussions with workers outside work time.[55]

Hoang Thach produces one-third of all VNCC's cement. Some parts of VNCC are scheduled to be equitized, but not Hoang Thach, according to Tinh, "as the state still wants to use it as a tool to control the market". The plant has 2,759 workers, of whom 466 are women. There are 400 engineers, 1,689 production workers, and 557 office workers. The average salary in 2005 was VND3 to 3.5 million (US$200–233) per month, a high workers' salary in Vietnam.[56] The director's salary cannot exceed the top rate allowed in the Labour Code. There is a regular eight-hour working day, from 7.00–11.30 a.m, and 1.30–5.00 p.m. Workers either live nearby or in one of three company dormitories.

According to Tinh, while the trade union's job is "to protect rights and benefits of workers", it also has a "common goal" with management "to accomplish the government plan". The union participates in management, and the head of the trade union is a member of the board of directors. Indeed, both unionists and workers we spoke to gave the impression of a great deal of workers' participation in decision-making, to a greater degree than at Bai Bang. While the workers' congress is the major forum, there are a number of other meetings, conferences and other methods of participation. Every week, there is an open day for soliciting opinions from workers. One person from Hoang Thach's management board is assigned to sit there for the day to receive anyone who wants to talk or make an inquiry. Every month, each unit holds a meeting to discuss problems with the union; the union heads then hold a meeting and bring up workers' opinions and concerns to management. "Workers can be very open about opinions and suggestions," said one worker. Both types of meetings take place during working hours, as do all union meetings. If they choose to, workers can also request a meeting with management about issues as they arise, and the union may even organize a workers' conference when a problem arises. Finally, the union also collects workers' anonymous suggestions and comments from boxes placed around the plant.

Workers said that Hoang Thach holds two workers' congresses, at the beginning and at the end of the year. Workers in each section prepare for them by holding a meeting coordinated by the grassroots union to discuss issues, and all these "mini-congresses" build up to the big congress. According to Tinh, the union has an important input into the congress as it has "considerable knowledge to provide the workers with ideas about whether the plan is feasible".

Interviews with Hoang Thach workers led me to feel that congress decisions here had greater authority than at Bai Bang. The memorandum signed by congress representatives and the director obliges management to implement production plans passed in accordance to workers' comments. A nine-member people's inspection board elected by the congress assesses and monitors proper implementation and an assessment report is presented at the next congress, based on interviews with workers.

While the director is chosen by the government via VNCC (from a number of nominees), my impression was that the workers' confidence votes had a strong influence on this decision. According to workers, "labour conferences in each unit vote for the directors of the units who in turn vote for the company director, and the deputies", taking into account the workers' confidence vote. According to Tinh, "a big guy from the government comes to find out how the workers voted". In other words, this government official is mindful of workers' opinions on the various candidates before making a decision.

The CPV unit is also a powerful force in the enterprise. There are 670 party members in Hoang Thach, about a quarter of the total workforce, and the party committee consists of 21 members. A party representative sits on the board of directors, and the head of the party unit is one of the deputy directors, while the director and union head are usually CPV members. The party unit in an SOE is at the same bureaucratic level as that of the district. Tinh is of the opinion that in SOEs, "the major leader is the party", and workers too say that the party's decisions over all sorts of things are channelled down through party members in the various units, such as the youth union, trade union, and the board of directors. The mass organizations are also represented in the SOE. There is the women's unit, which is part of the trade union. The women's unit consists of twenty-six sub-units, one for each section of the company, whose role is to collect women's opinions and share work-related and other issues reported by each of the small groups which meet monthly. Every section also has a unit of the youth union, which implements the political programmes of each district where the company is located. The youth union participates in many local youth activities such as conferences, festivals, and recreational activities, educational programmes, and cultural and sporting events. Because the women's and the youth unions are seen as doing important work for the company, their activities can take place during work hours.

The workers' congress also decides how to spend the welfare fund and bonuses, which can amount to over a million dollars. These funds account for 50 per cent of the after-tax profit, with the rest set aside for production expansion. The fund is used to cover a large number of programmes, ranging from sports and financial assistance to families in trouble to gifts for festive occasions and vacations in Vietnam and even abroad, along with poverty reduction programmes outside the enterprise. The company is particularly good at taking care of workers' health. One worker even said "this is one of the best companies for health". Every year workers receive a free medical check-up, and those in potentially hazardous environments get a special bonus. If a health problem is detected, "the worker is sent to a special hospital to be treated". One young worker said he chose to work at a state company "because they have better benefits packages than other sectors, whether private and foreign". Another young worker added that "state firms have a more human work environment and human relations inside the company".

Readers who are sceptical that such SOEs still exist in Vietnam should be convinced that they do if they read reports written by the consultant economists engaged in the audit of the sector, who in 2002 estimated that "excess labour" at Hoang Thach was around 75 per cent (or if the benchmark was other developing countries, around 60 per cent), or about 1,500–1,650 employees of the total workforce of 2,606. The consultants judged that its "'appropriate manning level' should be 949" (Ernst & Young 2004*b*, pp. 8, 91–92). Interestingly, Tinh from the union said that Hoang Thach has *increased* its workforce to 2,759 workers in 2005 after the audit. In other words, the Vietnamese government had not taken the advice of these neo-liberal consultants.

At Hoang Thach 1,086 tonnes of cement were produced per employee annually (the most productive ratio in VNCC was 1,756 tonnes at Ha Tien I). By contrast, the joint ventures Chinfon and Holcim produced 4,200 and 4,400 respectively, and cement companies in Thailand produce 6,000 tonnes per employee (Ernst & Young 2004*c*, p. 95). However, using the discourse of "SOE inefficiency" to try to explain the huge gap between the figures cannot help explain how the Vietnamese cement industry became successful and close to the cheapest in the region. The consultants themselves acknowledge that there is a social dimension in SOE industrial production. As revealed in their complaint that "there is virtually no realistic option for downsizing due to the *very high mandates for social and community responsibility*, the prevailing state regulatory framework and the position of *primary employer in an isolated location, supporting extended families*" (Ernst & Young 2004*b*, p. 92, my emphasis).[57] Thus the cement SOEs play a very important social role in their regions.

Case 3: The Quang Ninh Coal Mines

The Quang Ninh coal mines was chosen to counterpoise Bai Bang and Hoang Thach to show that not all SOEs have an enterprise culture where workers still participate in management. What occurred in 1999 in the mines was an example of an SOE acting against workers' interests. Greenfield's earlier research on these mines provides the background: Vinacoal (the state coal corporation) bosses in collusion with unregulated "bandit" private mines seriously undermined the jobs and incomes of Vinacoal miners (Greenfield 2000, pp. 251–54). Vinacoal's alliance with foreign capital led to a profit-driven strategy of over-reliance on exports. Following the Asian crisis, exports to the region fell, leaving a large stockpile in 1999 which led to mass retrenchment. While Greenfield's criticism is compelling, I disagree with his conclusion that these events represented an outright victory of a coalition between SOE management, the party–state and the workplace trade union, whose imperative was to introduce capitalist "efficiency" (ibid., pp. 260, 262–63). On the contrary, there was a twist in the story. Vinacoal's downsizing of the workforce led to a belated struggle within the party–state that thwarted an outright victory.

In May 1999, the Quang Ninh workers' congress voted that of the 85,000 employees, the 70,000 workers on long-term contracts would not lose their jobs (Nguyen and Luu 2000). Based on this decision, Vinacoal sacked the remaining 15,273 workers who were on short-term contracts. However, some 50,000 permanent workers were put on temporary rotational retrenchment and paid 70 per cent of their basic wage,[58] leaving 18,000 permanent workers unaffected.[59] White-collar and managerial staff were paid only 50 per cent of their salaries for four months (Chu 1999).[60]

While the official union reactions may have been weak, Greenfield's assertion that they backed management needs some qualification. My interviews with union officials indicated that they were strongly opposed to the mine closures, and argued that laid-off permanent workers should get their jobs back.[61] However, while the government did order Vinacoal to end the rotational retrenchments of the 50,000 miners, they were put on four-day work weeks and their wages were reduced by 15–20 per cent for six months (Duc Hung 1999). The VGCL also saved the contracts of short-term workers who were relatives of permanent workers (Ung and Quang 2000b). In the end, out of 15,000 workers slated to lose their jobs, only 5,500 actually did, according to the Vinacoal union head.[62] The VGCL was in fact highly critical of Vinacoal. One Lao Dong piece, which slammed cement and power SOEs for buying "bandit coal", accused the Vinacoal subsidiary, Dong Bac, of hiring thousands of seasonal workers under reduced employment conditions, equating it to "bandit mining" (Chu Tuong 1999b). Nevertheless, workers clearly suffered from Vinacoal's mismanagement and profiteering, and the unions were unable to prevent this during the height of the crisis.

Subsequent developments, however, cast doubt on the view that Vinacoal scored an outright victory in league with the party–state. For instance, the State Inspectorate launched an investigation involving the government, the unions, and Vinacoal. The report in July 2000 was scathing:

> Vinacoal purposefully exaggerated how much coal it had stockpiled. By doing so, it was able to inflate costs ... and so seek state approval to delay loan repayments and take out more loans. ... Vinacoal reported ... that its coal stockpiles had reached 4.34 million tonnes by the end of 1998 ... it asked for government permission to export at lower than regulated prices, to cut its number of miners and lower salaries. The actual total of stockpiled coal by the end of 1998 was just 2.42 million tonnes. (Tu Huong 2000)

The report held Vinacoal's directors and management board responsible. One manager had signed dozens of contracts at "lower than normal export prices", incurring losses of hundreds of thousands of U.S. dollars. Other allegations concern cash "drained away through investments and infrastructure", "illegal trading of foreign hard currency and unlawful financial and operational management moves" (ibid.). One manager, head of an affiliate in a joint venture with a U.S. firm, fled to the United States, but was jailed upon his return to Vietnam.[63]

The VGCL, the Vinacoal union, and the Industrial Unions of Vietnam conducted their own investigation about Vincoal's management's corrupt practices and demanded that the four officials most responsible be sacked, be given the "highest financial penalty" and face a criminal court, and that Vinacoal should return VND12 billion (about US$800,000) to the state. VGCL deputy head, Do Duc Ngo, claimed "the entire problem was the fault of management", but that the Vinacoal trade union was also responsible for not knowing what was happening, for not expressing its views, and having "very limited" participation in management.[64]

The fact that the VGCL, *Lao Dong*, and the State Inspectorate all challenged Vinacoal is evidence that the party–state is not monolithic. Different societal interests are represented within it, well beyond the commercial interests of enterprise management. It is unclear whether the mine workers actually staged a strike but clearly they were angry, and the VGCL's legitimacy may have been compromised had it done nothing. The fact that the union, though an arm of the party–state, took a proactive role without apparent direct pressure from mass workers' actions indicates it is not totally inactive.

Vinacoal's actions do not suggest a watershed victory for profit orientation at the expense of workers and society; and it may be surmised that the struggle within the party–state helped prevent such an outright triumph. First, the workforce increased from 85,000 in 1999 to 95,000 in 2005.[65] While this may be partly due to expanded coal production, the Miyazawa audit recognized grudgingly that Vinacoal is "required to maintain an excessive workforce to meet community and social objectives" with "no flexibility to restructure their labour force", and it has "no intention" of doing so, due to its "social responsibilities" (Jonker/Ernst & Young 2004, pp. 13, 54, 105). Even retrenching those on temporary contracts is now more difficult since the revised Labour Code of 2003 because companies are allowed to hire temporary workers for only one contract term — if the contract is renewed even once, the worker must be made permanent (ibid., appendix, p. 60).

In addition, profits are actually low for a company allegedly taken over by capitalist logic, too low even to generate operating cash flows, according to the Miyazawa audit. Vinacoal is mandated to sell coal at a lower than market price first to the steel, cement, fertilizer, and electricity SOEs before it can export. In 2003, coal prices for these sectors were US$4.50 per tonne lower than the export price, and even the normal domestic price was US$3 lower than export prices. In short, Vinacoal was made to sell at a little above production cost (ibid., pp. 4, 8–9).[66] Further, Vinacoal's non-coal businesses established in 1999 to absorb redundant labour from the coalfields are a heavy financial burden on the company (ibid., p. 14).[67] While allowing other sectors of the economy to gain from cheap coal, Vinacoal has been made to sacrifice itself for the public good.

Finally, according to the Miyazawa audit, "average mine labour costs" are VND 2.5 to 3 million per month, "far higher than the average salary in Quang Ninh", and this "impacts the salary of this region". Salary and related expenses represent 33–54 per cent of the cost of production, which "does not reflect the competitive advantage of low labour costs" (ibid., pp. 9, 54).[68]

WORKERS RESIST PRIVATIZATION

The forces of equitization work to undermine, indeed to undo, the better work conditions and job security enjoyed by Vietnamese workers in SOEs. Equitization has two main goals: to inject extra capital into SOEs and transform management so as to undermine the role played by the state, party, trade unions, mass organizations, and workers' congresses that are seen as cumbersome and inefficient. After equitization, the shareholders' meeting becomes the management board, and profit becomes the main goal of the enterprise. Parallel to equitization is the drive to eliminate the practice of appointing directors, including the various steps of "recommendation and voting for directors"; this refers to a change in the process by which state corporations will hire general directors, which "economists welcome" (Anh Hieu 2005). By removing all the other bodies, the director's power is further strengthened. Equitization is therefore the real threat to the traditional SOE management. While equitization has proceeded faster in light export-oriented industries, since 2004 government policy has been to extend it to most sectors. Once again, however, a struggle inside the party–state has held up the process.

Equitization was piloted in 1992.[69] In the early stages, state and workers together held 80–100 per cent of the shares.[70] Shares were provided to workers to mobilize idle capital, and to make workers feel that they were "real owners" and so would work more efficiently (Do 1991, pp. 62–63; Greenfield 1994, p. 219, quoting Thanh Phong 1993). While party leader Do Muoi claimed "workers as masters" by being shareholders could "rid the system of the disease of bribery and corruption", Prime Minister Vo Van Kiet believed workers should simply be able to buy shares like anyone else. At the opposite end of the spectrum in the debate, the theoretician Nguyen The Kiet thought that workers' share ownership was merely one step further towards privatization in that workers were being exploited "by more subtle methods" (Greenfield 1994, pp. 218–20).[71]

Of the 776 SOEs equitized by 2001 (accounting for only 2 per cent of SOE capital), workers held most shares in 453 of them and the state was the majority shareholder in 66 of them, and only in 35 of them did outsiders hold most shares. In the initial equitization phase, 40 per cent of all shares went to workers, 9 per cent to managers, 34 per cent to the state, and 17 per cent to private shareholders. By 2001, however, the percentage of shares held by workers had dropped to 35 per cent, as they sold shares to private individuals, whose share increased from 13 to 20 per cent. Workers' "influence as stakeholders" stagnated, while that of the director and the management board increased. The degree to which management and other shareholders could influence the appointment of directors also rose sharply in relation to workers (CIEM 2002, pp. 7, 17, 38, 39, 47–49, 53). Thus, even this version of equitization could not ensure "workers' mastery".

Following the Ninth Congress, the influence of the market-oriented wing of the CPV increased. Legislation in 2002 dropped the pretense that workers were masters.[72] Preferential shares to workers were capped at 50 per cent, while upper limits on share ownership for managers, individuals, and private firms were abolished (CIEM 2002, p. 60), facilitating buy-outs of worker shares. In a survey of 400 workers in two Ho Chi Minh City firms, 220 had initially bought shares but by 2004 only 52 had retained them (Nguyen L.H. 2004). The deepening of equitization is negatively impacting on workers' participation at the workplace, in terms of job security and benefits. Once managers own the firm, workers are turned into "wage earners only" who have no more say in profit distribution, reinvestment plans, or social insurance schemes (ibid.).

As a result, equitization has been held up. It is still often reported to be "slow" and "behind schedule" (World Bank and ADB 2002, pp. 22–24; EIU 2004a). While some 3,000 SOEs had been equitized by 2006, they only accounted for 12 per cent of SOE capital (EIU 2006). It is not only the socialist-oriented wing of the CPV or some SOE managers who were likely to lose their privileged positions who have held it up.[73] Resistance has also come from workers and trade unions. As noted by the World Bank, equitization was "difficult to implement without the consent of the director and a majority of the workforce" (World Bank and ADB 2002, pp. 22, 26).[74]

A conflict between VGCL-led labour and the equitized enterprises has emerged. According to Chau Nhat Binh from the VGCL,

> as international integration, marketization and equitization proceeds, there are increasing conflicts between managers and workers. ... Equitized firms are curtailing the management role of unions and party cells. Equitization means the shareholders' meeting makes all decisions. Workers are told they will vote as shareholders, so they do not need a congress. However, they control few shares and eventually sell them.[75]

According to Tran Trun Phuc, the VGCL "requested the state to issue regulations allowing workers to still hold a congress." But "it would only be allowed to discuss workers' issues, and even on these would have little power."[76] Binh adds that "many workers now want the unions right out of management, to clarify their role, lest they start advocating on behalf of an even more market-driven management".[77]

According to the deputy chair of the VGCL in Ho Chi Minh City:

> In the past workers could become managers — there were many notable examples. Post-equitization the role of trade unions is unclear. The owners of production are now the controllers of production and workers are wage labourers ... (now) we really only supervise management and it is an illusion to talk of workers' management. This is undermining the concept of the workers state.[78]

These forthright statements by leaders of the CPV-run union federation were supplemented by daily articles in the VGCL's newspaper *Lao Dong*, which denounced the loss of union power and violations of workers' rights. Headlines proclaimed unions have become "functionless", workers' rights are "forgotten" or congress "disappears" (Duong 2005; Dang 2005; Quang and Tran 2005; Quang 2005). One article asserted that "working relations are now relations between bosses and workers for hire" (Quang and Dang 2006). *Lao Dong* reported favourably on strikes and struggles in equitized enterprises (as it does on strikes at foreign or private firms). The VGCL claims that only 8 per cent of strikes are in state firms.[79] Below are two such examples.

Four hundred workers at Minh Khai, a textile SOE undergoing equitization went on strike in October 2005. Under the heading "The rights of workers are violated", and with a front-cover photo of striking workers, *Lao Dong* supported their grievances, which included harsh conditions, low salaries, no bonuses, no leave, and "no grassroots democracy" (Thu and Dang 2005). The article also accuses the factory trade union of collaborating with management, asking "Where is the grassroots trade union?" (ibid.).[80]

In another case, *Lao Dong* reported that workers in an equitized construction materials' SOE discovered that management had colluded with outsiders to seize a large proportion of shares. The court ruled in the workers' favour and declared the new management illegal, but the new management maintained control because the provincial people's committee was willing to tolerate the situation. When the court demanded the new management hand the company seal back to the worker-shareholders, the deputy director took the seal home. For four months, no business took place. Workesrs could not work and the unused machinery was "paralyzed". *Lao Dong* applauded dozens of workers who led a "sit-in" protest against the people's committee (Cong 2005).

In these two examples, the party-led trade union leadership stood with the workers against a management that was rorting the system. Both cases involved direct action by workers. As equitization is official CPV policy, this boldness by the CPV-led VGCL indicates that a form of social opposition is tolerated within party structures, a type of "pluralism" fundamental to Vietnamese politics.

This allows certain conclusions to be drawn about relations between workers and sections of the party–state. On the one hand, the VGCL, acting partly under pressure from their worker-base, plays the role of a "transmission-belt" from the ranks upwards (just as they can be a transmission-belt from the party–state leadership downwards). On the other, such official sanction for "illegal" workers' protests helps embolden workers to keep up the struggle.

Some academics are also critical of equitization. Truong Thi Minh Sam and Bui Duc Hai of the Southern Institute of Social Sciences, for example, wrote of the "strong criticism of equitization" throughout society and in the media (Truong and Bui 2004, p. 2). There is "an emerging new thinking" they claim, which "challenges the very idea of equitization" (ibid.).[81] They believe this resistance, including from inside the party–state, can partly be explained by the inheritance of the war and revolution, which left a great ideological impact on Vietnam, especially among the two million party members as a big force at the grassroots level (not the elites), and millions of ordinary veterans ... this is a kind of civil society which has its own voice and influence from the local to the central level. They are working in equitized SOEs where they are suffering from worsened conditions or even made redundant. ... (ibid., p. 11)

Aside from this mass base, they also claim "the party's intellectual old guards [sic] are forming a true civil society organization to fight against corruption in the process of equitization. ... These voices could hamper adventurous steps of the National Assembly" (ibid.).

Discourse on Vietnamese politics tends to see the old guard as "conservatives" who are out of touch with "reality". Truong and Bui, in contrast, see them as a civil society, with a mass base committed to socialist ideals, in reaction against the reality of growing exploitation and injustice fostered by the market and privatization.[82]

CONCLUSION

The onset of *Doi Moi* and the interaction of the state sector with the international market and growing private sector led to pressures on SOEs to put capitalist profitability and efficiency ahead of their traditional social roles. This had an impact on SOE workers, particularly in terms of their position as "masters" of production.

Nevertheless, despite their more profit-driven nature, most state enterprises still generally provide significantly better pay and conditions to their workers than do other sectors and allow workers some role in management as has been described in this chapter. Thus, while the market economy weakened the workers' formal status as "masters", inherited aspects of their traditional role prevented SOE workers from being reduced to mere commodities.

Initial *Doi Moi* changes strengthened the power of the director *vis-à-vis* the state, the party unit, the trade union, and the workers' congress, reflecting the relative autonomy granted to SOEs. However, the party and state later reimposed a degree of control over SOEs and their directors. From the other side, the power of SOE workers, trade unions, and workers' congresses were weakened at first in relation to the directors, who strove to reduce the role of the workers as the SOEs were run like commercial enterprises. Workers challenged this and the SOE-led economic recovery in the 1990s gave them confidence to reassert their strength. With many directors acting arbitrarily and engaging in large-scale theft of state property, the state upgraded the formal position of workers with a grassroots democracy decree, reaffirming the central role of the workers' congress, though as shown in this chapter, the effects of this remain uneven.

Hence, despite many changes, the SOE management structure is still composed of various actors representing different societal interests. Such a complex structure represents, at least theoretically and often in practice, a degree of social impact from the bottom over production. As a result this structure is being constantly targeted by SOE-reform advocates who believe SOE management needs to become more autonomous and totally profit-orientated.

Equitization aims at further undermining this traditional structure to hasten the transformation of these SOEs into purely profit-oriented enterprises. Even where workers initially have had a majority of shares, many have ended up selling them to managers. As equitized SOEs become more profit-oriented, they attack workers' traditional roles, plant antagonism, and elicit conflict with labour. Market pressure on state enterprises does not simply pit rank-and-file workers against management; rather working class and societal opposition are also expressed via elements of the state and party, reflecting their origins and the ideological basis of their continued legitimacy. The labour-oriented stance taken by the VGCL, and in particular that of its campaigning newspaper, *Lao Dong,* reflects this significance.

Many analysts believe the slow speed of equitization and the stubbornness of old SOE structures is due to resistance to "reform" from self-seeking officials who have vested interests in the old structure, alongside those wearing ideological blinkers. These are often alleged to be the two sources of the so-called conservative bloc within Vietnamese politics. However, there are also self-seekers in management who have vested interests precisely in equitization, while workers and potential losers in other sections of society also have legitimate interests in preserving the traditional structure. Therefore, so-called "resistance to reform" should be seen in a different light. The resistance put up by workers in the two case studies discussed above show how SOE workers do not easily accept being turned into commodities, a condition imposed on the new working class constituted mainly by recent rural migrants experiencing gruelling exploitation in private and foreign firms in export processing zones.

Therefore, the insistence by the socialist-oriented wing of the party to maintain a leading role in the state sector reflects the real presence in Vietnamese society of a positive, if contradictory, role of that sector within the socioeconomy, and of the social classes which benefit in some form from its continued presence and traditional structure.

While equitization to date has only mainly advanced in areas more fully exposed to the world market, government policy aims to equitize most areas. Therefore, the confrontations over equitization discussed in the previous section are not irrelevant to the more strategic industries such as paper and cement; as illustrated in the case studies above, workers in these industries are still holding onto a strong position of maintaining some degree of "master" status. Their real struggle to defy commodification may yet lie ahead.

Notes

1   This was one of the strategic goals listed in the CPV's 8th Congress in 1996, "to establish, consolidate and enhance the status of workers as masters in social production". Communist Party of Vietnam (CPV), "Political Report of the 7th National Committee to the 8th National Congress" (1996), in *75 Years of the Communist Party of Vietnam 1930–2005: A Selection of Documents from Nine Party Congresses* (Hanoi: The Gioi Publishers, 2005). Lenin claimed workers' "supervision and control" of nationalized factories was the difference between mere "confiscation" and "socialization". Vladimir Illich Lenin, "Left-Wing Childishness and the Petty-Bourgeois Mentality", *Collected Works*, vol. 27, 4th English ed. (Moscow: Progress Publishers, 1972 [1918]), pp. 323–34.

2   Ben Kerkvliet cites Brently Womack's view that Vietnam's system is both "authoritarian" and "mass-regarding" or "quasi-democratic", in "Politics and Society in the Mid 1990s", in *Dilemmas of Development: Vietnam Update 1994,* edited by Benedict J.T. Kerkvliet (Canberra: Research School of Pacific and Asian Studies, ANU, 1995), pp. 7–9. There is a reluctance to use open forms of repression against collective action, although the state does act against individual or small group protests, most notably against dissident intellectuals.

3   Nguyen Xuan Con, interview, Hanoi, November 2005. Adam Fforde and Stefan de Vylder state that "workers often accounted for 50 per cent of the members of enterprise councils" in *From Plan to Market: The Economic Transition in Vietnam* (Boulder: Westview Press, 1996), p. 256. As this study focuses on the post-*Doi Moi* system, I wasn't able to do in-depth interviews on the issue of how democratic pre-*Doi Moi* elections were.

4   Nguyen Xuan Con, interview, op. cit. Melanie Beresford makes the same claim
     in "The Political Economy of Dismantling the Bureaucratic Centralism and
     Subsidy System in Vietnam", in *Southeast Asia in the 1990s: Authoritarianism,
     Democracy and Capitalism,* edited by Kevin Hewison, Richard Robison, and
     Gary Rodan (St Leonard's: Allen and Unwin, 1993), p. 226.
5   According to Nguyen Xuan Con (op. cit.), the enterprise council and group
     of four were the official and unofficial leading bodies, respectively. Ton Thien
     Chieu of the Institute of Sociology in the Academy of Social Sciences and
     Humanities says that the official name of the group of four was *Ban Lanh
     Dao* (leading board). Interview, Hanoi, 25 November 2005.
6   Dung Du Duc, Head of Trade Union, Northern Airlines Services Company
     (NASCO, a subsidiary of Vietnam Airlines), interview, Hanoi, July 2005.
7   Nguyen Phuong Hoa, Head of Trade Union, Textile Research Institute, Vinatex,
     interview, Hanoi, November 2005. Hoa was previously the head of two other
     trade unions: first in a state wood company (Cong Ty Go Cau Duong) and
     then in a company under Vinatex.
8   See also Beresford who argues that pre-*Doi Moi* Vietnam was not really a
     "command economy" but rather was "a system in which the demands of con-
     flicting interest groups within society were negotiated through the mediation
     of the state apparatus". Melanie Beresford, "Vietnam: The Transition from
     Central Planning", in *The Political Economy of Southeast Asia*, edited by
     Kevin Hewison, Richard Robison, and Gary Rodan (Oxford: Oxford University
     Press, 2001), p. 228.
9   Council of Ministers, Decree 50-HDBT, "Regulations on State-Owned Industrial
     Enterprises", 22 March 1988. This decree added further substance to the first
     landmark legislation increasing the power of the director and ceding SOEs
     more autonomy, Council of Ministers, Decision 217-HDBT, "Renovation
     of Planning and Socialist Business Cost-Accounting in State Enterprises",
     14 November 1987.
10   Decision 217-HDBT, op. cit., Decree 50-HDBT, op. cit.
11   Council of Ministers, 2 June 1988, Decree 98-HDBT, "Regulations on the
     Right of Mastery of Workers Collectives in State-Owned Enterprises".
12   Until 1989 Vietnam was still involved in Cambodia and was under an
     international embargo, while suffering heavily from the previous war without
     any reparations. Inflation had risen to hundreds of per cent in the late 1980s.
13   Greenfield writes in relation to Vinacoal, the coal-mining SOE, that even "the
     threat of competition for employment and the removal of the constraints on
     managers to fire workers did not have its full effect until the spread of over
     a thousand 'bandit' mines…Contracting out and cooperation with the private
     sector by state mine managers saw workers forced into the unregulated
     small-scale private mines (with) intense competition and unrestrained profit

maximization." Gerard Greenfield, "The Development of Capitalism in Vietnam", *Socialist Register* 30 (1994): 212.

[14] Council of Ministers, 10 May 1990, Decision 143 HDBT, "Reviewing the Implementation of Resolution 217-HDBT, Decree 50 HDBT and Decree 98 HDBT and Working to Continue the Renovation of the Management of State Enterprises".

[15] The Prime Minister, Decision 90-TTG and 91-TTG, 7 March 1994. These corporations are commonly known as "Corporations 90 and 91" after the numbers of these decisions. The Corporations 91 consist of the largest, most strategic, corporations.

[16] The President of the Socialist Republic of Vietnam, Law on State Enterprises, 30 April 1995.

[17] A deputy director of the Northern Food Corporation said that the head of the union is one of the "leaders" who "always" has a voice in management meetings; interview, Hanoi, June 2005. Similarly, a deputy director of the Vietnam Tobacco Corporation said the trade union leader participated in "every" meeting of the board of directors; interview, Hanoi, July 2005. Similar statements were made by management personnel in the Tea and Paper corporations (Nguyen Khac Thinh, Head, Administrative Department, Vietnam Tea Corporation, interview, Hanoi, July 2005; Pham Van Tu, Management Board member, Vietnam Paper Corporation, interview, Hanoi, August 2005). In Sugar Corporation 1, a separate 'supervisory board' exists alongside the HDQT, including the trade union head and heads of departments, according to Mr Khanh, Head of Office, Vietnam Sugar Corporation 1, interview, Hanoi, September 2005. In Song Da Corporation, the head of the trade union is an actual member of the HDQT, according to Mr. Tinh, Song Da Corporation, interview, Hanoi, 8 August 2005. Clearly, there are many variations.

[18] This is the structure for state corporations only. In SOE subsidiaries of the corporations, and in ordinary SOEs outside the corporations, there is no HDQT; the enterprise council was replaced by a simple board of directors, consisting of a director and several deputies. The corporation HDQT appoints the director of the affiliate SOEs, facilitating government control. However, workers conduct a "vote of confidence" for the director and the other positions.

[19] Law on State Enterprises 1995.

[20] Nguyen Xuan Con, interview (see note 3). Gerard Greenfield, in "From Class to Commodity: Workers and Capitalist Industrialisation in Vietnam" (Ph.D. dissertation, University of New South Wales, 2000), p. 9, makes similar points, quoting Hoang Chi Bao and Nguyen Thanh Tuan, "Vai tro cua cac nghiep doan trong co che thi truong" [The role of unions under the market mechanism], *Lao Dong & Cong Doan* [Labour & trade union review] 150 (September 1993).

21 Ton Thien Chieu, interview (see note 5). A survey of SOE workers that Chieu was involved with in the 1990s showed that 47.4 per cent viewed the union as their best representative in any conflict with management. Ton Thien Chieu, "Quan he xa hoi trong xi nghiep cua cong nhan cong nghiep" [The social relations in enterprises of industrial workers], *Xa Hoi Hoc* [Sociology] 2, no. 54 (1996): 38–57.

22 Greenfield's study, "From Class to Commodity", provides a good example, that of the mass retrenchments in Vinacoal in 1999.

23 Government [of Vietnam], 11 May 1998, Decree 29/1998/ND-CP, "Regulations on the Implementation of Democracy at the Commune Level".

24 Government [of Vietnam], 13 February 1999, Decree No. 07/1999/ND-CP, "Promulgating the Regulations on Exercising Democracy in State Enterprises".

25 According to Nguyen Xuan Con (see note 5), the greater power given to directors had led to corruption, and "the decree was introduced to control this power".

26 Decree No. 07/1999/ND-CP; my emphasis.

27 Ibid.

28 The "diagnostic audit of Vietnam's important state enterprises (SOEs)" was "implemented under the supervision of the Ministry of Finance with technical support from the World Bank and funding support from Japan's Miyazawa Fund and other bilateral donors, notably Danida and AusAID". Its goals were to "strengthen Vietnam's capacity to compete in international and domestic markets", to advance SOE reform, and to assess "the commercial viability of the SOEs". Ernst & Young and A & C Sandwell, *Final Summary Report: Vietnam National Paper Corporation*, Operational Reviews of State-Owned Enterprises in the Steel and Paper Industries (Hanoi: Ministry of Finance and Miyazawa Fund, 2004[a]), p. 12. As such the audit provides a good idea of international donors' views, informed by economic efficiency. See reference list for the full list of reports.

29 The World Bank's earlier estimate that "income per worker in the private non-farm rural sector is roughly *one-fifth* that of the state non-farm rural sector" indicates a very stark difference in some areas. World Bank, *Vietnam: Advancing Rural Development from Vision to Action* (Hanoi: World Bank, 1998), p. 18.

30 Average wages in 2002 were 2.5 million in Bim Son Cement and Ha Tien 2 Cement, and 2.9 million in Ha Tien 1 Cement, other VNCC plants.

31 "Negligence Causes Increase in Work Accidents: Union", *Viet Nam News*, 15 January 2002.

32 "Violations of Labour Law on the Rise", *Viet Nam News*, 25 May 2005.

33 Vu Xuan Phu, Department of Health Economics, University of Public Health, Hanoi, "Health Insurance Members by Categories and Regions 1997, Vietnam

Health Insurance Association" (1998), p. 6, paper provided during interview, Hanoi, December 2005. Many companies especially in the non-state owned sector avoid participating in social and health insurance. Trinh Thi Hoa from Vietnam Social Insurance explains that many companies, especially in the non-SOE sector, avoid participating in social and health insurance. Trinh Thi Hoa, "Social Insurance: Status and Prospects", *Vietnam's Socio Economic Development* (Summer 2004).

[34] VGCL, "Country Report", document distributed by Chau Nhat Binh, International Department, VGCL, at the Workshop on Unions in Transitional Economies, Asia Monitor Resource Centre, Hong Kong and Oxfam-Solidarity (Belgium), Hanoi, June 2005.

[35] Nguyen Van T. (pseudonym), worker quoted in Nguyen Lan Huong, "Redundant Workers in SOE Equitization", paper presented at Workshop on Equitization in Vietnam, Southern Institute of Social Sciences, Ho Chi Minh City, October 2004. The papers at this conference contain a wealth of information on the post-equitization deterioration of workers' participation, benefits, and job security.

[36] Tran Trung Phuc, Director, Socio-Economic Policy Department, VGCL, interview, Hanoi, November 2005. In various discussions, quite different figures were given for the welfare fund, but never below 30 per cent.

[37] The study showed that 62 per cent of workers in the textile mill took an interest in their work, one-third higher than in the surveyed mechanical and rubber factories; 41 per cent of textile workers were satisfied with their working conditions, four times more than the others; 65 per cent assessed management–worker relations were good in the textile firm, compared to 35 and 26 per cent in the rubber and mechanical plants, respectively; in the textile factory, 62 per cent thought management cared about workers, compared to only 19 and 15 per cent, respectively, in the other two.

[38] A similar point was made by Tran Thi Van Anh, the editor of *Khoa Hoc Phu Nu* [Women's Studies journal]. While unions were far stronger in SOEs, and workers' conditions are therefore generally better, "in some cases they are not very good if the SOE has little cash and thus has not been able to upgrade equipment". Tran Thi Van Anh, interview, Hanoi, November 2005.

[39] Another study showing that female garment workers in Vietnam were better off than those in Bangladesh connected this to there being "more state-owned enterprises" and noted that "state regulation of the economy meant workers generally enjoyed higher levels of formal protection, labour standards and unionization, particularly in the state owned sectors". Kabeer, Naila, Simeen Mahmud, and Tran Thi Van Anh, "The Poverty Impacts of Female Employment in Vietnam and Bangladesh", *id21 Global Issues*, 24 June 2003 <http://www.id21.org/society/insights47art4.html 2003> (accessed 15 August 2009).

40   Dai Van Hoi and Nguyen Xinh, site visit to Bai Bang Pulp and Paper Mill,
      Phu Tho, 30 November 2005. Hoi is the chair and Xinh the deputy chair of
      the Bai Bang trade union. Both are CPV members. Xinh was a former soldier
      in the war with China in 1979.

41   Pham Van Tu, Management Board, Vinapimex, interview, Hanoi, 16 May 2007.
      The Miyazawa audit notes that global prices "range from 20 to 30 USD/cubic
      metres … mills in Indonesia pay in the 23 to 25 USD/cm range" but logs in
      Vietnam sell for the equivalent of "a mill gate price of 23 to 31 USD/cm".
      Ernst & Young and A.C. Sandwell, *Final Summary Report: Bai Bang Paper
      Company*, Operational Reviews of State-Owned Enterprises in the Steel and
      Paper Industries (Hanoi: Ministry of Finance and Miyazawa Fund, 2004[*b*]),
      p. 84. Bai Bang prices "are slightly above the domestic log averages". Even
      when they compare with world prices, this "ignores fibre quality — the
      international levels reflect freshly cut, clean sound wood … whereas domestic
      prices may not" (ibid.).

42   Tu from Vinapimex management claimed that "the state more or less commands
      our companies to buy from farmers,", but the companies "are often reluctant,
      as it is unprofitable," Pham Van Tu interview, op. cit. Vinapimex set up a
      woodchip plant in Quang Ninh Province to use all this timber. The chips are
      sent to Japan to be pulped, and then Vinapimex has to re-import the pulp at
      a much higher price.

43   In the paper mill we met with: the chair of the trade union; a woman in
      charge of quality control and chemical checking who was former head of a
      sectional women's unit; a member of the administration department; a deputy
      head of one of the workshops; and a shift leader. In the maintenance section
      we also met five people.

44   We were only able to stay two days around town, but met with numerous
      workers over the weekend. I'm especially grateful to my interpreter and
      unofficial assistant, Ms. Hoang, for facilitating this. Unofficial meeting places
      included eating venues, *bia hoi* (pubs) and markets. Most discussions could
      not take place for long, as we engaged in often fleeting conversations, though
      some were willing to talk at greater length before having to wander off.
      One female worker, Ms. Hang, who said she worked in the paper mill as a
      machinist, was particularly informative. We were also able to visit the house
      of two Bai Bang workers, Mr. Chien and Ms. Dung, who were relatives of
      a friend in Hanoi. They invited several other workers over for a casual chat.
      We also visited these workers again in April 2007.

45   Goliath: Business Knowledge on Demand, "Bai Bang Paper Co. <http://goliath.
      ecnext.com/coms2/product-compint-0001155056-page.html> (accessed 29
      August 2009). Bai Bang's own brochure claims 6,000 employees, <http://www.vica.
      vnn.vn/uni/hop_tac/engl/baibang/introduction.htm> (accessed 29 August 2009).

46   Average wages were VND1.35 million at Cogido and VND1.7 million at Tan
      Mai, two other major SOE paper plants.

47   Dung and Chien, Bai Bang workers, house visit, April 2007. Dung, an
      electrician, working there since 1982, was then earning VND6 million.

48   Presumably, it was the workers' choice to not wear boots; management can
      mainly be blamed for not enforcing boot-wearing against this habit, unless
      there had been demands for management to provide boots — but this was
      not specifically mentioned.

49   According to the union leaders Dai Van Hoi and Nguyen Xinh.

50   The "welfare" in the welfare fund does not include the cost of social and
      health insurance, which are compulsory legal deductions from company funds
      from *pre-tax* profit. Also, while the cost of workers' holidays (including travel
      and accommodation) are covered by the fund, annual paid leave is not from
      the fund, but a mandatory part of the salary.

51   Goliath: "Bai Bang Paper Co.".

52   Hoang Thach is located in Minh Tan Commune, Kim Mon District in Hai
      Duong Province.

53   Tinh is also a CPV member, and was a soldier in the American War.

54   In the mechanical section, we met the supervisor Mr. Luong, also deputy
      head of trade union in that section, and five workers: Mr. Hai, Ms. Hang,
      Mr. Duong, Mr. Quang, and Mr. Hung. The last three were relatively young,
      and Ms. Hang was about 40. Their jobs or roles were not stated, though
      Mr. Quang appeared to have some connection to the youth union. In the
      mechanical repair team we met Mr. Con, a supervisor, Ms. Hoa, deputy head
      of the union for that section, Mr. Thang, Mr. Thanh, and Mr. Trung. The four
      men were middle-aged, and Ms. Hoa was about 40.

55   Again, we could only stay two days in the neighbourhood to meet with
      workers. I am grateful to the invaluable assistance of another interpreter
      who acted as unofficial assistant, Ms. Vo Mai Trang. The unofficial meeting
      places were similar to those for Bai Bang. Most discussions were short,
      fleeting, and informal. Our best discussion was with three men having an
      early breakfast, who said they had seen us the previous day in the plant.
      We did not record their names. Though our encounters were not lengthy,
      we spoke to a significant number of people. Both here and at Bai Bang, it
      was not difficult to start up conversations once people spotted a foreigner
      sitting nearby.

56   This was confirmed in both official and unofficial meetings. This sits well
      with the Miyazawa audit's estimate of the average salary of VND2.7 million
      a month in 2001. Ernst & Young, *Final Report: Vietnam National Cement
      Company*, Operational Reviews of State-Owned Enterprises in the Cement
      Industry (Hanoi: Ministry of Finance and Miyazawa Fund, 2004[a]), p. 60.

57   They made the same comments about the Bim Son cement SOE, another VNCC affiliate. Ernst & Young, *Final Report: Bim Son Cement Company*, Operational Reviews of State-Owned Enterprises in the Cement Industry (Hanoi: Ministry of Finance and Miyazawa Fund, 2004[c]), p. 95.

58   Another 1,000 miners were moved to Vinacoal garment factories and 1,200 were retired with early pensions. Xuan Quang. "Tong Lien Doan lam viec voi CD nganh cong nghiep: Du kien chi 50 ti dong tra luong ngung viec cho gan 5 van cong nhan nganh than" [General Confederation works with industrial branch of trade union: Proposal to pay 50 billion dong in wages for work stoppages for 50,000 coal workers], *Lao Dong*, 4 June 1999.

59   This is backed by *Vietnam Investment Review*, which claimed 52,000 workers would receive 70 per cent of their salary during the mine stoppages, and "14,000 workers will be left with permanent jobs" ("Coal workers mining an unproductive future", 7–13 June 1999). Adding the 2,000 moved or retired and the 15,000 sacked seasonal workers, we get a total of 83,000 workers, close to the entire workforce, given rubbery figures in the Vietnamese media.

60   It is not clear whether "white collar staff" includes managers. However, Mr Nghiep, Director, Personnel Department, and Mr Cu, Deputy Director, Personnel Department, Vinacoal, claimed that "all of us had to work for half our salaries", interview, Hanoi, October 2005.

61   Tran Trung Phuc, VGCL, interview; Chau Nhat Binh, VGCL, interview.

62   Quoted in Ung Duy Ninh and Quang Chinh, "Ca nhan nao sai pham, du o bat cu cuong vi nao cung phai bi xu ly ky luat" [Every violator, whatever their position, must be disciplined], *Lao Dong*, 6 July 2000(*a*). The authors also claimed that by 2000, 77,500 miners were working, suggesting an original total of 83,000. Other articles also suggested fewer lay-offs. One quoted Vinacoal official Dinh Quang Trung as saying that the company was trying to cut the number of workers from 78,000 to 76,000 by sending them abroad or finding them work in garment factories, which suggests 7,000 lay-offs at that time. Duc Hung, "Coal Corporation Set for Hefty Losses of $3m", *Vietnam Investment Review*, 20–26 September 1999.

63   Mr Nghiep and Mr Cu, Vinacoal, op. cit.

64   The head of the Vinacoal union, Tran Khoa Thu, accepted this but said that while legally it should participate in management, the government has continually refused its requests to have a representative on management. Ung and Quang, "Ca nhan nao sai pham".

65   Mr Nghiep and Mr Cu, Vinacoal, op. cit.

66   The mandatory sales to the four state-owned sectors account for 50 per cent of all domestic sales. Vu Long, "Furore Over Coal Prices", *Vietnam Investment Review*, 13–19 (December 2004).

67   The net profit of its coal business is on average 3 per cent, and of its non-coal businesses 2 per cent. Barlow Jonker and Ernst & Young, *Final Report: Vietnam Coal Company*, Operational Reviews of State-Owned Enterprises in the Coal Industry (Hanoi: Ministry of Finance and Miyazawa Fund, 2004), p. 109. "The Bai Tu Long Garment joint venture has incurred losses since its establishment in 1999. By 2004, its accumulated loss was 11,184 million dong" (ibid., p. 89).

68   Vinacoal explained that these rises were due to cost of living increases and government decrees. The consultants called this "questionable business practice" which can "make a business uncompetitive" (ibid., p. 54).

69   Decision 202-HDBT, June 1992.

70   Table: "Equitized State-Owned Enterprises up to 1 January 1998", in Ton Tich Qui, "Equitization of State-owned Enterprises", *Vietnam's Socio-Economic Development* 14 (Summer 1998): 15.

71   Vo Van Kiet's view was shared by the head of the Privatization Bureau, Nguyen Van Tuong. When the majority of shares in the refrigeration company REE were sold to its workers, Tuong objected to this, warning that "a number of enterprises had the misunderstanding from the start that equitization simply meant division of property to workers." Nguyen Van Tuong, "Equitization Chief Calls for More State Involvement", *Vietnam Investment Review* 13–19 (December 1993).

72   Decree 64/ND-CP (19 June 2002).

73   An example of such comments is the Economist Intelligence Unit's assessment on equitization that "there is a high risk that its progress will be hampered by recalcitrant managers and vested interests", in "Country Report: Updater", 13 September 2004 <http://www.eiu.com.virtual.anu.edu.au/index.asp?layout=displayIssueArticle&issue_id=547593454&opt=full>. From the left, Gabriel Kolko, in *Vietnam: Anatomy of a Peace* (London: Routledge, 1997), asserted that SOE bosses opposed equitization because it "threatens" the de facto "ownership" they already have (p. 60), though he later notes that equitization would "quickly result in managerial takeovers" (p. 61), in other words, that many managers benefit precisely from equitization. Kolko comments in a footnote that workers were also opposed, "because a large part of SOE profits ... go to them in welfare payments" (p. 173).

74   The 2002 decree dealt with this. Binh explains "when SOEs could voluntarily choose equitization, workers had a big say. But now when the government directs a firm to equitize, it has to." Chau Nhat Binh, International Department, VGCL, interview, Hanoi, June 2005.

75   Interview, June 2005.

76   Interview with Tran Trung Phuc, Director, Socio-Economic Policy Department, VGCL, Hanoi, November 2005.

77   Interview, June 2005.
78   Quoted by Mark Evans, "Embedding Market Reform through Statecraft:
      The Case of Equitization in Vietnam", paper presented at Workshop on
      Equitization in Vietnam, Southern Institute of Social Sciences, Ho Chi Minh
      City, October 2004.
79   "Violations of Labour Law on the Rise", *Viet Nam News,* 25 May 2005. The
      VGCL figures show a total of 879 strikes between January 1995 and May
      2005, of which 565 (65 per cent) were in foreign-invested enterprises, 237
      (27 per cent) in private enterprises, and 77 (or 8 per cent) at SOEs.
80   Chau Nhat Binh from the VGCL, who had been visiting the strike site,
      commented that both the state company management and the "pocket union"
      were "disgusting". Interview, Hanoi, October 2005.
81   In this passage from their conference paper at the October 2004 conference
      on equitization, Truong and Bui are referring to another conference on SOE
      restructuring, held earlier on 15–16 March 2004.
82   At this earlier national conference on SOE restructuring on 15–16 March 2004,
      the assessment was made that equitization was resulting in "the robbery of
      state assets, and ownership is moving into the hands of management, which
      leads to social discontent ... [it has] developed with tricks and frauds".

References

Anh Hieu. "PM's New Policies May Alter SoC Hiring Process". *Viet Nam News,*
      12 April 2005.
Bai Bang Pulp and Paper Company. <http://www.vica.vnn.vn/uni/hop_tac/engl/
      baibang/introduction.htm>, accessed 29 August 2009.
Belser, Patrick and Martin Rama. *State Ownership and Labor Redundancy: Estimates
      Based on Enterprise-level Data from Vietnam.* Washington, D.C.: World Bank,
      Development Research Group, Public Service Delivery, 2001.
Beresford, Melanie. "The Political Economy of Dismantling the Bureaucratic
      Centralism and Subsidy System in Vietnam". In *Southeast Asia in the 1990s:
      Authoritarianism, Democracy and Capitalism,* edited by Kevin Hewison,
      Richard Robison, and Gary Rodan, pp. 215–36. St Leonard's: Allen and
      Unwin, 1993.
————. "Vietnam: The Transition from Central Planning". In *The Political Economy
      of South-East Asia,* edited by Kevin Hewison, Richard Robison, and Gary
      Rodan, pp. 206–32. Oxford: Oxford University Press, 2001.
Beresford, Melanie and Dang Phong. *Authority Relations and Economic Decision-
      Making in Vietnam.* Copenhagen: Nordic Institute of Asian Studies Press, 1998.
Central Institute for Economic Management (CIEM). "Viet Nam's Equitised
      Enterprises: An Ex-Post Study of Performance, Problems and Implications for

Policy". Hanoi: CIEM, August 2002. Available online at <http://siteresources. worldbank.org/INTVIETNAMINVIETNAMESE/Resources/other_reports_post_ equitization.pdf>.

Communist Party of Vietnam (CPV). "Political Report of the 7th National Committee to the 8th National Congress" (1996). In *75 Years of the Communist Party of Vietnam 1930–2005: A Selection of Documents from Nine Party Congresses.* Hanoi: The Gioi Publishers, 2005.

Cong Thang. "Cty san xuat betong vat tu xay dung Ha Tay: Cong nhan 'an va' UBND tinh" [Concrete and construction materials company Ha Tay: Workers 'stage sit-down' at province People's Committee]. *Lao Dong,* 26 November 2005.

Chu Tuong. "Tho mo vuot kho" [Miners overcome hardship]. *Lao Dong,* 4 June 1999.

———. "Khong mua than tho phi!" [Don't buy bandit coal!]. *Lao Dong,* 8 June 1999(*b*).

Dang Quang Dieu. "Du thao luat doanh nghiep thong nhat: Quen quyen loi cua nguoi lao dong!" [Draft unified enterprise law: Forgets the rights of workers!]. *Lao Dong,* 26 October 2005.

Do Duc Dinh. "The Public Sector in Vietnam". In *Doi Moi: Vietnam's Renovation Policy and Performance,* edited by Dean K. Forbes, Terence H. Hull, David G. Marr, and Brian Brogan, pp. 62–63. Canberra: Department of Political and Social Change, Research School of Pacific and Asian Studies, The Australian National University, 1991.

Duc Hung. "Coal Corporation Set for Hefty Losses of $3m". *Vietnam Investment Review,* 20–26 September 1999.

Duong Boi Ngoc. "Hoi thao 'Co phan hoa doanh nghipe nha nuoc va hoat dong cong doan': Khong the thieu dan chu co so" [Workshop 'Equitization of state enterprises and the activities of trade unions': Grassroots democracy must not be weakened], *Lao Dong,* 25 October 2005.

Economist Intelligence Unit (EIU). "Country Report: Vietnam", 1 April 2004*a* <http://www.eiu.com.virtual.anu.edu.au/index.asp?layout=displayIssueArticle &issue_id=1817054381&opt=full>.

———. "Country Report: Updater", 13 September 2004*b* <http://www.eiu.com. virtual.anu.edu.au/index.asp?layout=displayIssueArticle&issue_id=547593454& opt=full>.

———. "Country Report: Vietnam", 10 April 2006 <http://www.eiu.com.virtual.anu. edu.au/index.asp?layout=displayIssueArticle&issue_id=610351846&opt=full>.

Evans, Mark. "Embedding Market Reform through Statecraft: The Case of Equiti-zation in Vietnam". Paper presented at Workshop on Equitization in Vietnam, Southern Institute of Social Sciences, Ho Chi Minh City, October 2004.

Fforde, Adam and Stefan de Vylder. *From Plan to Market: The Economic Transition in Vietnam.* Boulder: Westview Press, 1996.

Goliath Business Knowledge on Demand. "Bai Bang Paper Co." <http://goliath.ecnext.com/coms2/product-compint-0001155056-page.html> (accessed 29 August 2009).

Greenfield, Gerard. "The Development of Capitalism in Vietnam". *Socialist Register* 30 (1994): 203–34.

———. "From Class to Commodity: Workers and Capitalist Industrialisation in Vietnam". Ph.D. dissertation, University of New South Wales, 2000.

Hoang Chi Bao and Nguyen Thanh Tuan. "Vai tro cua cac nghiep doan trong co che thi truong" [The role of unions under the market mechanism]. *Lao Dong & Cong Doan* [Labour & trade union review] 150 (September 1993).

Kabeer, Naila. "Local Production, Global Production: A Comparison of Women Workers Across the Trade Divide". Paper presented at Workshop on Globalisation and Poverty in Vietnam, Department for International Development (UK), Hanoi, September 2002.

Kabeer, Naila, Simeen Mahmud, and Tran Thi Van Anh. "The Poverty Impacts of Female Employment in Vietnam and Bangladesh". *id21 Global Issues,* 24 June 2003 <http://www.id21.org/society/insights47art4.html 2003> (accessed 15 August 2009).

Kerkvliet, Benedict J.T. "Politics and Society in the Mid 1990s". In *Dilemmas of Development: Vietnam Update 1994,* edited by Benedict J.T. Kerkvliet, pp. 5–43. Canberra: RSPAS, ANU, 1995.

———. "An Approach to Analysing State-Society Relations in Vietnam". *Sojourn* 16, no. 2 (2001): 238–78.

Kolko, Gabriel. *Vietnam: Anatomy of a Peace.* London: Routledge, 1997.

Le Kha Phieu. "Phat huy quyen lam chu cua nhan dan, xay dung va thuc hien thiet che dan chu o co so" [Bring into play the right of mastery of the people, build and effect democracy at the grassroots]. *Tap Chi Cong San* [Journal of the CPV] no. 3 (February 1998): 3–7.

Lenin, Vladimir Illich. "Left-Wing Childishness and the Petty-Bourgeois Mentality". In V. I. Lenin, *Collected Works*, vol. 27, 4th English ed. Moscow: Progress Publishers, 1972 [1918], pp. 323–34.

Mekong Economics. "SOE Reform in Vietnam: Background Paper". Hanoi: Mekong Economics, November 2002 <http://www.mekongeconomics.com/Document/Publications/2002/MKE%20SOE%20Reform%20in%20Vietnam.pdf>.

Navdi, Khalid and Enrique Blanco De Armas. "Globalisation and the Vietnamese Garment Industry". Paper presented at Workshop on Globalisation and Poverty in Vietnam, Department for International Development (UK), Hanoi, September 2002.

Nguyen An Dinh and Luu Quang Dinh. "Toi khong choi bo trach nhiem, nhung can hieu dung" [I don't deny responsibility, but it is necessary to understand correctly]. *Lao Dong,* 10 July 2000.

Nguyen Hai Huu. "Social safety net in the current macroeconomic situation". Paper presented at forum on Macroeconomic Stabilization: Challenges and Policy Options, CIEM and Deutsche Gesellschaft für Technische Zusammenarbeit (GTZ), Hanoi, 2 October 2008.

Nguyen Lan Huong. "Redundant Workers in SOE Equitization". Paper presented at Workshop on Equitization in Vietnam, Southern Institute of Social Sciences, Ho Chi Minh City, October 2004.

———. "Labour's Mastery through Owning of Shares". Paper presented at Workshop on Equitization in Vietnam, Southern Institute of Social Sciences, Ho Chi Minh City, October 2004.

Nguyen Minh Thong. "Bai hoc rut ra tu thuc hien quy che dan chu co so o doanh nghiep nha nuoc" [Lessons learnt from implementing grassroots democracy in SOEs]. *Tap Chi Cong San* 20 (October 2004): 45–49, 54.

Nguyen Van Linh. *Vietnam: Urgent Problems*. Hanoi: Foreign Languages Publishing House, 1988.

Nguyen Van Tuong. "Equitization Chief Calls for More State Involvement". *Vietnam Investment Review*, 13–19 December 1993.

Painter, M. "The Politics of Economic Restructuring in Vietnam: The Case of State-Owned Enterprise Reform". *Contemporary Southeast Asia* 25, no. 1 (April 2003): 20–43.

Porter, Gareth. *Vietnam: The Politics of Bureaucratic Socialism*. Ithaca: Cornell University Press, 1993.

Quang Chinh and Tran Nuong. "Quyen loi nguoi lao dong bi vi pham" [The rights of workers are being violated]. *Lao Dong*, 27 October 2005.

Quang Chinh. "Hau co phan hoa doanh nghiep nha nuoc: Vai tro cong doan dan bi vo hieu hoa" [Post-equitization of state enterprises: The role of the trade unions gradually becomes functionless]. *Lao Dong*, 21 November 2005.

Quang Chinh and Dang Tien. "Hau co phan hoa cac doanh nghiep nha nuoc: Vai tro cong doan dang dan mo nhat!" [Post-equitization of state enterprises: The role of the trade union gradually fades away]. *Lao Dong*, 23 February 2006.

Quang Duan. "Vietnam's state enterprises too much for nothing". *Thanh Nien News*, English edition, 25 July 2006. <http://www.thanhniennews.com/2006/Pages/20067252025580.aspx>.

Stern, Lewis. *Renovating the Vietnamese Communist Party: Nguyen Van Linh and the Programme for Organizational Reform 1987–91*. Singapore: Institute of Southeast Asian Studies, 1993.

Tien Hai. "Ve hoat dong cua to chuc dang trong cac doanh nghiep nha nuoc" [Regarding the activities of the party organization in state enterprises]. *Tap Chi Cong San*, no. 14 (July 1998): 27–29.

Thanh Phong. "Business Undertaking a Motive Force of Production". *Vietnamese Trade Unions*, no. 2, 1993.

Thu Huong and Dang Tien. "Cong nhan cong ty det Minh Khai (ha Noi) dinh cong: Quyen loi lao dong bi vi pham" [Workers at textile company Minh Khai (Hanoi) on strike: The rights of the workers are violated]. *Lao Dong*, 21 October 2005(*a*).

————. "Cong nhan cong ty det Minh Khai (ha Noi) dinh cong: Cong doan co so dung o dau" [Workers at textile company Minh Khai (Hanoi) on strike: Where is the grassroots trade union?]. *Lao Dong*, 22 October 2005(*b*).

Ton Thien Chieu. "Quan he xa hoi trong xi nghiep cua cong nhan cong nghiep" [The social relations in enterprises of industrial workers]. *Xa Hoi Hoc* [Sociology] 2, no. 54 (1996): 38–57.

Ton Tich Qui. "Equitization of State-owned Enterprises". *Vietnam's Socio-Economic Development* 14 (Summer 1998): 10–15.

Trinh Duy Luan, "Changes of Labour Relations in Industry". *Vietnam's Socio-Economic Development* 12 (Winter 1997): 29–38.

Trinh Thi Hoa. "Social Insurance: Status and Prospects". *Vietnam's Socio-Economic Development* 38 (Summer 2004): 18–26.

Truong Thi Minh Sam and Bui Duc Hai. "An Overview of the Most Crucial Period Of Equitization in Vietnam". Paper presented at Workshop on Equitization in Vietnam, Southern Institute of Social Sciences, Ho Chi Minh City, October 2004.

Tsang, Daniel C. "Vietnam Today: Interview with Ngo Vinh Long". *Critical Asian Studies* 34, no. 3 (2002): 459–64.

Tu Huong. "State Alleges Stockpile Fraud". *Vietnam Investment Review*, 10–16 July 2000.

Ung Duy Ninh and Quang Chinh. "Ca nhan nao sai pham, du o bat cu cuong vi nao cung phai bi xu ly ky luat" [Every violator, whatever their position, must be disciplined]. *Lao Dong*, 6 July 2000(*a*).

Ung Duy Ninh and Quang Chinh. "Cong doan co phan trach nhiem voi nhung sai pham cua nganh than" [Trade unions are partly responsible for the mistakes in the coal sector], *Lao Dong*, 10 July 2000(*b*).

Vo Tri Thanh. "Vietnam Two Years after WTO Admission: What Lessons can be Learnt?" Paper presented at Vietnam Update Conference, The Australian National University, Canberra, 6–7 November 2008.

Vu Long. "Furore over Coal Prices". *Vietnam Investment Review*, 13–19 December 2004.

World Bank. *Advancing Rural Development: From Vision to Action.* Hanoi: World Bank, 1998.

World Bank and Asia Development Bank (ADB). *Vietnam: Delivering on Its Promise.* Hanoi: World Bank and ADB, 2002.

Xuan Quang. "Tong Lien Doan lam viec voi CD nganh cong nghiep: Du kien chi 50 ti dong tra luong ngung viec cho gan 5 van cong nhan nganh than"

[General Confederation of Labour works with industrial branch of trade union: Proposal to pay 50 billion dong in wages for work stoppages for 50,000 coal workers]. *Lao Dong,* 4 June 1999.

Official proclamations and legislation

Council of Ministers. Decision 217-HDBT, "Renovation of Planning and Socialist Business Cost-Accounting in State Enterprises", 14 November 1987.

———. Decree 50-HDBT, "Regulations on State-Owned Industrial Enterprises", 22 March 1988.

———. Decree 98-HDBT, "Regulations on the Right of Mastery of Workers Collectives in State-Owned Enterprises", 2 June 1988.

———. Decision 143-HDBT, "Reviewing the Implementation of Resolution 217-HDBT, Decree 50 HDBT and Decree 98 HDBT and Working to Continue the Renovation of the Management of State Enterprises", 10 May 1990.

———. Decision 202-HDBT, "Implementing Experiments to Convert State Enterprises to Share Holding Companies", June 1992.

Government [of Vietnam]. Decree 29/1998/ND-CP, "Regulations on the Implementation of Democracy at the Commune Level", 11 May 1998.

———. Decree 7/1999/ND-CP, "Promulgating the Regulations on Exercising Democracy in State Enterprises", 13 February 1999.

———. Decree 64/ND-CP, "Regarding the Transformation of State-Owned Enterprises to Joint Stock Companies", 19 June 2002.

President of the Socialist Republic of Vietnam. *Law on State Enterprises,* 30 April 1995.

Prime Minister. "Work to Re-arrange State Enterprises", Decision 90-TTG, 7 March 1994.

Prime Minister. "Pilot Work to Establish Business Groups", Decision 91-TTG, 7 March 1994.

Miyazawa audit reports (Ministry of Finance)

Ernst & Young. *Final Report: Vietnam National Cement Company.* Operational Reviews of State-Owned Enterprises in the Cement Industry. Hanoi: Ministry of Finance and Miyazawa Fund, 2004(*a*).

———. *Final Report: Hoang Thach Cement Company.* Operational Reviews of State-Owned Enterprises in the Cement Industry. Hanoi: Ministry of Finance and Miyazawa Fund, 2004(*b*).

———. *Final Report: Bim Son Cement Company.* Operational Reviews of State-Owned Enterprises in the Cement Industry. Hanoi: Ministry of Finance and Miyazawa Fund, 2004(*c*).

Ernst & Young and A & C Sandiwell. *Final Summary Report: Vietnam National Paper Corporation.* Operational Reviews of State-Owned Enterprises in the Steel and Paper Industries. Hanoi: Ministry of Finance and Miyazawa Fund, 2004(*a*).

————. *Final Summary Report: Bai Bang Paper Company.* Operational Reviews of State-Owned Enterprises in the Steel and Paper Industries. Hanoi: Ministry of Finance and Miyazawa Fund, 2004(*b*).

Jonker, Barlow and Ernst & Young. *Final Report: Vietnam Coal Company.* Operational Reviews of State-Owned Enterprises in the Coal Industry. Hanoi: Ministry of Finance and Miyazawa Fund, 2004.

Packard, Le Anh Tu and VICA Consultants. *The Diagnostic Audit of Vietnam's State Enterprises, Final Policy Paper.* Hanoi: Ministry of Finance and Miyazawa Fund, 2004.

4

THE REDIVISION OF LABOUR IN A RED RIVER DELTA VILLAGE IN A GLOBALIZED ECONOMY

Nguyen Phuong Le

Vietnam's rural population is changing enormously as the country increasingly integrates with the global economy. Some of the most radical of these changes are occuring in migration patterns, a redistribution of labour, and the status of women. This chapter aims to analyze these changes in greater depth by investigating a traditional craft village in northern Vietnam. How have livelihoods transformed in the craft village? What are the mechanisms of migration into and out of the village? How are gender divisions of labour changing in the village?

This great transition in agricultural livelihoods in Vietnam began earlier, of course, starting with initial decollectivization in the early 1980s and more recent acceleration via land reforms in the early 1990s. In the Red River Delta region, where the field research for this chapter was carried out, rural livelihoods have been transformed further by state rural industrialization policies, especially those aimed at reviving and developing traditional craft villages. As the slogan goes, "leaving the rice field, but not the countryside" (*ly nong bat ly huong*). As a result, rural people no longer rely on farming as a sole source of income, and their livelihood strategies have increasingly focused on non-agricultural activities.

Under *Doi Moi*'s move toward a market-oriented economy, state regulations on rural labour have been loosened so that people can independently make decisions about their occupations and workplaces. Thus, *Doi Moi* policies have also propelled domestic labour migration flows. Labour migration patterns have become complex as can be seen in the case of traditional craft villages such as Kim Thieu in the Red River Delta where my research was conducted; not only do villagers migrate to work and do business elsewhere, including inland and abroad, but a number of migrants from other regions come to make their living in these villages as regular/long-term or casual contract labourers. Labour relations have also become more complex, with several concurrent and sometimes contradictory systems running — capitalist principles alongside a subsistence economy, as well as reciprocal relationships and patron–client exploitation.

Indeed, the new economic relationships that have grown out of this geographical mobility have given rise to new labour relations at the workplace as well as new gender relations patterns. In some craft-based industries, such as woodcarving, the high demand for labour absorbs vitually the entire local male and female village workforce. This is significant because, women workers today are able to participate actively in a field which used to be considered men's work and from which they were excluded. Women are also increasingly playing key roles in linking the traditional craft industries to the domestic and global market. In doing so, they face new challenges at various levels, including within the household or family, the community, and in the labour market itself.

FRAMEWORK AND RESEARCH METHODOLOGY

The Concept of the Division of Labour

The division of labour is generally defined as a process of specialization in which workers are assigned specific, circumscribed tasks and roles, a system intended to increase the productivity of labour. Historically, the growth of an increasingly complex division of labour is closely associated with the rise of capitalism, the growth of trade, and the complexity of industrial processes. As we shall see in this case study, the globalization of the woodcarving industry in one region of Vietnam has created a new division of labour.

The concept of the division of labour, or economic specialization, has been debated by many famous thinkers such as Adam Smith, Karl Marx, and Emile Durkheim as well as contemporary scholars such as Doreen Massey (1984; 1994). Most have concentrated on the issue of the "rationality" of labour division within a sector, a region, a family, and an economy.

This chapter looks at the division of labour in production processes at the village and family levels. My discussion here will centre on how labour migration and changing gender roles in production are transforming labour relations in the village and within households. I will argue that the division of labour in rural Vietnam has been changing in multiple directions at the same time. The reason for this multiplicity lies in the fact that local people are the main actors who always manage and situate the process of division of labour in their particular contexts. Thus, the phenomenon of rural migrant labour mobility is more complex than generally depicted either in scholarly or official sources. In addition, gender divisions of labour today are also negotiable. There are divisions not only between men and women, but also among different classes of men and women. Hence, my field data will be used as a critique of the conventional debates on rural labour migration and the gender division of labour in Vietnam.

Migration and Gender

Most studies of migration within Vietnam focus on rural-to-urban migration and the occupational movement from agriculture to industry. The countryside is defined as economically less developed with fewer opportunities to improve one's income and standard of living, while towns and cities are considered more advanced with better income opportunities as well as the possibility of a better quality of life (Wouterse and Taylor 2007; Winkels and Adger 2002; Cohen 2006; Dang *et al.* 2003). Rural-to-rural and urban-to-rural migrations are largely overlooked. In this study, I try to demonstrate the multiple layers of labour migration relating to the revival and development of a traditional craft-making industry. There are four major streams of labour migration in rural areas: long-term inward migration, casual migration, outward migration, and homeward or return migration. In addition, this study will also look at economic, social, and cultural motives for migration.

There is a substantial amount of literature on gendered work divisions. These can be categorized into three main arguments. The first supposes that the traditional sexual division of labour in the family confined women to certain kinds of work closely related to their reproductive roles, hence restricting them to a comparatively narrow range of occupations. Women also bring their roles from the domestic sphere to the workplace so that they tend to work in industries such as clothing and textiles, footwear, nursing, food processing, and services. The second line of argument explains gender discrimination as a result of biological differences, such as having inherited "nimble fingers", which make them more suited to certain types of work. In addition, women's reproductive roles and their biological characteristics supposedly make them more docile and willing to accept discipline and tedious, repetitive, and monotonous tasks. The third line of argument looks at gendered work differentiation through the lens of cultural constraints. For reasons of class and social status, women were excluded from certain kinds of occupations defined as being exclusively male. Furthermore, male incomes were higher compared to those for women because the work men performed was judged to more valuable. These conventional explanations about gender divisions at work have tended to confirm their ties with the domestic sphere and hence with limited spatial mobility. In contrast, the data and life stories examined in this chapter will be used to argue that gendered work divisions are not fixed but change in accordance with historical, social, and economic contexts.

Research Methodology and Site

I spent almost a year in the fieldwork site gathering ethnographic data, participating in all the "everyday life" activities of local people in order to understand the way in which labour has been divided into different economic activities. Participatory rural appraisal techniques such as group meetings, participant-observation, and oral history recording were employed to obtain information from different villagers. In-depth interviews were also used to gather data from forty typical households involved in the craft industry, including key informants such as head of the communal women's union and the village headman.

Information and data were collected to understand the division of labour in the family and in the workplace. Individual case histories concentrated on the ways in which village women negotiated their entry into "non-traditional occupations". All the data were analyzed by qualitative methods, and were mainly based on interviews with villagers rather than on statistically available information.

Kim Thieu Village

This is a case study of Kim Thieu village, in the Red River Delta, about 30 km northeast of Hanoi. Kim Thieu is a traditional craft village with an age-old history, though nobody can say when the woodcarving industry itself began. Local legend has it that at the time of the Chinese invasions, some thousands of Vietnamese woodcarvers were forced to work in China as slaves. Villagers say that woodcarving in their village owes its existence to the founding of Thang Long (the ancient citadel in Hanoi) as the capital under the Ly Dynasty (in the eleventh century). In modern times, a woodcarving cooperative was established in the late 1950s. Twenty-seven years later, however, the cooperative collapsed along with the demise of collectivization.

After *Doi Moi*, the woodcarving industry was revived and developed as an important way to improve household livelihoods. In 2007, Kim Thieu had 1,726 inhabitants who lived in 411 households (*ho*) of which 315 households were involved in traditional woodcarving. The total cultivated area of the village is 36.72 hectares, and the agricultural land area per capita is about 200m², which is considered the lowest in the region. As they cannot live on agriculture alone, people have been obliged to make a living by combining a number of different activities, but farming and woodcarving remain the most important ones (see Table 4.1). About

TABLE 4.1

Kim Thieu Village: Population, Labour, and Income Sources

Indicators	Unit	Total	Farming	Handicrafts	Services	Others
Total Population (Local residents only)	Persons	1,726	142 (8.23%)	1,394 (80.76%)	170 (9.84%)	20 (1.17%)
Local Labourers	Persons	977	82 (8.39%)	799 (81.78%)	76 (7.78%)	20 (2.05%)
Main Source of Income	Households	411	33 (8.03%)	315 (76.64%)	48 (1.17%)	15 (3.65%)

Source: Bac Ninh Province Department of Statistics, Bac Ninh Yearly Statistics Yearbook, 2007 (in Vietnamese).

70 per cent of households in the village still cultivate the land allocated to them by the state since 1988, although much of their income now derives from woodcarving.

As can be seen from the Table 4.1, woodcarving provides the major source of income at both the individual and household levels. The revival of the woodcarving industry has absorbed not only male but also female villagers, as well as a number of migrants who work as either regular or casual workers. According to estimates by local officials, there are about 500 regular and 200 casual migrant workers working daily in the woodcarving industry and seasonally in the farming sector in the village. For this reason, labour relations in the woodcarving industry and in agriculture have changed remarkably: the new division of labour at the village level as well as within families has allowed villagers to engage in both farming and craftmaking simultaneously.

CHANGES IN RURAL LIVELIHOOD STRATEGIES

The woodcarving industry in Kim Thieu has grown significantly since its revival and has been generating a large proportion of household income in the village for the past two decades. Households engage in the woodcarving and furniture-making industry in different ways, however. Among the 315 households who engage in woodcarving, 264 households operate their own family workshops. The workshop owners are classified as producers, while the other carpenters, woodcarvers, or mother-of-pearl sculptors — all of whom are involved at various stages of production but do not make or market the finished products — are categorized as outsourced workers.

A wide range of family workshops exist, varying according to the kind of woodcarving, scale of production, target market, and labour employed. Table 4.2 shows village producers categorized according to their scale of production. In 2007, depending on their scale of production, woodcarving generated 40 to 100 per cent of individual household income in Kim Thieu.

While Elson (1997) and Rigg (2001, 2008) claim that the invasion of off-farm economic activities in Southeast Asia has degraded the role of farming, most people in Kim Thieu continue to farm even if their income is mostly generated from working in the craft industry. The area of farm land cultivated by families is related to the scale of their woodcarving operations, however. The bigger the woodcarving business, the smaller the land area farmed; this is particularly true of paddy fields. Table 4.3

TABLE 4.2

Categorization of Woodcarving Producers in the Village by Scale of Production

Production scale	No. of Households (%)	Types of product	Targeted market	Type of Labour
Large	70 (26.52%)	Furniture	Domestic and China	Contract workers, Satellite factories, Family labour
Medium	89 (33.71%)	Furniture	Domestic and China	Family labour and Contract workers
Small	105 (39.77%)	Furniture Sculpture	Mainly Domestic	Mostly family labour

Source: Author's household survey, 2007.

TABLE 4.3

Classification of Households by Livelihood Strategies

Groups	% of Total households	Woodcarving Industry	Farming Activity
Group 1	30%	Large-scale factory owners	Do not farm; lend out land.
Group 2	10%	Large-scale factory owners	Self-sufficient farming; lend out part of the land
Group 3	30%	Medium or small factory owners	Farming allocated land and borrowed land
Group 4	20%	Skilled labourer (framing, carving, and whittling)	Farming allocated land and large-scale borrowed land
Group 5	10%	Unskilled casual labourers	Large-scale farming

Source: Author's household survey, 2007.

shows five groups of households, categorized according to the proportions of farming and craftmaking in their total household income.

The first group made up the 30 per cent of total households in the village who completely live on their earnings in the woodcarving industry and have given up farming. They still keep their farm land for a number of reasons, however. Moreover, they do not want to let their land lay fallow and instead lend it to other family members or villagers who are willing to continue farming. It should be noted that several of those in the category of non-farmers still consider woodcarving as a sideline because the industry is heavily dependent on unpredictable international markets, making their livelihoods insecure. They see themselves as temporarily still trying it out to see whether they could make a living from woodcarving and unsure whether their family labour could successfully encompass both farming and craftmaking.

> My family stopped farming three years ago as we do not have enough labour for both craftmaking and farming at the same time. I lent my farm land to my parents-in-law until our family would have enough labour for cultivation by ourselves. Some people asked me why I didn't sell the farm land, but I think land is very important in my life. If I sell it now, it would bring me only a small amount of money in comparison with what I could earn from the woodcarving industry. Also, when I want to return to farming, I would not be able to buy it again because farm land is increasingly scarce in my village. (Loi, a 38-year-old man, October 2006)

Another important reason for keeping farm land but not cultivating it is to maintain property rights. Unlike Loi, Hoa kept her farm land in the hope that the state will allow her to change its land use. For her, income from agriculture at present is much smaller than what she can earn from woodcarving, so she has stopped farming. She plans to expand the scale of the family factory, but her problem is that she does not have the space to do so. She expects that in future her farm allotment will be converted to non-agricultural purposes, particularly for building more woodcarving workshops.

The second group, which constitutes only 10 per cent of households, consisted of those who have large workshops but still cultivate rice for themselves on some land while renting out the remaining land. The reasons why this group people still keep farming even if they can make a lot of money from woodcarving is that agriculture provides security in bad times when the demand for wood products falls. There have been times when these families have not had enough money to buy food. For this reason, farming, especially rice cultivation, still plays an important role in sustaining their livelihoods. Moreover, most workshop owners need a large amount of rice not only for family consumption, but also for feeding their regular contract labourers.

We have a large family to feed. Aside from our seven family members, we have to feed three hired labourers who permanently work for our factory. So, we consume about 150 kg of rice per month. As we grow rice by ourselves, we can save half of the money, though we also have to spend money and labour on rice growing. However, the expenditure for rice production is spread out over the whole year, so it isn't a financial burden. By contrast, if we must buy rice, we will have to spend a large amount of money all at once. Most villagers here say that their rice growing can be considered as a way of saving money. (Cat, a 65-year-old, November 2006)

For some, the reasons for continuing to grow rice are both nutritional, tied to the well-being of the family, and cultural, that is, for the purposes of ritual feasts. As one elderly female informant explained, the rice grown by her family was tastier and had fewer impurities than rice bought in the local market. Villagers also emphasized that their home-grown rice was safer to eat because it is not grown with chemical fertilizers. They also needed to grow glutinous rice, in particular, because it has an important role on special occasions such as *Tet*, ancestor worship feasts, and the annual village festival.

My husband is the oldest son of his family, so he must be responsible for organizing many ancestor worshipping feasts a year. We need a lot of glutinous rice to cook "*xoi*" (glutinous rice with green bean) at such feasts. As an oldest daughter-in-law, I must serve my husband's relatives with hearty meals, especially very tasty *xoi*. For this reason, I try to preserve some land to grow glutinous rice. (Diep, a 50-year-old woman, May 2007)

For villagers who fall into the remaining third, fourth, and fifth groups (see Table 4.3), which together make up 60 per cent of the households, farming plays a more important role in household income and livelihoods in comparison with the first two groups. The average area cultivated by villagers in the third group varied from four to six *sao*,[1] although some households cultivate eight *sao* every season. These households decided to keep growing rice on such a large scale for three reasons. First, there was excess labour since the family was quite heterogeneous. While some family members could work as skilled carpenters and carvers, others could only do simpler tasks such as cleaning and polishing the finished items. Second, some workshop-owning families provided meals for their contract workers, who would eat together with the family. Third, these households still reared pigs, and it was necessary to have rice to supplement their feed.

Apart from all these reasons, some villagers also considered farming as an economic strategy from which they could make a profit. Vuong, for instance, explained that her family did not consume much rice, so she often bought their supply of rice from a familiar stall in the local market. The rice that she produced herself was kept both in reserve for the family's own consumption, as well as for sale in case the market price increased. In fact, she cultivated rice on borrowed land as well as on the family plot.

The fourth group was made up of those who had not established woodcarving factories of their own. They were simply engaged in one or some stages of the woodcarving production process, as contract or outsourced labourers — making frames, carving, whittling, or painting. While many villagers explained that they could not establish their own workshops because of a lack of appropriate skills or capital, others who had ample skills and capital chose to work as contract labourers because they were risk-averse. Nguyen, who was a highly skilled woodcarver, was one of the wealthier villagers who had good reason for wanting to remain as an outsourced worker, as she explained:

> My family used to operate a woodcarving factory. However, we faced bankruptcy in the mid-1990s, because a tricky trader did not pay us a lot of money. Since that time, I have decided to work as a contract labourer for some big factories in the village. For me, working as a contract labourer cannot bring me as much money as being a factory owner, but we don't need to think of cost and benefit relationships, as well as of rent-seeking. (Nguyen, November 2007)

Contract workers' employment also fluctuates and is dependent on variations in factory production. For this reason, the contract workers had no plans to give up farming. Most of them cultivated all their allocated land, as well as land borrowed from others, mostly from their siblings and relatives. According to most interviewees, they grew rice for their own consumption, for feeding their livestock, and for selling to other households in the village, including interestingly to those whom they leased the land from.

The last group is made up of those who had neither the skills nor the financial capital to establish their own factories. For these people, farming remained the focus of their livelihood. They tended to expand their rice cultivation by borrowing unused plots from anyone who did not wish to cultivate their own. Woodcarving was merely seen as one of a number of subsidiary economic activities, because of its contribution to their household economy. Those whose main focus was farming only participated in the woodcarving industry as unskilled casual labourers, when they finished all their farmwork.

In sum, the wide mix of different livelihood strategies depicted here could be considered as the villagers' way of coping with fluctuating market demand for the woodcraft industry products. On the other hand, there were varied reasons for villagers maintaining their farm land and agricultural activities. Many large-scale producers kept their fields, not in order to farm, but to maintain their property rights and to wait for new economic opportunities, rather than to invest anew. Similarly, some large- and medium-scale woodcarving producers also retained small farms, in order to maintain their property rights and provide their families with a reliable supply of nutritious food. In contrast, the small woodcarving producers, as well as contracted or outsourced workers, continued to perceive farming, particularly rice cultivation, as an important livelihood strategy. Hence, even in the case of a largely non-agricultural village economy such as that of Kim Thieu, there were some villagers who continued to cultivate rice for commercial purposes.

DIVISION OF LABOUR FOR LIVELIHOOD ARTICULATION

Labour Processes and Type of Labourers

As described, the Kim Thieu villagers displayed a variety of skills and skill levels, financial capacity, access to markets, and social capital. In the woodcarving industry itself, they have become either workshop owners, outsourced workers, or contract labourers. There are also a number of villagers who are not involved in the craft industry at all.

Figure 4.1 shows that the production process in the woodworking industry is generally divided into ten stages, which are carried out by different types of workers, including family labour, and regular and casual contract workers who are either villagers or outsiders. As mentioned, several skilled villagers who lack access to markets and financial and social capital do not have their own factories but work as contract workers for other family workshops and private companies in Kim Thieu as well as in the nearby villages. Moreover, while some stages of the production process, including sawing, designing, polishing, and furniture assembling are carried out in family workshops, others such as carving, whittling, inlaying mother-of-pearl, and painting are done both at the workshops and elsewhere.

FIGURE 4.1
The Process of Wood Production and Division of Labour

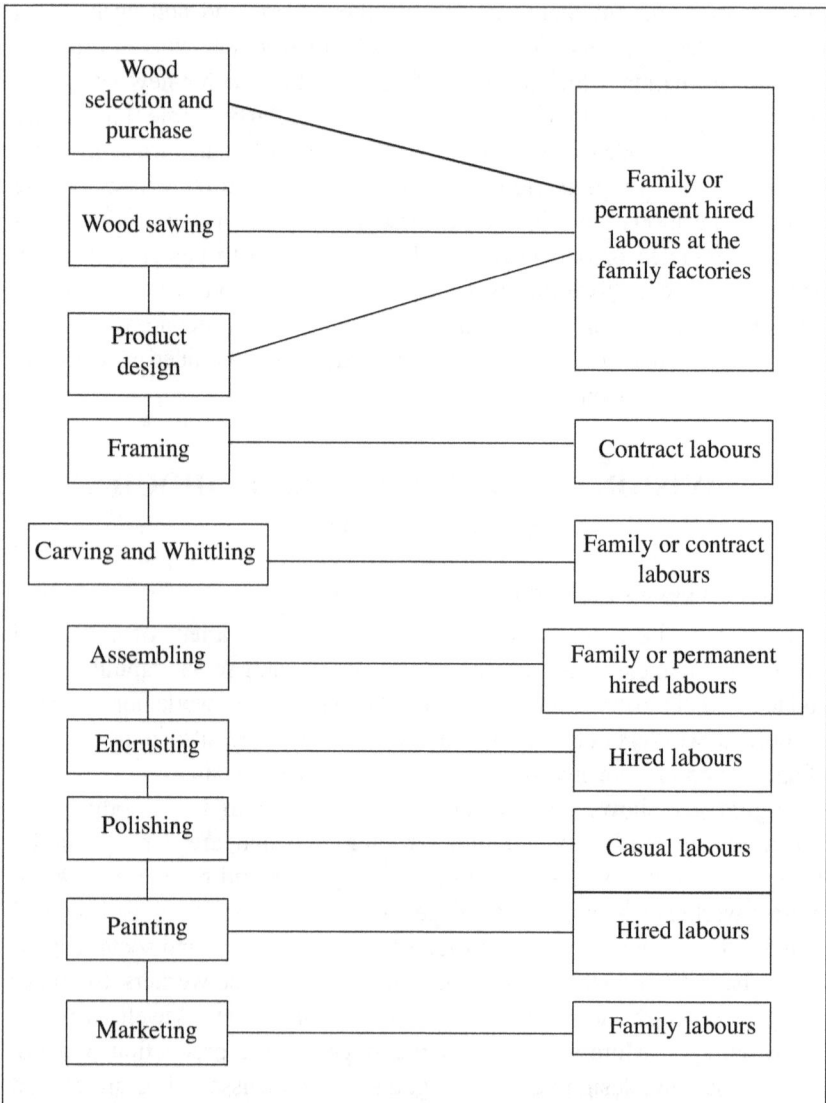

LOCAL OUTSOURCED WORKERS

The outsourced workers are responsible only for one stage of the production process, such as framing, carving, whittling, or painting.

Framers

The first group of outsourced workers is composed of those who specialize in making wooden frames for the furniture according to the pre-drawn templates. Before the commoditization of woodcarving, the owners of the workshop had to do the framing themselves, which took up a lot of their time and energy. Today, they send the pieces of wood, with the designs, to other households who have special framing machines. When I visited the village, there were five households responsible just for the framing stage. These households had equipped their factories with one to four framing machines, each run by a male worker. This meant that each factory owner also needed one to four male workers. In 2006, they had to pay VND300,000 per tea table set, typically consisting of a table and three or four chairs, which would take a worker three days to complete. Thus, a framer could earn nearly VND100,000 (about US$6) per day before deducting for machine fuel costs. Although this wage rate was not enough to make them wealthy, it was much higher than the income they could gain from either farming or more basic woodwork.

Carvers and Whittlers

Nearly one hundred households have family members who handled outsourced carving and whittling. Carving is the stage in which wood is shaped according to the draft designs, whereas whittling is the phase in which the carved pictures are brought to life. To qualify as a carver, one has to spend two to four years learning and practising, whereas to become a whittler, one only needs six months. The wage rates for carving are as much as two or three times higher than for whittling. In 2007 it was VND100,000 to 150,000 per day for a woodcarver, but only VND50,000 to 60,000 per day for a whittler. Most woodcarvers are men while almost all the whittlers are women, which reflects the gendered division of labour we will discuss in detail later.

Such outsourcing work was also handled by some of the big workshops like Nguyen's. Nguyen was the most skilled female woodcarver in Kim Thieu village. She and her husband, Viet, have been running a workshop which has specialized in woodcarving since 1996. Their workshop handles the carving for two big producers in Kim Thieu, and even for some others in a nearby village. Nguyen and her husband earned a total net income from woodcarving of about VND10 million a month in 2007.

Painters

One minor group of outsourced workers in the production process are the painters. Similar to the framers and carvers, the painters specialize either in providing services full-time, or doing painting jobs part-time when they have little to do in their own workshops. All the painters are men, as are those who saw and assemble the wood. It is said that painting is more suited to men because it requires the use of machinery and good health. Regardless of whether this is a convincing reason, it certainly reflects reality. Painters are paid on a piecework basis — in 2007 they were earning VND1,000,000 for painting a set of tea tables, from which they had to deduct the cost of paint.

In conclusion, various stages of woodcarving and furniture-making take place in Kim Thieu with the exception of the sculpting, inserting, and polishing of the mother-of-pearl inlay, which is mostly carried out by regular or daily hired labourers from other communities where off-farm job opportunities are rare.

IN-MIGRANT LABOURERS IN KIM THIEU VILLAGE

Regular Migrant Labourers

Mother-of-Pearl Sculptors

All the mother-of-pearl sculptors come from a village famous for pearl inlay work in Phu Xuyen District, Ha Tay Province. During my fieldwork, there were fifteen teams of inlay workers who had been at Kim Thieu for almost a decade. Each group had a team leader or manager who was concurrently an inlay worker. The team leaders usually brought their families along. The inlay teams rented village houses for living and working in because their work did not require a large space. Aside from the team leader's family, there were also five to seven co-workers, mostly men. Most of the team leaders' wives did some inlay work but had a more important role as cook for the team and family.

Phuong was the leader of an inlay team that had been working in Kim Thieu for six years at the time of the fieldwork. Phuong had worked in another team before establishing his own. Aside from his own team members, there were also five other sculptors working for him as hired labourers. Like other teams, Phuong and his workers rented an old house from a family which had moved to a new house in the village centre. According to Phuong, some inlay team leaders had even bought residential land and built their own houses in Kim Thieu because they wanted to settle there permanently. Of course, property had to be bought in the name of locals, because as outsiders they were not allowed to buy residential land or houses in the village. Phuong too was considering if he should buy a house in Kim Thieu, especially after the state household registration system (*ho khau*) was abolished in 2007.[2]

Phuong's team was contracted to provide for the inlay stage of five medium-sized family woodwork factories in Kim Thieu. Each year Phuong's group was able to inlay from fifty to sixty tea table sets and about ten wardrobes. The main material, mother-of-pearl, was usually purchased in Phu Xuyen. Phuong and his wife could earn VND15 to 20 million a year, after deducting all costs, including pearl-shell, food, accommodation, and the wages of the hired workers (i.e. those who were not part of the family). While this amount of money was quite small in comparison with the income of the households who ran large or medium-sized woodcarving workshops, it was higher than farmers' and migrants' earnings. While Phuong's income was not high, he regarded it as stable, and with better working conditions since the pearl sculptors did not have to toil in harsh conditions under the sun or in the rain, or inhaling dust and noxious chemicals.

All of Phuong's co-workers lived with his family in the rented house. They were fed three meals per day and paid VND600,000 to 800,000 per month in three or four installments a year. Phuong would pay his team members in advance when they needed money urgently. Almost all the pearl sculptors spent the whole year in Kim Thieu, returning to their hometown only on special occasions. Like Phuong, most migrant sculptors still retained their home farms, which they lent to parents, siblings, or other relatives to make use of, as a form of social security. They considered working in Kim Thieu as a temporary livelihood strategy, as they might one day have to return home to their farms if there were any problems in the woodcarving industry.

Carpenters and Woodcarvers

Besides the pearl sculptors, there were a number of woodcarvers and carpenters working in the village as regular migrant labourers. The number of contracted woodcarvers and carpenters working in a household varied from two to ten, depending on the size of the workshop. The route through which these people had become regular contract labourers was quite different from the former group. Most of them were either apprentices or ex-apprentices who had been taught by the village artisans themselves. Thus, the relationship between these migrant labourers and the workshop owners was not only one of employees and employers, but also as clients and patrons. Unlike the pearl sculptors, the migrant woodcarvers and carpenters lived and worked together with the workshop owners' families.

By 2007, Dong and Nong have been working in Sinh's furniture workshop for four years, the first two years as apprentices and hired carpenters. They were responsible for sawing wood and assembling furniture. During their apprenticeship, they did not have to pay any fees, except for the cost of 15 kg of rice monthly for their own consumption. After finishing their apprenticeship, Nong and Dong were paid as contract workers. They were fed three meals a day and paid VND1.2 million a month. They both worked and lived with Sinh's family, though their hometown was only 7 km from Kim Thieu. During my fieldwork, I observed no distinction between these hired labourers and family workers in terms of workload, meals, sleeping spaces, and other daily activities. However, some social and gender distinctions could be detected. For instance, in some cases, female family members were more powerful than male apprentices and often asked the latter to help with farm work during the peak season without paying them.

Outsourcing households such as Nguyen's (described earlier) also employed external workers. Nguyen and her husband both handled outsourced contracts for woodcarving workshops in the village and trained apprentices. There were frequently ten apprentices studying carving and fifteen others studying whittling in her household. When the workshop was set up, Nguyen had required each apprentice to contribute 13 kg of milled rice per month for their own consumption. Since 1999 she had stopped demanding such a contribution because it was an insignificant amount, given her income. Nguyen's apprentices no longer need to pay tuition fees nor contribute rice, and were paid according to their level of skill. Those who completed the woodcarving training course and stayed on to work as subcontractors in Nguyen's workshop were fed three meals and paid VND55,000 each day. Those who had just started their apprenticeship were also fed three meals, but paid VND10,000 per workday. Both contract workers and apprentices could receive advance payments of a maximum of three months when they needed the money.

Like Sinh, Nguyen allowed her apprentices and contract workers to work and live with her family. The model in which the regular contract labourers work and live together with the owner's family was popular only among the small and medium workshops. Hoa and her husband, for instance, did not have such a relationship with their contract labourers because the shop floor where workers worked and lived was located separately from their house. Nevertheless, Hoa and her husband sometimes organized small parties at home for all their contract workers. When necessary, they were also prepared to give their workers advances, as expected in a patron–client relationship.

Casual Migrant Labourers in Kim Thieu Village

Apart from long-term migrant labourers, there are also casual and daily hired woodcarvers, as well as in the farming sector in Kim Thieu village. Whereas the former group was mostly made up of male skilled labourers, the latter was mainly made up of female and unskilled workers. The casual and daily contract labourers go to Kim Thieu to seek jobs after they have finished their own farm work. They gather at a place next to the village — the *cho lao dong* or "labour marketplace" — where they wait for local villagers to come and hire them early each morning. The distances from their own villages to Kim Thieu varies from 4 to 20 km. Despite coming from different places with varied sociocultural conditions, these female migrant workers share one characteristic in common: their economic status is related to agricultural production.

Most hired labourers come to work for the woodworking industry in Kim Thieu, but some accept any job as long as they can earn money. Nearly all casual migrant labourers work as polishers, which is the least skilled but most labour-intensive stage of the woodworking process. Job opportunities and wage rates were inconsistent, but varied according to the skill, experience, health, as well as any verbal agreement made between themselves and the workshop owners. In 2006, those who could machine-polish wooden items were paid between VND32,000 to 35,000 while manual labourers received only between VND20,000 to 25,000 per eight hour workday. At the end of 2008, these wage rates had significantly increased: VND60,000 for machine operators and VND40,000 per workday for manual labourers.

Although all female hired labourers went to work in Kim Thieu to make extra money for their family, their attitudes towards job-seeking were not identical. For some women, working in Kim Thieu earned them desperately needed cash that could help them to repay debts and buy food, but for others it was only a small auxiliary income. One day when I visited the village, there were twenty women who could not be hired by villagers. Many of them were very sad when they could not be hired. One of them said, however, "No problem! There is a lot of work waiting for me. My village has large land areas for cash crops such as vegetables, onion, and tomato, so if I don't work here, I will go back to work in my field" (November 2006).

Others preferred to go home as a way of getting a fair wage for their labour. They reasoned: "There are not many producers hiring labour today, so they want to lower the wage. If we accept that wage level, we have to accept it next time also" (November 2006).

By refusing to work for such a low wage, these female workers were resisting the devaluation of their wage rate, using their refusal as a "weapon of the weak" in the labour market.

PATRON–CLIENT RELATIONSHIP OR EXPLOITATION?

We have thus far described a number of social and work relationships among different groups in Kim Thieu. Surprisingly it was only among these casual female workers that we found strong feelings that the pay offered was unfair and that they preferred not to take on jobs rather than be exploited. They were an exception to the cases discussed so far of hired migrant workers who were willing to live and work under a patron–client system. Yet, unlike labourers who had been working in the capitalist factories (private enterprises), most of these contract workers did not complain about the low wages. The reason could be that most of them often saw their wages from woodcarving as being much higher than what they could earn from farming. Many thought that low wages were at least better than underemployment, or not having any off-farm work at all.

Another reason why these contract workers never felt exploited was that most of the factory owners also worked alongside them as labourers. According to Alexander Chayanov (1966), owners such as these are more likely to accept "self-exploitation" by lengthening their working day and intensifying their unpaid family labour in the production process in order to produce more and thus earn more. Self-exploitation of family labour in Kim Thieu was seen as necessary not only for meeting basic needs, but also for improving general living standards through maximum utilization of the family workforce.

Contract labourers from other villages, particularly those who worked in inlay, carving, and whittling, were exploited through the piecework contracts, though the price for each piece had been negotiated and agreed on by both parties. Daily wage rates varied from one worker to another. The owners might pay some workers a lower daily wage rate telling them that either their skills were not up to standard or that they did not work hard enough. By concealing exploitation in the piece-rate system, the confrontation between the owners and the workers was thus avoided (Jamaree 1996).

The apprentice system too could be considered as a "soft" tactic of labour exploitation. Generally, the length of the training was determined by the trainers, who were also the factory owners, rather than by the trainees. To be qualified as a skilled woodcarver, whittler, or carpenter, an apprentice had to learn from and work alongside a master craftsman. The tasks assigned them often varied from the simplest to the most complicated. During their apprenticeship, they were paid at a much lower rate than that of a skilled worker. The apprenticeship wage rate usually remained unchanged until the end of the training course when the apprentices could begin to undertake complicated tasks.

My fieldwork in Kim Thieu revealed that teenage apprentices were usually paid at a lower rate than adult apprentices even when the quality of their work was not that different. Moreover, apprentices were more exploited than skilled workers because they were often required to do other types of work besides woodcarving, such as cooking, house cleaning, and farming.

The patron–client relationship between workshop owners and migrant workers can also be seen as the teacher–apprentice relationship. In the northern Vietnamese tradition, teachers, regardless of their educational level, must be respected by their students. As local people would say:

"Someone who taught you even half a letter must be called your teacher" (*Nhat tu vi su ban tu vi su*). As an expression of their gratitude, workers who used to be apprentices would often stay on to work for their former teachers as long-term contract labourers even when they were paid low wages. Nong and Dong who worked in Sinh's workshop are an example. There is also another subtle form of exploitation by the workshop owner-teacher, when he or she withholds transmitting all the necessary knowledge to the apprentice. In order to gain as much knowledge as possible, the student tends to voluntarily prolong the training period and hence is unintentionally trapped into providing their labour under apprenticeship conditions for longer.

Another manifestation of the patron–client relation is the system of paying workers only a few times, or even once, a year, rather than regularly. When workers needed money urgently, they had to ask their employer for an advance. This payment system gives the factory owners power over their skilled labourers by making it more difficult for them to quit and so binding them to a long-term work relationship. In addition, the worker, having received prepayment to tide them over, might even feel indebted to the owners. As a result, they keep working there even if they did not want to.

OUTWARD LABOUR MIGRATION

Let us now turn to marketing-related outward migration which is also integral to the craft industry. These wood products are sold mostly in inland cities and in the Puzhai free trade zone. Hence, a number of villagers have to work outside as entrepreneurs, shopkeepers, and to assemble the furniture, which is transported disassembled. Rather than simply in response to push and pull factors, as described by migration scholars, most Kim Thieu choose to migrate as a consequence of their active involvement in the woodcraft industry, particularly the final stages of the supply chain, to work in distribution and sales. Such emigrants from Kim Thieu village can be categorized into three groups:

- woodcraft business-owning shopkeepers who sell their products in the big cities and abroad;
- wood traders, whose business is related to timber exploitation and transportation from Laos to the village; and

- people who have established woodcarving workshops outside the village.

The shopkeepers form the biggest group of emigrant labour. They are mainly responsible for selling and marketing the products in the inland cities, such as Ho Chi Minh City, Nha Trang, Vinh, and Hai Phong, and in the border trading zone between Vietnam and China. They often go back and forth from the village to the shop, instead of living permanently away from the village, and travel either individually or as a group.

The wood traders usually travel in groups to source and buy timber in the forests of Laos. Then they transport the timber to the village for sale to local wood traders or producers. Whilst the female shopkeepers are able to go back and forth between the village and their place of trade, the male wood traders have to work abroad as long-term migrant labourers. One informant, Tuan, described how his team members stayed and worked together in Laos the whole year round. Normally, they only visited their hometown twice a year, in order to sell the wood when they had collected a volume of 500 cubic metres or more. Some had been away from their families for as long as two years because of difficulties obtaining suitable wood in Laos.

Unlike the first two groups, the last one consists of migrant families who have established private woodcarving workshops outside the village. Almost all these families have migrated to the south, to places such as Khanh Hoa, Ho Chi Minh City, and Binh Duong. Most of the migrant families cannot conduct business away from their village on a long-term basis for several reasons. Duc's family was among those few villagers who went to Nha Trang and established a woodcarving factory there in 1999. However, he decided to close the factory in early 2007 in order to return to the village because he believed that his children would have many difficulties when they grew up in that "strange land". Similar to the migrant pearl sculptors, these emigrant labourers have tended to retain their farm land by lending it to their relatives while making a living outside their village. It is also a common practice for them to retain their residential land and their houses in the village. This means they are able to move back and forth between their workplace and their hometown. Their farm land has little to do with agricultural production, but everything to do with home and a sense of community. It can be said that these emigrant families have opened up a new urban-to-rural migration channel.

In short, labour migration relating to the woodcarving industry in Kim Thieu village is a very diverse phenomenon. With respect to spatial mobility, four paths of labour migration have emerged in Kim Thieu village: rural-to-urban; rural-to-rural; urban-to-rural; and transnational migration. Rural labourers migrate not only from the traditional to the modern and from farm to non-farm sectors, but also from farm to farm and from the modern (formal industry) to the traditional (cottage industry). Therefore, labour migration related to the development of the woodcarving industry in Kim Thieu could be used to show that migration in Vietnam is not merely uni-directional. Here we have added a new dimension to several previous studies that focus only on labour migration flows from rural to urban areas and from farming to non-farming sectors (see Wouterse and Taylor 2007; Winkels and Adger 2002; Cohen 2006; Dang *et al.* 2003).

CHANGING GENDER DIVISION OF LABOUR

In addition to local versus in-migration as variables that create hierarchical relations, gender is another dimension that has undergone change because of new social and work roles and relationships. Before agricultural collectivization, villagers lived mainly on yields from farming, livestock rearing, and only partially on their woodcraft products. Craftmaking was considered as a supplementary activity for the household economy. Peasants would concentrate first and foremost on farming, using only their leisure time for craftwork. The oral histories of Kim Thieu villagers indicate that artisans who had to go work outside the village were mostly landless peasants.

Nevertheless, woodcarving was culturally held in high esteem. In traditional Vietnamese society, only men could participate in woodwork for two reasons. First, carpentry and woodcarving were related to the construction of sacred buildings such as temples, pagodas, communal houses, the imperial palace, and roof-making, all of which women were traditionally excluded from for cultural reasons. Second, being a wood craftsman and selling the items required a mobility which women in traditional patriarchal Vietnamese society did not enjoy.

By the end of the 1950s, the Vietnamese government implemented reforms on agriculture and the rural economy by collectivizing all means of production. Under collectivization, all households in the village were organized into either agricultural or handicraft cooperatives. The era of cooperatives contributed to the equalization of male-female relations. For instance, unmarried daughters and daughters-in-law who formerly constituted unpaid family labour became paid members of agricultural collectives. Women workers were supposed to be remunerated at the same level as their male family members. In practice, however, female workers were assigned to simpler tasks, which earned lower wage rates in the craft industry.

The gender division of labour in the woodcarving industry has significantly changed again since the early 1990s with an increasing number of female labourers engaging in production and marketing. It should be noted, however, that the changes in the gender division of labour have occurred differently in various kinds of household workshops in accordance with their scale of production. Women in households which run large-scale woodcarving businesses usually work as entrepreneurs, managers, shopkeepers, and traders. In medium-sized family-run workshops, women usually work as shopkeepers. Some women also participate in the actual making of the wooden items or furniture. The following section provides examples of women working in each category, although it can be seen that many women play multiple roles across the spectrum of production and marketing activities in the woodcraft industry.

Women's Roles in the Woodcraft Industry

Managers, Entrepreneurs, and Traders

Hoa is a company manager. She is responsible for seeking new contracts with Chinese customers, tracking changes in market demand for the wood products, and selling them, while her husband is responsible for organizing the necessary material for making furniture, buying the wood, subcontracting to other workshops, and hiring other villagers for some stages which cannot be done in their own workshop, such as framing, carving, and whittling. Hoa herself sometimes works on the shop floor directly, adjusting and packing finished items. She also helps her husband manage and monitor production at home and at their satellite workshops.

Most women whose families run large and medium-scale woodcarving workshops assist their husbands in managing production. Loi's wife, for instance, works as a polisher as well as manager of the family workshop. While Loi works alongside their contract workers assembling furniture, his wife inspects the work of the carvers and whittlers. Loi's wife is also responsible for cooking for the family and regular contract labourers who live and have meals with them. Like other village women, she contributes to her household economy not only as a money earner in her own right but also manages the household budget.

As has been mentioned, to sell their products, about twenty of Kim Thieu's large and medium-scale woodcraft producers rent shops all over the country and forty rent shops in the Puzhai trade zone at the Sino-Vietnamese border. Notably, all these furniture shops are run by women.

While almost all female entrepreneurs, shopkeepers, and managerial staff are from families which run either large or medium-scale workshops, female carvers, whittlers, and polishing workers are generally those whose families either have small workshops or only work as outsourcing units. Some highly skilled female woodcarvers give up carving to manage their workshops when their business expands.

Woodcarvers, Whittlers, and Polishers

Although women can theoretically participate in carving the wooden items, in practice, it seems to be an exclusively male realm. Even when dozens of women received specialized training in woodwork during the period of collectivization, none of them could carve as well as the men. According to several villagers, carving is the most difficult stage because the carvers must be very skilful and in good health. The skill here does not only come from having "nimble fingers", but it must be a combination of dexterity and imagination. In the villagers' perception, carving is hard work which needs both strength and skill and both male and female informants said that it should be done by men rather than by women. Indeed I only came across three female woodcarvers who possessed skills considered comparable to male artisans.

Whittling, on the other hand, is said to require "nimble fingers". I was astonished to see such gender bias, which was confirmed by San's comment: "women should be responsible for whittling because they are more dexterous than us (men)" (Oct 2006). Although women can start learning how to whittle at any age, it is believed that the younger the better. Ever since women started taking on whittling, men are hardly to be seen working as whittlers.

Furniture polishing is mainly done by daily hired female workers. It is also undertaken, however, by village women who do not have the skills to either carve or whittle. These women participate in the production process as a "reserve army". This group of village women consists of:

those who are over sixty years of age and hence considered to be too old to learn carving and whittling; those who do not seem to be interested in learning carving or whittling, although they were born into and live in woodcarving families; and daughters-in-law who came from places without a woodcarving tradition.

In summary, there is a gender division of labour in the woodcarving industry. Yet women have increasingly been occupying various positions at production sites and in marketing the crafts and as a result, their wage rates have improved substantially. Certain stages of the production process, such as purchasing material, sawing, framing, furniture assembling, and painting remain within the purview of men. Both women and men believed that such kinds of work should belong to men because they involved the use of machinery and special skills. With the exception of a few women who could carve as well as men, most women were assigned to simpler manual duties. In the workshops, both village and migrant women specialized in whittling in particular, a task which is monotonous but requires a high level of dexterity and patience.

While more women have been engaged in the woodcarving industry since the 1990s, fewer and fewer village men work in the fields any more. The task has been taken up entirely by village women. Where previously higher status men monopolized household decision-making, in Kim Thieu women could make all decisions related to farming, from seed selection to distribution of the harvest. This does not mean that the women who have decision-making power are engaged in farming themselves. Among the women there is also a heirarchy. Those with little or no woodcarving skills take up farming although they may not like it. Old or middle-age women are therefore more likely to be farming than younger women.

Despite mechanization, farming is still hard labour; families that are sufficiently wealthy prefer to hire outside labour rather than have women in the family cultivate the land. There are two reasons for this. The first is a question of opportunity cost: the women can earn more in the workshops. For instance, a whittler can earn VND80,000 per day, double a farmhand's daily fee of VND40,000. Second, some young women do not like to do "dirty" and "hard" tasks even if they can save some money. Working under the hot sun, knee-deep in mud, is very hard labour.

As described earlier, there are also a number of female day labourers who come to work in the village as hired workers from early morning to evening. Unlike the Kim Thieu women, these female labourers are willing to bear the drudgery to earn some extra cash. On top of that, farm work is sometimes "supplemented" by both male and female permanent labourers who work for the family factories. These labourers, hired as permanent woodcarving workers, sometimes also have to help out during planting and harvest seasons without pay. This kind of labour exploitation goes under the guise of "asking for help". As permanent hired labourers often live in the owner's households, it is very difficult for them to refuse such ad hoc "requests". Such arrangements have allowed some women to empower themselves by not having to toil in the field; on the other hand, it also creates an hierarchical relationship between these women as the employers and their hired workers.

CONCLUSION

The revival and development of traditional craft villages is widely perceived by government and locals alike as one strategy towards solving the problem of surplus rural labour in Vietnam. As has been demonstrated, the expansion of the woodcarving industry in Kim Thieu village has caused multiple changes in the division of rural labour through attracting immigrants to work in the village as well as through local women taking on roles in areas which they were previously excluded from. At the same time, the participation of immigrant labourers and female workers in the traditional woodcarving industry has made a significant contribution to the growth of this sector. The new distribution of labour in the woodcarving industry, as well as in the farming sector in Kim Thieu, shows that rural-to-rural migration is a popular mobility strategy for labourers in the Red River Delta region in northern Vietnam, creating a new rural labour market. In addition, the active engagement of female labourers at different stages of the woodcarving industry cycle, as well as in farming, has contributed to new forms of gender discrimination in the workplace and to a change in women's economic role within rural households.

The other area of social change is in the dynamics of labour relations in the woodwork industry. The revival of the industry has been based on what could be termed exploitative and patronage-based relations. The concepts of exploitation, as well as of patron-client relations, need to be redefined in the context of the traditional woodcarving industry in Kim Thieu, however, as has been shown in this study. While there are instances where the patrons take advantage of their clients through various means such as apprenticeships and payment systems, the relationships are not merely exploitative. We see "exploitation" not only in the sense that private enterprise factory owners exploit their workers, but by working alongside their employees, the owners also "exploit" themselves. On the other hand, while the workers have not been transformed into proletarians in the subjective sense, objectively they are wage labourers without owning any means of production. Yet most of the Kim Thieu workers neither expressed nor demonstrated a sense of being exploited in their work. It could be concluded that the division of labour in the woodcarving village of Kim Thieu has become more complicated in the context of the ongoing commoditization and globalization of the rural economy.

Notes

[1]   1 *sao* = 360 m^2.

[2]   In the old household registration system, each person had to register their permanent place of residence. Since 2007, migrant workers have been allowed to register as regular residents in a place they have worked in for more than one year.

References

Chayanov, Alexander V. *The Theory of Peasant Economy*. Homewood: American Economic Association, 1966.

Dang Nguyen Anh, C. Tacoli, and Hoang Xuan Thanh. "Migration in Vietnam: A Review of Information on Current Trends and Patterns, and Their Policy Implications". Paper presented at the Regional Conference on Migration, Development and Pro-Poor Policy Choices in Asia, Dhaka, Bangladesh, 22–24 June 2003 <http://www.livelihoods.org/hot_topics/docs/Dhaka_CP_7.pdf> (accessed 6 February 2007).

Elson, R.E. *The End of the Peasantry in Southeast Asia: A Social and Economic History of Peasant Livelihood, 1800–1990s*. New York: St. Martin's Press, 1997.

Jamaree Pitackwong. "Disorganized Development: Changing Forms of Work and Livelihood in Rural Northern Thailand". Ph.D. dissertation, University of London, 1996.

Lande, Carl. "Networks and Groups in Southeast Asia: Some Observations on the Group Theory of Politics". *American Political Science Review* 67, no. 1 (1973): 103–27.

Luttrell, Cecilia. "An Institutional Approach to Livelihood Resilience in Vietnam". Ph.D. dissertation, University of East Anglia, 2001.

Massey, Doreen. *Spatial Divisions of Labor: Social Structures and the Geography of Production*. New York: Routledge, 1984.

————. *Space, Place and Gender*. Cambrige: Polity Press, 1994.

Popkin, Samuel L. *The Rational Peasant: The Political Economy of Rural Society in Vietnam*. London: University of California Press, 1979.

Rigg, Jonathan. *More than the Soil: Rural Change in Southeast Asia*. Singapore: Prentice-Hall, 2001.

Winkels, Alexandra and W. Neil Adger. "Sustainable Livelihoods and Migration in Vietnam: The Importance of Social Capital as Access to Resources". Paper presented in symposium, Sustainable Food Security and Managing Natural Resources in Southeast Asia: Challenges for the Twenty-first Century, Chiangmai, 8–11 January 2002.

Wouterse, Fleur and J. Edward Taylor. "Migration and Income Diversification: Evidence from Burkina Faso". *World Development* 36, no. 4 (2007): 625–40.

5

CORPORATE SOCIAL RESPONSIBILITY IN SOCIALIST VIETNAM
Implementation, Challenges, and Local Solutions

Angie Ngoc Tran

More than thirteen years have passed since the 1996 media exposé of the sweatshop working conditions endured by Honduran workers assembling clothes for Kathie Lee Gifford's brand led to federal-level investigations of sweatshop abuses in the United States, as well as elsewhere around the world. This media exposure prompted non-governmental organizations (NGOs) and ethical consumers to criticize brand name corporate buyers more aggressively, giving rise to the need for social reporting of working conditions. The ensuing Corporate Social Responsibility (CSR) initiatives in turn have led to a proliferation of codes of conduct (CoCs) and monitoring schemes to help inform consumers on whether the goods that they buy have been produced under exploitative conditions. There are also, of course, many CSR-like initiatives dating back to the 1970s, which include philanthropy and ethical investment. This chapter focuses on labour standards compliance, the problems in implementing them, and their effects on workers on the factory floor.

The CSR initiative gained further legitimacy at the World Economic Forum in Davos in January 1999, when UN Secretary-General Kofi Annan urged multinational corporations (MNCs) to voluntarily incorporate the nine principles established by Global Compact, a UN body established by Annan himself to set standards on human rights, labour, and the environment for the international business community.[1] These initiatives focus attention on the global manufacturing supply chain's multi-level subcontracting practices and the resulting difficulty of monitoring labour standards at subcontractors' production sites in the developing world.

This chapter examines what the introduction of CSR to Vietnam in 2000 meant for the global supply chain and the actions and interactions of the stakeholders. By stakeholders, I mean those who have a stake in their interests, rights, and entitlements in the CSR context. From the Vietnamese side they include workers, The Vietnam General Confederation of Labour (VGCL), the labour press, the Ministry of Labour, Invalids and Social Affairs (MOLISA), local state officials, and the Vietnamese Chamber of Commerce and Industry (VCCI). The global actors include institutions such as the World Bank, the International Labour Organization (ILO), MNCs, international NGOs, and foreign subcontractors. To be sure, each of these stakeholders have very different levels of power to influence this process. The chapter focuses on challenges for labour standards compliance and monitoring regimes. It seeks answers to the following questions: what has CSR meant to Vietnamese stakeholders since its introduction into Vietnam? How does the multi-level global supply chain affect the implementation of CSR and the monitoring of the corporate codes? How does the tripartite structure work at both national and local levels, in light of the global economic crisis? To what extent can local initiatives undertaken by local state, labour unions, and the labour press improve collective bargaining agreements (CBAs) and labour standards?

The data for this chapter include fieldwork interviews with the key stakeholders from 2003 to June 2009, secondary data including reports from newspapers, studies from relevant state ministries and agencies, research by scholars and experts, and Internet materials, as well as observations and conversations from factory visits. The interviewees included labour union representatives (at central, city, district, and workplace levels), state officials (in MOLISA, from central to local levels), ILO officials in Hanoi, MNC representatives working on CSR, Vietnamese journalists in labour newspapers, representatives of CoC certifying and monitoring companies, CSR specialists, consultants and researchers, and migrant workers in safe spaces of their choice outside the factories.

This topic is a sensitive one in the context of a one-party state which characterizes itself as operating in a "market economy with socialist orientation" while integrating itself ever more deeply into the neoliberal global economy. As discussed elsewhere, investigative journalists in Vietnam are valuable, reliable resources, not only because they have easier access to information and to decisions made by the key stakeholders (both domestic and foreign), but also because they have created a public forum for workers' complaints about CSR violations.[2]

CODES OF CONDUCT AND THE VIETNAMESE LABOUR CODE

Most labour standards manifested in CoCs are developed from the core ILO conventions: occupational health and safety, freedom of association, freedom from harassment and abuse, the right to collective bargaining, non-discrimination in employment, minimum wage payment and benefits, prohibition on forced labour, regulated hours of work, and prohibition of child labour (Douglas 2001; Fung *et al.* 2001; Harvey *et al.* 2003). Most MNCs and NGOs have incorporated these standards into their own codes. However, not all of them include politically sensitive conventions such as the right to collective bargaining and independent labour unions (freedom of association).[3] In Vietnam, labour unions have been working with the ILO and MOLISA on collective bargaining agreements (CBAs), but have steered away from independent labour unions.

Many CoCs include a statement which recognizes the need to "comply with all applicable laws of the country of manufacture", which in this case means compliance with the Vietnamese Labour Code. This would include all relevant labour legislation on the minimum wage, unemployment insurance, and contributions to social security, health care, and union funds. The Labour Code, ratified in June 1994 and put into effect in January 1995, is quite progressive. It encompasses all work and pay conditions, non-wage benefits, special stipulations for women workers, as well as the right to strike.[4]

However, the clause "compliance with local labour legislation" is often violated. A recent article from an influential labour newspaper, *Nguoi Lao Dong* (Labourer), discussed some of the reasons for this, some of which have to do with contradictions in Vietnam's own policy implementation.[5] For one, the state and its apparatuses often do not enforce the law in a proper and timely manner.[6] For instance, unemployment insurance was added to the Labour Code in 2002 but was not enforced until 2009; at the time of writing there is still a lack of adequate guidance for its implementation. Another example is that of legally stipulated benefits for female workers. For instance, vocational training for back-up jobs in case of lay-offs, or tax breaks for factories that hire many female workers are legal requirements but they seldom happen in reality. Compliance with the Labour Code often has to rely on the prime minister's resolutions and on circulars issued by MOLISA. The resulting lack of coordination and/or alignment between the Labour Code and proper implementation instructions have contributed to thousands of "illegal" labour strikes in the last fifteen years.

There are also reasons arising from external causes, such as the discrepancies between most CoCs and the Vietnamese Labour Code. The Vietnamese Code allows only 200 hours of overtime work per year (or a maximum of 300 hours in textile/garment industries, with the approval of the labour unions). However, most CoCs allow a maximum of 12 hours of overtime a week (or a maximum of 60 hours a week), which could add up to 624 hours per year, more than double the permitted overtime.[7] Moreover, while most CoCs do not allow continuous overtime, they fail to specify the rest time required between two periods of overtime. The labour law requires that management should contribute 15 per cent to social insurance based on the workers' entire wage package, and 2 per cent to health insurance, with workers contributing 6 per cent, but many factories base their calculation of fringe benefits on the much lower basic wage, which is pegged at exactly the official minimum wage. This results in underpayment and a lower level of social and health benefits for workers.

Other legal benefits for female workers are difficult to enforce because of subcontracting in the supply chain. Women workers are supposed to have paid breaks (fifteen minutes per day for those who are nursing or menstruating and one hour of rest for women in and after the seventh month of pregnancy). However, with high production quotas and very poor wages, many pregnant workers in need of money do not take their breaks, and even work overtime without extra pay. Thus, these breaks are not really "paid" since pregnant workers still have to meet their daily quota and work twenty-six days per month or lose their attendance bonus.

There are two systems of minimum wage in Vietnam, one for the domestic and public sector and one for the foreign direct investment (FDI) sector. Monthly minimum wages for the FDI sector in 2008 was VND1,000,000 for Hanoi and Ho Chi Minh City (HCMC), VND900,000 for outlying areas around these two cities and districts of other major provinces, and VND800,000 for the rest of the country. In the domestic sector, it was VND540,000, about 30 per cent less than the FDI sector. However, as shown in Michael Karadjis's chapter, on average workers in the state sector are paid higher than their minimum wage rate and their salaries rise at a faster rate than those in the FDI sector. The government has also been trying to bridge the gap between these two sectors. In 2009, the FDI sector's minimum wages were increased to VND1.2 million, VND1 million, and VND920.000, respectively, which amounts to an increase in the range of 15 to 20 per cent, but in the domestic and public sector it rose to VND650,00 as of May 2009, a 20 per cent increase.[8]

The minimum wage for the FDI sector was increased in 2006, 2008, and 2009. The state raised it by 40 per cent in the beginning of 2006 in response to workers' protests, after seven years of no increase. In 2007, there was another wave of protests, with workers demanding wage adjustments to keep up with staggering inflation (as high as 13 per cent), which was raising the prices of food and housing and disproportionately affecting their livelihoods. In response, the state raised the base minimum wage in FDI companies by about 13 per cent in 2008. The situation worsened, with an inflation rate of 19 per cent in March 2008 (25 per cent in May 2008), when food prices rose 30 per cent and housing 20 per cent. These increases seriously reduced workers' access to basic necessities. When many companies delayed paying these inflation-adjusted minimum wages, a wave of massive spontaneous strikes erupted in the first quarter of 2008.[9] Starting in January 2009, the state initiated another round of minimum wage increases for the FDI sector: VND1.2 million in Hanoi and HCMC; VND1 million in these two cities' suburbs and other key industrial, commercial or oil-rich cities and provinces (such as Hai Phong, Ha Long, Vung Tau, Thu Dau Mot, Dong Nai and Binh Duong provinces), and VND920,000 in other regions (Sunoo *et al.* 2009, p. 36).

There are two broad types of labour standards. First, MNCs and retail companies each generated their own CoCs (the World Bank estimated that there were over 1,000 such codes). For instance, Nike, Adidas, and Ikea used their own codes in Vietnam and relied on private monitoring to check on compliance.[10] These MNC codes are based on international conventions related to working and social conditions. Some, such as the Ikea and Mountain Equipment Co-op[11] codes also mention compliance with national laws and regulations. Second, there are private international NGOs such as the Fair Labour Association (FLA) and Social Accountability International (SAI), which created SA8000, an international standard for improving working conditions based on the principles of the ILO and various UN labour conventions.[12]

Clearly, many Vietnamese contract factories have to comply with multiple CoCs, because a factory can have multiple international clients. In addition, many corporate buyers place orders with a number of different suppliers in order to minimize production risk factors. In a survey conducted by the Institute of Labour Science and Social Affairs (ILSSA) in MOLISA and financed by the World Bank in 2004, there were thirty-five different CoCs applying to eighteen of the twenty-four textile and footwear factories sampled, meaning that, on average, each factory had to comply with almost two CoCs.[13] Before delving deeper into the workings of CSR in Vietnam, it may be useful to briefly examine what the term means to its various stakeholders.

THE MEANING OF CSR IN VIETNAM TO THE KEY STAKEHOLDERS

The Vietnamese translation of "corporate social responsibility" is "*trach nhiem xa hoi doanh nghiep*". The key word is "*xa hoi*", meaning social, which carries both a residual sense of the Marxist-Leninist concepts of "socialist", "socialism", and a meaning to do with "society", or things pertaining to society. This has resulted in the use in Vietnam of the new expression "socialization" (*xa hoi hoa*), which embodies activities related to the dispersal of responsibilities away from the state,[14] such as "social work" or "charity work" (*viec xa hoi, viec tu thien*). These expressions can mean very different things to different people.

The General Public's Perspective

Most people in socialist Vietnam understand "social responsibility" as charitable work, along the lines of doing good deeds, over and above one's regular realm of activity. For instance, a *Nguoi Lao Dong* article reported that Nike staff in Ho Chi Minh City (HCMC) spent a day helping poor households in Dong Nai to improve their houses, and donated US$22,500 to fix their houses and water wells.[15] While this was a commendable community service, it was not about labour standards, nor did it resolve issues critical to workers' survival, such as wages, work hours, and benefits.

One explanation for this is that the Vietnamese public is not familiar with the fact that CSR initiatives originated from anti-sweatshop campaigns in the wealthy countries:

> At present in Vietnam, many people and a lot of factories still do not understand properly about CSR. Many factories still consider that performing CSR is doing "charity work", not taking care of their workers. Worse yet, in the current economic crisis, many factories in Vietnam expect workers to share the difficulties, rather than enforcing CSR.[16]

Supplier Factory Management's Perspective

From the supplier management's perspective, CSR is mostly understood as "philanthropy, certification-led and customer-driven". Suppliers in Vietnam are aware that compliance with CSR improves their business image and can attract more clients and orders. Moreover, CSR compliance can be considered a long-term investment with potential economic benefits in terms of productivity, quality, competitiveness, and the retention of skilled workers. Through compliance with CoCs, they can acquire certification. However, suppliers also fear that, as a mandatory requirement, CoC compliance may become a new form of protectionism (Tencati 2007; Nguyen Quang Vinh 2007).

The MNCs' Perspective

MNCs mostly interpret CSR in terms of labour standards, for fear of being accused by the global anti-sweatshop movement of violating labour rights; many big brands also engage in some philanthropy, however. With their own CoCs and social departments to attend to compliance, MNCs train their suppliers on CSR issues and hire local consultants for internal monitoring (Sunoo *et al.* 2009). Their concerns for workers focus on labour training with a view to achieving higher productivity, a lower turnover rate, a higher quality final product, and improved conflict resolution (Tencati 2007). Overall, there is the potential for a win-win situation, if higher labour productivity is matched with higher salaries, but that scenario requires much better CBAs. This will be analyzed in the last section.

The Vietnamese Trade Unions' Perspective

The labour unions' understanding of CSR has been squarely focused on labour standards such as wages, work hours and benefits, wage rises, bonuses, and allowances, but the unions' awareness of the relevance of CSR in their work has some way to go. So far, at the time of writing, there has not been any nationwide VGCL campaign specifically on CSR, but rather embedding CSR as one component in the CBAs campaign. However, at the factory level, there are more conscious efforts to promote CSR implementation by raising labour standards.

TRIPARTISM PROPOSED AS A SOLUTION

The concept of "multiple stakeholders" in the CSR process has been popularized by scholars, international NGOs, and multilateral institutions such as the World Bank and the ILO. Its roots lie in the fact that the ILO itself is a tripartite international body, consisting of the peak levels of the state, employers' organizations, and trade unions. The ILO in Vietnam has been promoting the concept of a tripartite structure (*co che ba ben*), by which the three parties engage in social dialogue to improve labour–management relations. The tripartite structure at the national level includes MOLISA, the VGCL, the VCCI, and the Vietnamese Cooperatives Alliance (VCA) (Sunoo *et al.* 2009, pp. 13–14). The ILO's stated intention was to provide technical assistance on interest-based negotiations and to enhance the VGCL's role in the growing private sector.

Vietnam rejoined the ILO in 1993. Since then it has focused on three main industrial relations projects: conflict resolution and mediation, social dialogue at work, and CBAs.[17] Starting from the memorandum of understanding (MOU) signed in 2000 when then-U.S. president Bill Clinton visited Vietnam, the ILO has collaborated with MOLISA to oversee six labour-related projects funded by the U.S. Department of Labor, and helped to draft amendments to the Labour Code in 2002.[18] In that context, the ILO office has been working closely with MOLISA officials, providing technical assistance and training to the VGCL on skills with regard to interest-based negotiations, and has facilitated the VGCL's role in the growing private sector.[19]

The World Bank, the U.S. government, and MNCs have also been funding studies carried out by ILO and MOLISA to introduce CSR concepts to Vietnam, but my observations suggest that these studies are more concerned with the interests of management than those of workers. Following a six-day visit to Vietnam in 2002, World Bank personnel issued a report on the athletic shoe industry that promoted the "multiple stakeholder" concept (World Bank 2002, p. 18). Between 2004 and 2006, the World Bank and the United States stepped up pressure on the Vietnamese state to adopt CSR regimes in Vietnam, providing it with "technical assistance" on how to strengthen them (ILSSA 2004, p. 1). In 2004, they commissioned ILSSA, the research arm of MOLISA, to undertake a study on CSR and labour-related practices, which made some interesting findings on overtime violations.[20] In 2006, the Swiss State Secretariat for Economic Affairs, and the U.S. Department of Labor and Department of State commissioned the ILO, MOLISA, and the VCCI to conduct two other studies focusing on CSR implementation in Vietnam.[21] Moreover, as described later, in mid-2009 and 2010, the ILO and the International Finance Corporation (IFC, part of the World Bank group) have started working with MOLISA and VGCL on the "Better Work" project to pilot the signing of CBAs in the textile and garment enterprises. Thus, these international bodies and foreign governments have been actively pushing Vietnam in the direction of tripartism and social dialogue.

MINISTRY OF LABOUR, INVALIDS, AND SOCIAL AFFAIRS

MOLISA advises the Vietnamese state on labour–management negotiations. In April 2009, the Prime Minister formed a Centre for the Development of Industrial Relations, headed by a high-ranking, experienced official from MOLISA, Mr. Nguyen Manh Cuong. In his interview with a *Nguoi Lao Dong* journalist, Mr. Cuong explained that this new institution provides state support for labour–management relations in a market economy based on the prinnciple of rule by law and emphasizing regular industrial negotiations to avoid the eruption of conflict. Relations between labour and management bring stability and mutual benefit when both sides find a balance in the reasonable distribution of the enterprise's profits. When this balance is missing, conflicts and strikes will erupt. This equilibrium is based on two foundations: the rights (*quyen*) of both sides being regulated by law, and the contention over interests (*loi ich*) being resolved through dialogue and negotiations/bargaining. This Centre's purview is to support negotiations before, during, and after conflict erupts.[22]

Mr. Cuong further explained why the VGCL has been focusing on CBAs to obtain higher-than-minimum benefits for workers: "In industrialized countries, most strikes are about interests. In Vietnam, previously most labour strikes were about rights; but lately the conflicts gradually move towards struggling for interests".[23] However, with regard to workers' protests, my view is that most agendas are still about a combination of basic rights (minimum wages, work hours, and benefits) and interests (pay rises based on wage tables, with steps according to skill levels, and bonuses, especially the thirteenth-month salary that workers used to receive in the state sector).

VIETNAMESE CHAMBER OF COMMERCE AND INDUSTRY

The VCCI is a state-sanctioned organization of employers for both foreign and domestic investors, formed in the 1990s as Vietnam developed its fully-fledged market system (Sunoo *et al.* 2009, p. 13).[24] Its function is to represent management in the private sector, influence policy-making, and implement trade-related policies. The Prime Ministerial Decision no. 123 in June 2003 officially acknowledged the VCCI as the principal non-governmental association representing the interests of the private sector, including small and medium enterprises; following that decision, in the same year the VCCI formed the Small and Medium Enterprise Promotion Centre.[25]

With time, the VCCI became stronger, with members coming from all sectors of the economy, especially from joint-stock companies that were formerly state-owned enterprises (SOEs) run primarily by retired state officials with connections to the state and the party. As such, they lobby the state in their own interest, not unlike lobbyists in capitalist countries. The VCCI influences policy-making by participating in important debates on the minimum wage, industrial relations, and CBAs. It provides services, such as trademarks, certificates of origin, and advice on intellectual property compliance.[26] It has three bilingual websites to reach out to various audiences: the Small and Medium Enterprise Promotion Centre, the Finance Newsletter, and the Vietnam Business Forum.[27]

As of May 2009, over 2,000 members were listed on the VCCI website, reflecting all types of ownership (state-owned, joint-stock, limited shareholding companies, FDI enterprises), sectors of the economy (manufacturing, agriculture, services, extractive), and geographical regions.[28] For instance, the Vietnam Textile and Garment Association (VITAS) has been working with the VCCI on the registration and issuance of certificates of origin. To prevent trade fraud, VITAS provides the VCCI with information about producers' capacity and the average price of each category.[29]

Nonetheless, in the labour press the VGCL has been critical of the VCCI's effectiveness, saying that it does not truly represent domestic and foreign management in the private sector as stipulated by law. It argues that the VCCI does not have a nationwide presence, with offices in only eight out of sixty-four cities, nor can it control the budgets of its member firms.[30] The VGCL is of the opinion that the VCCI lacks the legal representation for management to participate meaningfully in a tripartite structure at both national and local levels. Views expressed in a tripartite meeting with representatives from the Parliamentary Committee on Social Issues, the HCMC Labour Federation, the HCMC Export Processing Zone Authority (HEPZA) representing management, HCMC Party leaders, and private enterprises showed some of these internal problems. As one journalists explains "By law, the VGCL represents workers; the VCCI and the VCA (Vietnamese Cooperatives Alliance) represent management. But neither the VCCI nor the VCA have capacity to "reach down" to the workplace level — where most conflicts take place — and they are only present in several large cities".[31]

The union as well as some enterprise representatives at that tripartite meeting also pointed out that FDI management are similarly incapacitated, as "most presidents of FDI factories are employees [of supplier MNCs whose headquarters are outside of Vietnam] so they have no power to make decisions on issues related to their corporation's finance".[32] In any case, the VCCI does not actually represent many FDI factories. The large ones do not need VCCI, because they prefer to have direct access to the office of the Prime Minister via their chambers of commerce to lobby for their interests (Sunoo *et al.* 2009). Finally, the connection between the VCCI and the CSR initiative is tenuous:

> VCCI and VCA have programs to promote CSR but do not achieve any real results because they cannot organize managers in most enterprises, especially in FDI factories. Most FDI factories are concerned primarily

about their profits. When they mention CSR, it is only form over substance. Many FDI contract factories display the Code of Conduct [subscribed to by the brands for which they produce] in their main lobbies, but mainly for show and self-advertisement. In short, implementing CSR in Vietnam is still an uphill struggle.[33]

In practice, collective bargaining at the factory level does not need the VCCI to come in and represent management. The real challenge is to have on-site managers who can make immediate decisions in response to workers' demands.

VGCL AND THE LABOUR MEDIA

Labour unions in Vietnam are organized by administrative area (city, district, workplace levels), by industrial sector (such as textile/garment, commerce, railroads), and by state corporations (privatized former SOEs now report directly to the VGCL). By December 2008, total union membership was about 6.24 million members, 3 million of whom were female.[34] By ownership type, the domestic private sector has 1.55 million union members; the state sector 1.36 million; and the FDI sector 1.1 million.[35] Interestingly, the domestic private sector has surpassed the state sector in union membership, the effect of a shrinking state sector, and the mushrooming foreign and domestic private sector, now 42 per cent of total membership. Moreover, the VGCL requires the formation of labour unions in export processing zones such as HEPZA, a requirement that is unusual in other developing countries. These zones, formed in 2000 due to the concentration of FDI factories in HCMC, were the sites of major worker-initiated protests that resulted in minimum wage increases of 40 per cent in 2006 (Tran 2007*b*).

In the face of thousands of labour protests since 1995, the VGCL and the state have been groping for solutions. The Tenth Congress of the VGCL in November 2008 ratified a five-year plan of action (2009–13) that encompasses three main goals:

- to increase membership by 1.5 million;
- to improve the capacity of workplace labour unions and provide training for union representatives; and
- to pilot test CBA procedures in the textile and garment industries, which employ over 2 million workers nationwide under all types of [enterprise] ownership.

Mr Sunoo of the ILO Hanoi office pointed out two major turning points arising from this congress. First, upper-level labour unions at city and district levels now have permission and protocols to intervene and support workplace labour unions, which are widely acknowledged as the weakest link in the VGCL. Second, the union's emphasis was to be on workers' interests rather than the political education of union cadres.[36]

Preliminary findings show that SOEs and large FDI factories have complied with CoCs. SOEs fared better on compliance with female workers' rights, but smaller FDI factories have failed to comply with such rights and with wage standards, nor have they registered their wage scales, including job positions, steps, and coefficients, with the local labour administration.[37]

After being wary of the CSR initiative for some years, labour union leaders have begun to see its potential usefulness and to reclaim the focus on labour standards while being conscious of the need to remedy their own weaknesses, especially with regard to workplace labour unions, in bargaining with management.

> We currently focus on industry-wide collective bargaining [without a ceiling wage] to provide a framework for further negotiations at local levels [with flexibility to bargain for higher wages]. *CSR is more style over substance, but we realize that the unions have to establish our own strength first before we can bargain effectively with MNCs* [my emphasis]. The proverbial 'tripartite' structure pushed for by ILO and MOLISA does not really work, because the VCCI does not represent management, since many enterprises did not join the VCCI.[38]

This critical assessment of the tripartite structure from a central-level union leader also makes sense in that at the workplace level where factory management bargains with labour representatives, there is no VCCI representation. At the local level, labour union leaders are familiar with the CSR initiative and the companies' interests. Mr Nguyen Huy Can, President of the HCMC Labour Federation, pointed out the nature and intention of CSR activities:

> Most multinationals use CSR as a form of free advertisement for their companies. They receive tax exemption for their social and charitable activities, having their company names listed on the flyers and banners for these events. Also, they want to give 'favours' to workers as one-time allowances, rather than the long-term obligations stated on collective bargaining agreements. As such, MNCs gain flexibility without responsibility for workers' compensation.[39]

Mr Can is insightful in his sharp criticism of MNCs' intentions, which is tax exemption and free advertising for their social and charitable activities. He acknowledges that CBAs guaranteeing long-term obligations to workers would be important, but not one-off "favours". These one-off allowances are not only short-term but also perpetuate patron–client relations between MNCs/suppliers and workers.[40]

The labour press functions as the official forum of the VGCL, with ebbs and flows in freedom to report. For instance, there was relatively greater freedom in 2005 and 2006: the state allowed the media (both Vietnamese and English) to provide various forums for workers' complaints, to give legal advice on workers' rights and benefits, and to report on the workers' protests that led to the 2006 and 2008 minimum wage increases. Moreover, the labour press reported internal debates among state bureaucracies that publicized some progressive positions arguing for *independent* labour representation, in the absence of workplace unions (Tran 2007*a*). For instance, thanks to sustained labour press coverage of workers' persistent protests from 2005 to 2008 demanding payment of unpaid social security and healthcare benefits contributions, Hue Phong, a Taiwanese-owned and managed company registered as a domestic enterprise under the name of a Chinese Vietnamese, was required to pay debts of over VND5 billion (US$312,500) owed to workers.[41] This is just one of many cases where contract factories only comply when workers protest, bringing the key parties to the negotiating table.

However, the labour press, very much ensconced *within* the state structure, has to walk a fine line between representing workers' rights and responding to the political agendas of the state and the labour unions. There has been a reluctance in the labour press to report on labour–management issues since Vietnam joined the WTO in November 2006, and in a similar vein, the press has not been critical on the subject of CSR. In private conversations over the years, however, some seasoned labour journalists have told of potential benefits of CoCs not being realized due to ineffectual enforcement and high monitoring costs. Yet thus far there have been no specific press reports on cases of non-compliance by brands/corporate buyers — the targets have always been the suppliers. Consequently, direct reporting on CSR activities has been minimal; in the few articles on the topic, the focus has been on the philanthropy and not on code compliance issues.

An interesting recent development on permissible space for the labour press' coverage is reliance on the "rule *by* law" to criticize the shortcomings of state policies and state apparatuses.[42] Many new laws have recently been added to the Labour Code, dealing with matters such as a minimum wage, unemployment insurance, social security and healthcare insurance, CBAs in textile and garment industries, and labour union fees in the FDI sector.[43] Common complaints have to do with inadequate instructions to explain and implement those new laws. In 2009, some journalists and legal authorities in HCMC challenged MOLISA on the legality of Decision No. 1846 on pilot CBAs in the textile/garment industries, as being neither a legal document nor an implementation document, and cited mistakes when MOLISA gave representation to VITAS and its Labour Unions Department in CBA negotiations. An article in *Nguoi Lao Dong* reported that both the VGCL and VCCI criticized MOLISA, the author of Decision No. 1846, questioning MOLISA's purview: "MOLISA overstepped its boundaries by naming specific representatives from VCCI and VGCL".[44] They complained that MOLISA had "replaced" their roles by imposing conditions on organizations not under its purview and jurisdiction: VITAS and its Labour Unions Department, the VGCL (the general labour unions) and the VCCI (the employers' association).[45]

How do these stakeholders — such as workers, domestic subcontractors, foreign contract factories/suppliers, corporate buyers/brands, monitoring companies, labour unions, labour press, MOLISA officials — fare in the multi-level global supply chain, the production system that underlies labour–management relations in the market economy?

GLOBAL SUPPLY CHAIN AND CHALLENGES TO MONITORING

How does a multi-level global supply chain affect code monitoring in Vietnam? Why are some of the most basic stipulations of the Vietnamese Labour Code — work hours, pay, social security/health contributions, and conditions for women workers — not properly enforced?[46] First, we shall examine the challenges which multi-level subcontracting in the global supply chain poses for monitoring.

Multi-level Manufacturing and Unauthorized Subcontracting

One rule of thumb is that, the more layers a supply chain has, the more invisible are workers at the bottom of the chain and the harder it is to monitor CoC compliance. It is likely that many corporate buyers/brands do not know all of the subcontractors who manufacture their products. In the flexible global supply chain, when rush deliveries of small batches are required or when risks are involved, workers on the bottom rung (mostly in small factories or household units, more than three levels down the supply chain) are often invisible to monitors and thus are not protected (Lee 1997; Fung *et al.* 2001; O'Rourke 2003).[47]

At the top of the chain are the corporate buyers/brands (MNCs) that place orders with their suppliers, either foreign or domestic. Taiwanese and South Korean companies own and manage most large suppliers in Vietnam, having established long-term relations with the brands/corporate buyers. Over time, as business relations develop, the MNCs also place orders directly with large domestic Vietnamese factories, including some large former SOEs that have been transformed into joint-stock companies.[48] At the lowest level are the *unlicensed, unauthorized* subcontracting factories. These are mostly small domestic factories filling orders for the larger contract factories/suppliers. These Vietnamese factories are legal, in that they register with the Vietnamese government and pay taxes, but they are not licensed by brands to produce for them. Their existence may be unknown to the MNCs, or the MNCs may prefer to close their eyes to their existence. As such, they are not subjected to CoC scrutiny, so these unlicensed factories are not monitored.

Workers' Pay and Benefits in the Global Supply Chain

Uneven power relations exist in the global supply chain between MNCs, their contract factories, and the domestic subcontractors, leading to fierce competition to drive down the price in order to win contracts (Arnold and Hartman, p. 685). In the case of Vietnam, with an abundance of contract factories and domestic suppliers, corporate buyers can demand the lowest contract prices and fastest turnaround delivery terms in this race to the bottom. The distribution of earnings is grossly unequal, favouring corporate buyers and contract factories at the expense of income and benefits for workers. On average, for a pair of shoes for which an end-consumer pays US$100, a multinational would pay a contractor a freight-on-board price of only US$16, out of which US$5 goes towards (mostly imported) raw materials, US$2 for local management, and US$2 for local labour, leaving US$7 for the contract factory's profit. In sum, the MNC took a massive 84 per cent of the sales price, while workers received only 2 per cent in

2008. Recent development in 2010 shows that workers receive even less: only 1 per cent.[49]

Workers' take-home pay is based on a combination of piece-rates, an hourly minimum wage, overtime work, and a bonus structure (Nghiem 2006). The minimum wage is not a living wage because, even with the 2008 state-mandated increase adjusted to inflation, it still does not match the huge inflation rate. However, it is important to note the high daily productivity targets in FDI contract factories. In a fine-grained study of three garment factories in Hanoi (one SOE, one joint-venture between state and South Korean capital, and one private local workshop), Nghiem found that the joint-venture factory used both a piece-rate and a daily quota system to ensure high productivity. When workers became more proficient at their assembling skills, the daily quota went up from 600 to 700 pieces a day (October to December 2002), but wages did not go up, which actually meant a decline in the piece-rate (Nghiem 2006, pp. 79–82). Thus management does not increase workers' salary when their productivity increases.

Facing low piece-rates and staggering inflation starting in 2007, workers in both FDI and domestic factories faced a dilemma of being exhausted by overtime work, but still needed to work overtime to make a living. On average they earned 1.3 to 1.5 million VND per month (less than US$100).[50] Most workers in big cities are female migrants from poor provinces and villages, who need money not only for their own survival but also for their families back home. Under such work pressure, without adequate food and rest, workers became fatigued and some even fainted on the factory floor.[51] Such exhaustion occurred in both compliant and non-compliant factories: "Most workers, even in compliant companies, work overtime and receive low wages."[52] A female migrant worker who worked at a Taiwanese factory in Linh Trung EPZ (HCMC) told me: "We went on strike because of too much overtime to make up for the low wages. We worked from Monday to Saturday; now we also have to work on Sundays. Only after we went on strike did management raise wages."[53]

In a study focusing on the problems of trafficking in women and children and the preliminary effects of CSR, Huynh Ngoc Tuyet interviewed 300 migrant workers in a district of HCMC with many FDI factories. The study revealed that workers are willing to work overtime to make up for low piece-rates and non-liveable minimum wages, but only under certain conditions:

- Limits on the number of overtime hours per day;
- Limits on the number of days with overtime per week;
- Ability to take a break for a few hours between shifts;
- Adequate hourly compensation for overtime work;
- Transparency in overtime wage calculations; and
- Allowances for non-wage benefits such as breaks and meals while on overtime (Huynh 2005).

Excessive overtime work is hard to control for a number of reasons, and this applies to all types of ownership. First, CoCs allow more overtime than does the Labour Code, undermining legal enforcement. Second, in order to survive, workers have no choice but to appear as if they work overtime *voluntarily*. Management takes advantage of workers' survival needs, and transfers to them the responsibility to "choose". Voluntarism is actually a hidden form of forced labour. In practice, mandatory overtime is normal when there are rush orders to fill (Huynh 2005, pp. 14–15; Nghiem 2006, p. 68), because many labour contracts require workers to sign a form agreeing to work overtime at any time when needed. Most workers whom I interviewed have signed such a form, fearing that they would lose their job if they refused. Uneven power relations render refusal of overtime very difficult. Third, some management paid workers overtime on condition that they worked all twenty-six days in a month (the "perfect attendance" requires that workers not miss any of the twenty-six workdays) (ILSSA 2004, pp. 19, 32). Also, if workers had "perfect attendance", they would receive a small attendance bonus (*tien chuyen can*, up to about US$10–12 per month). Management rationale was to prevent labour absenteeism, to enhance labour relations and to help workers cope with inflation.[54]

Fourth, the lack of transparency in calculating overtime wages not only results in workers being cheated but also means a lower contribution by management to workers' social security and healthcare benefits, as a percentage of the wage package (Huynh 2005): the smaller the wage package, the lower the contribution. There are many ways by which management cheats on social and health insurance funds. One method is not to add overtime pay and wage increases to the base salary. Another method is more drastic: some FDI factory owners flee Vietnam or open new factories in other provinces to avoid these responsibilities. Out of a list of seventeen companies with social security debts in the south, 53 per cent were joint-ventures, 41 per cent Asian FDI, and 6 per cent Vietnamese factories.[55]

Finally, another common practice is the way that management exerts control over workers' benefits to cope with production fluctuations in the global supply chain. Management manipulate workers' days off by making them take leave when orders are low, and euphemistically express this as a concern for workers' health. Even in some FDI companies that are reasonably code-compliant, workers can in fact choose only six out of the twelve days off per year to which they are entitled; the other six days are determined by the company when work is slow.[56]

Challenges in CoC Monitoring

As can be seen, violations of CoCs and the law are rampant. Has social monitoring not accomplished anything?

First, multi-level global supply chains make monitoring nearly impossible. At the corporate buyers' level, MNCs diversify their risks by spreading their orders to many contract factories. For instance, Nike places about 5 per cent of their total order with each contract factory.[57] Because of such risk diversification, most subcontractors in Vietnam manufacture for more than one brand-name retailer (such as Nike, Adidas, Reebok, and Clarks) in order to utilize their capacity. This makes the monitoring of different CoCs requested by different brands even more difficult. Fortunately, the ILO-Better Work project on CBAs in some key textile/garment/shoe factories has been negotiating so that each contract factory will only have to comply with *one* CoC, which would improve monitoring.[58]

Many domestic subcontractors are left unmonitored in the multi-layered supply chain, however. Unauthorized subcontracting is prevalent at the contract factory level, especially during peak seasons when quick deliveries are demanded. Even when practices of unauthorized subcontracting have been discovered and remediation (i.e. recommended changes to non-compliant factories to correct their violations within a certain time frame) called for, there has been no follow-up to see if the remediation had been undertaken or was effective.[59]

MNCs' internal monitoring serves their own interests, and has many loopholes. Some MNCs hire accounting firms to undertake internal monitoring of supplier factories on their behalf. Naturally, these monitoring companies report to their clients and not to the workers.[60] Even when a violation is detected, as reported in a FLA tracking chart in 2002, the brands shifted their responsibility to their suppliers:

Unauthorized subcontracting is against Adidas policy and in breach of the manufacturing contract. *These issues will be followed up internally.* The issue of subcontracting and whether our suppliers check the working conditions of their subcontractors are covered by the Standards of Excellence rating tool. Suppliers who fail to inform subcontractors of our standards or check on the working conditions before placing orders will score very poorly in this section of the rating tool. This will have an impact ultimately on the overall performance of the factory, and how orders are placed there. In respect of [sic] the local partner, the same principles apply. *Adidas will hold its business partner responsible for working conditions in the factory and for informing local partners about the SOE and our expectations regarding labour and HSE requirements.* (FLA Tracking Chart, 2002, my emphases).

Second, following up on such implementation is difficult. In this case, Adidas knew about its supplier's unauthorized practice and made a "threat" to the supplier that it would stop placing orders. However, it is impossible for outsiders to verify the outcomes of this case because "these issues will be followed-up internally" and that specific information under the "Remediation" column such as "Target Completion Date" and "Remediation Updates" were not specified in this case.[61]

Moreover, contract factories/suppliers are very skilled at hiding violations of overtime, pay, and social and health benefits. Carey Zeiger, the president of Global Standards, a monitoring company that works closely with MNCs, shed light on overtime work violations, and unreliable record-keeping with the practice of double and triple book-keeping on work hours:

Having double books or triple books on work hours are common management practices. The common practice is sixty hours per week [Note: in peak seasons]. It's not hard to cover up and they are good at it: swiping a time card, entering it into the computer and then clearing it. We talk to workers, check production records, stay there for the whole day. We often found inaccurate records with different workers, so messages to the corporate buyers [MNCs] are not honest using the practice of double book-keeping.[62]

It is thus conceivable that the brands may receive inaccurate records from their suppliers, and act on these records in good faith. However, to be consistent with their CoCs they should be vigilant, demand remedial action, or discontinue contracts with non-compliant suppliers. The actions that the brands may take are voluntary, and much more transparent information is needed (i.e., via the Internet) to allow ethical consumers to monitor and hold the brands accountable to their CoCs obligations. More on this topic is found in the discussion of the Sambu Vina case below.

Moreover, some factory owners told me that they were informed in advance when these monitors would be visiting to audit the factory.[63] Such advance alerts undermine the very purpose of monitoring. Frank, a monitor specializing in compliance consulting, admitted that auditors missed many violations and that shared interests among corporate clients, monitoring companies, and suppliers benefit everyone but the workers.[64]

Third, cost is a big constraint, even when contract factories have the incentive to implement the CoCs in order to get more corporate orders. The outlays required to cover the full extent of the monitoring and compliance are prohibitively expensive, especially for small factories.

> The MNCs transfer monitoring expenses to their suppliers, who have to pay us directly for auditing and monitoring. Suppliers also have to pay for remediation costs, such as fixing facilities or building additional ones [Note: restrooms for workers based on certain ratios of workers]. There are many hidden costs incurred by suppliers. In general, suppliers have twelve months to form labour unions, which are required by law. The VGCL could give more support on this. ... The process starts with monitoring, reporting, and having an action plan. Often factories have thirty to ninety days to take corrective action, followed by auditing and training, etc. The key intention is for capacity-building activities which will lead to sustainable improvement of working conditions. Follow-up visits often occur within two to three months. We found that close to 100 per cent of labour violations are on the management side.[65]

To cope with such constraints, the ratcheting labour standards (RLS), which prioritize domestic control over a country's labour regulatory regime recommended a *cost-sharing scheme* in which the corporate buyers would share costs with their local suppliers for both monitoring and compliance with the CoC (Fung *et al.*, pp. 13–14). This would be implemented via a council of monitors from the state, labour unions, and local NGOs because they understand their country's constraints and conditions to make feasible changes gradually (Fung *et al.*, pp. 36–37).

However, this suggestion has not been taken up. MNCs are not willing to contribute to the costs; many contract factories/suppliers refuse to implement labour standards because they are costly;[66] and as I demonstrate in the Sambu Vina case study, corporate buyers seldom discontinue ordering from non-compliant factories.

Consequences for Workers

Low piece-rates and high daily quota requirements, especially with an inflation rate of over 20 per cent in 2008, increase workers' health risks. In-depth interviews in 2008 with two migrant workers in a big Taiwanese factory in HCMC that produces for several high-profile MNC shoe retailers revealed how the pressure to meet the daily quota combined with low pay resulted in fatigue and accidents on the factory floor. Moreover, the interviews showed how line-leaders contributed to the exploitation and commodification of workers. A worker from a central province said:

> We stopped work to have lunch while this tiny young female worker continued working to glue part of the inner sole to the shoe. Shoe soles piled up at her station. Then I heard the first loud scream. She was in great pain as, she had accidentally put her hand beneath the hot glue machine. Workers did not seem to be alarmed by this: they were either eating, or working away at their station to keep up with the daily quota. I rushed to her side, then came her second scream of agony. With the top skin stuck to that machine, the wound exposed the white layer underneath. … The third scream was much weaker: she was as white as a sheet and had almost fainted. Together with other workers, we took her out of the station. It took management 30 minutes to finish all the paperwork before she could be taken to the hospital for treatment. It really upset me when some nearby workers shrugged it off and said: "Well, this happens on a daily basis". I'm also upset that when the line-leader came down, he immediately checked the machine without regard for the poor worker, and removed the burnt skin without any emotions. I have not seen her back since then.[67]

When I asked follow-up questions about other workers' indifference on the line, a sense of peer pressure for survival became evident. Another worker chimed in:

> Everyone relies on bonuses to make ends meet, because our basic wages are very low and do not provide a living. Most of us already eat breakfast only every other morning and eat fruit with rice to fill our stomachs. So, in order to get bonuses based on hard work and full attendance, no one on the assembly line can make any mistake. If anything happens to one worker, everyone on the whole line is affected

and will not receive any bonus. There are times, I know, when workers have actually hidden accident cases in order for other workers to receive bonuses. I could not believe how, when some women had accidents, instead of worrying about their injuries, they were afraid of being scolded by their immediate bosses and by their fellow workers for letting them down.[68]

This does not mean workers are not conscious of their rights and interests. There have been moments of crisis and desperation when workers have risen up in collective action to fight for their rights, as described in other chapters in this volume.

CHALLENGES WITH TRIPARTITE NEGOTIATIONS AT THE FACTORY LEVEL

As we have seen, there are many problems in contract factories. The tripartite system that has been set up in Vietnam is not working on the shop floor. One reason is that enterprise-level unions are mostly ineffective in FDI factories, because union representatives are paid by management. Worse still, many union staff are from human resource departments. Workers' grievances are routinely ignored, compounded by ambiguity about on-site management's power to deal with workers' demands. All decisions need approval from foreign suppliers' headquarters located in their home countries. The same situation applies to MNC offices in Vietnam.

It is not clear who should be accountable to workers and who has the final say: suppliers, brands, or both. To resolve this problem, the Tenth Congress of the VGCL has promoted CBAs in which upper-level labour unions can directly assist enterprise union representatives in critical factory-level negotiations. Recently, this CBA protocol has been developed and disseminated widely in Vietnam (Sunoo *et al.* 2009: 43–45).[69]

The local union leaders understand the possibilities of such ambiguity, and stress that the brands make the final decisions on workers' economic demands. Truong Lam Danh, the Vice President of the HCMC Labour Federation, explained:

The "real bosses", who can make the decision on raising workers' wages, are precisely the global corporate buyers who place orders in Vietnam. Thus, local suppliers who are at the negotiating table have no power to come to any resolution. That impasse has led to many strikes. Therefore, at the negotiating table, when we came to resolve the conflicts, local suppliers often say: "We need to seek opinions and approval from our mother company", or to ask the brand MNCs to raise the subcontracting price so that they can raise workers' wages.[70]

CASE STUDY OF CONTRACT FACTORY
SAMBU VINA

The Sambu Vina case shows the complexity of implementing and enforcing labour standards in a global supply chain, even where a multinational is well-intentioned. Sambu Vina is a wholly owned South Korean supplier in Hoc Mon District in HCMC which manufactures sports bags and backpacks for a Canadian multinational, Mountain Equipment Cooperative (MEC). The MEC website highlights their Ethical Sourcing Programme, which claims to "continue to vigilantly monitor our supply chain". It provides easy links to their reports: the 2007 Accountability Report, the 2007 Sourcing Report of Non-Compliant Factories worldwide, and the 2008 Vendor List. It promotes proactive local governments and holds suppliers responsible for working conditions and labour standards: "Local authorities must play an active and effective role to regulate the industries they oversee".[71]

In the 2007 Sourcing Report of Non-Compliant Factories, I found that four suppliers in Vietnam, identified only by their ID numbers, had violations in all major areas: wages and benefits; health and safety conditions; local laws; grievance policy; and incomplete documentation.[72] Checking this in the Vietnamese labour newspapers, I found that one of the four suppliers was Sambu Vina Ltd Company, where 2,183 workers went on strike for two days in March 2006 to demand that the South Korean management raise the minimum wage by 40 per cent in accordance with Prime Ministerial Decree 03, which had gone into effect a month earlier.[73]

Again in June 2008, over 2,000 workers stopped work to demand a 20 per cent increase in their basic wage to catch up with inflation, especially for food and housing expenses. After several rounds of negotiations, the final outcome was that a 15 per cent wage increase would be added to their permanent base salaries, and the remaining 5 per cent was to be spread out as holiday bonuses.

In response to workers' actions, the city and district state and union leaders came to the negotiating table. Management agreed only to a one-off bonus of 20 per cent, which would not be added to the base salaries (thus no increase in salary-based benefits), so workers stopped work. This prompted representatives of MOLISA in HCMC, the HCMC Labour Federation, Hoc Mon District People's Committee and other local state agencies to converge at Sambu Vina to resolve the conflict. Then, management negotiated for an 11 per cent increase to be added to the base salaries (with an assumed increase in benefits), with the remaining 9 per cent as a one-off bonus.[74] That was unacceptable to workers, so they stopped work again. One day later, further negotiations among the Hoc Mon district authorities, the factory manager, and union representatives resulted in a 15 per cent increase to base salaries, plus a monthly bonus of VND50,000. Management also agreed to pay workers for the two days that they had spent on strike (21 and 23 June). Special holiday bonuses were increased to 150 per cent, in which 30 per cent was to be paid on 30 April and 1 May; 30 per cent on 2 September, and the remaining 90 per cent to be paid for *Tet* (the Vietnamese New Year). Workers eventually returned to work on the fifth day.[75] This case demonstrates the progress from rights-based (minimum wage increase in 2006) to interests-based struggles (wage and benefits increases in 2008).

LOCAL AND INTERNATIONAL INITIATIVES

Most VGCL efforts are not aimed directly at implementing CSR but rather at embedding it in relevant campaigns, such as for collective bargaining. Concerned that the waves of wildcat strikes did not follow legal strike procedures, in June 2008 the Central Committee signed into effect the VCP-mandated Directive 22, which, among other things, promotes the tripartite structure with a pro-labour slant and CBAs at the economic sector, and regional, levels.[76] It shows the party's intention to maintain total control and leadership in all facets of labour–management relations, utilizing state apparatuses and quasi-state organizations, including the VGCL and VCCI.

The HCMC People's Committee and Labour Federation understood the real issues on the ground, and came up with pragmatic ways to implement Directive 22. For instance, in June 2008 Madame Huynh Thi Nhan, former Vice Minister of MOLISA, and Mr. Mai Duc Chinh, Vice President of the VGCL, initiated the "Four Reals" (Bon That) Directive to overcome union weaknesses in collective bargaining and to support workplace labour unions.[77] The Four Reals — "real counterparts" (*doi tac*), "real negotiations" (*dam phan*), "real issues" (*noi dung*), and "real implementation" (*thi hanh*) — set out to address the previously noted limitations of labour–management negotiations (Sunoo *et al.* 2009: 47–48).

Though introduced recently, the Directive has already been incorporated into the ILO's *Human Resource Survival Guide*. However, this is a difficult time to implement it, given reduced corporate orders resulting in massive layoffs and underemployment. With no orders coming in, management has legitimate reasons to postpone workers' demands for higher wages and benefits. On the contrary, workers have been expected to share the difficulties of reduced orders by agreeing to reductions in pay and benefits, no periodic wage increase, and late salary payment. Meanwhile the "counterpart" problem in FDI factories remains unchanged: "Many factory owners are still only employees and thus cannot make decisions, and Vietnam still only subcontracts for most brands."[78]

Local leaders in strike-prone districts have promoted local monitoring by setting up interdepartmental monitoring teams consisting of state and labour union officials at city, district, and hamlet levels to monitor FDI licensees' operations and to prevent FDI owners from fleeing the factories and the country while owing workers wages, social security and healthcare benefits.[79]

Efforts to promote CBAs gained momentum in 2008 with more attention from the HCMC Labor Federation and the VGCL with ILO support, but with limited results.[80] A candid VGCL study based on "available reports" from the labour unions at the city and provincial levels nevertheless offered helpful insights to assess the existing CBAs.[81] The statistical findings were as expected, with the state sector ranked the highest: 94 per cent of SOEs and 86 per cent of state corporations had CBAs, as had 60 per cent of FDI, and 57 per cent of private domestic enterprises. Of all the cities, HCMC achieved the highest level: 77 per cent signed CBAs. On average, only 63 per cent of all unionized factories at the city/province level had signed CBAs; actually, if one considered all the factories which are required to establish labour unions, then the percentage of signed CBAs over a larger hypothetical unionized base would be smaller (26 per cent).

However, the content of these CBAs is of limited quality. Most clauses are still identical to the bare minimum stipulated in the Labour Code. Reports from some major cities/provinces suggest that about 40 per cent of the signed CBAs reflect equitable sharing of rights and responsibilities between labour and management; only 10 per cent successfully bargained for workers' benefits *higher* than the legal minimum; and the remaining 50 per cent duplicated exactly what were required by the labour laws, rendering them little different from individual labour contracts. In some cases, vague language could lead to workers being worse off than before the CBAs were signed.[82]

The problems with CBAs are caused by both internal and external factors.[83] First, there is the failure of the state to provide adequate legal guidance for the implementation of Chapter 5 of the Labour Code, which deals with CBAs. Second, enterprise labour unions are weak and lack the capacity to enforce the bargaining process within a limited period of time. Many enterprise union representatives, especially in the non-state sector, lack the requisite negotiating skills to bargain, thus further eroding workers' confidence in them. Third, management in the private sector, especially in small and medium-size firms, often refuses to sign CBAs with terms higher than minimum wages and benefits.

On 25 December 2008, Decision No. 1846, "Pilot Testing Negotiations, and Signing Collective Bargaining Agreement in the Textile and Garment Industries", was introduced to provide guidance on details of the CBA process, such as who should be in charge and how to implement it. This pilot program covers only the textile and garment industries, employing over two million workers nationwide.

As part of the "Better Work" project — partly financed by the International Finance Corporation (IFC), a financial arm of the World Bank — the ILO has been assisting the VGCL in this pilot project targeting 150 factories, which started in 2009 and is to continue for two years.[84] The project aims to improve social dialogue in the factories and to strengthen the capacity of workplace labour unions to represent workers better in CBAs. At the time of writing, the basic framework agreement at the peak sectoral level (*thoa thuan khung*) had been drawn up, including such things as minimum wages, salary table with steps, timeline for pay raises, regular and overtime hours, compensation for exposure to toxic material, and working conditions. However, the global economic crisis has delayed the signing to the end of 2009, and some agreed terms have to be re-negotiated. It is expected that, after the sectoral agreement is signed, negotiations at the factory and regional levels will take place, with the aim of negotiating conditions higher than the minimum to match the costs of living and needs of each region.[85]

CONCLUSION

With regard to the questions posed at the beginning of the chapter, the evidence shows unambiguously that, as far as delivering the promised labour standards in most CoCs goes, CSR in Vietnam is largely tokenistic and widely equated merely with charitable work. On the other hand, at both central and local levels the VGCL is very conscious that CSR relates to labour standards. However, CSR has thus far been included as only one component in its campaigns, such as that on CBAs.

For corporate buyers (or brands) intending to comply with labour standards, the multi-level subcontracting nature of the global supply chain makes it difficult for monitoring to uncover code violations in the unlicensed factories at the bottom of the production chain. While certified contract factories are supposed by their pledges on labour standards to be accountable for workers' conditions, the inability to verify the connections between these factories' labour violations (as in the case of Sambu Vina) and the brands' disciplinary actions renders CSR no more than an empty promise.

The original intention of CSR was to hold the brands accountable for their promises to the final consumers of their "ethical sourcing program" and for "vigilantly monitoring the supply chain". Without transparent disciplinary action to pressure non-compliant contract factories into remedying their violations, the codes are almost useless. Thus, it is rather misleading to call the brands "stakeholders", because nothing is really "at stake" if they can turn a blind eye and shift responsibility to their contract suppliers so that they themselves can avoid public scrutiny.

The tripartite structure pushed by the World Bank and the ILO and adopted by MOLISA thus far has not worked in practice, due to the unequal power relationships between labour and capital. While the ILO provides some useful technical guidance on how tripartism might work, it is the *local* authorities, including both the state and the unions that can put it into genuine effect by overcoming problems at the factory level. Local authorities have recognized the power of transnational capital, realizing that the VCCI does not have the structure and capacity to represent domestic capital at the factory level and cannot represent the FDI factories at all. Most FDI factories do not want to engage in tripartite or collective bargaining, fearing that it may have a negative effect on their profitability; further, large FDI factories have access to the Vietnamese state directly through their own chambers of commerce, making the VCCI representation irrelevant. While it is commendable that the VGCL has long recognized the weakness of enterprise level labour unions and tried hard to address the problem, more research is needed to analyze the impacts of some relatively recent developments: the signed Pilot CBA[86] in textile/garment industries in April 2010; more direct intervention of upper-level labour unions to intervene in CBAs and labour–management conflicts at the factory level (initiative from the Tenth Congress of the VGCL); and increasing numbers of CBAs signed with higher quality (benefits and bonuses beyond the Labour Code stipulations)

The grossly uneven power relationship in the multi-level global supply chain means that strengthening collective bargaining power is important. As Vietnam integrates more deeply with the global market system, most workers have raised their sights from fighting for rights to fighting for interests, and a stronger collective bargaining capacity will be needed to achieve this.

The state and the labour unions are conscious of the potential benefits of CBAs in negotiating effectively with management and the need to empower enterprise labour unions. But they need to resolve the fundamental conflict of interests and financial dependence of enterprise union representatives — who are employed by management — on their employers before workplace unions can improve their representation of workers.

Fundamentally, however, the problem results from internal contradictions within the socialist state, rather than from these other problems. On the one hand, the state appeases global capitalism by recognizing CSR, which benefits capital and pays lip service to the needs of workers. On the other, it also tries to make capital comply with the law of the land; indeed, the laws lean towards empowering labour unions and strengthening collective bargaining. However, these laws are only weakly enforced, and the resulting mixed messages reflect the state's ambivalence.

One bright spot has been the role of the labour press. Developments in 2008 and up to mid-2009 show that the press is permitted to criticize the state and its apparatuses based on the "rule *by* law". The labour press has been able to report critically on those contradictions as well as to reveal tensions among state entities that operate at the expense of the workers. Press activities have prised open a space for transparency and for empowering the workers.

In conclusion, the party–state and the VGCL still control all facets of labour–management relations. The original deadline for the final drafting phase and ratification of the revision of the Labour Code was November 2010, but the ratification process is delayed at least until the end of 2012 (the eighth Parliament session). At the time of writing, there is no sign of any practical mechanism allowing workers to represent themselves in non-unionized factories. Even in unionized factories, workers' participation in the collective bargaining process is often assumed; whether they can participate *meaningfully*, given the reality of compromised workplace unions and exploitative working conditions in the multilevel global supply chain, is not verified. Thus, more research is needed to explore critically and to assess the *real* extent of "workers' participation".

Notes

I would like to acknowledge the support from the Centre for Asia Pacific Social Transformation Studies (CAPSTRANS), University of Wollongong, Australia, where I did the research for this chapter during my Visiting Fellowship in Summer 2007. The analysis, writing up, and revision had been conducted with generous support from Stanford University and the National University of Singapore as part of the Lee Kong Chian NUS-Stanford Distinguished Fellowship on Southeast Asia, May to November 2008. The final revision was done at California State University, Monterey Bay in Spring 2009. I'd also like to thank Anita Chan, David Marr, and other anonymous reviewers on the previous draft for their feedback, advice and insights. Appreciation also goes to my partner, Joe Lubow, who has supported me throughout this project.

1   Kofi Anan's speech is available online at <http://www.un.org/News/Press/docs/1999/19990201.sgsm6881.html>. See also the Global Compact website: <http://www.unglobalcompact.org/>.

2   On the role of the labour newspapers in Vietnam, see Angie Ngoc Tran, "The Third Sleeve: Emerging Labor Newspapers and the Response of Labor Unions and the State to Workers' Resistance in Vietnam", *Labor Studies Journal* 32, no. 3 (September 2007): 257–79. Due to limited press and association freedoms in Vietnam, I have used pseudonyms for most interviewees and correspondents.

3   For instance, Worldwide Responsible Apparel Production (WRAP) does not explicitly recognize the right to collective bargaining, while Social Accountability International's SA8000 standards recognize "parallel means" or different forms of labour unions (i.e. beyond the VGCL). Informally, I was told that SAI operations were banned from Vietnam, allegedly due to this proposition. Regarding a *liveable* wage beyond the minimum wage, while most CoCs require only the local minimum wage, SA8000 and Worker Rights Consortium (WRC) codes ask for some sort of "*fair living wage*" which is

higher than a minimum wage meeting basic needs (such as food, housing, and clothing), to provide some discretionary income for a household. SA8000 codes also support some modest family savings; see William Douglas, "Who's Who in Codes of Conduct", New Economy Information Service, 2 January 2001 <http://www.newecon.org> (accessed October 2008). Some South Asian scholars have initiated research on a *regional* minimum wage, using a common survey in developing countries with comparable economic development levels, to prevent the current practice of MNCs "racing to the bottom". Anita Chan, phone conversation, July 2007.

[4]   For an analysis of the law on strikes, see Angie Ngoc Tran, "Alternatives to the 'Race to the Bottom' in Vietnam: Minimum Wage Strikes and their Aftermath", *Labor Studies Journal* 32, no. 4 (December 2007): 430–51.

[5]   Le Thuy, "15 Years after the Labour Code: Many Stipulations are Obsolete and not Enforceable, *Nguoi Lao Dong*, 5 May 2009 <http://www.nld.com.vn/20090505122151420P0C1010/nhieu-quy-dinh-loi-thoi-khong-kha-thi.htm> (accessed 19 May 2009).

[6]   Ibid.

[7]   ILSSA, "Study on Corporate Social Responsibility Labour-Related Practices" (Hanoi: MOLISA, February 2004), pp. 20–21, 39–40. ILSSA is a research think tank in MOLISA.

[8]   VietNamNet/VNS, Effective 1 January 2011, the 2011 minimum wage increases for the FDI sector (107/2010/NĐ-CP) in the four zones are: VND1.55 million (districts in downtowns of Hanoi and HCMC); VND1.35 million (suburbs of Hanoi and HCMC and downtowns of key industrial cities), VND1.17 million (growing provinces and districts) and VND1.10 million (the rest of the country). The 2011 minimum wage increases (108/2010/NĐ-CP) for the domestic sector in the four zones are: VND1.35 million, VND1.20 million, VND1.05 million, and VND830,000. "Minimum wage rises today: Look at Vietnam", 1 May 2009 <http://www.lookatvietnam.com/2009/05/minimum-wage-rises-today.html> (accessed 5 May 2009). This includes members of the armed forces, state agencies, socio-political organizations, and state-owned companies. It also raises their pensions and social insurance. See ASEAN Affairs, "Vietnam to Raise Minimum Wage to Revive Economy" <http://www.aseanaffairs.com/vietnam_govt_to_raise_minimum_wage_to_revive_economy> (accessed 5 May 2009).

[9]   Tran Nam Duong, "Minimum Wage is Not the Basic Wage", *Nguoi Lao Dong* [Labourer], 22 January 2008 <http://www.nld.com.vn/213304P1010C1012/luong-toi-thieu-khong-phai-la-luong-can-ban.htm> (accessed July 2008) and "Factories Have to Adjust Wages for All Workers", *Nguoi Lao Dong,* 25 January 2008 <http://www.nld.com.vn/213621P0C1010/doanh-nghiep-phai-dieu-chinh-luong-cho-tat-ca-nld.htm> (accessed July 2008).

[10] Nike Corporate Responsibility Report (Fiscal Year 2005–2006) <http://www.nikebiz.com/> (accessed 5 May 2008); Ikea IWAY code of conduct (factory visit at Yujin Kreves, 2007); Adidas code of conduct/worksplace standards are available at <http://www.adidas-group.com/en/sustainability/suppliers_and_workers/code_of_conduct/default.aspx>; and how they work with suppliers (monitoring and verification policy) is: <http://www.adidas-group.com/en/sustainability/suppliers_and_workers/how_we_work_with_suppliers/default.aspx>

[11] MEC does not have a complete CoC; theirs is adapted from the FLA Code and the Core conventions of ILO <http://www.mec.ca/Main/content_text.jsp?FOLDER%3C%3Efolder_id=2534374302883571> (accessed 2 June 2010).

[12] See note 3 on SAI's position in Vietnam.

[13] ILSSA, "Study on Corporate Social Responsibility Labour-Related Practices" (Hanoi: MOLISA, February 2004), pp. 20–21, 30, 39–40.

[14] I thank David Marr for this excellent point.

[15] Kim Chi, "Helping 98 Poor Households to Improve their Livelihoods", *Nguoi Lao Dong*, 25 April 2007 <http://www.nld.com.vn/187312P0C1010/ho-tro-98-ho-dan-ngheo-cai-thien-dieu-kien-song.htm> (accessed July 2008).

[16] Correspondence with Journalist Nguyen, April 2009.

[17] Interviews with Rosemarie Greve, Director of ILO Hanoi, and Jan Sunoo, Chief ILO Technical Advisor, October 2003.

[18] Interview with Nguyen Manh Cuong, then in MOLISA, October 2003.

[19] Interview with Sunoo, op. cit.

[20] See note 11.

[21] These studies focused on management interests, CSR services for MNCs (such as CSR training, consultancy, accreditation, and certification in some CoCs) and interviewed managers and staff only, not workers. ILO and VCCI, "Market Assessment: Factory-Level Integrated Management and Labour Services in Vietnam", Factory Improvement Programme (FIP) (Hanoi: ILO and VCCI, January 2006), pp. 35–36, 67. In this report, most CSR problems were blamed on women workers, not the brands or their suppliers; ILO and VCCI, "Final Report: Pilot Programme in Vietnam", FIP (Hanoi: ILO and VCCI, October 2005), p. 17. However, one study raised important weaknesses: ineffectual enterprise labour unions and inexperienced human resource managers, lack of transparency or efficient resolution mechanisms at the workplace, and the lack of ongoing communication among workers, unions, and management (ILO and VCCI 2006, p. 29).

[22] Pham Ho, "Moving from 'post-Strike' to 'pre-Conflict' Negotiations", *Nguoi Lao Dong*, 3 April 2009 <http://www.nld.com.vn/20090403125216500P0C1010/chuyen-hau-dinh-cong-sang-tien-tranh-chap.htm> (accessed 30 April 2009).

[23] Ibid.

24   The other state-sanctioned employers' association is the VCA, with membership from agricultural cooperatives and small-scale businesses.

25   Interview with Ms. Pham Thu Hang, Small and Medium-sized Enterprises Department, VCCI, October 2003.

26   Interviews with Phung Quang Huy and Vu Tien Loc, representatives from VCCI, August 2004.

27   The Small and Medium Enterprise Promotion Center <http://smenet.com.vn/> which is the same as the main VCCI website: <http://www.vcci.vn/>; the Vietnam Business Forum <http://vccinews.com/>. The Finance Newsletter site is no longer available (as of June 2010). Between 2009 and 2010, VCCI added more online services, in both Vietnamese and English, such as: Certificate of Origin <http://covcci.com.vn/>; Dien Dan Cac Doanh Nghiep Vietnam <http://www.vibonline.com.vn/vi-VN/Home/default.aspx> (focusing on laws, proposals, disputes, petitions, etc); VNemart: Making Online Trade Success (site uses English) <http://www.vnemart.com.vn/>; Van Phong Gioi Su Dung Lao Dong: <http://vnemployers.com.vn/Home/Default.aspx/>, Dien Dan Doanh Nghiep Vietnam: <http://dddn.com.vn/> (focusing on general and commercial news); and VN Business directory <http://www.vidc.com.vn/>.

28   VCCI <http://www.vcci.com.vn/vcci/hoi-vien/danh-ba/phonebook_listing?b_start:int=1980&-C> (accessed 10 May 2009).

29   "Granting Garment Export Certificates to US", 28 April 2009 <http://vibforum.vcci.com.vn/news_detail.asp?news_id=16374&cate=1>.

30   Interviews with Journalist Nguyen, September 2008; Mr. Chau, April 2008.

31   Pham Ho, "Labour conflicts resolution: Not yet in sight", *Nguoi Lao Dong,* 10 February 2009 <http://www.nld.com.vn/20090210101332702P0C1010/giai-quyet-tranh-chap-lao-dong-chua-co-loi-ra.htm> (accessed 30 April 2009).

32   Ibid.

33   Correspondence with Mr Chau Nhat Binh, International Relations Department, VGCL, May 2009.

34   Correspondence with Mr Tran Van Ly, International Relations Department, VGCL, 2007, 2009.

35   Correspondence with Mr Chau in April 2008 and May 2009 (see note 33). The remaining union members were in local retail, and self-employed in small workshops, etc.

36   Conversation with Mr Sunoo, June 2009.

37   Correspondence with Mr Chau, May 2009.

38   Conversation with Mr Chau, April 2008.

39   Interview with Nguyen Huy Can in August 2007.

40   I thank David Marr for this insight.

41   Conversation with Nguyen Thi Dan. August 2007; Vinh Tung, "Sambu Vina, Ltd: Agreed to Raise Wages and Bonuses", *Nguoi Lao Dong*, 25 June 2008

<http://www.trachnhiemxahoi.net/default.aspx?portalid=1&tabid=360&itemid=2306> (accessed 17 May 2009).

42 This is not to be confused with rule *of* law, which implies a separation of powers between the state and judiciary and would make the state subject to the law — not the intention of the Vietnamese state. See Melanie Beresford, "Book review: *Vietnam and the Rule of Law* by Carlyle A. Thayer and David G. Marr", *Journal of Asian Studies* 54, no. 3 (August 1995): 910–12.

43 Le Thuy, "15 Years after the Labour Code".

44 Le Thuy and and Nam Duong, "Decision 1846 of MOLISA on Pilot Testing CBAs in Textile and Garment Industries: Too Many Mistakes", *Nguoi Lao Dong,* 24 February 2009 <http://www.nld.com.vn/2009022401325466P0C1010/qua-nhieu-sai-sot.htm> (accessed 30 April 2009).

45 Ibid.

46 Of course there are other workers' common complaint, for example, restricting time in the restroom, failure to give female workers paid rest time during pregnancy and nursing, the use of short-term contract to avoid employer responsibility (ILSSA 2004, pp. 31–32).

47 This was also confirmed in my interview with Carey Zeiger, president, Global Standards, 2006 and in correspondence with Journalist Lan, 2007.

48 See <http://www.nike.com/nikebiz/nikeresponsibility/pdfs/Nike_CRR_Factory_List_C.pdf> (accessed 9 May 2009).

49 Pham Ho, "Raising Wages: Solutions are in the Hands of Enterprises", *Nguoi Lao Dong,* 31 October 2007 <http://www.nld.com.vn/206301P0C1010/nang-luong-dap-an-trong-tay-doanh-nghiep.htm> (accessed 30 April 2009). Personal correspondence with Journalist Lan (pseudonym) and Researcher Huynh, March 2008. They based their opinions on data from several big contract factories in the South. Nam Duong, Le Thuy, "Cong Nhan Cong Ty POUCHEN VN Ngung Viec: Cong nhan van buc xuc", Nguoi Lao Dong, 8 April 2010 <http://nld.com.vn/20100407095333675P0C1010/cong-nhan-van-buc-xuc.htm> (accessed 5 June 2010).

50 Nam Duong, "Hơn 100 cong nhan ngung viec vi tang ca qua suc", *Nguoi Lao Dong*, 18 May 2008 <http://nld.com.vn/225178P0C1010/hon-100-cn-ngung-viec-vi-tang-ca-qua-suc.htm> (accessed 30 April 2009). Nhom Phong Vien Cong Doan, "Chong choi trong con bao gia: Moi nua thang đa het veo tien luong", *Nguoi Lao Dong*, 7 November 2007 <http://nld.com.vn/206856P0C1010/moi-nua-thang-da-het-veo-tien-luong.htm> (accessed 30 April 2009).

51 Yen Trinh and Dieu Hien, "Cong nhan kiet suc ngat xiu, chu doanh nghiep tho ơ", *Tuoi Tre Online*, 23 January 2008 <http://tuoitre.vn/Chinh-tri-Xa-hoi/240031/Cong-nhan-kiet-suc-ngat-xiu-chu-doanh-nghiep-tho-o.html> (accessed 30 April 2009).

52   Correspondence with Journalist Lan in June 2007; Vinh Tung, "Cong ty TNHH Tasko Vina (huyen Hoc Mon-TPHCM): Cong nhan ngat xiu hang loat do tang ca qua suc", *Nguoi Lao Dong*, 18 January 2008 <http://nld.com. vn/212987P0C1010/cong-nhan-ngat-xiu-hang-loat-do-tang-ca-qua-suc.htm> (accessed 30 April 2009).

53   Interview with Worker Dieu, August 2006.

54   Interview with Worker Ha, September 2008; Kim Chi, "Cong ty SEDO VINA (Quan Go Vap- TPHCM): Cong khai don gia, luong, thuong", *Nguoi Lao Dong*, 9 September 2008 <http://nld.com.vn/238640P0C1010/cong-khai-don-gia-luong-thuong.htm>; H. Dung, "Da Nang: Tren 1.000 cong nhan Cong ty TNHH Valley view Viet Nam ngung viec tap the", *Nguoi Lao Dong*, 11 September 2008 <http://nld.com.vn/238866P0C1010/tren-1000-cong-nhan-cong-ty-tnhh-valley-view-viet-nam-ngung-viec-tap-the.htm> (accessed 1 May 2009); D. Long, "Hon 530 CN tiep tuc ngung viec", *Nguoi Lao Dong*, 15 September 2008 <http://nld.com.vn/239338P1010C1012/hon-530-cn-tiep-tuc-ngung-viec.htm> (accessed 1 May 2009); Khanh Linh and Hong Dao, "CD gop phan lam lanh manh quan he lao dong Hai hoa loi ich doanh nghiep va cong nhan", *Nguoi Lao Dong*, 16 September 2008 <http://nld.com.vn/239468P0C1010/hai-hoa-loi-ich-doanh-nghiep-va-cong-nhan.htm> (accessed 1 May 2009).

55   Pham Ho, "Cac Doanh nghiep no Bao Hiem Xa Hoi 2.156 ti dong: Bat Luc Bat Luc, phai giai quyet dut diem bang bien phap manh", *Nguoi Lao Dong*, 26 November 2007 <http://nld.com.vn/208443P0C1010/phai-giai-quyet-dut-diem-bang-bien-phap-manh.htm> (accessed 30 April 2009) (quoting Bao Hiem Xa Hoi HCMC as his source); Nam Duong, "Diem mat cac doanh nghiep chay i no BHXH", *Nguoi Lao Dong*, 18 February 2008 <http://nld. com.vn/215497P0C1010/diem-mat-cac-doanh-nghiep-chay-i-no-bhxh.htm> (accessed 30 April 2009).

56   Interview with Worker Thao, August 2007.

57   Personal communication with Ms. Huynh Ngoc Tuyet, September 2008.

58   Conversation with Sunoo, June 2009.

59   For instance, Global Standard monitors correctly reported to FLA on how an official Adidas contract factory (reported as an anonymous factory) placed orders with unlicensed Vietnamese factories: "The factory ships far more than it produces. ... Monitors saw records of orders from at least four Vietnamese suppliers and understood that these were not approved by Adidas" (FLA Tracking Chart in 2002).

60   Interview with Mr Pham Ngoc Doan, Director of Go Vap District Labour Union, 2006.

61   I found that FLA tracking charts in later years are more transparent on such information.

[62]   Interview with Carey Zeiger in 2006.

[63]   Personal communication with Ms. Thuy, owner of a Vietnamese garment factory in HCMC, August 2007.

[64]   T.A. Frank, "Is There Any Way to Stop Wal-Mart & Co. from Sweatshop Profiteering?" *Washington Monthly*, 29 April 2008 <http://www.alternet.org/workplace/83767> (accessed 1 May 2008).

[65]   Zeiger, interview, op. cit.

[66]   Personal communications with Journalist Lan, June 2007; Mr. Tran Van Ly, May 2009.

[67]   Interview with Worker Huyen in 2008.

[68]   Interview with Worker Ha in 2008.

[69]   In the *Foreign Manager's Human Resource Survival Guide*, the four steps to collective bargaining include: Preparation, Negotiation, Union ratification, and Conclusion and Education (Sunoo *et al.* 2009, pp. 43–45). First (the Preparation phase), workers give their complaints to the Union Negotiating Committee (elected or appointed by the enterprise union executive board), whose members then go around the factory to survey and document their grievances and suggestions. Then, the Negotiation phase is a closed-door meeting in which the Union Negotiating Committee works with the Employer Negotiating Committee (the union counterpart) to come up with a Tentative Agreement; workers have no input during this phase. In the Ratification phase, workers are supposed to ratify the tentative agreement through a secret ballot; if more than 50 per cent do not ratify the contract, then the Union Team has to return to the table to re-negotiate. A mediator can assist at this point. A vote to strike can be taken if agreement cannot be reached even with the help of a mediator, or both sides can take their disagreements to arbitration. In the Conclusion and Education phase, when *both* sides agree to the CBA, with copies filed with the local state authorities, distributed to all workers and posted on the Union Bulletin Boards, as well as to supervisors and managers, the CBA is signed.

[70]   Duong Minh Duc, "Doi song cong nhan lao dong trong cac KCX-KCN: Lam them ca de song", *Lao Dong*, 10 December 2007 <http://www.laodong.com.vn/Home/Lam-them-ca-de-song/200712/68154.laodong>.

[71]   See <http://www.mec.ca/Main/content_text.jsp?FOLDER%3C%3Efolder_id=2534374302883570&bmUID=1242581060651> (accessed 17 May 2009).

[72]   See <http://images.mec.ca/media/Images/pdf/non_compliance_chart_v1_m56577569830701764.pdf> (accessed 18 May 2009).

[73]   Nguyen Luu <http://dantri.com.vn/c133/s133-106009/hon-2000-cong-nhan-cong-ty-sambu-vina-dinh-cong.htm> (accessed 17 May 2009).

[74]   Duong Minh Duc, "Sambu Vina Ltd. HCMC: Over 2,000 Workers Continued to Stop Work", *Lao Dong*, 24 June 2008 <http://laodong.vn/Home/congdoan/tranhchapld/2008/6/94461.laodong> (accessed 18 May 2009).

75   Vinh Tung, "Sambu Vina, Ltd: Agreed to Raise Wages and Bonuses", *Nguoi Lao Dong*, 25 June 2008 <http://www.trachnhiemxahoi.net/default.aspx?port alid=1&tabid=360&itemid=2306> (accessed 17 May 2009).

76   The discourse in Directive 22 is pro-labour with clear party–state control: "The main reason for all those 'unruly' strikes [tranh chap lao dong dan den dinh cong khong dung trinh tu phap luat lao dong] is that management fails to implement fully the Labour Code stipulations, to pay appropriate attention to the legal rights and interests of workers; living conditions and cultural activities in EPZs and industrial zones are still inadequate; many non-state companies still do not form labour unions, even if they did, most are not effective representatives to protect legal rights and interests of workers". Central Committee of The Communist Party of Vietnam, Directive No 22-CT/TW: Chi thi so 22-CT/TW cua Ban Bi thu TW ve xay dung quan he lao dong hai hoa, on dinh, tien bo trong doanh nghiep (Directive 22-CT/TW of the Central Committee of the Party: on the development of harmonious, stable, and progressive labor relations in enterprises), Hanoi, 05 June 2008 <http://amchamvietnam.com/3451>.

77   Personal communications with Journalist Nguyen (pseudonym), September 2008; Sunoo *et al.* 2009, pp. 47–48.

78   Correspondence with Journalist Nguyen (pseudonym) in April and May 2009.

79   Pham Ho, "Workers got a Run-around, Their Rights and Interests are Not Met!" *Nguoi Lao Dong*, 28 May 2009 <http://www.nld.com.vn/20090527105232211 P0C1010/cn-bi-sang-tay-quyen-loi-khong-ai-giai-quyet.htm> (accessed 30 May 2009); Local leaders in strike-prone districts have promoted local monitoring by setting up interdepartmental monitoring teams consisting of state and labour union officials at city, district, and hamlet levels to monitor FDI licensees' operations and to prevent FDI owners from fleeing the factories and the country while owing workers wages, social security and healthcare benefits. Pham Ho, "Cac Doanh nghiep no Bao Hiem Xa Hoi 2.156 ti dong: Bat Luc, phai giai quyet dut diem bang bien phap manh", *Nguoi Lao Dong*, 26 November 2007 <http://nld.com.vn/208443P0C1010/phai-giai-quyet-dut-diem-bang-bien-phap-manh.htm> (accessed 30 April 2009) (quoting Bao Hiem Xa Hoi HCMC as his source); Nam Duong, "Diem mat cac doanh nghiep chay i no BHXH", *Nguoi Lao Dong*, 18 February 2008 <http://nld.com.vn/215497P0C1010/diem-mat-cac-doanh-nghiep-chay-i-no-bhxh.htm> (accessed 30 April 2009).

80   Vinh Tung, "Lam viec voi LDLD TPHCM, Chu tich Tong LDLD VN Dang Ngoc Tung: Can bo Cong doan phai biet cach thuong thao voi doanh nghiep", *Nguoi Lao Dong*, 20 May 2008 <http://nld.com.vn/225383P0C1010/can-bo-cong-doan-phai-biet-cach-thuong-thao-voi-doanh-nghiep.htm> (accessed 30 April 2009).

81   Dang Quang Dieu, "Realities and Solutions to Improve the Quality of CBAs", *Cong Doan* <http://www.congdoanvn.org.vn/details.asp?l=1&c=248&c2=248 &m=3131, 21 May 2009> (accessed 25 May 2009).

[82]   Ibid.
[83]   Ibid.; Sunoo *et al.* 2009, pp. 42–44.
[84]   Conversation with Mr. Sunoo, June 2009; Correspondence with Mr. Chau, May 2009.
[85]   Correspondence with Mr. Chau, June 2009; Sunoo *et al.* 2009, p. 48.
[86]   N. Quyet, "Ky thoa uoc lao dong tap the nganh det may VN", *Nguoi Lao Dong*, 27 April 2010 <http://nld.com.vn/20100427125858236P0C1010/ky-thoa-uoc-lao-dong-tap-the-nganh-det-may-vn.htm> (accessed 5 June 2010).

References

Arnold, Denis G. and Laura P. Hartman. "Worker Rights and Low Wage Industrialization: How to Avoid Sweatshops". *Human Rights Quarterly* 28 (2006): 676–700.

ASEAN Affairs, "Vietnam to Raise Minimum Wage to Revive Economy" <http://www.aseanaffairs.com/vietnam_govt_to_raise_minimum_wage_to_revive_economy> (accessed 5 May 2009).

Beresford, Melanie. "Book Review: *Vietnam and the Rule of Law* by Carlyle A. Thayer and David G. Marr". *Journal of Asian Studies* 54, no. 3 (August 1995): 910–12.

Center for Development and Integration (CDI) <http://www.cdivietnam.org/default.aspx?portalid=26&tabid=245> (accessed 29 April 2009).

Dang Quang Dieu. "Realities and Solutions to Improve the Quality of CBAs", *Cong Doan* <http://www.congdoanvn.org.vn/details.asp?l=1&c=248&c2=248&m=3131, 21 May 2009> (accessed 25 May 2009).

Dinh, Tran Trung Hau. "Nike Strike Ends in Vietnam, Contract Factory Closed after Worker Brawl". Associated Press, 2 April 2008.

Douglas, William. "Who's Who in Codes of Conduct" <http://www.newecon.org, 2 January 2001> (accessed October 2008).

Duong Minh Duc. "Sambu Vina Ltd. HCMC: Over 2,000 Workers Continued to Stop Work". *Lao Dong*, 24 June 2008 <http://laodong.vn/Home/congdoan/tranhchapld/2008/6/94461.laodong> (accessed 18 May 2009).

Fair Labour Association. "History" <http://www.fairlabor.org/about_us_history_a1.html> (accessed 29 April 2009).

Frank, T.A. "Is There Any Way to Stop Wal-Mart & Co. from Sweatshop Profiteering?" *Washington Monthly*, 29 April 2008 <http://www.alternet.org/workplace/83767> (accessed 1 May 2008).

Fung, Archon, Dara O'Rourke, and Charles Sabel. *Can We Put an End to Sweatshops?* Boston: Beacon Press, 2001.

Harvey, Pharis J., *et al.* "Developing Effective Mechanisms for Implementing Labour Rights in the Global Economy". Washington D.C.: International Labor Rights Fund, 10 May 2000 <http://www.laborrights.org/files/developing_mechanisms.pdf>.

Hay, Phil and Stevan Jackson. "Economies Perform Better in Coordinated Labor Markets: Impact of Globalization Spurs Interest in Labor Standards around the World". World Bank Press Release, 12 February 2003 <http://go.worldbank.org/2L1S4UZIB1>.

Human Rights Watch. "Not Yet a Workers' Paradise: Vietnam's Suppression of the Independent Workers' Movement". New York: Human Rights Watch, 4 May 2009, <http://www.hrw.org/en/reports/2009/05/03/not-yet-workers-paradise-0>.

Hung H. "Collective Work Stoppage at Ching Luh, Long An: Workers and Company Management Not Yet Come to a Resolution". *Nguoi Lao Dong* 2 April 2008 <http://www.nld.com.vn/219920P0C1010/cong-nhan-va-bgd-cong-ty-chua-dat-duoc-thoa-thuan.htm> (accessed 2 April 2008).

————. "Strike at Ching Luh — Long An: Workers and Company Management Not Yet Come to a Resolution". *Labourer*, 3 April 2008. <http://www.nld.com.vn/220142P0C1010/cong-nhan-va-lanh-dao-chua-dat-thoa-thuan.htm> (accessed 3 April 2008).

Huynh Ngoc Tuyet. "Report on the Findings from the Survey on Prevention of Women and Children Trafficking and Enhancing Corporate Social Responsibility". Go Vap District People's Committee, ActionAid Vietnam (Southern Office), and Development Assistance Project, 2005.

Institute of Labour Science and Social Affairs (ILSSA). "Study on Corporate Social Responsibility Labour-Related Practices". Hanoi: MOLISA, 2004.

International Labour Organization (ILO) and Vietnamese Chamber of Commerce and Industry (VCCI). *Final Report: Pilot Programme in Vietnam.* Factory Improvement Programme (FIP). Hanoi: ILO and VCCI, October 2005.

————. *Market Assessment: Factory-Level Integrated Management and Labour Services in Vietnam.* Factory Improvement Programme (FIP). Hanoi: ILO and VCCI, January 2006.

————. "Better Work" <http://www.ilo.org/global/What_we_do/Projects/lang--en/WCMS_084616/index.htm> (accessed 29 April 2009).

————. *Successful Collective Bargaining in Vietnam.* Training DVD. March 2009.

Justice, D. "The New Codes of Conduct and the Social Partners". *International Confederation of Free Trade Unions*, 2001.

Kim Chi. "Nike Viet Nam: Ho tro 98 ho dan ngheo cai thien dieu kien song". *Nguoi Lao Dong*, 25 April 2007 <http://www.nld.com.vn/187312P0C1010/ho-tro-98-ho-dan-ngheo-caithien-dieu-kien-song.htm> (accessed July 2008).

Le Thuy. "15 Years after the Labour Code: Many Stipulations are Obsolete and Not Enforceable". *Nguoi Lao Dong,* 5 May 2009, <http://www.nld.com.vn/20090505122151420P0C1010/nhieu-quy-dinh-loi-thoi-khong-kha-thi.htm> (accessed 19 May 2009).

Le Thuy and Nam Duong. "Decision 1846 of MOLISA on Pilot Testing CBAs in Textile and Garment Industries: Too Many Mistakes". *Nguoi Lao Dong,*

24 February 2009 <http://www.nld.com.vn/2009022401325466P0C1010/qua-nhieu-sai-sot.htm> (accessed 30 April 2009).

Lee, E. "Globalization and Labour Standards: A Review of Issues". *International Labour Review* 136, no. 2 (1997): 173–89.

Mountain Equipment Coop (MEC) <http://www.mec.ca/Main/content_text. jsp?FOLDER%3C%3Efolder_id=2534374302883570&bmUID=1242581060651> (accessed 17 May 2009).

——— <http://images.mec.ca/media/Images/pdf/non_compliance_chart_v1_m56577569830701764.pdf> (accessed 18 May 2009).

Nghiem Lien Huong. "Work Culture, Gender and Class in Vietnam: Ethnographies of Three Garment Workshops in Hanoi". Ph.D. dissertation. Amsterdam: University of Amsterdam, n.d.

Nguyen Luu. "Hơn 2000 cong nhan Cong ty SAMBU Vina đinh cong". *Dan Tri*, 11 March 2006 <http://dantri.com.vn/c133/s133-106009/hon-2000-cong-nhan-cong-tysambu-vina-dinh-cong.htm> (accessed 17 May 2009).

Nguyen Quang Vinh. "Current Status of CSR in Viet Nam". Presentation, July 2007 <http://www.adbi.org/files/session1_05_nguyen_q_vinh.pdf> (accessed 15 May 2009).

Nike. Nike Corporate Responsibility Report (Fiscal Year 2005–2006) <http://www.nikebiz.com/> (accessed 5 May 2008).

O'Rourke, Dara. "Outsourcing Regulation: Analyzing Nongovernmental Systems of Labor Standards and Monitoring". *Policy Studies Journal* 31, no. 1 (February 2003): 1–29.

———. "Monitoring the Monitors: A Critique of Corporate Third-Party Labor Monitoring". In *Corporate Responsibility and Labour Rights: Codes of Conduct in the Global Economy*, edited by R. Jenkins, R. Pearson and G. Seyfang, pp. 196–208. London: Earthscan, 2002.

Pham Ho. "Xac lap mat bang tien cong tren thi truong lao đong: Nang luong: Đap an trong tay doanh nghiệp". *Nguoi Lao Dong,* 31 October 2007 <http://www.nld.com.vn/206301P0C1010/nangluong-dap-an-trong-tay-doanh-nghiep.htm> (accessed 30 April 2009).

———. "Labour Conflicts Resolution: Not Yet in Sight". *Nguoi Lao Dong,* 10 February 2009 <http://www.nld.com.vn/20090210101332702P0C1010/giai-quyet-tranh-chap-lao-dong-chua-co-loi-ra.htm> (accessed 30 April 2009).

———. "Moving from 'Post-strike' to 'Pre-conflict' Negotiations". *Nguoi Lao Dong*, 3 April 2009 <http://www.nld.com.vn/20090403125216500P0C1010/chuyen-hau-dinh-cong-sang-tien-tranh-chap.htm> (accessed 30 April 2009).

———. "Workers Got a Run-around, Their Rights and Interests are Not Met!" *Nguoi Lao Dong*, 28 May 2009 <http://www.nld.com.vn/20090527105232211P0C1010/cn-bi-sang-tay-quyen-loi-khong-ai-giai-quyet.htm> (accessed 30 May 2009).

SGS Group. "In Brief" <http://www.sgs.com/about_sgs/in_brief.htm> (accessed 29 April 2009).

Sunoo, Jan Jung-Min, Chang Hee Lee, and Do Quynh Chi. *Vietnam: A Foreign Manager's HR Survival Guide*. Hanoi: International Labour Organization, 2009.

Tencati, Antonio. "The Case of CSR in Viet Nam: How CSR Affects Developing Countries". Department of Management. Bocconi University, 2008 <*www.isbee.org/index.php?option=com_docman&task=doc_download&gid=213&Itemid=39*> (accessed 5 May 2009).

Tran, Angie Ngoc. "Global Subcontracting and Women Workers in Comparative Perspective". In *Globalization and Third World Socialism: Cuba and Vietnam*, edited by Claes Brundenius and John Weeks. Houndmills: Palgrave Macmillan, 2001.

————. "Gender Expectations of Vietnamese Garment Workers: Viet Nam's Re-Integration into the World Economy". In *Gender, Household, State: Doi Moi in Viet Nam*, edited by Jayne Werner and Daniele Belanger. Southeast Asia Program Publication (SEAP) Series, Cornell University Press, 2002.

————. "The Third Sleeve: Emerging Labor Newspapers and the Response of Labor Unions and the State to Workers' Resistance in Vietnam". *Labor Studies Journal* 32, no. 3 (2007a): 257–79.

————. "Alternatives to the 'Race to the Bottom' in Vietnam: Minimum Wage Strikes and Their Aftermath". *Labor Studies Journal* 32, no. 4 (2007b): 430–51.

Tran Nam Duong. "Minimum Wage is Not the Basic Wage". *Nguoi Lao Dong*, 22 January 2008 <http://www.nld.com.vn/213304P1010C1012/luong-toi-thieu-khong-phai-la-luong-can-ban.htm> (accessed July 2008).

————. "Factories Have to Adjust Wages for All Workers". *Nguoi Lao Dong*, 25 January 2008 <http://www.nld.com.vn/213621P0C1010/doanh-nghiep-phai-dieu-chinh-luong-cho-tat-ca-nld.htm> (accessed July 2008).

Vietnamese Chamber of Commerce and Industry. 6 May 2005 <http://www.vcci.com.vn/thongtin_kinhte/tinvcci/multilingual_news.2006-12-21.0151/chitiet> (accessed July 2007)

————. List of VCCI Members <http://www.vcci.com.vn/vcci/hoi-vien/danh-ba/phonebook_listing?b_start:int=1980&-C=> (accessed 10 May 2009).

————. "Granting Garment Export Certificates to the U.S" <http://vibforum.vcci.com.vn/news_detail.asp?news_id=16374&cate=1> (accessed 10 May 2009).

VietNamNet/VNS. "Minimum Wage Rises Today: Look At Vietnam". 1 May 2009 <http://www.lookatvietnam.com/2009/05/minimum-wage-rises-today.html> (accessed 5 May 2009).

Vinh Tung. "Sambu Vina, Ltd: Agreed to Raise Wages and Bonuses". *Nguoi Lao Dong*, 25 June 2008 <http://www.trachnhiemxahoi.net/default.aspx?portalid=1&tabid=360&itemid=2306> (accessed 17 May 2009).

6

WORKERS' PROTESTS IN CONTEMPORARY VIETNAM

Benedict J. Tria Kerkvliet

Since the mid-1990s public protests in Vietnam have been increasing compared to the 1976–1995 period. Particularly numerous have been demonstrations by peasants and workers. This article examines protests by urban workers in private and state-owned factories and other types of workplaces.

Most of these workers' public protests have taken the form of strikes, the primary focus of my analysis. I address two sets of questions. One set concerns the protests themselves. What are workers pressing for, and why? What happens during strikes? Where do they occur, and are they peaceful, disruptive, or violent? How are they organized? And how do they occur, given that thus far they have all been illegal? The other set of questions concerns the consequences of these protests. What are the outcomes? What happens to the workers involved? How do employers respond? What are the reactions of state authorities, including those in the official labour confederation, and what do those reactions reveal about Vietnam's political system?

Although labour protests in contemporary Vietnam are my main concern, I compare them, insofar as available sources allow, to similar phenomena in the southern part of Vietnam (then the Republic of Vietnam [RVN]) during 1954–75, prior to the country's reunification.[1] Because many of the strikes today occur in the southern half of Vietnam, a comparison between current and past protests reveals some differences between labour protests today and those of some fifty years earlier. Another goal of this study is to compare the forms and consequences of labour unrest in the two political settings — the anticommunist, semi-democratic/semi-authoritarian RVN that together with the United States was fighting internal wars, and the current, largely authoritarian, Communist Party-governed Socialist Republic of Vietnam (SRV). The analysis shows some similarities in what workers sought and the consequences of their protests. The contrasts, however, are more remarkable and help to highlight the significance of today's labour unrest for the present political system.

For the pre-1975 period in southern Vietnam, I rely on secondary literature. For labour unrest in recent years, which has only begun to attract scholarly attention, I draw heavily on over 750 Vietnamese news reports from the 1990s until late 2008 about labour conditions, unrest, and related matters.[2] No doubt research using other sources, especially interviews with workers and other relevant actors, would enhance this study. But I have not had the opportunity to do that. Fortunately, a few other researchers have published pertinent interview material that I can draw on. Given my emphasis on public expressions, news reports are a justifiable source. The newspaper accounts are typically based on the journalists' interviews with and observations of where the workers are employed, where they live, and what happened when they are on strike. Thus news stories help to publicize workers' complaints, amplify their protests, and get government authorities' attention.[3]

FORMS OF PUBLIC PROTEST

In the public record, strikes [*dinh cong, bai cong*] are the most well publicized form of workers' protest in recent years. Historically, too, strikes have been a common way for Vietnamese workers to express discontent since the late nineteenth or early twentieth century under French colonial rule.[4] Between 1954–75, while the country was administratively and politically divided — as Edmund Werhle explores in his chapter with specific reference to the Vietnamese Confederation of Labour — RVN authorities in the south had to deal with a large number of workers' strikes.[5] After reunification in 1975, strikes began in the late 1980s, possibly earlier. In the nineties, available evidence suggests that there were fewer than forty strikes per year. Since 1995–96, however, the numbers have been rising (see Table 6.1).[6]

TABLE 6.1
Strikes in Vietnam, 1995–2008

Year	Number	% in Ho Chi Minh City
1995	60	48
1996	59	49
1997	59	63
1998	62	71
1999	67	49
2000	71	48
2001	89	43
2002	100	44
2003	139	41
2004	125	35
2005	147	NA
2006	350[a]	NA
2007	541	NA
2008	762	NA
Total	2,631	

Notes: [a] Estimate based on figures as of August 2006. NA indicates information not available.

Sources: "Tranh chap LD va dinh cong gia tang: Han che bang cach nao?" [Labour conflicts and strikes increasing: How can they be limited?], *Lao Dong*, 24 May 2005 <http://www. laodong.com.vn/pls/bld/folder$.view_item_detail(130531> (accessed 5 May 2006); Do Ngoc Dang, "Ve Tinh Hinh Dinh cong" [Strike situation], 29 August 2006, at website of Tong Lien Doan Lao Dong [VGCL] <http://www.congdoanvn.org.vn/prindocument. asp?MessageID=712> (accessed 20 October 2006); "CD phai thich ung voi thay doi co cau LD" [Trade union must adjust to changing structure of labour], *Lao Dong*, 11 January 2008 <http://www.laodong.com.vn/Home/congdoan/2008/1/72615.laodong> (accessed 14 March 2008); and a Tong Lien Doan Lao Dong official, cited in "Dinh cong nam sau cao hon nam truoc" [More strikes than previous year], BBC Vietnamese, 9 January 2009 <http://www.bbc.co.uk/vietnamese/vietnam/story/ 2009/01/090109_strikes_statistics.shtml > (accessed 14 January 2009).

The increasing number of strikes correlates with the increasing number of enterprises that are entirely or partly foreign-owned. Even though they employ less than 8 per cent of the 20.4 million Vietnamese working in non-agricultural and non-fishing industries, these enterprises have been the site of about 70 per cent of reported strikes between 1995 and mid-2007.[7] The remaining 30 per cent took place in Vietnamese privately-owned businesses and state-owned enterprises (SOEs), the latter taking up less than 10 per cent based on 2006 data.[8] Most strikes in foreign-invested enterprises occur in factories wholly or partly-owned by Taiwanese (39 per cent of those strikes) and South Koreans (29 per cent).[9]

Strikes are only a small fraction of all labour disputes and conflicts [*tranh chap lao dong*], which in 1995–2000 numbered around fifty thousand and no doubt have been far more numerous since the year 2000.[10] Many disputes and conflicts are brief, essentially private quarrels between individual workers and their immediate supervisors. Others involve workers sending complaints, in writing or through intermediaries, to managers and employers. Workers occasionally stage a simultaneous "slow-down" [*lan cong*]. For example, one day in 2006 at a footwear factory in the Mekong Delta owned by the Vinh Long provincial government and a foreign investor, managers suddenly announced that each worker's quota would increase from 120 to 160 shoes per day. Sixty shoemakers, instead of working faster, abruptly slowed down.[11] In Ho Chi Minh City (HCMC) in late December 2007, three hundred seamstresses in the Japanese-owned Wonderful Saigon Garment factory stopped sewing at precisely 11 a.m. For the next several hours, the women workers continued to sit behind their silent machines.[12]

Frequently individuals or small groups of labourers take their complaints to outsiders. Workers appeal to government officials to help deal with employers. Usually these complainants are government employees or workers in SOEs or former SOEs that have been converted to shareholding companies [*cong ty co phan*].[13] Perhaps due to their employers' link to state authorities, the workers reason that higher authorities might be willing to take action, just as villagers often petition higher authorities to punish or remove misbehaving local officials. People employed in establishments not attached to the government perhaps see no point in approaching public officials, although there has been at least one significant exception, which I shall discuss at the end of the next section. Workers in enterprises of other ownership types frequently turn to local trade union offices of the

Tong Lien Doan Lao Dong [Vietnam General Confederation of Labour] (VGCL) or one of its affiliated trade unions [*cong doan*].[14]

Journalists and newspapers are often the first outsider sources to whom aggrieved workers turn for assistance, especially those known to be sympathetic to workers' problems.[15] In July 2005, for instance, about ten employees of a private clothing manufacturer went to a *Lao Dong* office with a litany of objections about how the Vietnamese owners treated workers and even failed to pay them. The ensuing news report, which included both the workers' complaints and the owner's response, ended with a plea that workers be paid the wages owed to them.[16] Rather than going in person to a newspaper's office or even telephoning, some workers, such as hundreds of employees at a chain of bookstores, emailed their complaints to journalists.[17]

As in most other countries and in southern Vietnam during 1954–75, strikes in contemporary Vietnam usually occur only after other efforts fail to reach a resolution or even draw attention to their concerns. That slow-down at the Wonderful Saigon Garment factory in late 2007 occurred after many petitions from workers to management "'were just ignored'", according to one worker.[18] Only when the 300 women stopped sewing did managers consent to meet with representatives of the disgruntled employees. Sewing resumed once serious discussions began between management and the representatives. When an impasse came in early January 2008, the workers launched a strike that lasted about three days before the company made acceptable concessions.[19] Another example of a strike being a last resort occurred in May 2005 at the large Hong Kong-owned Keyhing Toy factory in Da Nang, central Vietnam.[20] Workers had frequently sent written complaints about numerous issues to managers and to the main office but received no positive response. Many petitions either "went astray" or were simply rejected. Ultimately, said one employee, "workers were only able to 'talk' by going on strike", which 10,000 did for a few days until a settlement was negotiated.[21]

WORKERS' DEMANDS AND OBJECTIVES

During the last fifteen years workers have voiced many criticisms and demands, the majority of which are about the wages and treatment they receive from employers. Some accounts estimate that wage disputes are central to more than 75 per cent of strikes.[22] The specifics regarding wages vary. Workers who have not been paid for weeks, sometimes months, demand the money owed to them. Other workers accuse employers of paying less than the hourly and daily rates promised to them, which in some cases are even written into their labour contracts. Piecework employees may object to higher daily production quotas without additional pay. Another frequent criticism is that employers do not turn over to Vietnam's social security system, *Bao Hiem Xa Hoi*, the money deducted from workers' wages for that purpose. Employers instead use these deductions to cover their operating costs or even, in some instances, to give managers extra pay. As described in Suhong Chae's chapter, another frequently contentious issue is the annual bonus workers expect to receive just before the Vietnamese New Year [*Tet Nguyen Dan*] but which employers, especially foreign ones, often try to avoid paying or pay in only small amounts.[23]

The most common demand regarding wages is that they be raised. This was a claim in some of the first cases of contemporary labour discontent and continued through 2008. Even though wages have increased over that period, they have not kept pace, many workers insist, with rising costs of living or even with people's basic needs.[24] A demand frequently voiced in the 1990s and early 2000s was that employers should pay at least the legal minimum wage, which the government had raised a number of times.[25] Meanwhile, many employers — especially private and foreign-invested companies — essentially have made the minimum wage the maximum for all but a few employees. For most production workers, pay increments beyond the minimum are minuscule.[26] This situation helps explain why workers in recent years have pressed for wages higher than the official minimum. That, primarily, was the reason behind the demand of many of the 140,000 workers who joined strikes in late 2005 and early 2006.[27] Since early 2006, workers in several private and foreign-invested companies have clamoured for wages beyond the government-stipulated minimum. Strikers at the Wonderful Saigon Garment factory in January 2008, for instance, wanted 30 per cent more than the new minimum that had just taken effect.[28]

Second only to demands for higher wages are workers' insistence that employers treat them humanely. Workers object to physical abuse, such as when supervisors and managers kick, slap, or punch them, sometimes resulting in bloody injuries that require stitches and even hospitalization. One supervisor in a Hanoi factory owned by Canon, Inc., after turning down two workers' request to take time off for personal reasons, made sure the women did not leave by tying their legs to their work stations.[29] Verbal abuse and other indignities are common. Many company managers and supervisors insult and swear at employees. Numerous enterprises prohibit workers from talking to each other while working and physically punish, dock wages, or dismiss employees caught chatting. Employers have also fired employees for other reasons that workers deem unjustified, such as simply being pregnant.[30] Frequently, enterprises even regulate employee trips to the bathroom. Typically in these places, a worker must get permission to go, is limited to two trips per shift, and is fined if she or he stays in the toilet longer than the company's prescribed time.[31] Another sore point for workers is the food they are given in company canteens. Although meals are provided by some companies for free or at subsidized prices, often the food is tasteless and has little nutritional value; it may even be contaminated. Yet several enterprises prohibit workers from taking meals elsewhere or bringing their own food.[32] Another common workers' objection is the length of the work day. According to the Labour Code and contracts between employers and employees, a work day is supposed to be eight hours long. But this is the exception rather than the norm for most workers who publicly criticize their conditions. These workers object to managers requiring them to labour twelve to fourteen hours or even longer, for six, sometimes seven, days a week with little or no additional pay.

Mistreatment, according to many news accounts, is most atrocious in foreign-invested companies. The reasons may in some cases be due to foreign managers and directors having low regard for Vietnamese employees. But Vietnamese can also be mean to their compatriots. Some directors and floor managers in state-owned and private enterprises have made workers labour to the point of exhaustion and abused them in other ways, including cheating them of their wages.[33] Furthermore, even in foreign-invested companies, Vietnamese supervisors are frequently the ones "disciplining" Vietnamese workers. The floor manager who bound the female workers' legs in that Canon, Inc. factory in Hanoi, for instance, was a Vietnamese woman.

Elderly Vietnamese in southern Vietnam today who worked in factories during the RVN era would see many similarities between workers' complaints then and now. Physical and verbal abuse, humiliation, work shifts lasting eleven to twelve hours a day for six or seven days a week without extra pay, and miserable wages (which became even more pathetic as inflation exceeded 60 per cent in 1966 and 100 per cent in 1974) were among the most common issues around which southern Vietnamese workers rallied between 1954 and 1975. And similar to conditions in present-day Vietnam, many of those angry workers in the RVN period laboured in factories owned by American, Taiwanese, and other foreign companies.[34]

One big difference between then and now, however, is that the war and related matters figured prominently in southerners' grievances. Petitioning and striking workers frequently spoke against the war, compulsory military service, the Thieu government, corruption, unfair elections, and American imperialism.[35] Only some of this can be attributed to influences among labourers from the National Liberation Front and the Communist Party of Vietnam (CPV). Many other groups and organizations with no attachment to the revolutionary movement were outspoken about these matters and joined forces with like-minded workers.

Exemplifying the litany of complaints from today's workers about wages and treatment is a list that employees at the Keyhing Toy factory presented in 2005. The company had not raised wages in years yet several times had increased the volume of goods that it expected each worker to produce. Workers who failed to meet these daily quotas were fined. They laboured from 6:30 a.m. until 8:30 p.m., and the one hour of rest they were supposed to get at midday was often shorter. Workers often fainted on the job, from exhaustion and paint fumes, and supervisors responded not with sympathy but with chastisement. A worker who had fainted needed to beg permission to rest, and her pay was docked if she exceeded the allotted recovery time.[36] Supervisors, mostly Vietnamese, frequently insulted and swore at workers and arbitrarily penalized them through pay reductions. Workers also suspected that company officials were responsible for the theft of employees' bicycles parked inside the factory compound. Managers raised the prices for meals in the canteen and forbade workers from eating their own food at work. For every one thousand workers, the company provided only one jug of water each shift. Perhaps that was a tactic to reduce workers' trips to the toilet. In any event, each worker was allowed only two toilet visits per day and was fined for trips beyond that. "It's embarrassing to talk about this," said one worker to a reporter, "yet reasons for the strike started with this and other seemingly little things."[37]

Underlying both sets of major issues — wages and treatment — is the push for decent treatment and living conditions. As one close observer in Vietnam noted, workers object to employers and supervisors treating them "like slaves".[38] In appeals for help to TV stations, husbands of factory workers in the north wrote that employers treat the women like "lemons squeezed to the last drop and then thrown away".[39] A major cause of strikes, explained a labourer in HCMC, is that if workers have to toil such long hours every day, "we'll surely die early".[40] With long work days, many employees have little time for anything else. They go to work early, come home late, sleep, then repeat the routine day after day, often going more than a week without letting up, either because they cannot get permission from their supervisors to rest or because, to boost their income a bit, they take on extra shifts, even additional jobs.[41] Yet despite the long hours and hard work, their wages remain meagre, so they live poorly. Many workers reside in dingy, cramped quarters often shared with others. A reporter likened workers' rooming houses to chicken coops [*chuong ga*].[42] One worker described his residence as a "rat's nest" [*o chuot*].[43] But he, like many fellow workers, could not afford a better place. Housing is particularly poor for the 70 per cent of workers, most of them women, who migrate from many parts of the county to find employment in Vietnam's industrial zones.[44] Most of these workers rent tiny apartments or rooms, typically sharing bed spaces, cooking facilities, and bathrooms with others. Most discontented workers, whether locals or migrants, eat primarily vegetables and rice, not by choice but by necessity. And still, such workers report, 70–90 per cent of their income is spent on bare essentials.

All workers, surveys show, want enough time and money to enjoy little excursions, read newspapers, see a film, and eat nice food. But for most, these are "luxuries" [*xa xi*] that, as one worker said, "we don't dare dream about".[45] What little they manage to save they typically send home to relatives, set aside for their children's school expenses, and spend on medical care when they get sick. With inflation rising significantly in the last few years, many labourers say they can no longer save anything and now eat even less than they did before.[46]

Contemporary Vietnamese workers direct almost all their public complaints to employers, whom they expect to meet their demands. Unlike their counterparts in southern Vietnam in the 1960s and early 1970s, they rarely blame the government for their misery.[47] Occasionally they do criticize trade unions for, as a participant in a strike against a Hanoi textile factory told a journalist, "ignoring" [*lo di*] complaints that workers ask to be conveyed to management.[48] Given that the unions are under the state-endorsed VGCL, such criticisms may be indirectly aimed at state officials.

From time to time, workers in private and foreign-invested enterprises have sent complaints directly to national leaders of the Vietnamese state, partly to solicit help from those authorities and partly to criticize national agencies for paying insufficient attention to workers' needs. A letter that eleven workers sent to the secretary-general of the CPV, the party's Political Bureau, and the Ministry of Labour, Invalids, and Social Affairs (MOLISA) is a remarkable example of this line of action.[49] Writing in early 2006, these workers blamed the Party and government for taking their farm land, thereby forcing them to sell their labour and become "slaves" [*no le*] and "servants" [*toi moi*], and thus "exploited" [*boc lot*] by factory owners and government officials alike. They called on national authorities to live up to the ideals and ideology of communism and protect workers, particularly to see to it that workers are paid better — equivalent, they demanded, to the wages that workers receive in Singapore, South Korea, Thailand, and elsewhere in the region. Their letter also claims that official trade unions fail to help workers and thus should be dissolved, leaving workers free to form their own organizations. Indeed, a few months later, in October 2006, two of the eleven workers who wrote that letter were among the leaders of the newly established Hiep Hoi Doan Ket Cong-Nong Viet Nam [United Workers-Farmers Association] (UWFA), which publicly claimed to be an independent organization representing the interests of oppressed labourers and peasants. It also accused the Vietnamese government of violating human rights and called on international organizations to help workers fight for their basic rights.[50] Authorities' reactions are discussed later in this essay.

STRIKE ACTIVITIES

According to news accounts, strike activities in contemporary Vietnam have been confined to the workplace and, with few exceptions, have been peaceful. A typical pattern is as follows: Strikers congregate outside the factory where they work and wait for answers from management to the demands that their representatives have conveyed verbally and/or in writing. While waiting, they talk among themselves, exercise, and read newspapers. They also talk to journalists who have rushed to the scene and explain why they have stopped working and what actions they want management to take — raise wages, reduce work hours, treat employees properly, and so forth.[51] Sometimes they block driveways and gates to prevent people and vehicles from entering or leaving the factories they are picketing.[52] Rarely do they have banners and posters, fly the Vietnamese flag, or carry pictures of Ho Chi Minh — props commonly displayed when angry villagers march to protest outside government and Party offices. Nor, so far as I can tell, have striking workers had marches of their own to offices or other locations beyond their site of employment.

One unusual type of strike occurred in November 2007 at the Tae Kwang Vina factory, a producer of Nike brand shoes. Thousands of the company's 14,000 workers, nearly all of them women, refused one morning to get off the buses that had transported them to work. They remained seated in dozens of buses parked along a street within the Dong Nai industrial zone while some fellow workers peacefully stood outside the factory gate to present their demands to the company's managers for higher wages. They claimed that, in the face of rapidly rising prices, including higher fares for the company bus that took them to work, they could not keep their heads above water [*khong the song noi*].[53]

I have found no figures averaging how long strikes normally last or how many people participate. Judging from news accounts, I estimate that the typical strike in recent years has lasted three to five days. The shortest ones last less than a day; the longest, until very recently, have spanned about two weeks. Breaking that record was the 24-day strike in 2008 at the Hue Phong shoe factory in HCMC.[54] Some reports suggest that strikes have been getting longer since around 2005, especially in the industrial zones in and near HCMC.[55] The size of strikes may also be increasing, probably reflecting larger workforces in assembly plants. Reports in 1999 indicate that the smallest strike as of August that year involved 18 workers, and the largest strike had 5,000 participants.[56] Since then the largest numbers have more than tripled to nearly 18,000 people at the Freetrend Company strike in HCMC in December 2005, and 20,000 at the Pou Chen factory strike in nearby Dong Nai Province in March 2006 — virtually the entire workforce in these two Taiwanese-owned shoe manufacturing companies.[57] In 2006, strikes in HCMC involved an average of 4,627 workers each.[58] Scattered figures suggest that the average strike elsewhere in Vietnam in 2006–07 was smaller, involving perhaps 700 to 1,000 workers.

The few occasions on which striking workers have become violent usually involved employees breaking things belonging to their employers. In an early example, employees striking because of unpaid wages and other matters in 2000 destroyed machinery at Ly Vuong, a manufacturer in the outskirts of HCMC.[59] Occasionally, strikers and company officials have come to blows. In 2002, workers at the entrance of the Doanh Duc furniture factory in Binh Duong Province said they had to defend themselves against Taiwanese technicians who started hitting some strikers with pipes. Not until police fired shots in the air did the scuffle stop.[60] During some strikes, including one at the Da Nang Keyhing factory in 2005, frustrated workers assembled outside locked gates, waiting for managers' responses or trying to meet with managers, lost their tempers and used their brute strength in numbers to break through the gates and then smash windows and other property inside the factory compound.[61] In another example, during a strike in 2006 at the Japanese-owned Mabuchi Motors electronics factory, managerial staff reportedly provoked a fight with some male workers that also resulted in police intervention.[62] Striking workers have sometimes used threats and coercion to get reluctant co-workers to join the strike.[63]

Workers in South Vietnam during the 1950s to early 1970s, like their counterparts today, carried out most of their strike activities at their places of employment. And then, as now, violence occasionally broke out between workers and managerial staff members. One difference from today's strikes is that in the RVN period, strike participants often clashed with the government police and soldiers, and workers on different sides of a dispute sometimes fought physically. Examples include fights between a hundred or more workers supporting a lengthy strike in late 1971 at Vidopin, a battery manufacturing company, and a smaller number of workers who wanted to return to work. Several men and women were injured and one company car was set ablaze.[64]

Unlike workers in contemporary Vietnam, thus far anyway, agitated southern workers in the 1960s and early 1970s frequently marched through streets, carrying their protests away from their work sites to other parts of their cities and towns. Usually on those occasions workers were participating in demonstrations that also included employees from other companies and factories and people from different sectors of society, such as students, Buddhist monks, Catholic clergy, and anti-war activists. Often these public protests were not only about working conditions but also about overtly political issues. There were also numerous sympathy strikes in the South, in which employees stopped working not because of grievances with their employers per se but because they supported work stoppages by labourers elsewhere. The only sympathy strikes in contemporary Vietnam that I have seen mentioned occurred in early 2006.[65] Additionally, before 1975 southern

Vietnam had several general strikes, which do not occur in Vietnam today. In 1964, 1968, 1970, 1971, and possibly other years, Saigon workers of various professions — electricians, bus drivers, factory labourers, garment makers, cleaners — simultaneously refused to work and thus shut down much of the city for a day or more. General strikes also occurred in other cities, such as Quang Tri, Hue, and Da Nang.[66]

MODEST ORGANIZATIONS

General strikes were possible in pre-1975 South Vietnam partly because employees linked their complaints about work conditions and employers to their criticism of government policies and officials. Two additional factors also account for these massive labour protests. Striking workers in the South during the 1950s to early 1970s were usually members of unions, indicating that strikes often had trade union leadership. The workers striking at Vidopin in 1971 were in the Far East Battery Company Trade Union [Nghiep Doan Cong Nhan Cong Ty Pin Vien Dong], which in turn was affiliated with the Vietnam General Confederation of Labour [Tong Lien Doan Lao Dong Viet Nam] (not to be confused with the organization of the same name that exists today). Many workers who opposed the strike were also organized, but in a different union affiliated with a different federation.[67] As of the late 1960s, the RVN had 525 trade unions with about 400,000 members, about one-fifth of the non-farming labour force. Most unions, in turn, were attached to one of the eleven or twelve federations whose strength and size waxed and waned during the 1960s and early 1970s.[68]

The second factor is that striking workers then often had support from people and organizations that emphasized other issues while also being concerned with workers' problems or that at least saw workers as allies for other causes. Supporting the striking Vidopin workers in 1971, for instance, were a Catholic youth organization, some priests, and several students. Assistance from such groups, in the form of food, other material aid, and manpower, was common. Frequently the sympathizing organizations were publicly known and legal in the eyes of the Saigon government; support also came from the CPV, the National Liberation Front, and other covert organizations.[69]

In contemporary Vietnam there are few signs of significant support for troubled workers from other sectors of society. Some Vietnamese organizations do help industrial workers, often by conveying complaints to employers and mediating between employers and employees. These groups, however, reportedly shun involvement in strikes and other confrontations.[70] Buddhist groups, particularly the large but unauthorized Giao Hoi Phat Giao Vietnam Thong Nhat [Unified Buddhist Church of Vietnam], have publicly expressed solidarity with many strikes, as have a few outspoken critics of Vietnam's political system.[71] It is uncertain, however, whether such supporters have gone beyond words to give material or other assistance. They or others might do so discreetly, hiding their activities to avoid detection by and repression from government officials and thus making it difficult for journalists and researchers to know the extent of such support.

Striking workers today are also not particularly well organized. Organizations that theoretically could lead and coordinate workers' actions include the several thousand government-authorized trade unions and the single legal confederation to which they belong, the VGCL. But as of August 2006, according to the VGCL, not one strike over the years has been led by a trade union.[72] Moreover, according to the VGCL, only about 10 per cent of the non-state enterprises — the sites where most public discontent among workers occurs — even have a union presence, often because owners will not countenance them. This position appears to have become more pronounced in recent years.[73] Hence, somewhere between 70 and 80 per cent of strikes have taken place in enterprises without trade unions.[74] Where trade unions exist, their officials are often not attuned to workers' concerns, not permitted by company officials to be active, or beholden to company owners for their jobs and special privileges.[75]

Two known unauthorized organizations claiming to represent workers' interests are the UWFA, mentioned earlier, and the Cong Doan Doc Lap Viet Nam [Independent Trade Union of Vietnam] (ITUV). Both organizations publicly announced their existence in October 2006 on the Internet.[76] Whether they were active underground earlier is unclear. In any event, neither has claimed credit for organizing strikes before or since then, and I have found no evidence to suggest their involvement in workers' public expressions of discontent.

Most strikes in contemporary Vietnam have had minimal organization and planning, and some seem to erupt spontaneously. When they begin, most strikes have no identifiable spokespersons. Only when strikes are under way do a few individuals emerge, sometimes through a voting process, to negotiate on behalf of the workers. That hundreds, even thousands, of people rapidly join in collective activity is partly due to their shared frustrations over working conditions and desire for a better life.[77] Reinforcing this are networks among workers in the same site who can be relatives, friends, and roommates working at other factories in close proximity, or workers who have links with fellow workers from the same region, province, or even district and village.[78] A Vietnamese official overseeing one of HCMC's industrial zones observed that typically those who lead or initiate a strike are workers from the same town or village [*nhom cong nhan dong huong*].[79] Networks and shared circumstances account for the high rates of participation in most strikes; typically well over a majority, often more than 80 per cent, of workers join. Mobile phones, which have become common in recent years even among low-income Vietnamese, facilitate the coordination of collective actions.[80]

Available evidence suggests that abrupt and offensive actions by employers often provoke workers to react immediately and collectively. An example is a strike at the Vietnamese-owned Dong Anh shoe factory in the outskirts of Hanoi. The 3,500 employees, 90 per cent of them women, had long endured a work routine of twelve hours per day, six or seven days per week, at wages scarcely above the minimum for most employees. They received minuscule extra pay for the overtime beyond the lawful eight-hour day, and no additional pay for Saturdays and Sundays. Workers had written numerous complaints to company managers and the office of a local trade union, but had received no relief. One afternoon in December 2006, upon returning to their work stations after a lunch break, workers heard managers announce that the company would raise wages but at the same time would increase the quota for each worker. This speed-up only meant an even more stressful work regime and no net monetary gain. Almost simultaneously, virtually all of the labourers walked out.[81]

Walkouts can be instigated by a strong sense of indignation and solidarity with abused fellow workers. For example, in December 2006 forty employees in a package-making company in HCMC instantaneously stopped working after seeing a foreman beat up a fellow worker so badly that police had to rush him to an emergency medical centre.[82] A worker in a foreign-owned garment factory in Binh Duong Province wrote that vicious treatment was even harder to bear than low wages and other miserable working conditions. "One time a foreign manager in the company made some employees sit outside under the hot sun. That was their punishment for merely having talked while working. Seeing those women baking in the sun, crying and sobbing, made all of us so angry that we went on strike."[83]

Often strikes begin with only a few employees. As the news spreads from one part of a factory to another, more join, especially if employers further aggravate the situation. An example of this occurred at Nikkiso, a Japanese-owned medical equipment manufacturing company in HCMC. In the context of tensions between employees and employer over money, a group of about twenty workers went on strike one morning in early February 2007. They wanted a pay rise — at least equal to the increase received in early 2006 — and a proper *Tet* bonus. As word of their action and the company's indifference spread, more workers joined the effort. Soon all six hundred of the day-shift workers were striking, forcing management to begin negotiations.[84]

An analogous phenomenon, but on a larger scale, is when a strike in one factory prompts strikes in nearby enterprises, which in turn stimulate more strikes. This results, journalists and workers say, in waves [*lan song*] of walkouts within a short time in numerous enterprises. Perhaps half of the strikes in recent years have occured in Vietnam's industrial and export zones, where foreign-funded factories are concentrated. Strikes generally take place between December through February, when there are widespread frustrations over low wages and unfulfilled expectations of pay increases and annual bonuses. It is said, for example, that strikes in early 2006 at a few companies in one of HCMC's industrial zones influenced other workers within the zone and workers elsewhere in the city to stop work. Soon thereafter, industrial workers in nearby Binh Duong Province, prompted by this wave of protests, walked off the job too.[85] Sometimes, a successful strike encourages workers at a neighbouring factory to protest as well. Explaining why she joined the January 2006 strike at the Vietnamese-owned Hai Vinh shoe manufacturing company in HCMC, one woman said, "Workers at the Freetrend company [a nearby Taiwanese-owned shoe factory] fought and got a raise, so we can do the same."[86]

Several large strikes since the mid-2000s showed signs of some planning by one or more groups from within the factories. Leading such planning, Angie Tran finds, are "experienced older workers who understand workers' rights", know management's "recurring labor violations," have the respect of fellow workers, and have well-established networks, including good contacts with journalists.[87] Without knowing the full details, one can only speculate that strike preparations probably involve quiet meetings among initiators and within their circles of fellow workers to discuss demands, timing, and tactics. Planning might also involve preparing leaflets to be passed hand-to-hand among employees just prior to the walkout and scrawling imperatives to action in graffiti on the walls of toilets within the enterprise. For example, the strike at Freetrend in late December 2005 initially had no one to speak on behalf of workers, to convey their demands to management. Yet some organizing began after word spread that the wage increases likely to emerge from negotiations between the company directors and trade union officers at Freetrend would be far short of their expectations. Several disgusted employees then began to mobilize fellow workers. On the day before the strike, a group distributed leaflets urging fellow workers to unite in opposition to the proposed new wages. The next morning, nearly all of the enterprise's 18,000 employees stopped work, forcing negotiations two days later that resulted in a more substantial wage increase.[88]

CONSEQUENCES

Strikes in contemporary Vietnam usually do bring positive results for workers in the short run and sometimes in the long term. Companies typically decide rather quickly to address workers' demands rather than let work stoppages drag on.[89] Because a high proportion of an enterprise's workforce joins the strike, production comes to a complete or near-complete halt — the cost of which may soon exceed that of making concessions. Strikes in foreign-invested enterprises also spur managers to act on issues they had ignored, even after receiving workers' petitions and letters of complaint. One reason for not being responsive earlier is that managers in many foreign-invested companies have little decision-making power over wages, bonuses, and workday regimes. Those decisions are made at company headquarters in Taiwan, Japan, South Korea, or elsewhere. Mere employee complaints are not deemed serious enough for managers to report back to the head office. The pressure of a strike, on the other hand, pushes managers to make headquarters take urgent notice and get involved in negotiations.[90]

Vietnamese government authorities frequently urge managers to negotiate and reach a settlement with striking workers. Such government intervention in strikes has been commonplace since the late 1990s and is authorized in the Labour Code as amended in 2007. Local offices of trade unions and VGCL branches also frequently get involved even if the company with the industrial dispute has no union. Often these union officials are sympathetic to the protesting workers and urge companies to make concessions.[91]

Because all the strikes that have occurred in contemporary Vietnam have been illegal (see below), one might expect company managers and owners to use this as a weapon. Yet few companies have, at least publicly. Rarely, for instance, are striking workers fired for missing work — a recourse companies might lawfully take against absent employees.[92] It is likely that companies essentially ignore this illegality because they themselves have violated laws, including the Labour Code, in many ways. Both local and national government officials have often publicly stated that virtually all strikes are caused by employers who breach the law by failing to pay workers for months, paying workers less than their lawful wages, mistreating workers, hiring people without giving them proper contracts, and withholding health and social security contributions. Numerous examples as well as several provincial and national surveys of companies' labour practices back up these claims.[93] Even some business leaders have blamed strikes on employers who break the law.[94]

Although most strikes have forced employers to make concessions to their employees, the improvements have not endured in numerous cases. Conditions improve for a while but then deteriorate, prompting workers to object and even go on strike again. Hence, several companies have had more than one walkout within the last dozen years. Perhaps a record holder is the Hue Phong shoe manufacturer in HCMC, which has had at least six strikes since its establishment in 1992. The first strike took place in 1997; the most recent were two in 2008. Workers' recurrent demands include better pay, decent food in the company's canteen, and a halt to physical and verbal abuse. After each strike, Hue Phong authorities make concessions and promise to treat workers better, yet maltreatment and bad working conditions resume. The company's owners may also be learning how to outlast the resolve of striking workers. After 4,000 employees were on strike for nearly a month in 2008, most returned to the factory with only a modest pay increase. The owners refused to make any further concessions. The strikers gave up, said a journalist, because they were desperate for an income. Some government officials with experience in trying to resolve Hue Phong's industrial relations problems have concluded that the company is interested only in "exhausting and exploiting labour", not managing and maintaining good relations with workers.[95]

In some cases, a company retaliates against certain workers who went on strike after the upheaval settles down and the company has made compromises. Companies find or invent reasons to dismiss employees they suspect are leaders or instigators of labour disputes.[96] In January 2006, a Korean garment factory in Bac Giang Province north of Hanoi laid off 100 of its 2,000 employees for no clear reasons. The only thing the dismissed workers had in common was that seven months earlier they had all been conspicuously involved in a strike that won employees higher wages.[97]

In pre-1975 southern Vietnam, too, workers' protests pressured employers to make concessions. Available sources are vague but refer to several strikes that resulted in pay rises, reinstatement of fired workers, and promises of better treatment by employers. Some companies experienced multiple strikes within a short period, which suggests that settlements were not necessarily long-lasting. For example, workers at Stanvac, a U.S. oil company, went on strike twice in 1961 to demand higher wages.[98] Textile workers at Vimytex and Vinatexco, both with Taiwanese, American, and Vietnamese owners, walked off the job at least twice, maybe more, in the early and mid-1960s.[99]

Because workers' protests in pre-1975 southern Vietnam frequently went beyond complaints about employment conditions, and given the support that workers received from other sectors of society, one significant consequence of their strikes and other actions was to augment political struggles. Publicly active workers, especially those in unions and federations, were important for political movements in the South.[100] Research to date, insofar as I can tell, does not enable us to assess just how significant the contributions of workers' public criticisms were to broader political dynamics. Clear, however, is that many strikes were related to other political activity in the South during the 1950s to mid-1970s. This political dimension and the fact that many strikes were deemed illegal by the RVN government, which was fighting a war for its own survival, help to explain why authorities were frequently hostile toward protesting workers.[101]

Sometimes government officials took measures to resolve strikes peacefully and even intervene to protect workers from employers' hostility.[102] The RVN government, unlike today's government in Vietnam, also allowed independent trade unions. Nevertheless, available sources suggest that RVN government officials were often partial to owners and managers but hostile, even violent, toward workers. Repressive tactics included arrests and incarcerations of numerous trade union activists, who were frequently imprisoned for months without charges or trials. Then, in order to incarcerate them even longer, authorities labelled these people communists or revolutionaries.[103] The violence that occurred during workers' strikes and demonstrations, available evidence suggests, was often inflicted by police and soldiers who, perhaps under orders from their superiors, clubbed, shot, sprayed toxic chemicals, and occasionally killed strike participants.[104]

Authorities in contemporary Vietnam are more tolerant of workers' public criticisms than were RVN officials, and they appear to be more partial to employees than to employers. The most severe repression to date that I am aware of is the arrest and imprisonment of several members of the UWFA, one of the two independent labour organizations. Among those arrested between late 2006 and early 2007 were five leaders who, after trials and court appeals, were sentenced to prison terms ranging from eighteen months to five years. The charges against them included spreading anti-state propaganda, joining reactionary organizations, and abusing their democratic rights by saying negative and false things about the regime. In prison they suffered many abuses, including being put in stocks [*cum*] for several days in a row. Two of the five prisoners, having served their sentences, were released in December 2008.[105] Police harass leaders of the other organization, the ITUV, some of whom have lost their jobs. One ITUV leader was arrested in 2007 and imprisoned for nine months, although apparently not for her labour union involvement but for other political activism that, a court ruled, had caused "public disorder".[106] Thus far, authorities appear to be treating the ITUV less harshly than they do the UWFA.

Repression against striking workers seems to be rare. Neither of these two independent organizations has reported any such incidents, although one underground political party has.[107] Newspaper accounts refer to police (usually the security police [*cong an*]) arriving to stop fights between workers and management, resulting sometimes in clashes between police and strikers. Only occasionally do news items report police hitting or attacking peaceful strike participants.[108] And no striking workers, to my knowledge, have been arrested.[109]

That authorities have not been more heavy-handed is remarkable given that all strikes to date have been unlawful. None have followed the process prescribed by law through which aggrieved workers are permitted to strike. In particular, strikes occur before employees and employers begin to negotiate.[110]

Perhaps one reason why Vietnamese authorities have tolerated trans-gressions of the law about strikes is that workers have confined their concerns to their employment conditions. Moreover, they are not well organized, either at the workplace or across different work sites. Additionally, unlike their pre-1975 counterparts, workers in contemporary Vietnam have not linked their concerns and demands to other causes or organizations, and few other groups have tried to link up with them.

Another explanation is that the CPV-government sees workers as an essential part of its constituency. Workers and peasants, officials frequently say, are the two main pillars of the party. At the same time, party and government authorities are also eager to develop a market economy and are especially eager to make Vietnam attractive to foreign investors. From time to time, contradictions and tensions between these two stances appear. Some local and national officials have signalled their partiality to employers, especially foreign-invested companies. A prominent instance of this partiality was when the country's president, Tran Duc Luong, reportedly apologized in April 2006 to the chair of an association of Japanese businesses for strikes at companies with Japanese investors.[111] But just a few weeks earlier, another national official, Nguyen Van An, president of the National Assembly, said that as a "last resort", after getting no satisfaction from employers or authorities, workers "go on strike; it's their only weapon." He reportedly added that just because strikes have yet to follow formal procedures does not make them illegitimate.[112]

Officials have not criminalized strikes and strikers despite their violation of the law.[113] Instead, a notable reaction among authorities has been to tolerate, even support, aggrieved workers and to blame strikes primarily on companies, especially foreign-invested ones, for violating labour laws and workers' rights. As several National Assembly delegates have stated, strikes resulting from employer violations of the law should not be deemed illegal.[114]

Some authorities have sympathized with the companies, suggesting recently, for instance, that workers who strike illegally should compensate their employers for lost production.[115] But more members of the National Assembly, leaders in the VGCL, and provincial and district officials put the onus of any losses on the company managers and owners themselves and advocate that intense pressure should be put on them to adhere to the Labour Code — particularly provisions about wages, weekly work hours, treatment of employees, and workers' contributions to social security and health programmes. Inspections of enterprises, they say, need to be more frequent, fines and other punishments for violations of labour laws should be increased, and the agency responsible for monitoring companies and their treatment of employees needs more resources.[116]

Officials have also considered ways to bring Labour Code provisions regarding strikes more in line with, as the MOLISA minister and others reportedly put it, "reality" and "life" [*thuc tien, cuoc song*].[117] Rather than trying to get workers to comply with existing laws, many authorities have advocated changing the law to better conform with the conditions workers face. Put another way, workers' public criticisms, especially their strikes, have significantly influenced national policy and law-making processes.[118]

This realignment can be traced by briefly examining the evolution of the Labour Code (see Anita Chan's chapter for a detailed analysis of the Code). In the early 1990s, laws made no provisions for strikes. Yet there were two dozen walkouts in the late 1980s and nearly six dozen in 1992 and 1993. This and other pressures prompted party and government authorities to act. After much discussion, little of it in the public domain, they drafted a new Labour Code in 1994, which took affect in 1995.[119] The Code affirmed the right of workers to strike. To be legal, however, a strike had to meet several conditions. From then through 2006, another 1,300 strikes occurred, none of them complying with these conditions. The strikes and other factors induced authorities to re-examine provisions in the Labour Code regarding disputes (chapter 14), which were revised in November 2006 and took effect in July 2007. This time some deliberations, especially several National Assembly sessions in 2006, were reported in the mass media. They reveal two aspects of the debates pertinent to my point about workers' criticisms and protests being influential.

The first revealing aspect of the debates concerns the role of official trade unions. A major condition in the 1995 law was that strikes, to be legal, had to be led by a trade union within the VGCL. Several National Assembly delegates, VGCL leaders, and MOLISA officials favoured retaining this provision. But others, including some within the VGCL, argued that this provision was unrealistic: many enterprises have no trade union and in those that do, the officers are frequently inattentive to workers' needs, are complacent, or are obligated to company owners and managers.[120] Although this view did not entirely prevail, it did have a significant impact. The revised Labour Code of 2007 (Article 172*a*) says that in enterprises without an official trade union, workers may choose their own representatives to organize and lead strikes.

The second issue is whether strikes can be about collective "rights" [*quyen*] as well as "interests" [*loi ich*]. "Rights" have to do with entitlements in laws and labour contracts; "interests" have to do with matters not covered in those documents. Previously, the Labour Code made no such distinction. In 2006, several National Assembly delegates and other officials argued that the distinction was necessary, particularly for strikes. Strikes should be fuelled only by disputes over interests. Disputes over rights should be settled by authorities responsible for resolving conflicting interpretations of laws and contracts. This is necessary, they said, in order to foster a good environment for investors. Others disagreed. Distinguishing between rights and interests sounds simple, they argued, but is actually complicated and impracticable. One assembly delegate, for example, said the two are a pair, and trying to separate rights from interests will deprive workers of their right to strike [*quyen dinh cong*]. Another delegate said that workers do not make these distinctions, and legal experts themselves have difficulties doing so.[121] In the end, the revised law contains definitions for rights and interests that figure in some provisions for how to resolve disputes. But those differences do not apply to strikes, which can be over either rights or interests, or both.

CONCLUSION

Despite revisions in the law aimed at better accommodating workers' circumstances, strikes have continued to fall short of meeting all legal requirements. Government authorities continue to tolerate this shortcoming, and employers remain essentially quiet about it. Workers are likely to continue to protest as long as enterprise owners and managers mistreat and underpay them.

Helping workers persist with their collective struggles is the knowledge, from their experience thus far, anyway, that the CPV government is generally sympathetic toward them. Even though local officials in the state's trade unions are not particularly attentive to workers' concerns prior to strikes, during negotiations with employers they often help to resolve issues and emphasize the legitimacy of workers' complaints. Government and trade union authorities frequently publicly chastise employers for abusing workers. And by not persecuting workers for joining strikes that do not comply with legal provisions, authorities have backed up their verbal support with action. Government lawmakers have also taken workers' circumstances and concerns into consideration when revamping the Labour Code; this is evidence that bottom-up pressures outside the formal institutions of policymaking can be influential in this Communist Party-governed political system.[122]

The mass media, especially the newspapers from which much of the material for this study comes, plays a significant role in this interaction between workers and authorities. Although media coverage is doubtless restricted, it has nonetheless described a wide range of workers' conditions and protests. Government and party authorities cannot ignore such accounts, and apparently they can repress neither the protests nor the news accounts, or they have chosen not to try. Instead, they have attempted to respond to workers' concerns. News coverage also affects employers. By investigating workers' conditions and complaints, reporting their protests, and being a place to which labourers can turn for assistance, major newspapers have made employers aware that angry employees can readily get their concerns amplified far beyond the confines of the workplace.

Compared to the government in Vietnam today, that of the RVN during 1954–75 appears to have been far less sympathetic to distressed workers and more inclined to see their public protests as threats. Officials viewed workers' protests in the South before 1975 as threats because often their demands went well beyond their immediate employment conditions and they demonstrated not only at their work sites but in the streets and at government office buildings. They were also more organized than their counterparts are today; workers often teamed up with other groups to become part of a movement calling for significant political change.

Were something like that to emerge in contemporary Vietnam, authorities' reactions could turn more hostile. Authorities may well be trying to prevent workers' protests from branching out into other concerns and linking up with people from other walks of life. This may be part of the reason why officials have tried to be reasonably attentive to workers' troubles with employers. It is also probably one reason why authorities have quickly suppressed the two small, independent organizations claiming to represent labour and advocate political change.

Notes

An earlier version of this chapter is published in the *Journal of Vietnamese Studies* 5, no. 1 (2010): 162–204. I am grateful to the journal for permission to republish the material in this volume. I also gratefully acknowledge the assistance of Pham Thu Thuy of the Department of Political and Social Change, The Australian National University, who collected and organized into computer files many of the Internet versions of materials used for this article. I also thank the Australian Research Council for a grant that has partly financed this research; Michael Karadjis, for sharing his photocopies of several 2005 newspaper stories; and Anita Chan, Dang Dinh Trung, David Marr, Philip Taylor, Angie Ngoc Tran, the three anonymous *JVS* reviewers, and Trang Cao and other members of the journal's production team and Dayaneetha De Silva for correcting errors and making helpful suggestions on previous versions.

[1] There probably were few workers' public protests in northern Vietnam during 1954–75, judging from the one scholarly investigation I am aware of on that period's industrial relations. See Tuong Vu, "Workers and the Socialist State: North Vietnam's State-Labor Relations, 1945–1970", *Communist and Post-Communist Studies* 38 (2005): 329–56.

[2] The primary method by which Pham Thu Thuy and I collected news reports was to regularly monitor, since 2004, three national newspapers that have reported extensively on labourers' conditions, complaints, and strikes as well as actions of the Vietnam General Confederation of Labour (VGCL), CPV, and government. Two newspapers — *Lao Dong* [Labour], published by the VGCL national office, and *Nguoi Lao Dong* [Labourer], published by the HCMC branch of the VGCL — are the sources for most of the accounts. *Thanh Nien* [Youth], published by the Youth Association, is the third newspaper we monitored regularly since 2004. I have other articles — less systematically gathered than those from these three newspapers — published in 1992, 1993, 1995, 1996, and 2000. The supplementary method for finding reports was to perform online (Google) searches for information about particular enterprises, organizations, individuals, strikes, and other events. That method frequently led to additional news sources inside and outside Vietnam.

[3] I am reasonably confident that Vietnamese journalists report rather well what workers tell them. I base this on having read a large number of news accounts stretching over several years, using a diversity of news sources, talking to Vietnamese researchers interested in labour issues, and reading studies by scholars who have interviewed workers. This is not to say the reporting is even-handed for all sides of the strikes and related events. Some reports are; many, however, focus on workers and their problems, complaints, ambitions, and demands. Given my interest in understanding precisely those views, that focus is helpful.

[4] *Giai Cap Cong Nhan Viet Nam* [Vietnam's working class] (Hanoi: Su That, 1961), pp. 65, 99–109.

⁵   Edmund F. Wehrle, *Between a River and a Mountain: The AFL-CIO and the Vietnam War* (Ann Arbor: University of Michigan Press, 2005), p. 69; Ton Vy, "Workers' Struggle", *Vietnamese Studies*, no. 8 (1966): 93–98.

⁶   The sources for most such statistics on strikes reported in Vietnamese newspapers are the Ministry of Labour, Disabled Veterans, and Social Affairs (MOLISA) [*Bo Lao Dong, Thuong Binh, va Xa Hoi*] and the VGCL. What counts as a strike is not clear. Workers talk about *dinh cong* [strike] but they also speak of *ngung lam viec* [stop work]. I presume both are included in tallies of strikes.

⁷   The figure for proportion of strikes at enterprises with foreign investment comes from the VGCL as reported in "Quan he lao dong nhieu bat on" [Many uncertainties in labour relations], *Lao Dong*, 6 September 2007 <http://www.laodong.com.vn/Home/congdoan/2007/9/53933.laodong> (accessed 10 September 2007). The workforce figures are based on data in *Nien Giam Thong Ke Statistical Yearbook of Vietnam 2008* (Hanoi: Thong Ke), pp. 19–22.

⁸   "Vi sao cac dinh cong deu trai luat?" [Why are strikes contrary to the law?], *VNEconomy*, 3 February 2006, VGCL website <http://www.congdoanvn.org.vn/print document.asp?MessageID=282> (accessed 20 October 2006).

⁹   "Tranh chap LD va dinh cong gia tang: Han che bang cach nao?" [Labour conflicts and strikes increasing: How can they be limited?], *Lao Dong*, 24 May 2005 <http://www.laodong.com.vn/pls/bld/folder$.view_item_detail(130531)> (accessed 5 May 2006).

¹⁰   "Lam gi de han che tranh chap, dinh cong?" [How can conflicts and strikes be limited?], *Nguoi Lao Dong,* 3 November 2000, p. 3. I have not found figures for the number of all disputes since 2000.

¹¹   "Thay gi qua cuoc lan cong o Cty LD Ty Xuan?" [What's to be seen from the slow-down at Ty Xuan Company?], *Lao Dong*, 23 October 2006 <http://www.laodong.com.vn/Home/congdoan/tranhchapld/2006/10/8081.laodong> (accessed 25 October 2006).

¹²   "Vu lan cong cua 300 cong nhan Cty TNHH Wonderful" [Slow-down by 300 workers at the Wonderful Saigon Garment Company], *Lao Dong*, 31 December 2007 <http://www.laodong.com.vn/Home/congdoan/2007/12/71187.laodong> (accessed 11 February 2008).

¹³   For examples, see *Dai Doan Ket* [Great Unity (newspaper of the Fatherland Front)], 26 July 2000, p. 6, and 2 August 2000, p. 6; and Angie Ngoc Tran, "Sewing for the Global Economy", in *Critical Globalization Studies*, edited by Richard P. Appelbaum and William I. Robinson (New York: Routledge, 2005), p. 389.

¹⁴   "Han che ca quyen lam me cua nguoi lao dong" [Limits on Workers' Motherhood Rights], *Lao Dong*, 31 October 2006 <http://www.laodong.com.vn/Home/congdoan/tranhchapld/2006/10/9129.laodong> (accessed 2 November 2006).

15 *Nguoi Lao Dong, Lao Dong,* and *Thanh Nien* are among such newspapers, and these are widely circulated and read in Vietnam. For a revealing analysis of news coverage about workers' protests, see Angie Ngoc Tran, "The Third Sleeve: Emerging Labour Newspapers and the Response of Labour Unions and the State to Workers Resistance in Vietnam", *Labour Studies Journal* 32 (September 2007): 257–79. Of course, many newspapers and magazines pay little attention to workers or are more partial to employers and businesses.

16 "Cong nhan Xi nghiep may Bach Hoa 1: Xin nghi viec, khong duoc tra luong?" [Unpaid garment makers at Bach Hoa 1 Enterprise to stop work], *Lao Dong,* 4 July 2005 <hhtp://www.laodong.com.vn/pls/bld/folder$.view_ item_detail(133579)> (accessed 4 May 2006). I do not know whether workers' conditions improved.

17 "Doanh nghiep sach Than Nghia — TPHCM" [Than Nghia Books HCMC], *Lao Dong,* 31 July 2007 <hhtp://www.laodong.com.vn/Home/congdoan/tranhchapld/ 2007/7/48269.laodong> (accessed 1 August 2007).

18 "Vu lan cong cua 300 cong nhan Cty TNHH Wonderful" (see note 12).

19 "Hai vu dinh cong ve luong" [Two strikes over wages], *Lao Dong,* 10 January 2008 <http://www.laodong.com.vn/Hai_vu_dinh_cong_ve_luong__thuong_ chua_co_hoi_ket/1300919.epi> (accessed 15 January 2008); "Tiep tuc co 4 vu dinh cong ve luong — thuong" [Four continuing strikes over wages and bonuses], *Lao Dong,* 11 January 2008 <http://www.laodong.vn/Home/ congdoan/2008/1/72616.laodong> (accessed 15 January 2008); "Luong, thuong chua tuong xung voi cong lao dong" [Wages and bonuses not yet acceptable to workers], *Lao Dong,* 14 January 2008 <http://www.laodong.com.vn/Home/ congdoan/tranh chapld/2008/1/72907.laodong> (accessed 11 February 2008).

20 A strike was a "last resort" for those wanting or needing to remain employed at the factory. For other workers, their last resort was to quit, which reportedly hundreds of Keyhing Toy factory employees had done over several years. See "Chi co the noi bang dinh cong!" [Can speak only by going on strike], *Lao Dong,* 12 May 2005 <http://www.laodong.com.vn/pls/bld/folder$.view_item_ detail(129565)> (accessed 5 May 2006).

21 Ibid.; "Chi moi nhuong bo 3/8 'yeu sach' cua CN" [Conceding only 3/8 of workers' demands], *Lao Dong,* 13 May 2005 <http://www.laodong.com.vn/ pls/bld/folder$.view_item_detail(129710)> (accessed 5 May 2006); and "100% yeu sach cua cong nhan duoc dap ung" [100 per cent of workers' demands met], *Lao Dong,* 14 May 2005, p. 1ff.

22 See, for instance, "Ve Tinh Hinh Dinh cong …" [The strike situation], 28 August 2006, VGCL website <http://www.congdoanvn.org.vn/printdocument. asp?MessageID=712> (accessed 20 October 2006); "Tranh chap LD va dinh cong gia tang: Han che bang cach nao?" [Labour conflicts and strikes increasing: How can they be limited?], *Lao Dong,* 24 May 2005 <http://

www.laodong.com.vn/pls/bld/folder$.view_item _detail(130531> (accessed 5 May 2006); "Khong nen xem loi nhuan la tat ca" [No need to see profits as everything], *Nguoi Lao Dong*, 11 July 2007 <http://www.nld.com.vn/tintuc/ cong-doan/194987.asp> (accessed 11 July 2007); "Giam thieu cac vu phan ung ngung viec tap the" [Reducing collective work stoppages], *Bao Dong Nai* [Dong Nai Province newspaper], 25 July 2007 <http://www.baodongnai. com.vn/default.aspx?tabid=585&idmid=&ItemID=20918> (accessed 7 August 2007); "Dinh cong" [Strike]; *Nguoi Lao Dong*, 27 August 2007 <http://www. nld.com.vn/tintuc/cong-doan/200511.asp> (accessed 28 August 2007) .

23   The New Year bonus, Suhong Chae shows, was a key demand in a 1993 strike, one of the earliest against a foreign-invested manufacturer in contemporary Vietnam. See also Chae's fine analysis in, "Spinning Work and Leaving Life: The Politics of Production in a Capitalistic Multinational Textile Factory in Vietnam" (Ph.D. dissertation, City University of New York, 2003), pp. 77–86. For news coverage of workers' grievances about bonuses, see December and January issues of *Lao Dong*, *Nguoi Lao Dong*, and *Thanh Nien*, 2004–09.

24   This claim was particularly acute in 2008 and helps to explain the sharp increase in strikes during that year when the inflation rate averaged 23 per cent, nearly three times that of 2007. See Radio Free Asia's interview with Le Dang Doanh, a prominent economist in Vietnam, 26 May 2008 <http:// www.rfa.org/vietnamese/in_depth/Interview_with_economist_LeDangDoanh_ about_wave_of_labour_strikes_in_Vietnam_NNguyen-05262008103135.html> (accessed 27 May 2008). For details on inflation figures, see "Vietnam's 2008 Average Inflation at 22.97 pct", Reuters, 25 December 2008 <http://uk.reuters. com/article/idUKHAN40610920081225> (accessed 18 September 2009).

25   Examples of workers telling employers to pay minimum wages are reported in *Vietnam Investment Review*, 19–25 December 1994, and Reuters, 16 August 1999.

26   Radio Free Asia report, citing a study by the Vien Cong Nhan va Cong Doan [Workers and Trade Union Institute], 1 November 2007 <http://www.rfa. org/vietnamese/in_depth/2007/11/01/ VnWorkerLowWagesAndInsufficientCar eP2_GMinh/> (accessed 2 November 2007); and "Dinh cong la cong cu cuoi cung" [Striking is the last resort], *Lao Dong*, 16 August 2008 <http://www. laodong.com.vn/Home/congdoan/2008/8/102446.laodong> (accessed 20 August 2008).

27   Duong Van Sao and Vu Minh Tien, "Dinh cong Thoi Gian Qua: Nhin tu Goc do Cong Doan" [Recent strikes: Seen from a trade union perspective], *Lao Dong & Cong Doan* [Labour and Trade Union (a journal published by VGCL)], 10 April 2006; "Dinh cong doi nang luong toi thieu lan rong" [Strike calls for higher minimum wage], *Lao Dong*, 6 January 2006 <http://www.laodong. com.vn/pls/bld/folder$. view_item_detail(147169> (accessed 4 May 2006);

"Kien quyet xu ly nhung hanh vi qua khich" [Resolutely addressing extreme actions], *Bao Binh Duong* [Binh Duong provincial newspaper], 6 January 2006 <http://www.baobinhduong.org.vn/detail.aspx?ltem= 1229&Kind=8> (accessed 23 May 2007).

[28] "Luong, thuong chua tuong xung voi cong lao dong" (see note 19). A decree that took effect in February 2006 set VND870,000 per month as the minimum wage for workers in foreign-invested establishments in Hanoi and HCMC and lesser amounts for those in other areas (Nghi-Dinh 03/2006/ND-CP). A later decree, which took effect in January 2008, raised that figure to VND1,000,000, with commensurate boosts for those employed by foreign-invested enterprises in other parts of the country (Nghi-Dinh 168/2007/ND-CP). Additional decrees for 2008 set minimum wages for workers in domestic enterprises (Nghi Dinh 166/2007/ ND-CP and Nghi Dinh 167/2007/ ND-CP).

[29] "Hai cong nhan bi troi chan tai noi lam viec" [Two workers' legs tied at workplace], VietNamNet, 12 April 2007 <http://www.vietnamnet.vn/xahoi/laodong/2007/04/683865/> (accessed 19 April 2007).

[30] See, for example, "Sa thai lao dong nu trai luat" [Illegal firing of female employee], *Lao Dong*, 28 March 2006 <http://www.laodong.com.vn/pls/bld/folder$.view_item_detail(152616> (accessed 4 May 2006). Firing a pregnant employee also violates Vietnam's Labour Code.

[31] For examples, see "Giam thieu cac vu phan ung ngung viec tap the" (see note 22); "Dinh cong o Cong ty TNHH Rau Nha Xanh (Lam Dong)" [Strike at Rau Nha Xanh Company in Lam Dong], *Lao Dong*, 21 July 2006 <http://www.laodong.com.vn/pls/bld/folder$.view_item_detail(134903> (accessed 4 May 2006); and "Cong ty TNHH Kido Hanoi (Hung Yen): 1.700 CN dinh cong doi tang luong" [Hanoi Kido Company: 1,700 strikers demand wage hikes], *Lao Dong*, 12 April 2007 <http://www.laodong.com.vn/Home/congdoan/tranhchapld/2007/4/31748.laodong> (accessed 17 April 2007).

[32] Two enterprising journalists, after investigating food issues at several factories in and around HCMC, found that the money employers spent on food provided to workers was well below what nutritious meals would cost. The journalists also estimated that a quarter of the nearly forty strikes in the city during the first half of 2007 were related to food issues. See "Bua an ngay cang te" [Meals worsen by the day], *Nguoi Lao Dong*, 2 July 2007 <http://www.nld.com.vn/tintuc/cong-doan/194162.asp> (accessed 5 July 2007). Also see Angie Ngoc Tran's account of workers refusing to eat bad meals that factory cafeterias served: Angie Ngoc Tran, "Contested 'Flexibility': Networks of Place, Gender, and Class in Vietnamese Workers' Resistance", in *Taking Southeast Asia to Market: Commodities, Nature, and People in the Neoliberal Age*, edited by Joseph Nevins and Nancy Lee Peluso (Ithaca: Cornell University Press, 2008), pp. 64–65.

33 Examples include a building materials company in Dac Lac Province; the Minh Khai weaving company, a SOE in Hanoi; and XNX Da Giay Sai Gon, a former SOE shoe manufacturer in HCMC that has been privatized. See "Lanh dao vo trach nhiem, cong nhan bi bo roi" [Worker wrongly dismissed], *Lao Dong*, 27 December 2004 <http://www.laodong.com.vn /pls/bld/folder$. view_item_ detail(120405> (accessed 5 May 2006); "Cong nhan Cong ty det Minh Khai (Hanoi) dinh cong" [Workers strike at Minh Khai Weaving Company], *Lao Dong*, 21 October 2005 <http://www.laodong.com.vn/pls/bld/ folder$.view_item_detail(141488)> (accessed May 4, 2006); and "Khong thuc hien theo quy dinh" [Improper implementation], *Lao Dong*, 3 July 2006 <http:// www. laodong.com.vn/new/congdoan/index.html> (accessed 4 July 2006).

34 Wehrle, *Between a River and a Mountain*, pp. 69, 95; Ton Vy, "Workers' Struggle", pp. 93–98; Cao Van Luong, *Cong Nhan Mien Nam Viet Nam trong cuoc Khang Chien Chong My Cuu Nuoc* [Southern Vietnamese workers during the War for National Salvation against the United States] (Hanoi: Khoa Hoc Xa Hoi, 1977), pp. 66–67 and 72–74; Nguyen Quang Quynh, *Nhung Van De Lao Dong va Xa Hoi Hien Dai* [Current labour and social issues] (Saigon: Lua Thieng, 1974), pp. 115–58. For inflation figures, see Bureau of Labour Statistics, *Labour Law and Practice in the Republic of Viet-Nam* (Washington, D.C.: U.S. Department of Labour, 1968), p. 66; and Cao Van Luong, *Cong Nhan*, pp. 144–45.

35 Ton Vy, "Workers' Struggle", pp. 93–98; Cao Van Luong, *Cong Nhan*, pp. 107–15, 128–41.

36 "Chi co the 'noi' bang dinh cong!" (see note 20).

37 Ibid.

38 "… *doi xu cong nhan nhu no le* …", Le Tri Tue, quoted by Radio Free Asia, 1 May 2007, from Mang Y. Kien [Opinion Network] <http://ykien. net/blog/?p=1225> (accessed 3 May 2007).

39 Tran, "Sewing for the Global Economy", p. 389.

40 *Nguoi Lao Dong*, 29 August 2007 <http://www.nld.com.vn/tintuc/cong-doan/200603.asp> (accessed 30 August 2007).

41 One report says workers stopped work and declared a strike just to get a day of rest. "Vi sao cong nhan van dinh cong tu phat?" [Why do workers still strike spontaneously?], *Bao Binh Duong*, 24 February 2006 <http://www. baobinhduong.org.vn/detail.aspx?Item=2577&Kind=7> (accessed 23 May 2007).

42 "Nhoc nhan doi cong nhan" [The weary life of a worker], *Tuoi Tre*, 22 October 2007 <http://www.tuoitre.com.vn/Tianyon2/Index.aspx? ArticleID+225522&C hannelID=89> (accessed 4 April 2008).

43 "Noi buon com ao" [Sad way to live], *Lao Dong*, 28 February 2006 <http:// www.laodong.com.vn/pls/bld/folder$.view_item _detail(150350)> (accessed 4 May 2006).

44   Ibid.; and "Doi song cong nhan Vietnam thoi ky mo cua" [Vietnamese workers' lives in the Open Door period], Radio Free Asia, 31 October 2007 <http://www.rfa.org/vietnamese/in_depth/2007/10/31/VnWorkersSeriesPIPresentDayLaborForces_GMinh/> (accessed 2 November 2007).

45   "Doi song cong nhan o TPHCM" [Workers' lives in HCMC], *Sai Gon Giai Phong* [Saigon Liberation (newspaper published by HCMC branch of the CPV)], 23 August 2007 <http://www.sggp.org.vn/xahoi/2007/8/117054/#> (accessed 27 August 2007).

46   For accounts of workers' living conditions and summaries of studies, see three articles: "Bua an ngay cang te" (see note 32); and two articles in *Nguoi Lao Dong*, 4 July 2007, "That lung buoc bung den bao gio?" [Belt tightening for how long?] <http://www.nld.com.vn/tintuc/cong-doan/194274.asp> and; and "Co thuc moi vuc duoc dao" [To be ethical and honest, a person needs to be fed and clothed] <http://www.nld.com.vn/tintuc/cong-doan/quyen-nghia-vu/194361.asp> (accessed 5 July 2007). Also telling are "That da day vi chuyen ao com" [Pull in your stomach for the hard times], *Lao Dong*, 7 March 2008 <http://www.laodong.com.vn/Home/phongsu/2008/3/79370.laodong> (accessed 12 March 2008); "Cong nhan chong choi voi 'bao' tang gia" [Workers resist the storm of rising costs], *Tuoi Tre*, 19 July 2007 <http://www3.tuoitre.com.vn/Vieclam/Index.aspx?ArticleID=211149 &ChannelID=269> (accessed July 19, 2007); and "Cong nhan hang giay Nike dinh cong" [Nike shoemakers go on strike], BBC Vietnamese, 29 November 2007 <http://www.bbc.co.uk/vietnamese/vietnam/story/2007/11/071129_nike_factory_strike.shtml> (accessed 5 December 2007).

47   Considering that perhaps journalists in Vietnam are omitting from their news accounts workers' views of this kind, I have looked for, but have yet to find, such views in reports about workers in newsletters that dissidents in Vietnam publish, particularly *To Quoc* [Homeland] and *Tu Do Ngon Luan* [Free Speech].

48   "Cong nhan cong ty det Minh Khai (Hanoi) dinh cong" (see note 33). Also see Wang Hong-zen, "Asian Transnational Corporations and Labor Rights: Vietnamese Trade Unions in Taiwan-invested Companies", *Journal of Business Ethics* 56 (Spring 2005): 49.

49   The writers of the undated letter are Huynh Ngoc Canh, a labourer in the AMATA industrial zone in Dong Nai Province; Nguyen Tan Hoanh, from the Dien Ban industrial zone, Quang Nam Province; Nguyen Tan Dung, working in the Bien Hoa II industrial zone, Dong Nai; Duong Thai Phong, Huyen Tien, Truong Long, Vu Ha, Tran Ta, Vo Hai, and Nguyen Thi Tuyet, all from the Tan Binh and Vinh Loc industrial areas of HCMC; and Hoang Anh Tuan, working in the Gia Dinh shoe factory, Saigon. Found at Dan Chu Net <http://www.danchu.net/ArticlesChinhLuan/0.0.0.Collection.2006.I/HuynhNgocCanh.601.

htm> (accessed 25 April 2006). Also see Radio Free Asia's interview with one of the letter writers, Nguyen Tan Hoanh, 24 March 2006 <http://www. doi-thoai.com/baimoi0306_336. html> (accessed 21 April 2006).

50 Hiep Hoi Doan Ket Cong-Nong Vietnam [United Workers-Farmers Association], Ban Tuyen Bo [Official announcement], 30 October 2008, from Tu Do Ngon Luan website <http://www.tdngonluan.com/tailieu.htm> (accessed 23 February 2007). The two letter writers involved were Nguyen Tan Hoanh and Nguyen Thi Tuyet.

51 For examples of news accounts with photos, see "'Lien khuc' dinh cong" [Potpourri of strikes], *Thanh Nien*, 3 March 2006 <http://www3.thanhnien. com.vn/ Xahoi/2006/3/3/140573.tno> (accessed 13 April 2006); "Giam thieu cac vu phan ung ngung viec tap the" (see note 22); and "Quan he lao dong nhieu bat on" (see note 7).

52 An example is a strike at the South Korean-owned G.S. Company, a clothing manufacturer on the outskirts of HCMC. See "Hon mot tram CN dinh cong doi no luong" [Over 100 workers strike over unpaid wages], *Lao Dong*, 11 September 2006 <http://www.laodong.com.vn/pls/bld/display$. htnoidung(36,165993> (accessed 12 September 2006).

53 "Cong nhan hang giay Nike dinh cong" (see note 46).

54 "Cong nhan Hue Phong lai dinh cong" [Hue Phong workers strike again], VietNamNet, 11 April 2008 <http://vietnamnet.vn/xahoi/2008/04/777989/> (accessed 8 May 2008); "Vu Dinh cong Hue Phong Chua On" [Hue Phong strike not yet resolved], Vietnam News Network, 5 May 2008 <http://www. vnn-news.com/breve.php3?id_breve=11681> (accessed 8 May 2008).

55 "Giam thieu cac vu phan ung ngung viec tap the" (see note 22); Radio Free Asia, 4 March 2006 <http://www.rfa.org/vietnamese/in_depth/2006/03/04/ vnpress_review_NNguyen/> (accessed 8 February 2007).

56 "Vietnam: Labour strikes increased by 30%", Reuters, 16 August 1999, http://elisa.anu.edu.au:8080/current/0000026.bsk/AA6RC00C.htm> (accessed 20 August 1999).

57 "Gan 18.000 cong nhan dinh cong, doi nang luong toi thieu" [Nearly 18,000 workers strike for higher minimum wage], *Lao Dong*, 29 December 2005 <http://www.laodong.com.vn/pls/bld/folder$.view_item_ detail(146579)> (accessed 4 May 2006); and Nguyen Minh Quang, "20,000 cong nhan dinh cong, bieu tinh" [20,000 workers strike, demonstrate], DCVOnline, 14 March 2006, at TiengDanKeu [Cry of the people] website <http://www.tiengdankeu. net/, section Ho So Dinh cong [Strike folder]> (accessed 9 March 2007).

58 Calculated from figures in "Quyen loi nguoi lao dong trong hoi nhap kinh te" [Workers' rights in a world economy], *Lao Dong*, 15 May 2007 <http://www. laodong.com.vn/Home/congdoan/2007/5/36279.laodong> (accessed 21 May 2007).

59   "Vi sao cac cuoc dinh cong ngay cang nhieu hon, nong hon?" [Why are strikes becoming more numerous and heated?], *Nguoi Lao Dong*, 27 September 2000, p. 3.

60   Vietnam's Business Forum postings, 30 November and 1 December 2002, based on *Tuoi Tre* and *Lao Dong* news items <http://www.le.org/pipermail/vnbiz/2002-December/000286.html> (accessed 4 December 2006).

61   "Chi moi nhuong bo 3/8 'yeu sach' cua CN" (see note 21); "Dinh cong doi nang luong toi thieu lan rong" (see note 27).

62   "Lien khuc' dinh cong" (see note 51).

63   For a report of coercion by fellow workers in a strike, see "Lam quyen hanh xu trai luat" [Behaviour contrary to the law], *Nguoi Lao Dong*, 16 April 2007 <http://www.nld.com.vn/tintuc/cong-doan/quyen-nghia-vu/186443.asp> (accessed 18 April 2007).

64   Nguyen Quang Quynh, *Nhung Van De*, pp. 124–26.

65   Duong Van Sao and Vu Minh Tien, "Dinh cong thoi gian qua," p. 10.

66   Wehrle, *Between a River and a Mountain*, pp. 94–95; Cao Van Luong, *Cong Nhan*, 131–32; Ton Vy, "Workers' Struggle", p. 105; Nguyen Ngoc Linh, "The Working Man in Vietnam" [a booklet] (Saigon: Vietnam Council on Foreign Relations, not dated, circa 1970), pp. 3–4; Trinh Quang Quy, *Phong Trao Lao Dong Vietnam* [Vietnam Labour Movement] (Saigon: n.p., 1970), p. 73 (Vietnamese section), p. 102 (English section).

67   Nguyen Quang Quynh, *Nhung Van De*, pp. 118–19.

68   All but one of the figures here come from the Bureau of Labour Statistics, *Labor Law and Practice*, pp. 22, 43; and "Report on Trade Unions in Viet Nam", in U.S. Agency for International Development (USAID), Trade Union Branch, *Labor in Vietnam*, vol. 2 (1970), pp. 6–7. The proportion of workers in unions is my calculation, based on data in these two sources. The non-farming labour force includes the approximately 38,000 workers in rubber, tea, and coffee plantations, many of whom were unionized.

69   For some details, see Wehrle, *Between a River and a Mountain*; Cao Van Luong, *Cong Nhan*; and Tong Lien Doan Lao Dong Vietnam [General Confederation of Labour of Vietnam], *Lich Su Phong Trao Cong Nhan va Cong Doan Vietnam* [History of Vietnam's worker and union movement], vol. 2, 1954–1975 (Hanoi: Lao Dong, 2004), sections regarding South Vietnam.

70   For examples of such organizations in HCMC, see Joseph Hannah, "Local Non-Government Organization in Vietnam: Development, Civil Society and State-Society Relations" (Ph.D. dissertation, University of Washington, Seattle, 2007), pp. 184–90.

71   Examples of such support are the open letter of 27 March 2006, from Thich Quang Do, the well-known Unified Buddhist Church of Vietnam leader living in HCMC (published in *Thong Luan* [Open Discussion], a monthly journal

from France, 18–19 April 2006); and statements in 2006 by human rights advocates in Vietnam, Nguyen Chinh Ket, Do Nam Hai, Tran Anh Kim, Nguyen Phong, and Huynh Viet Lang (also known as Huynh Nguyen Dao), found at Dang Dan Chu Nhan Dan [People's Democratic Party] website <http://www.freewebs.com/dangdanchunhandan/> (accessed 23 February 2007), and Tu Do Ngon Luan website <http://www.tdngonluan.com/tailieu/tl_lmdcnq_khangthu_01.htm> (accessed 10 July 2009).

72 "Kien Nghi Dang ra nghi quyet ve giai cap cong nhan" [Party resolution produces decision regarding working class], *Lao Dong*, 25 August 2006, p. 2.

73 "Vi sao cac dinh cong deu trai luat?" (see note 8). In 2002, half of the non-state enterprises with more than ten employees had trade unions, a much higher proportion than in 2006. *Vietnam News Briefs*, 21 June 2002. Apparently using 2002 data, another source says 70 per cent of foreign-invested enterprises had trade unions; see Anita Chan and Wang Hong-zen, "The Impact of the State on Workers' Conditions: Comparing Taiwanese Factories in China and Vietnam", *Pacific Affairs* 77 (Winter 2004–2005): 640.

74 "Vi sao cac dinh cong deu trai luat?" (see note 8); "Giai phap han che dinh cong" [Addressing strike restrictions], *Phap Luat* [Law (a newspaper published by the Ministry of Justice)], 18 May 2006 <http://www.congdoanvn.org.vn/printdocument.asp?MessageID=440> (accessed 20 October 2006).

75 For examples, see "Vi sao cong nhan van dinh cong tu phat?" (see note 41); "Gioi chu khong chiu nhuong bo yeu sach tang luong" [Owners not yielding to demands for higher wages], *Lao Dong*, 19 May 2005 <http://www.laodong.com.vn/pls/bld/folder$.view_item_detail(130095> (accessed 5 May 2006); and Tran, "Contested 'Flexibility'", p. 67. For some reasons why the official trade unions are unable to be better advocates for workers, see Simon Clarke, Chang-Hee Lee, and Do Quynh Chi, "From Rights to Interests: The Challenge of Industrial Relations in Vietnam", *Journal of Industrial Relations* 49, no. 4 (2007): 545–68. Also see Chan and Wang, "Impact of the State", which finds that unions in Vietnam are more concerned with workers' problems than unions in China are.

76 ITUV's announcement, 20 October 2006, Dan Chim Viet [Viet Flock] (website) <http://www.danchimviet.com/php/modules.php?name=News&file=article&sid=2523> (accessed 16 January 2007).

77 A study of humour among factory workers provides some unusual evidence of such shared frustrations and desires. See Nghiem Lien Huong, "Jokes in a Garment Workshop in Hanoi: How does Humour Foster the Perception of Community in Social Movements?", supplementary issue, *International Review of Social History* 52 (2007): 209–23.

78 Tran, "Contesting 'Flexibility'", pp. 62–65. Of course, networks and shared circumstances are no guarantee for collaborative action. Networks can even

divide workers, a point made in Tran's article and in Chae, "Spinning Work", chapters 5 and 6.

[79] "Vi sao cong nhan van dinh cong tu phat?" (see note 41).

[80] Hoang Phuc Vinh, "Ve cuoc dinh cong cua 24,000 cong nhan Vietnam" [On the strikes of 24,000 workers], 28 December 2005, *Thong Luan*, 13 January 2006 <http://www.thongluan.org/vn/modules.php?name=News&file= article& sid=382> (accessed 12 January 2006); Tran, "Contesting 'Flexibility'", p. 65.

[81] "3.500 cong nhan dinh cong" [3,500 workers strike], *Lao Dong*, 12 December 2006 <http://www.laodong.com.vn/Home/congdoan/tranhchapld/2006/ 12/14746.laodong> (accessed 3 January 2007).

[82] "Hau qua tu vi pham nghiem trong luat lao dong" [Consequences of serious violations of the Labour Code], *Lao Dong*, 21 December 2006 <http:// www.laodong.com.vn/Home/congdoan/tranhchapld/2006/12/16021.laodong> (accessed 3 January 2007).

[83] "Cuc lam doi cong nhan!" [Workers' lives are very desperate!], *Tuoi Tre*, 20 October 2007 <http://www.tuoitre.com.vn/Tianyon2/Index.aspx?ArticleID=22 5252&ChannelID=118> (accessed 4 April 2008).

[84] "Cong nhan dinh cong doi nang luong va thuong tet" [Striking workers demand higher wages and Tet bonus], *Lao Dong*, 3 February 2007 <http://www. laodong.com.vn/Home/congdoan/tranhchapld/2007/2/22437.laodong> (accessed 15 February 2007).

[85] See "Don dap dinh cong khong chi vi luong" [Successive strikes are not just about wages], VietNamNet, 5 January 2007 <http://www.vietnamnet.vn/xahoi/ laodong/2006/01/529614/> (accessed 22 March 2007); "No luc ngan chan dinh cong" [Efforts to stop strikes], *Lao Dong*, 11 January 2006 <http://www. laodong.com.vn/pls/bld/folder$.view_item_detail(147530> (accessed 4 May 2006); and "'Lien khuc' dinh cong" (see note 51). For accounts of similar waves in late 2006 to early 2007, see "Can co cai nhin khac ve dinh cong" [Need to look at strikes differently], *Nguoi Lao Dong*, 17 December 2006 <http://www.nld.com.vn/tintuc/cong-doan/210108.asp> (accessed 20 December 2007); and "Ngan ngua nhung vu dinh cong lien quan den nang luong" [Strike prevention linked to wage hikes], *Bao Dong Nai*, 14 March 2007 <http:// www.baodongnai.com.vn/default.aspx?tabid=573&idmid=&ItemID=16906> (accessed 29 March 2007).

[86] "Nguoi lao dong dinh cong doi tang luong toi thieu tai cac doanh nghiep FDI o TP.Ho Chi Minh" [Striking labourers demand higher minimum wages at foreign-invested enterprises in HCMC], *Lao Dong*, 4 January 2006 <http://www.laodong. com.vn/pls/bld/folder$.view_item_detail(146952> (accessed 4 May 2006).

[87] Tran, "Contesting 'Flexibility,'", p. 64. Also see Simon Clarke, "The Changing Character of Strikes in Vietnam", *Post-Communist Economies* 18 (September 2006): 350.

88 "Gan 18.000 cong nhan dinh cong, doi nang luong toi thieu" (see note 57);
    "Hon 5.000 cong nhan dinh cong doi nang luong toi thieu" [More than
    5,000 workers strike for higher minimum wage], *Lao Dong*, 30 December
    2005 <http://www.laodong.com.vn/pls/bld/folder$.view_item_detail(146723>
    (accessed 4 May 2006). For additional details about the strike, see Angie
    Ngoc Tran, "Alternatives to the 'Race to the Bottom' in Vietnam: Minimum
    Wage Strikes and Their Aftermath", *Labor Studies Journal* 32 (December
    2007): 435–38.

89 "'Khoanh vung' giai quyet dinh cong" [Setting limits for resolving strikes],
    Nguoi Lao Dong, 26 February 2007 <http://www.nld.com.vn/tintuc/cong-
    doan/181365.asp> (accessed 16 March 2007).

90 For more on this last point, see the analysis in "Luong, thuong chua tuong
    xung voi cong lao Dong" (see note 19).

91 "Lam gi de han che tranh chap, dinh cong?" (see note 10) summarizes the
    involvement of local officials in resolving strikes during 1995–2000. For more
    recent evidence, see Clarke, "Changing Character", pp. 350, 352–54; "Kien
    quyet xu ly nhung hanh vi qua khich" (see note 27); "'Khoanh vung' giai
    quyet dinh cong" (see note 89); and "Tu cac cuoc dinh cong cua cong nhan tai
    tinh Binh Duong" [Workers' strikes in Binh Duong], *Thanh Nien*, 26 October
    2007, http://<http://www1.thanhnien. com.vn/doisong/2007/10/26/213781.tno>
    (accessed October 29, 2007). Besides labour conciliation boards and courts,
    says Article 168 of the amended Labour Code (2007), chairpersons of people's
    committees [*chu tich uy ban Nhan Dan*] at district, ward, town, and city levels
    have the authority to resolve some types of industrial disputes.

92 For one example, see "Vu dinh cong tai Cong ty TNHH Sao Vang (Hai
    Phong)" [Strike at Red Star Company, Hai Phong], *Tuoi Tre*, 22 February
    2006 <http://www.tuoitre.com.vn/Tianyon/PrintView.aspx?ArticleID= 124135
    &ChannelID=3> (accessed 23 February 2006).

93 For summaries of recent surveys, see "Thuc hien Bo luat lao dong tai Khanh
    Hoa" [Implementing the Labour Code in Khanh Hoa], *Lao Dong*, 9 February
    2007 <http://www.laodong.com.vn/Home/congdoan/tranhchapld/2007/2/23357.
    laodong> (accessed 15 February 2007); "Quan he lao dong nhieu bat on" (see
    note 7).

94 "Chia re nguoi lao dong voi cong doan?" [Dividing workers and unions?],
    Lao Dong, 11 December 2006 <http://www.laodong.com.vn/Home/congdoan/
    tranhchapld/2006/12/14664.laodong> (accessed 3 January 2007).

95 Quoted in "Vi sao cong nhan dinh cong trien mien?" [Why strikes are
    entangled], Saigon Net, 16 April 2008 <http://www.saigonnet.vn/detail.
    aspx?flag=1&item=44959> (accessed 8 May 2008). The same story indicates
    that the company's owner, although claiming to be Vietnamese, is actually
    from China. Additional stories on which this account of Hue Phong workers'

protests is based include "Vi sao cac cuoc dinh cong ngay cang nhieu hon, nong hon?" (see note 59); "Mat 10 ngay de khoi phuc san xuat" [Ten days needed to resume production], *Lao Dong*, 6 June 2005, pp. 1ff; "Cong nhan Hue Phong lai dinh cong" (see note 54); "Cong ty Hue Phong: tranh chap da duoc giai quyet" [Hue Phong strike resolved], VietNamNet, 22 April 2008, http://vietnamnet.vn/xahoi/2008/04/779729/> (accessed 8 May 2008); "Cong ty Hue Phong khong giai quyet dut diem" [Hue Phong strike not definitely resolved], Vietnam News Network, 2 May 2008 <http://www.vnn-news.com/breve.php3?id_breve=11665> (accessed 8 May 2008); "Vu dinh cong Hue Phong chua on" (see note 54); and "Vu tranh chap tai Cong ty Hue Phong — TPHCM" [Conflict at Hue Phong Company-HCMC], *Nguoi Lao Dong*, 5 May 2008 <http://www.nld.com.vn/tintuc/cong-doan/223736.asp> (accessed 8 May 2008).

[96]   Chae, "Spinning Work", pp. 125–27.

[97]   "Bac Giang: Hon 100 cong nhan may bi sa thai vo co" [Over 100 workers laid off without reasons], VietBao.vn, 6 January 2006, http://vietbao.vn/Xahoi/Bac-Giang-Hon-100-cong-nhan-may-bi-sa-thai-vo-co/70035915/157/> (accessed 7 May 2008); "Gioi chu khong chiu nhuong bo yeu sach tang luong" (see note 75); "Ket thuc thang loi sau 12 ngay dinh cong" [Victory after a 12-Day strike], *Lao Dong*, 25 May 2005 <http://www1.laodong.com.vn/pls/bld/display$.htnoidung(36,130595)> (accessed 7 May 2008).

[98]   Ton Vy, "Workers' Struggle", p. 101; Tong Lien Doan Lao Dong Vietnam, *Lich Su*, p. 186.

[99]   Tong Lien Doan Lao Dong Vietnam, *Lich Su*, pp. 187–88; Cao Van Luong, *Cong Nhan*, pp. 72–74; Wehrle, *Between a River and a Mountain*, p. 95.

[100] See discussions in Wehrle, *Between a River and a Mountain*; and Cao Van Luong, *Cong Nhan*.

[101] The Republic of Vietnam's Constitution protected workers' right to strike, but in order to be legal, strikes first needed to comply with numerous laws, which only some did. Also, with a 1964 decree that declared a state of emergency in the entire Republic, the government forbade all interruptions to economic activities, including strikes. The government also had laws against strikes with "political" objectives. See Nguyen Quang Quynh, *Nhung Van De*, pp. 150–52; and Trinh Quang Quy, *Phong Trao Lao Dong*, pp. 78–80 (Vietnamese section), pp. 110–13 (English section).

[102] Examples of RVN officials trying to help workers deal with their employers occurred during the Vidopen battery strike in 1971. See Nguyen Quang Quynh, *Nhung Van De*, pp. 120–21.

[103] For examples under different RVN administrations, see Don Luce and John Sommer, *Viet Nam: The Unheard Voices* (Ithaca: Cornell University Press, 1969), p. 261; Wehrle, *Between a River and a Mountain*, pp. 70–71, 183–84;

Trinh Quang Quy, *Phong Trao Lao Dong*, p. 72 (Vietnamese section), pp. 100–101 (English section).

[104] For examples, see Wehrle, *Between a River and a Mountain*, pp. 70–71, 127–29; Trinh Quang Quy, *Phong Trao Lao Dong*, pp. 73, 84–85 (Vietnamese section), pp. 102, 120–21 (English section); Hoang Quoc Viet, *Nhung Net So Luoc ve Lich Su Phong Trao Cong Nhan va Cong Doan Viet Nam* [Features of Vietnam's labour and trade union movement] (Hanoi: Lao Dong, 1959), pp. 56–57; Ton Vy, "Workers' Struggle", pp. 103–4; and Tong Lien Doan Lao Dong Vietnam, *Lich Su*, p. 190.

[105] *Dien Thu* [Electronic letter], a publication of the Dang Dan Chu Nhan Dan [People's Democracy Party], July 2007, pp. 4–5; "Viet Nam: Farmers' Union Crushed", worldwide appeal from Amnesty International, May 2007, circulated via Steve Denney's Vietnam News List (vnnews-l), 1 May 2007, <http://coombs. anu.edu.au/~vern/forum.html>; Nguyen Van Huy, "Hai Vu An Tho Bao Dang Luu Y" [Two brutal cases worth noticing], *Thong Luan*, February 2009, pp. 13–14. One of two prisoners released in December 2008 was Nguyen Tan Hoanh (also known as Doan Huy Chuong). He was also released in May 2008, perhaps for health reasons, but apparently had to return to prison until the end of the year. See interview with him by Radio Free Asia, 18 May 2008 <http://www.rfa.org/vietnamese/HumanRights/Nguyen-Tan-Hoanh-political-prisoner-set-free-VHung-05182008134432.html> (accessed 27 May 2008).

[106] "Tran Khai Thanh Thuy bi bat giam" [Tran Khai Thanh Thuy arrested], *Dan Chim Viet*, 22 April 2007 <http://www.danchimviet.com/php/modules. php?name=News&file=article&sid=3276> (accessed 15 June 2007); Committee to Protect Journalists, press release, New York, 4 February 2008; account by Dao Van Thuy of police harassing him, "Ky su Dao Van Thuy len an manh me nha cam quyen CSVN dan ap cong doan doc lap va ca nhan anh" [Dao Van Thuy charges Communist authorities with repression against independent trade union and himself], *Tu Do Ngon Luan* <http://www.tudongonluanonline. com/pages/tp.asp?TID=1857&CID=2&SID=3> (accessed 15 January 2007).

[107] "Cong an dung vu khi sieu am Dan ap cong nhan bieu tinh" [Security police use ultrasound to suppress workers' demonstration], *Dang Dan Chu Nhan Dan*, 15 February 2006 <http://www.freewebs.com/dangdanchunhandan/tailieu.htm> (accessed 27 October 2006).

[108] One such incident appears in "Quan he lao dong ngay cang ran nut" [Labour relations becoming more fractured], *Lao Dong*, 4 April 2007 <http://www. laodong.com.vn /Home/congdoan/tranhchapld/2007/4/30521.laodong> (accessed 17 April 2007).

[109] If such arrests occur, the three newspapers I am primarily using may not report them, but newsletters published by government critics in Vietnam would; yet I have thus far found no such reports there, either. Vietnamese and foreign

observers of strikes with whom I have spoken also have no information about strikers being arrested.

110 "Giai phap han che dinh cong" (see note 74); Truong Giang Long, "Giai Cap cong nhan Viet Nam — Thuc Trang va Suy Ngam" [Vietnam's working class: Reality and thought], *Tap Chi Cong San* [Journal of the Communist Party], 17 December 2007 <http://www.tapchicongsan.org.vn/details.asp?Object=4 &news_ ID=171239103> (accessed 5 May 2008).

111 Radio Free Asia, 19 April 2006 <http://www.rfa.org/ vietnamese/chuyenmuc/ YouthForum/ 2006/04/19/Vietnamese_Workers_talk_about_Their_lives_TMi/> (accessed 8 February 2007).

112 "Khong the coi cuoc dinh cong chua dung trinh tu, thu tuc la bat hop phap" [Should not see strikes that don't conform to formalities as illegal], *Thanh Nien*, 30 March 2006 <http://www3.thanhnien.com.vn/Xahoi/2006/3/30/143752. tno> (accessed 13 April 2006). For considerable evidence of debates among policymakers about how to protect workers while also keeping Vietnam attractive for investors, see Tran, "Alternatives to the 'Race to the Bottom'".

113 Tellingly, officials rarely say, at least not in public, that the strikes are "illegal" [*khong hop phap, khong hop le,* or *bat hop phap*]. Instead they describe the strikes as "spontaneous" [*tu phat*].

114 See, for example, the report of comments by delegate Nguyen Dinh Xuan of Tay Ninh Province during a National Assembly debate in June 2006 about revising the Labour Code. "Quoc hoi thao luan du an Luat sua doi bo sung mot so dieu cua Bo luat Lao dong" [National Assembly debates draft legislation and amendments to Labour Code], *Nhan Dan*, 7 June 2006 <http:// www.nhandan.com.vn/tinbai/?top=37&sub=130&Article=64235> (accessed 23 October 2006).

115 See discussions about a communiqué from MOLISA regarding such compensation: "Dinh cong va luat dinh cong tai Viet Nam" [Strikes and the law in Vietnam], Radio Free Asia, 6 June 2008 <http://www.rfa.org/vietnamese/ vietnam/xa-hoi/Strike-in-vietnam-NTran-06062008122012> (accessed 22 June 2008).

116 See, for example, "Dinh cong lam quan he lao dong lanh manh" [Strikes make wholesome labour relations], *Lao Dong*, 9 June 2006 <http://www.laodong. com.vn/new/congdoan/index.html> (accessed 13 June 2006); and "Cong doan o dau khi cong nhan dinh cong?" [Where is the trade union when workers strike?], *Tuoi Tre*, 28 October 2006 <http://www.tuoitre.com.vn/Tianyon/Index. aspx?ArticleID=169444&ChannelID=3> (accessed 2 November 2006). For an interview with the government's chief inspector for industrial relations, see "Giai phap thao 'ngoi' tranh chap lao dong?" [Defusing labour conflicts?], *Lao Dong*, 27 April 2006 <http://www.laodong.com.vn/pls/bld/folder$.view_ item_detail(155037> (accessed 28 April 2006).

117 "Quoc hoi nghe trinh sau du an luat" [National Assembly hears six reports on draft legislation], *Nhan Dan*, 1 June 2006 <http://www.nhandan.com. vn/tinbai/?top=37&sub=50&Article=63688> (accessed 24 October 2006).

118 A statement saying essentially this came from the VGCL's Legal Department [Ban Phap Luat Tong Lien Doan], 10 March 2006 <http://www.congdoanvn. org.vn/printdocument.asp?Message ID=275> (accessed 20 October 2006).

119 See the thoughtful analysis by Jonathan Stromseth, "Reform and Response in Vietnam: State-Society Relations and the Changing Political Economy" (Ph.D. dissertation, Columbia University, 1998), pp. 207–26.

120 For samples of these discussions, see "Cong nhan qua suc chiu dung moi dinh cong" [Workers put up with more than they can endure before striking], VietNamNet, 4 May 2006 <http://www.vietnamnet.vn/xahoi/ laodong/2006/05/567168/> (accessed 22 March 2007); "Noi chua co cong doan thi ai lanh dao dinh cong?" [Who leads strikes where no union exists?], *Lao Dong*, 11 August 2006 <http://www.congdoanvn.org.vn/printdocument. asp?MessageID=674> (accessed 20 October 2006); "Nguoi lao dong duoc cu ban dai dien de to chuc dinh cong" [Workers' representatives may organize strikes], *Tuoi Tre*, 27 September 2006 <http://www.tuoitre.com.vn/Tianyon/ Index.aspx?ArticleID=164055&ChannelID=3> (accessed 28 September 2006); "Dinh cong bat hop phap se phai boi thuong" [Illegal strikes will have to pay damages], VietNamNet, 27 October 2006 <http://www.vietnamnet.vn/service/ printversion.vnn?article_id=857706> (accessed 3 November 2006); "Cong doan o dau khi cong nhan dinh cong?" (see note 116).

121 For some news coverage of the discussions, see "Can thao go nguyen nhan dan den dinh cong" [Need to solve causes of strikes], *Lao Dong*, 5 June 2006 <http://www.laodong.com.vn/new/congdoan/index.html> (accessed 7 June 2006); " Khong dinh cong khi co tranh chap lao dong ve quyen?" [No strike when a labour conflict is about rights?], *Dai Doan Ket*, 11 August 2006, p. 1; "Hoi nghi Quoc Hoi" [National Assembly Conference], *Phap Luat*, 11 August 2006; "Chi duoc dinh cong khi chu khong chap hanh cach giai quyet cua co quan nha nuoc" [Strikes permitted only when employer does not abide by state offices' solutions], *Tien Phong*, 27 September 2006 <http://www.tien phongonline.com.vn/Tianyon/Index.aspx?ArticleID=61546&ChannelID=2> (accessed 28 September 2006); "Quoc hoi thao luan cac du an luat ve lao dong va viec lam" [National Assembly debates draft legislation regarding labour and work], *Nhan Dan*, 27 October 2006 <http://www.nhandan.com. vn/tinbai/?top=37&sub=50&Article=77577> (accessed 28 November 2006).

122 This conforms with the "dialogical" interpretation of Vietnam's political system. For an elaboration of that interpretation, see Hy V. Luong, "Postwar Vietnamese Society: An Overview of Transformational Dynamics", in *Postwar Vietnam: Dynamics of a Transforming Society*, edited by Hy V. Luong (Boulder:

Rowman and Littlefield, and Singapore: ISEAS, 2003), pp. 22–25; and Benedict J. Tria Kerkvliet, *The Power of Everyday Politics: How Vietnamese Peasants Transformed National Policy* (Ithaca: Cornell University Press, 2005), pp. 33–36.

References

Amnesty International. "Viet Nam: Farmers' Union Crushed", May 2007, circulated via Steve Denney's Vietnam News List (vnnews-l), 1 May 2007, <http://coombs. anu.edu.au/~vern/forum.html?>.

Bao Binh Duong [Binh Duong Province newspaper]. "Kien quyet xu ly nhung hanh vi qua khich" [Resolutely addressing extreme actions], 6 January 2006 <http://www.baobinhduong.org.vn/detail.aspx?Item=1229&Kind=8> (accessed 23 May 2007).

———. "Vi sao cong nhan van dinh cong tu phat?" [Why do workers still strike spontaneously?], 24 February 2006 <http://www.baobinhduong.org.vn/detail. aspx?Item=2577&Kind=7> (accessed 23 May 2007).

Bao Dong Nai [Dong Nai Province newspaper]. "Ngan ngua nhung vu dinh cong lien quan den nang luong" [Strike prevention linked to wage hikes], 14 March 2007 <http://www.baodongnai.com.vn/default.aspx?tabid=573 &idmid=&ItemID=16906> (accessed 29 March 2007).

———. "Giam thieu cac vu phan ung ngung viec tap the" [Reducing collective work stoppages], 25 July 2007 <http://www.baodongnai.com.vn/default. aspx?tabid=585&idmid=&ItemID=20918> (accessed 7 August 2007).

BBC Vietnamese. "Cong nhan hang giay Nike dinh cong" [Nike shoemakers go on strike], BBC Vietnamese, 29 November 2007 <http://www.bbc.co.uk/ vietnamese/vietnam/story/2007/11/071129_nike_factory_strike.shtml> (accessed 5 December 2007).

———. "Dinh cong nam sau cao hon nam truoc" [More strikes than previous year], 9 January 2009 <http://www.bbc.co.uk/vietnamese/vietnam/story/ 2009/01/090109_strikes_statistics.shtml> (accessed 14 January 2009).

Bureau of Labour Statistics. *Labour Law and Practice in the Republic of Viet-Nam.* Washington, D.C.: United States Department of Labour, 1968.

Cao Van Luong. *Cong Nhan Mien Nam Vietnam trong cuoc Khang Chien Chong My Cuu Nuoc* [Southern Vietnamese workers during the War for National Salvation against the United States]. Hanoi: Khoa Hoc Xa Hoi, 1977.

Chae, Suhong. "Spinning Work and Leaving Life: The Politics of Production in a Capitalistic Multinational Textile Factory in Vietnam". Ph.D. dissertation, City University of New York, 2003.

Chan, Anita and Wang Hong-zen. "The Impact of the State on Workers' Conditions: Comparing Taiwanese Factories in China and Vietnam". *Pacific Affairs* 77 (Winter 2004–2005): 629–46.

Clarke, Simon. "The Changing Character of Strikes in Vietnam". *Post-Communist Economies* 18 (September 2006): 345–61.

Clarke, Simon, Lee Chang-Hee, and Do Quynh Chi. "From Rights to Interests: The Challenge of Industrial Relations in Vietnam". *Journal of Industrial Relations* 49, no. 4 (2007): 545–68.

Committee to Protect Journalists. Press release, New York, 4 February 2008.

Dai Doan Ket. "Khong dinh cong khi co tranh chap lao dong ve quyen?" [No strike when a labour conflict is about rights?], 11 August 2006, p. 1.

Dan Chim Viet. "Tran Khai Thanh Thuy bi bat giam" [Tran Khai Thanh Thuy arrested], *Dan Chim Viet*, 22 April 2007 <http://www.danchimviet.com/php/modules.php?name=News&file=article&sid=3276> (accessed 15 June 2007).

Dan Chu Net. <http://www.danchu.net/ArticlesChinhLuan/0.0.0.Collection.2006.I/HuynhNgocCanh.601.htm> (accessed 25 April 2006).

Dang Dan Chu Nhan Dan [People's Democratic Party] website <http://www.freewebs.com/dangdanchunhandan/> (accessed 23 February 2007).

―――. "Cong an dung vu khi sieu am Dan ap cong nhan bieu tinh" [Security police use ultrasound to suppress workers' demonstration], *Dang Dan Chu Nhan Dan*, 15 February 2006 <http://www.freewebs.com/dangdanchunhandan/tailieu.htm> (accessed 27 October 2006).

Dien Thu [Electronic letter], a publication of the Dang Dan Chu Nhan Dan [People's Democracy Party], July 2007, pp. 4–5.

Duong Van Sao and Vu Minh Tien. "Dinh cong thoi gian qua — nhin tu goc do cong doan" [Recent strikes – seen from a trade union perspective], *Lao Dong & Cong Doan* [Labour & Trade Union], April 2006, pp. 10–11, 15.

Hannah, Joseph. "Local Non-Government Organization in Vietnam: Development, Civil Society and State-Society Relations". Ph.D. dissertation, University of Washington, Seattle, 2007.

Hiep Hoi Doan Ket Cong-Nong Vietnam [United Workers-Farmers Association]. Ban Tuyen Bo [Official announcement], 30 October 2008, *Tu Do Ngon Luan* <http://www.tdngonluan.com/tailieu.htm> (accessed 23 February 2007).

Hoang Phuc Vinh. "Ve cuoc Dinh cong cua 24,000 cong nhan Vietnam" [On the strikes of 24,000 workers], 28 December 2005, *Thong Luan* <http://www.thongluan.org/vn/ modules.php?name=News&file= article&sid=382> (accessed 12 January 2006).

Hoang Quoc Viet. *Nhung Net So Luoc ve Lich Su Phong Trao Cong Nhan va Cong DoanVietnam* [Features of Vietnam's labour and trade union movement]. Hanoi: Lao Dong, 1959.

Independent Trade Union of Vietnam. 20 October 2006, Dan Chim Viet [Viet Flock] <http://www.danchimviet.com/php/modules.php?name=News&file=article&sid=2523>(accesed 16 January 2007).

Kerkvliet, Benedict J. Tria. *The Power of Everyday Politics: How Vietnamese Peasants Transformed National Policy*. Ithaca: Cornell University Press, 2005.
Lao Dong. "Lanh dao vo trach nhiem, cong nhan bi bo roi" [Worker wrongly dismissed], 27 December 2004 <http://www.laodong.com.vn/pls/bld/folder$.view_item_ detail(120405> (accessed 5 May 2006).
———. "Chi co the noi bang dinh cong!" [Can speak only by going on strike], 12 May 2005 <http://www.laodong.com.vn/pls/bld/folder$.view_item_detail (129565)> (accessed 5 May 2006).
———. "Chi moi nhuong bo 3/8 'yeu sach' cua CN" [Conceding only 3/8 of workers' demands], 13 May 2005 <http://www.laodong.com.vn/pls/bld/folder$.view_item_detail(129710> (accessed 5 May 2006).
———. "100% yeu sach cua cong nhan duoc dap ung" [100% of workers' demands met], 14 May 2005, p. 1ff.
———. "Gioi chu khong chiu nhuong bo yeu sach tang luong" [Owners not yielding to demands for higher wages], 19 May 2005 <http://www.laodong.com.vn/pls/bld/folder$.view_item_detail(130095> (accessed 5 May 2006).
———. "Tranh chap LD va dinh cong gia tang: Han che bang cach nao?" [Labour conflicts and strikes increasing: How can they be limited?], 24 May 2005 <http://www.laodong.com.vn/pls/bld/folder$.view_item_detail(130531)> (accessed 5 May 2006).
———. "Ket thuc thang loi sau 12 ngay dinh cong" [Victory after a 12-Day strike], 25 May 2005 <http://www1.laodong.com.vn/pls/bld/display$.htnoidung (36,130595)> (accessed 7 May 2008).
———. "Mat 10 ngay de khoi phuc san xuat" [Ten days needed to resume production], 6 June 2005, pp 1ff.
———. "Cong nhan Xi nghiep may Bach Hoa 1: Xin nghi viec, khong duoc tra luong?" [Unpaid garment makers at Bach Hoa 1 Enterprise to stop work], 4 July 2005 <hhtp://www.laodong.com.vn/pls/bld/folder$.view_item_detail(133579)> (accessed 4 May 2006).
———. "Cong nhan cong ty det Minh Khai (Hanoi) dinh cong" [Minh Khai Company workers strike], 21 October 2005 <http://www.laodong.com.vn/pls/bld/folder$.view_item_detail(141488)> (accessed 4 May 2006).
———. "Gan 18.000 cong nhan dinh cong, doi nang luong toi thieu" [Nearly 18,000 workers strike for higher minimum wage], 29 December 2005 <http://www.laodong.com.vn/pls/bld/folder$.view_item_detail(146579)> (accessed 4 May 2006).
———. "Hon 5.000 cong nhan dinh cong doi nang luong toi thieu" [More than 5,000 workers strike for higher minimum wage], 30 December 2005 <http://www.laodong.com.vn/pls/bld/folder$.view_item_detail(146723> (accessed 4 May 2006).

————. "Nguoi lao dong dinh cong doi tang luong toi thieu tai cac doanh nghiep FDI o TP.Ho Chi Minh" [Striking labourers demand higher minimum wages at foreign-invested enterprises in HCMC], 4 January 2006 <http://www.laodong. com.vn/pls/bld/folder$.view_item_detail(146952> (accessed 4 May 2006).

————. "Dinh cong doi nang luong toi thieu lan rong" [Strike calls for higher minimum wage], 6 January 2006 <http://www.laodong.com.vn/pls/bld/folder$. view_item_detail(147169> (accessed 4 May 2006).

————. "No luc ngan chan dinh cong" [Efforts to stop strikes], 11 January 2006 <http://www.laodong.com.vn/pls/bld /folder$.view_item_detail(147530> (accessed 4 May 2006).

————. "Noi buon com ao" [Sad way to live], 28 February 2006 <http://www. laodong.com.vn/pls/bld/folder$.view_item_detail(150350)> (accessed 4 May 2006).

————. "Sa thai lao dong nu trai luat" [Illegal firing of female employee], 28 March 2006 <http://www.laodong.com.vn/pls/bld/folder$.view_item_detail(152616> (accessed 4 May 2006).

————. "Giai phap thao 'ngoi' tranh chap lao dong?" [Defusing labour conflicts?], 27 April 2006 <http://www.laodong.com.vn/pls/bld/folder$.view_item_detail (155037> (accessed 28 April 2006).

————. "Can thao go nguyen nhan dan den dinh cong" [Need to solve causes of strikes], 5 June 2006 <http://www.laodong.com.vn/new/congdoan/index.html> (accessed 7 June 2006).

————. "Dinh cong lam quan he lao dong lanh manh" [Strikes make wholesome labour relations], 9 June 2006 <http://www.laodong.com.vn/new/congdoan /index.html> (accessed 13 June 2006).

————. "Khong thuc hien theo quy dinh" [Improper implementation], 3 July 2006 <http://www.laodong.com.vn/new/congdoan/index.html> (accessed 4 July 2006).

————. "Dinh cong o Cong ty TNHH Rau Nha Xanh (Lam Dong)" [Strike at Rau Nha Xanh Company in Lam Dong], 21 July 2006 <http://www.laodong.com. vn/pls/bld/folder$.view_item_detail(134903> (accessed 4 May 2006).

————. "Noi chua co cong doan thi ai lanh dao dinh cong?" [Who leads strikes where no union exists?], 11 August 2006 <http://www.congdoanvn.org.vn/ printdocument.asp?MessageID=674> (accessed 20 October 2006).

————. "Kien nghi dang ra nghi quyet ve giai cap cong nhan" [Party resolution produces decision regarding working class], 25 August 2006, p. 2.

————. "Hon mot tram CN dinh cong *doi* no luong" [Over 100 workers strike over unpaid wages], *Lao Dong*, 11 September 2006 <http://www.laodong.com. vn/pls/bld/display$.htnoidung(36,165993> (accessed 12 September 2006).

————. "Thay gi qua cuoc lan cong o Cty LD Ty Xuan?" [What's to be seen from the slow-down at Ty Xuan Company?], 23 October 2006 <http://www.laodong

LaoDongNewsOct2006.com.vn/Home/congdoan/tranhchapld/2006/10/8081.
laodong> (accessed 25 October 2006).

———. "Han che ca quyen lam me cua nguoi lao dong" [Limits on Workers'
Motherhood Rights], 31 October 2006 <http://www.laodong.com.vn/Home/
congdoan/tranhchapld/2006/10/9129.laodong> (accessed 2 November
2006).

———. "Chia re nguoi lao dong voi cong Doan?" [Dividing workers and unions?],
11 December 2006 <http://www.laodong.com.vn/Home/congdoan/tranhchapld
/2006/12/14664.laodong> (accessed 3 January 2007).

———. "3.500 cong nhan dinh cong" [3,500 workers strike], 12 December 2006
<http://www.laodong.com.vn/Home/congdoan/tranhchapld/2006/12/14746.
laodong> (accessed 3 January 2007).

———. "Hau qua tu vi pham nghiem trong Luat lao dong" [Consequences of
serious violations of the Labour Code], 21 December 2006 <http://www.laodong.
com.vn/Home/congdoan/tranhchapld/2006/12/16021.laodong> (accessed
3 January 2007).

———. "Cong nhan dinh cong doi nang luong va thuong tet" [Striking workers
demand higher wages and Tet bonus], 3 February 2007 <http://www.laodong.
com.vn/Home/congdoan/tranhchapld/2007/2/22437.laodong> (accessed
15 February 2007).

———. "Thuc hien Bo luat Lao Dong tai Khanh Hoa" [Implementing Labour
Code in Khanh Hoa], 9 February 2007 <http://www.laodong.com.vn/Home/
congdoan/tranhchapld/2007/2/23357.laodong> (accessed 15 February 2007).

———. "Quan he lao dong ngay cang ran nut" [Labour relations becoming
more fractured], 4 April 2007 <http://www.laodong.com.vn/Home/congdoan/
tranhchapld/2007/4/30521.laodong> (accessed 17 April 2007).

———. "Cong ty TNHH Kido Hanoi (Hung Yen): 1.700 CN dinh cong doi tang
luong" [Hanoi Kido Company: 1,700 strikers demand wage hikes], 12 April
2007 <http://www.laodong.com.vn/Home/congdoan/tranhchapld/2007/4/31748.
laodong> (accessed 17 April 2007).

———. "Quyen loi nguoi lao dong trong hoi nhap kinh te" [Workers' rights
in a world economy], 15 May 2007 <http://www.laodong.com.vn/Home/
congdoan/2007/5/36279.laodong> (accessed 21 May 2007).

———. "Doanh nghiep sach Than Nghia — TPHCM" [Than Nghia Books HCMC],
31 July 2007 <hhtp://www.laodong.com.vn/Home/congdoan/tranhchapld/
2007/7/48269.laodong> (accessed 1 August 2007).

———. "Quan he lao dong nhieu bat on" [Many uncertainties for labour relations],
6 September 2007 <http://www.laodong.com.vn/Home/congdoan/2007/9/53933.
laodong> (accessed 10 September 2007).

———. "Vu lan cong cua 300 cong nhan Cty TNHH Wonderful" [Slow-down
by 300 workers at the Wonderful Saigon Garment Company], 31 December

2007 <http://www.laodong.com.vn/Home/congdoan/2007/12/71187.laodong> (accessed 11 February 2008).

———. "Hai vu dinh cong ve luong" [Two strikes over wages], 10 January 2008 <http://beta.baomoi.com/Home/KinhTe/LaoDong/www.laodong.com. vn/Hai_vu_ dinh_cong_ve_luong__thuong_chua_co_hoi_ket/1300919.epi> (accessed 15 January 2008)

———. "Tiep tuc co 4 vu dinh cong ve luong — thuong" [Four continuing strikes over wages and bonuses], 11 January 2008 <hhtp://www.laodong.vn/Home/ congdoan/2008/1/72616.laodong> (accessed 15 January 2008)

———. "Luong, thuong chua tuong xung voi cong lao dong" [Wages and bonuses not yet acceptable to workers], 14 January 2008 <http://www.laodong.com. vn/Home/congdoan/tranh chapld/2008/1/72907.laodong> (accessed 11 February 2008).

———. "'That da day vi chuyen ao com" ['Pull in your stomach' for the hard times], 7 March 2008 <http://www.laodong.com.vn/Home/phongsu/2008/3/79370. laodong> (accessed 12 March 2008).

———. "Dinh cong la cong cu cuoi cung" [Striking is the last resort], 16 August 2008,<http://www.laodong.com.vn/Home/congdoan/2008/8/102446.laodong> (accessed 20 August 2008).

Luce, Don, and John Sommer. *Viet Nam: The Unheard Voices*. Ithaca: Cornell University Press, 1969.

Luong, Hy V. "Postwar Vietnamese Society: An Overview of Transformational Dynamics". In *Postwar Vietnam: Dynamics of a Transforming Society*, edited by Hy V. Luong, pp. 1–26. Boulder: Rowman and Littlefield, and Singapore: ISEAS, 2003.

Nghiem Lien Huong. "Jokes in a Garment Workshop in Hanoi: How does Humour Foster the Perception of Community in Social Movements?". *International Review of Social History* 52 (2007): 209–23.

Nguoi Lao Dong. "Vi sao cac cuoc dinh cong ngay cang nhieu hon, nong hon?" [Why are strikes becoming more numerous and heated?], 27 September 2000, p. 3.

———. "Lam gi de han che tranh chap, dinh cong?" [How can conflicts and strikes be limited?], 3 November 2000, p. 3.

———. "Can co cai nhin khac ve dinh cong" [Need to look at strikes differently], 17 December 2006 <http://www.nld.com.vn/tintuc/cong-doan/210108.asp> (accessed 20 December 2007).

———. "'Khoanh vung' giai quyet dinh cong" [Setting limits for resolving strikes], 26 February 2007 <http://www.nld.com.vn/tintuc/cong-doan/181365. asp> (accessed 16 March 2007).

———. "Lam quyen hanh xu trai luat" [Behaviour contrary to law], 16 April 2007 <http://www.nld.com.vn/tintuc/cong-doan/quyen-nghia-vu/186443.asp> (accessed 18 April 2007).

———. "Bua an ngay cang te" [Meals worsen by the day], 2 July 2007 <http://www.nld.com.vn/tintuc/cong-doan/194162.asp> (accessed 5 July 2007).

———. "Co thuc moi vuc duoc dao" [To be ethical and honest, a person needs to be fed and clothed], 4 July 2007 <http://www.nld.com.vn/tintuc/cong-doan/quyen-nghia-vu/194361.asp> (accessed 5 July 2007).

———. "That lung buoc bung den bao gio?" [Belt tightening for how long?], 4 July 2007 <http://www.nld.com.vn/tintuc/cong-doan/194274.asp> (accessed 5 July 2007).

———. "Khong nen xem loi nhuan la tat ca" [No need to see profits as everything], 11 July 2007 <http://www.nld.com.vn/tintuc/cong-doan/194987.asp> (accessed 11 July 2007).

———. "Dinh cong" [Strike], 27 August 2007 <www.nld.com.vn/tintuc/cong-doan/200511.asp> (accessed August 28, 2007).

———. 29 August 2007 <http://www.nld.com.vn/tintuc/cong-doan/200603.asp> (accessed 30 August 2007).

———. "Vu tranh chap tai Cong ty Hue Phong-TPHCM" [Conflict at Hue Phong Company-HCMC], 5 May 2008 <http://www.nld.com.vn/tintuc/cong-doan/223736.asp> (accessed 8 May 2008).

Nguyen Ngoc Linh. "The Working Man in Vietnam". Saigon: Vietnam Council on Foreign Relations, not dated, circa 1970.

Nguyen Minh Quang. "20,000 cong nhan Dinh cong, Bieu Tinh" [20,000 workers strike, demonstrate], DCVOnline, 14 March 2006, at TiengDanKeu [Cry of the people] website <http://www.tiengdankeu.net/, section Ho So Dinh cong [Strike folder]> (accessed 9 March 2007).

Nguyen Quang Quynh. *Nhung Van De Lao Dong va Xa Hoi Hien Dai* [Current labour and social issues]. Saigon: Lua Thieng, 1974.

Nguyen Van Huy. "Hai Vu An Tho Bao Dang Luu Y" [Two brutal cases worth noticing]. *Thong Luan* (February 2009): 13–14.

Nhan Dan. "Quoc hoi nghe trinh sau du an luat" [National Assembly hears six reports on draft legislation], *Nhan Dan*, 1 June 2006 <http://www.nhandan.com.vn/tinbai/?top=37&sub=50&Article=63688> (accessed 24 October 2006).

———. "Quoc hoi thao luan du an Luat sua doi bo sung mot so Dieu cua Bo luat lao dong" [National Assembly debates draft legislation and amendments to Labour Code], *Nhan Dan*, 7 June 2006 <http://www.nhandan.com.vn/tinbai/?top=37&sub=130&Article=64235> (accessed 23 October 2006).

———. "Quoc hoi thao luan cac du an luat ve lao dong va viec lam" [National Assembly debates draft legislation regarding labour and work], *Nhan Dan*, 27 October 2006 <http://www.nhandan.com.vn/tinbai/?top=37&sub=50&Article=77577> (accessed 28 November 2006).

Nien Giam Thong Ke Statistical Yearbook of Vietnam 2008. Hanoi: Thong Ke.

Phap Luat [Law]. "Giai phap han che dinh cong" [Addressing strike restrictions], 18 May 2006 <http://www.congdoanvn.org.vn/printdocument.asp?MessageID =440> (accessed 20 October 2006).

————. "Hoi nghi Quoc Hoi" [National Assembly Conference], 11 August 2006, p. 3.

Radio Free Asia. 4 March 2006 <http://www.rfa.org/vietnamese/in_depth/2006/03/04/ vnpress_review_NNguyen/> (accessed 8 February 2007).

————. Interview with Nguyen Tan Hoanh, 24 March 2006 <http://www.doi-thoai. com/baimoi0306_336.html> (accessed 21 April 2006).

————. 19 April 2006 <http://www.rfa.org/vietnamese/chuyenmuc/YouthForum/ 2006/04/19/Vietnamese_Workers_talk_about_Their_lives_TMi/> (accessed 8 February 2007).

————. "Doi song cong nhan Vietnam thoi ky mo cua" [Vietnamese workers' lives in the Open Door period], 31 October 2007 <http://www.rfa.org/vietnamese/ in_depth/2007/10/31/VnWorkersSeriesPIPresentDayLaborForces_GMinh/> (accessed 2 November 2007).

————. 1 November 2007 <http://www.rfa.org/vietnamese/in_depth/2007/11/01/ VnWorkerLowWagesAndInsufficientCareP2_GMinh/> (accessed 2 November 2007).

————. Interview with Nguyen Tan Hoanh, 18 May 2008 <http://www.rfa. org/vietnamese/HumanRights/Nguyen-Tan-Hoanh-political-prisoner-set-free-VHung-05182008134432.html> (accessed 27 May 2008).

————. Interview with Le Dang Doanh, 26 May 2008 <http://www.rfa.org/ vietnamese/in_depth/Interview_with_economist_LeDangDoanh_about_wave_ of_labour_strikes_in_Vietnam_NNguyen-05262008103135.html> (accessed 27 May 2008).

————. "Dinh cong va luat dinh cong tai Vietnam" [Strikes and the law in Vietnam], 6 June 2008 <http://www.rfa.org/vietnamese/vietnam/xa-hoi/Strike-in-vietnam-NTran-06062008122012> (accessed 22 June 2008).

Reuters. "Vietnam: Labour Strikes Increased by 30%", 16 August 1999, <http:// elisa.anu.edu.au:8080/current/0000026.bsk/AA6RC00C.htm> (accessed 20 August 1999).

————. "Vietnam's 2008 Average Inflation at 22.97 pct", 25 December 2008, <http://uk.reuters.com/article/idUKHAN40610920081225> (accessed 18 September 2009).

Sai Gon Giai Phong [Saigon Liberation]. "Doi song cong nhan o TPHCM" [Workers' lives in HCMC], *Sai Gon Giai Phong* [Saigon Liberation (newspaper published by HCMC branch of the CPV)], 23 August 2007 <http://www.sggp. org.vn/xahoi/2007/8/117054/#> (accessed 27 August 2007).

Saigon Net. "Vi sao cong nhan dinh cong trien mien?" [Why strikes are entangled], 16 April 2008 <http://www.saigonnet.vn/detail.aspx?flag=1&item=44959> (accessed 8 May 2008).

Stromseth, Jonathan. "Reform and Response in Vietnam: State-Society Relations and the Changing Political Economy". Ph.D. dissertation, Columbia University, 1998.

Thanh Nien. "'Lien khuc' dinh cong" [Potpourri of strikes], 3 March 2006 <http://www3.thanhnien.com.vn/Xahoi/2006/3/3/140573.tno> (accessed 13 April 2006).

———. "Khong the coi cuoc dinh cong chua Dung trinh tu, thutuc la bat hop phap" [Should not see strikes that don't conform to fomalities as illegal], 30 March 2006 <http://www3.thanhnien.com.vn/Xahoi/2006/3/30/143752.tno> (accessed 13 April 2006).

———. "Tu cac cuoc dinh cong cua cong nhan tai tinh Binh Duong" [Workers' strikes in Binh Duong], *Thanh Nien*, 26 October 2007, http://<http://www1.than hnien.com.vn/doisong/2007/10/26/213781.tno> (accessed October 29, 2007).

Tien Phong. "Chi duoc dinh cong khi chukhong chap hanh cach giai quyet cua co quan nha nuoc" [Strikes permitted only when employer does not abide by state offices' solutions], 27 September 2006 <http://www.tien phongonline.com.vn/Tianyon/Index.aspx?ArticleID=61546&ChannelID=2> (accessed 28 September 2006).

Ton Vy. "Workers' Struggle". *Vietnamese Studies* 8 (1966): 93–98.

Tong Lien Doan Lao Dong Vietnam [VGCL]. *Lich Su Phong Trao Cong Nhan va Cong Doan Vietnam* [History of Vietnam's worker and union movement], vol. 2, 1954–1975. Hanoi: Lao Dong, 2004.

Tran, Angie Ngoc. "Sewing for the Global Economy". In *Critical Globalization Studies*, edited by Richard P. Appelbaum and William I. Robinson, pp. 379–92. New York: Routledge, 2005.

———. "The Third Sleeve: Emerging Labour Newspapers and the Response of Labour Unions and the State to Workers Resistance in Vietnam". *Labour Studies Journal* 32 (September 2007): 257–79.

———. "Alternatives to the 'Race to the Bottom' in Vietnam: Minimum Wage Strikes and Their Aftermath". *Labor Studies Journal* 32 (December 2007): 430–51.

———. "Contested 'Flexibility': Networks of Place, Gender, and Class in Vietnamese Workers' Resistance". In *Taking Southeast Asia to Market: Commodities, Nature, and People in the Neoliberal Age*, edited by Joseph Nevins and Nancy Lee Peluso, pp. 56–72. Ithaca: Cornell University Press, 2008.

Tran Van Giau. *Giai Cap Cong Nhan Viet Nam* [Vietnam's working class]. Hanoi: Su That, 1961.

Trinh Quang Quy. *Phong Trao Lao Dong Vietnam* [Vietnam Labour Movement]. Saigon: n.p., 1970.

Truong Giang Long, "Giai cap cong nhan Viet Nam — Thuc Trang va Suy Ngam" [Vietnam's working class: Reality and thought], *Tap Chi Cong San* [Journal of the Communist Party], 17 December 2007 <http://www.tapchicongsan.org.vn/details.asp?Object=4&news_ID=171239103> (accessed 5 May 2008).

Tu Do Ngon Luan. "Ky Su Dao Van Thuy Len An Manh Me Nha Cam Quyen CSVN Dan Ap Cong DoanDoc Lap Va Ca Nhan Anh" [Dao Van Thuy charges Communist authorities with repression against independent trade union and himself] <http://www.tudongonluanonline.com/pages/tp.asp?TID=1857&CID=2&SID=3> (accessed 15 January 2007).

————. <http://www.tdngonluan.com/tailieu/tl_lmdcnq_khangthu_01.htm> (accessed 10 July 2009).

Tuoi Tre [Youth]. "Vu dinh cong tai Cong ty TNHH Sao Vang (Hai Phong)" [Strike at Red Star Company, Hai Phong], 22 February 2006 <http://www.tuoitre.com.vn/Tianyon/PrintView.aspx?ArticleID=124135&ChannelID=3> (accessed 23 February 2006).

————. "Nguoi lao dong Duoc cu ban Dai dien De to chuc dinh cong" [Workers' representatives may organize strikes], 27 September 2006 <http://www.tuoitre.com.vn/Tianyon/Index.aspx?ArticleID=164055&ChannelID=3> (accessed 28 September 2006).

————. "Cong doan o dau khi cong nhan dinh cong?" [Where is the trade union when workers strike?], 28 October 2006 <http://www.tuoitre.com.vn/Tianyon/Index.aspx?ArticleID=169444&ChannelID=3> (accessed 2 November 2006).

————. "Cong nhan chong choi voi 'bao' tang gia" [Workers resist the storm of rising costs], 19 July 2007 <http://www3.tuoitre.com.vn/Vieclam/Index.aspx?ArticleID=211149 &ChannelID=269> (accessed 19 July 2007).

————. "Cuc lam doi cong nhan!" [Workers' lives are very desperate!], 20 October 2007 <http://www.tuoitre.com.vn/Tianyon2/Index.aspx?ArticleID=225252 &ChannelID=118> (accessed 4 April 2008).

————. "Nhoc nhan doi cong nhan" [The weary life of a worker], 22 October 2007 <http://www.tuoitre.com.vn/Tianyon2/Index.aspx?ArticleID+225522&ChannelID=89> (accessed 4 April 2008).

Tuong Vu. "Workers and the Socialist State: North Vietnam's State-Labor Relations, 1945–1970". *Communist and Post-Communist Studies* 38 (2005): 329–56.

United States Agency for International Development (USAID). Trade Union Branch, Labor Division. "Report on Trade Unions in Viet Nam". In *Labor in Vietnam*, vol. 2 (1970): 1–10.

VGCL. "Ve Tinh Hinh Dinh cong …" [The strike situation], 28 August 2006, 20 VGCL website,www.congdoanvn.org.vn/printdocument.asp?MessageID=712> (accessed October 2006).

VGCL. Legal Department [Ban Phap Luat Tong Lien Doan]. 10 March 2006 <http://www.congdoanvn.org.vn/printdocument.asp?Message ID=275> (accessed 20 October 2006).

VietBao. "Bac Giang: Hon 100 cong nhan may bi sa thai vo co" [Over 100 workers laid off without reasons], 6 January 2006, <http://vietbao.vn/Xa-hoi/Bac-Giang-Hon-100-cong-nhan-may-bi-sa-thai-vo-co/70035915/157/> (accessed 7 May 2008).

Vietnam News Network. "Cong Ty Hue Phong Khong Giai Quyet Dut Diem" [Hue Phong strike not definitely resolved], 2 May 2008 <http://www.vnn-news.com/breve.php3?id_breve=11665> (accessed 8 May 2008).

———. "Vu Dinh cong Hue Phong chua on" [Hue Phong strike not yet resolved], 5 May 2008 <http://www.vnn-news.com/breve.php3?id_breve=11681> (accessed 8 May 2008).

VNEconomy. "Vi sao cac dinh cong deu trai luat?" [Why are strikes contrary to the law?], 3 February 2006, VGCL website <http://www.congdoanvn.org.vn/print document.asp?MessageID=282> (accessed 20 October 2006).

VNExpress. "Can bo cong doan chua dam to chuc dinh cong" [Trade union officials have not yet dared to organize strikes], 16 July 2006, http://vnexpress.net/Vietnam/Xa-hoi/2006/07/3B9EBFF9/> (accessed 7 December 2007).

VietNamNet. "Cong nhan qua suc chiu dung moi dinh cong" [Workers put up with more than they can endure before striking], 4 May 2006 <http://www.vietnamnet.vn/xahoi/laodong/2006/05/567168/> (accessed 22 March 2007).

———. "Dinh cong bat hop phap se phai boi thuong" [Illegal strikes will have to pay damages], 27 October 2006 <http://www.vietnamnet.vn/service/printversion.vnn?article_id=857706> (accessed 3 November 2006).

———. "Don dap dinh cong khong chi vi luong" [Successive strikes are not just about wages], 5 January 2007 <http://www.vietnamnet.vn/xahoi/laodong/2006/01/529614/> (accessed 22 March 2007).

———. "Hai cong nhan bi troi chan tai noi lam viec" [Two workers' legs tied at workplace], 12 April 2007 <http://www.vietnamnet.vn/xahoi/laodong/2007/04/683865/> (accessed 19 April 2007).

———. "Cong nhan Hue Phong lai dinh cong" [Another Hue Phong strike], 11 April 2008, <http://vietnamnet.vn/xahoi/2008/04/777989/> (accessed 8 May 2008).

———. "Cong ty Hue Phong: Tranh chap da duoc giai quyet" [Hue Phong strike resolved], 22 April 2008, <http://vietnamnet.vn/xahoi/2008/04/779729/> (accessed 8 May 2008).

Wang Hong-zen. "Asian Transnational Corporations and Labor Rights: Vietnamese Trade Unions in Taiwan-invested Companies". *Journal of Business Ethics* 56 (Spring 2005): 43–53.

Wehrle, Edmund F. *Between a River and a Mountain: The AFL-CIO and the Vietnam War*. Ann Arbor: University of Michigan Press, 2005.

7

STRIKES IN VIETNAM AND CHINA IN TAIWANESE-OWNED FACTORIES
Diverging Industrial Relations Patterns

Anita Chan

In previous chapters we have seen that the number of strikes in Vietnam has exploded, especially in the country's export industries. This chapter takes the phenomenon of strikes in the export sector further by placing it in comparative perspective, using China as a foil. This can help to further our understanding of Vietnamese strikes and their implications for Vietnam's industrial relations system.

Even though Vietnam and China have emerged from similar histories of Communist Party rule, the labour laws of the two countries are a study in contrasts. Nowhere is the distinction more marked than in the regulation of strikes. Vietnam has legislated complex provisions detailing when and how strikes can legally occur, and specifying the negotiations that must precede a strike. The intent is to regulate labour discontent by providing workers with a collective bargaining platform and strike procedures when bargaining breaks down, so as to reduce the outbreak of wildcat strikes. Chinese law, in contrast, does not mention strike actions, and as a result they are neither legal nor illegal. We therefore might expect fewer strikes in Vietnam, where legal sanctions exist to regulate them; but the reverse is the case. Vietnam witnesses waves of wildcat strikes, whereas China observes far fewer strike actions. Also unexpected is that although the strikes in Vietnam are illegal, they are unimpeded by the authorities, who often in fact act in the interests of the strikers, whereas strikes in China which cannot be categorized as illegal are nonetheless normally vigorously suppressed by the authorities.[1]

To understand this sharp contrast in labour laws and their implementation, Section I of the chapter will compare the course of strikes in Vietnam and China. Section II will examine the underlying factors: the differences in the two countries' labour laws and legal regulatory regimes, the tripartite dispute-resolution institutions, the legal labour standards established by the governments, and the relationship between the government and the official trade union. Section III will analyze the trends in the two countries' industrial relations patterns.

It is appropriate to compare Vietnam and China given that both countries had had a planned command socialist economy and within the past several decades both have gone a long way toward dismantling that system, turning to the market, and integrating with global capitalism. But unlike most other former socialist states which have become multiparty political systems, the two Asian neighbours share in common the fact that they remain one-party regimes under their respective Communist parties. As Leninist states, both countries prohibit autonomous trade unions and instead grant a monopoly to official trade unions controlled by the party–state; the Vietnam General Confederation of Labour (VGCL) and the All-China Federation of Trade Unions (ACFTU). One question that arises is: Why, despite these similarities, are their industrial relations systems diverging?

It is important, when comparing industrial relations and factory strikes in both countries, to ensure that the factories examined share broadly similar characteristics. Accordingly, my field research has focused on factories owned and managed by Taiwanese companies to ensure the factories are run by corporations with a similar management style. In the same vein, the research focused largely on footwear factories. Different industries tend to have somewhat dissimilar work conditions, hire somewhat different types of workers, and give rise to somewhat different worker grievances and different courses of industrial action. Focusing largely on one industry — shoe manufacturing — in both countries avoids the pitfalls of studying dissimilar work situations. In each country, I conducted the field research on a region where Taiwanese-managed footwear factories are heavily concentrated.

I.
COMPARING STRIKES IN VIETNAM'S HCMC REGION AND IN CHINA'S PEARL RIVER DELTA

As noted, strikes have been far more common in Vietnam than in China. Strike waves began to erupt in Vietnam in 2006 (350 strikes) and reached a crescendo in 2008 (762 strikes),[2] dropping to 215 strikes in 2009,[3] a year of global economic recession. But once the economy picked up in early 2010, the strikes resumed. They have erupted most frequently in the export sector in Ho Chi Minh City (HCMC) and surrounding provinces, where Taiwanese-invested firms are concentrated. Firms from Taiwan, the third largest investor nation in Vietnam, operate some 2,000 to 3,000 factories there. According to the Taiwanese newspaper *Zhongguo Shibao*, Taiwanese firms have been particularly targeted by strikers, accounting for a disproportionate number of strikes and giving rise to alarm among the Taiwanese business community. In Binh Duong Province, home to more than 500 Taiwanese factories in 2006, a strike wave that year swept simultaneously through more than 50 of these factories, all of which came to a standstill for a period.[4] Strikes today remain a regular phenomenon. Taiwanese factory owners reportedly greet each other nowadays with the anxious query, "Has your factory been affected by a strike yet?", and in 2010 a Taiwanese blogger wrote that only when one has not been targeted by strikers is it newsworthy.[5]

In China, the counterpart of the HCMC region is in southern Guangdong Province, in Dongguan and Shenzhen, where Taiwanese factories similarly are concentrated. Labour-intensive industries relocated from Taiwan to Dongguan in abundance starting in the late 1980s.[6] As of 2008–09 Dongguan contained some 6,000 Taiwanese factories. Here too, there have been an increasing number of strikes, but they are negligible compared to the HCMC region. According to one report, "the number of strikes sometimes reaches three or four a day" in Dongguan, but this included factories owned by other nationals, not just Taiwanese.[7] Taiwanese investors who were interviewed who own factories in both Vietnam and China do not see strikes in China as a problem.

This difference poses an interesting question because it goes against a previous study that I participated in comparing management–labour practices in Taiwanese businesses in Vietnam and China (Chan and Wang 2004). Our findings went against the popular notions of cultural affinity: that people with the same ethnicity interact better. Instead we discovered that Taiwanese bosses treated Vietnamese workers better than they treated Chinese workers. Our article concluded that the attitude of the Vietnamese government and the official trade union toward labour violations by foreign investors has been the most salient factor influencing Taiwanese management's treatment of workers. So when newly collected data show that Vietnamese workers are actually prone to strike in protest more readily than their Chinese counterparts, this came as a surprise.

The new information comes from diverse sources. In particular, a number of research visits were made to each of these two regions, and factory managers were interviewed in both.[8] No attempt was made to conduct interviews with workers while inside the factories, but this was accomplished outside factory premises as workers left work at the end of a shift. In Vietnam, interviews were also conducted with VGCL officials and the Ministry of Labour, Invalids, and Social Affairs (MOLISA), with staff members of the International Labour Organization (ILO) in Vietnam, and with monitoring companies. In China we conducted fewer interviews with trade union and government officials in Guangdong Province who were not supportive of workers and this kind of academic research, but a considerable number of interviews were held with the staff of labour NGOs in Hong Kong and Shenzhen, who have a wealth of experience working with Chinese migrant workers. In contrast, in Vietnam very few such grassroots labour NGOs exist, and there was no opportunity to get in touch with them. In both countries, extensive interview sessions were held with locally based staff of a well-known Western-owned footwear company that sources from supplier factories in both Vietnam and China.

These field visits were complemented by a large amount of information gathered from documentary research. These include Chinese-language materials from Taiwan and China, media reports regarding labour disturbances in Vietnam written in Vietnamese and English, and some very detailed reports on Chinese strikes posted on the Internet by international and Hong Kong-based NGOs.

Coverage of strikes in the Vietnamese press is plentiful, in particular in *Lao Dong* (Labour) and *Nguoi Lao Dong* (Labourer), sometimes followed up by investigative reports complete with photographs of strikes and statistical data. The Chinese press had refrained from reporting on strikes in Guangdong's Pearl River Delta in the 1990s, but the press has been gradually granted greater freedom to cover stories and more Chinese have become active bloggers. As a consequence, news about strikes has started surfacing. But reports are seldom illustrated by photographs of mass protests, protest banners, or police vans. Images of street actions are off limits. However, Hong Kong photojournalists sometimes make up for this by rushing to the scene.

Vietnam keeps a record of the number of strikes, which is regularly reported in the press. For China, I have yet to come across similar official statistics, possibly because "strikes" are not considered as legitimate collective actions. Though there are now descriptions of strikes, there has not yet been any public discussion at the policy and law-making levels. China only releases figures on "labour disputes" (*laodong zhengyi*) or "mass incidents" (*qunzhong shijian*); but while such figures include strikes, these are umbrella terms for all kinds of upheavals. The official statistics for "labour disputes" entail officially recorded cases of individual or collective disputes that have been accepted for arbitration and litigation.[9] The term "mass incidents" refers to collective protests with the implication that violence has taken place, some of which could be strikes. The Chinese strike figures quoted earlier in this chapter are not official statistics.

In order to analyze the nature of strikes and industrial relations in both countries, it is best first to describe one representative example of a strike each in Vietnam and a strike in China to give readers a sense of what these are typically like. What instigates workers to take up a collective protest action? What are the workers' grievances, demands, and how do they behave during a strike? What is the level of worker solidarity? How does management respond? How do the trade union, local government, and police handle the incidents? Finally, how do the strikes end, what are the terms of settlement, and what roles are played by stakeholders, including labour advocates and the major corporations that purchase from the factory?

Vietnam: A Spontaneous Strike's Negotiated Conclusion

As a typical example, I have chosen a strike that broke out in one of the several factory sites of ABC Footwear Company (a pseudonym) in March 2006. ABC employed 50,000 workers at this one site. It was one of the earliest Taiwanese footwear factories established in Vietnam and supplies a single Western brand-name company. As required by Vietnam's Labour Code,[10] it allowed a trade union branch to be set up in 1996. The trade union has not been proactive in representing workers' interests, however. During an interview, the union chairperson described the relationship between the union, the workers, and the company as one of "partnership". His attitude was that the "the trade union will stand up for workers' interests if the company infringes the law. We will propose suggestions to the company, but if it does not accept them it is the company's responsibility, not the union's". (Thus, implicitly, if the workers stage a strike, it is the management's fault, not his.) From his vantage point, the trade union has to work in cooperation with various departments in the company and it is not his job to struggle on behalf of the workers.

Nevertheless, in the months leading up to the ABC strike, the trade union had notified management that the workers had some serious grievances. They were unhappy, for instance, about the reduction in their monthly "production quantity bonus" each time there was a new shoe model, when their productivity initially dropped. The management's attitude was that as long as the factory did not breach the law and the client's corporate code of conduct, this was good enough. It did not heed the trade union's advice. In a roundtable discussion that we held with trade union committee members at the factory in 2006, they expressed their frustration but said that they would not push management to the point that their relationship with management became confrontational. The result: workers did not trust the trade union and some of them even publicly challenged the trade union chairperson, calling upon him to step down.

In September 2005, at a time of high inflation, the Vietnamese government had announced an increase of some 40 per cent in the legal minimum wage for foreign direct investment (FDI) enterprises (VND870,000 [about US$55] per month for the HCMC region and Hanoi).[11] Factory managers complained that the announcement gave them too little time to arrange for a wage increase. The government then delayed the increase, to be effective as of 1 April 2006. However, workers were impatient with the half-year delay, and started a wave of strikes after the announcement. To appease the workers, the government gave in and rescheduled the date to 1 February, causing great confusion.

Despite the rise in the minimum wage, after workers returned to ABC Factory from the *Tet* holidays a wildcat strike broke out in early March

2006. On 10 March, a Friday, the company discovered call-for-strike flyers posted on walls and placed at a number of production lines. Management had no idea who organized this, nor did the workers whom we subsequently interviewed. Management immediately decided to give workers a day off on Monday in the hope of averting the strike, but not all workers were informed about the day off. On Monday, some workers turned up for work, but they were blocked by striking workers from entering the factory. A few angry workers started throwing stones at the office buildings. Some administrative staff managed to get to their offices, but anonymous internal phone calls intimidated them into leaving. As each staff member emerged from the factory gate, the crowds of strikers gathered outside cheered and applauded.

That morning, local government officials, including officials from the labour bureau and the provincial trade union, arrived to mediate the dispute. They talked to the workers and noted down their complaints. The police arrived as well but, according to management, "did nothing". When managers tried to take photos of the most active and vocal strikers, the police stopped them on the grounds that "it might irritate the crowd and would lead to unexpected consequences". Management pointed out to the police that the blockade was illegal, but the police did not take any action.

Management asked the trade union to present a list of the workers' demands, but the trade union could not represent the workers, nor would any strike leaders step forth. Under these circumstances, government officials and provincial trade union officials came to the negotiating table, putting forward the workers' demands to management representatives. The demands included: raising wages for senior workers; contributing to social security for workers; and paying a seniority allowance. Senior workers demanded a wage increase because when ABC had raised the basic wage in accordance to the mandatory minimum wage rise as of 1 February resulting in the junior workers' increase becoming proportionally higher in relation to their base wage than that of the senior workers' (which had been higher than minimum). The latter thought this unfair and agitated for a bigger increase. The company already had an informal annual incremental wage system policy based on seniority. During the negotiations, the workers demanded that this seniority system be included in the collective agreement — though this was an annual increment of merely VND25,000 (about US$1.80). Management accepted all three demands.

The negotiations lasted three days, and during that period the workers did not return to work. But *still* they were paid. When the negotiations were wrapped up, management warned that strikers who did not turn up for work on Thursday would get a demerit and no pay. The company could not legally fire those who did not turn up for work on Thursday because, according to the Labour Code, a company could only fire someone who has been absent from work for three successive days.

An interviewee who was representing management at the negotiations was convinced that "the Vietnamese government is behind the scenes. On the surface it appears to be taking a *laissez faire* attitude, but whenever there's a strike, it becomes a mediator and presses businesses to accept workers' demands".

China: Confrontation at a Stella Footwear Factory

This strike was widely reported inside and outside of China on the Internet, including in blogs. Several such reports tracked the development of the dispute over a period of several months.[12]

Stella Footwear Company (real name) is Taiwanese-owned. In 1991, like so many Taiwanese factories, it relocated from Taiwan to Dongguan city. A decade later it had expanded into five facilities in different parts of Guangdong Province, two of which were in Dongguan. It employed about 60,000 workers and supplied shoes to some ten brand name companies, including Nike, Reebok, Timberland, and Clarks. None of the five Stella factories contained trade union branches.

Working hours were long at these factories, up to eleven hours a day, six days a week. Workers were paid a so-called monthly basic wage for the first forty hours of the workweek. Like all factories in Dongguan, this basic monthly wage as of 2004 was CNY450 (US$54.50), set exactly at the official minimum wage (similar to Vietnam, where factories pay a basic wage that is exactly the official minimum wage).[13] With overtime, in 2004 workers on average made CNY700 a month at Stella. Eighty per cent of the workers lived in cramped company dormitories, for which they had to pay. After deductions for rent and food, they were left with only some CNY200 (US$24.20) per month in take-home pay. Without the overtime work of some twenty to twenty-six hours a week, the workers would have had no take-home pay at all.

In March 2004, Stella management suddenly reduced the amount of overtime work by giving workers two more days off a month, causing a reduced income of about CNY100 for each worker. The problem was that while working hours were reduced, the production quota remained unchanged, which effectively meant an increase in work intensity alongside a decrease in their monthly income. On pay day, when workers saw the pay cut in their wage package, they became angry. Some workers began calling in unison, "Higher wages! Better food!", and soon afterwards a crowd of more than a thousand workers started smashing machinery, rushed into staff offices, breaking windows, looting the factory grocery store, and overturning vehicles. A corps of thirty security guards could not control the crowd. The police were called. "In the chaos the workers had no leaders, no representatives, no organization, and no concrete demands. They dispersed as quickly as they rose up". News of the conflagration spread, and four out of five Stella factories were engulfed by violence. This onsite violence is not commonplace in Chinese industrial actions, however. The usual pattern of industrial action is for workers to take to the streets, marching to the local authorities to seek redress. The police then arrive in large numbers to try to stop the march, which can end in violence and arrests.

Ultimately, more than a thousand Stella workers were fired, seventy were arrested, and ten were charged by the local government for destroying property and were quickly sentenced to three to three-and-half-year jail terms. The youngest was only sixteen years old. Immediately, international and Hong Kong NGOs launched a protest campaign to release the ten convicted workers. Six Chinese lawyers, including a well-known human rights lawyer, were hired and came to Dongguan to represent the convicted workers. Campaign organizers urged the footwear brand name companies to use their leverage to write to the Dongguan local government to ask for their release. On 1 January 2005 all ten were released with suspended sentences. According to follow-up reports, work conditions reverted to what they had been in earlier months — the two days of monthly weekend overtime work were restored and monthly wages remained at previous levels. The brand name companies organized management–worker training sessions at the factories in the hope of establishing more stable labour relations.

I was able to talk to several Stella workers outside the factory in September 2007. They related that there was still a lot of overtime work and the pay was average. They also said that they were trying to organize other workers to agitate to set up a democratically elected union, which they hoped to register with the local district union one level above. At the time of writing, their hopes had not come to pass.

Comparing the Two Cases

I have chosen these two strikes in large part because they are representative of strikes in each country. One typical aspect is that in neither factory was an official workplace union involved. At ABC in Vietnam, although a union existed it played no role in the entire process. Despite its legal status, it was not even present at the negotiation table. In China, as noted, there were no unions at Stella's five production sites. This reflects a typical phenomenon in both countries — workplace unions often do not exist in the foreign-run export factories in China, or exist only in name, while in Vietnam, where they do exist, they are extremely weak and distrusted by workers (Wang 2005). However, Vietnamese workplace unions, as exemplified in ABC, may still serve as a channel of communication between management and labour to diffuse extreme tensions. But when a union cannot quietly convince management to resolve grievances, bottled-up frustration can turn into collective protest actions. In both countries, these strikes are "spontaneous", and in both countries there had been no formal representation made to management on behalf of the workers before strike actions began, though some worker activists inside ABC were organizing covertly. The Stella strike in contrast exploded into mass action without any covert planning.

Herein lies one of the differences between strikes in the two countries. As strike waves have spread across the HCMC region month after month and year upon year, Vietnamese workers have learned from each other about how to start a wildcat strike, and have become emboldened by their experience. Both the VGCL and Taiwanese investors have become convinced that groups of experienced underground labour activists have emerged.[14] One Taiwanese factory owner whose factory has been affected by strikes many times in the past decade is convinced that there are "professional strikers" moving from factory to factory instigating workers to rise up. While these suspicions cannot be confirmed, they are not unlikely.

In the mid-1990s, when I first embarked upon a comparative study of factory labour in Vietnam and China, it could be seen that Vietnamese workers in the export industries were more prone to resort to strike actions than Chinese workers. In fact, due to worries about the increasing labour unrest, the Vietnamese government, when revising the Labour Code in

1994, included a chapter on strikes in the hope that by laying down strike procedures, wildcat strikes would be avoided (Chan and Norlund 1999, pp. 177–204). Yet strikes continued unabated (see Ben Kerkvliet's chapter) and have become longer (Do Quynh Chi 2007). From newspaper and Internet reports, I have been able to collect a sample of 105 strikes that were reported during 2007, and as can be seen in Fig. 7.1, most of the strikes lasted one day; only in rare cases did they last more than five days, indicating that issues were generally resolved quite quickly.

The longest strike in Vietnam that I know of, which was well documented by daily press reports, occurred at Hue Phong, a Taiwanese-owned footwear factory, and lasted from 10 April to 5 May 2008.[15] This is a factory that has experienced a strike almost every other year during the past ten years because the management has never honoured the improvements it agreed to at the end of each strike.

FIGURE 7.1

Vietnam: Distribution of Length of Strikes as Reported in the Media from January to December 2007 (N = 105)

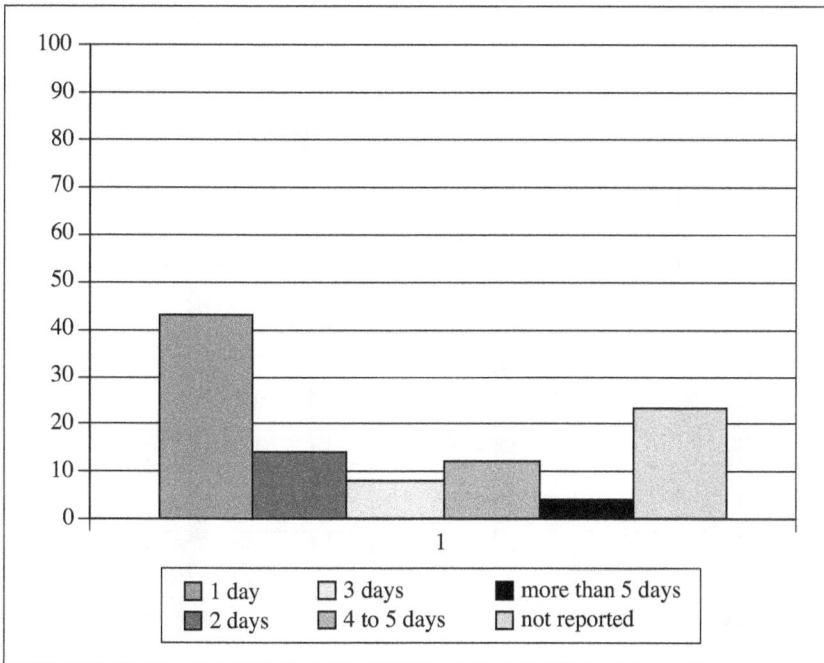

▣ 1 day	☐ 3 days	■ more than 5 days
■ 2 days	▨ 4 to 5 days	☐ not reported

Strikes usually peak each year a few months around the Vietnamese New Year: before *Tet*, workers mostly strike over year-end bonuses and after *Tet*, they strike for better wages and work conditions. But based on seventy published reports on strikes in 2007 that were collected online, after the *Tet* spike early in the year, strikes broke out again later in the year. In the first five months of 2008, there were 280 strikes, an average of 56 per month. By August 400 strikes had erupted, still averaging some 50 strikes in April, June, and July. In other words, by 2008, the period around *Tet* no longer marked the height of the annual strike cycle. The number of strikes climbed and stayed high all year round, reflecting the fact that the causes leading to strikes had changed. Increasingly, they had to do with workers' wages not catching up with a high inflation rate, which soared to 25.5 per cent in May 2008.[16]

FIGURE 7.2
Vietnam: Distribution of Number of Strikes in 2007 (N = 88).

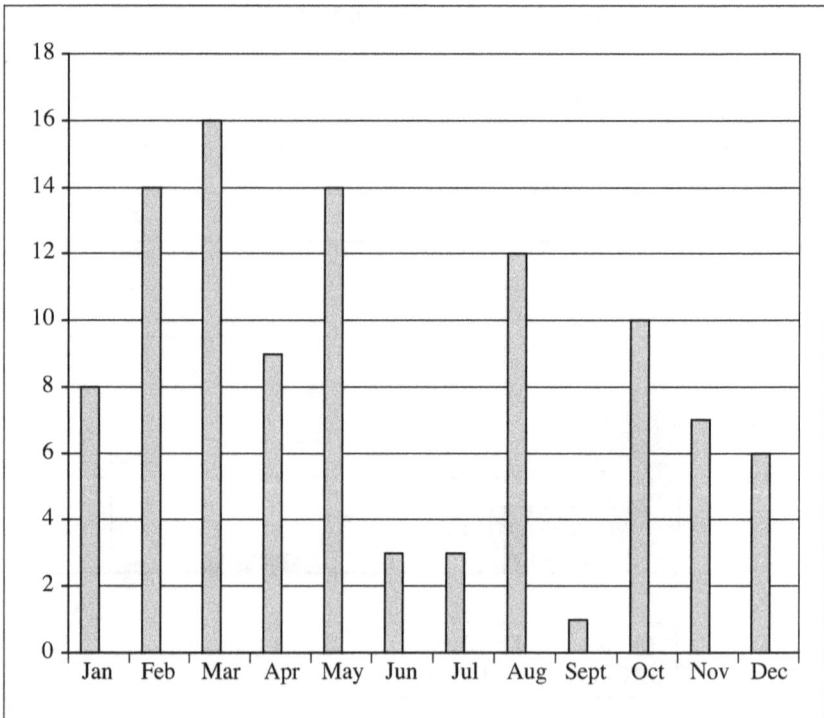

Workers' demands in the two countries are not the same, as well illustrated in the two case studies. At ABC, workers were asking for higher pay, better food, welfare coverage, a stepped wage structure, a seniority system, and dignified treatment. These demands are representative of those made by most Vietnamese workers. Based on a breakdown of the seventy strike cases in 2007, the most salient cause was low pay, followed by insufficient wage increases to offset galloping increases in the cost of living. The next most numerous set of complaints was related to the *Tet* bonus with workers claiming the bonus was not commensurate with their work contribution. Some complaints had to do with employers withholding the *Tet* bonus until the workers had returned after *Tet*. Too much overtime was also often an issue. Workers complained about being forced to work extra hours or shifts and not being awarded the legal overtime premium. Similarly, failure to pay health and social insurance regularly surfaced as a grievance, but generally was not the catalyst in sparking collective protests. Finally, some workers also demanded a decrease in work quotas and an increase in piece-rates. In short, these tend to be interest-based demands.

In contrast, Chinese workers most often strike for other reasons, with correspondingly different demands. The Stella case provides a good example. Wages here were a major issue, but the strike was not over an insufficient wage increase; on the contrary, it was over a wage decrease due to reduced work hours accompanied by faster-paced work. Often a wage decrease in the export industries in southern China takes the form of higher deductions for meals, rent, or utilities, a ploy used to obfuscate the wage decrease. This method can be used because quite a sizeable proportion of the workers there live in dormitories. In Vietnam, workers usually live in private housing and so this method of wage deduction is not useful from management's perspective.

What would have confused Vietnamese workers was that Stella workers fought only to maintain their previous wage level but not for a wage rise. While Vietnamese workers fight for reduced work hours, Stella workers fought to have their reduced overtime restored! By law they are entitled to four days of rest a month, but they fought to go to work for two of those four days. Because they had not fought for higher pay rates they could not afford to lose two days of overtime — an amount of overtime, notably, that exceeded the legal maximum number of hours of work. Also, instead of fighting for a reduction in their work quota, they were willing to maintain the previous quota. They did not take advantage of the strike to ask for shorter work hours and better pay. The workers at Stella showed a confused understanding of the integral relationship between wages, work hours, and work intensity. Their expectations and demands were considerably lower than that of the ABC workers in Vietnam.[17]

The Stella workers' lack of understanding of the kind of demands that could improve their wage and work conditions was not unusual. In China's Pearl River Delta, workers tend to have low expectations. Most labour disputes are over seriously delayed payments of wages. When the delay drags on for too long, in reality it becomes unpaid wages. Workers' claims of unpaid wages almost always spike just before Chinese New Year (the same national festive holiday as *Tet*), leading to a large amount of uncoordinated labour unrest. Unpaid wages reached a serious level in the 1990s in Guangdong Province, reaching CNY5.6 billion (about US$190 million) in 1998. To appease angry workers, local governments in places like Dongguan launched "chase back-wage campaigns" (Fang 2001). According to one survey, 72.6 per cent of Chinese migrant workers in the early 2000s suffered varying degrees of wage defaults.[18] In an effort to restore "social harmony", local governments have tried to use administrative methods to reduce the problem, but even then, in 2005 owed-wage cases still made up 41 per cent of labour dispute cases in the province.[19] In Vietnam, delayed wage payment cases also exist, but these pale in significance. As Simon Clark points out, "Low wages, rather than unpaid wages, was an issue cited in one-third of reports on strikes in the period 2002–04" (Clarke 2006, pp. 351–52). The irony of the protests before *Tet* and Chinese New Year is that while Vietnamese workers were protesting a delayed bonus payment or demanding a higher bonus, in China workers were trying to get paid, period.

There was one other type of serious workplace conflict in China that is often overlooked by observers — the issue of workers being denied permission to quit a job. This problem does not seem to exist in foreign-invested Asian factories in Vietnam. In China a widespread management practice has been to withhold a couple of months of wages at the time of recruitment as a method of preventing workers from quitting when they want to. The inability to leave a factory with their full pay and entitlements was a cause of great anxiety among Chinese migrant workers and was often a source of serious conflict on the shop floor, because supervisors

usually have had the power to decide whether to grant workers permission
to resign. Workers desperate to leave without permission have had to forfeit
the amount withheld at the time they started working.

The ABC Footwear and Stella cases also highlight a big difference
in how local governments and trade unions handle strikes in Vietnam
and China. Strikes in the HCMC region can be characterized as peaceful
despite occasional skirmishes between a factory's private security guards
and strikers. Take the ABC case as an example: workers stopped working
and assembled outside the factory gate with banners to attract attention.
Vietnamese workers generally restrain themselves from lashing out in
violence and demonstrate a sense of solidarity. Differences among the
workforce may emerge when strikers try to stop workers who do not
want to strike from entering the factory. Emotions can run high. The local
authorities, the district trade unions, and the media will quickly learn
about an incident either from the workers or from management and rush
to the scene. Upon arrival, the authorities try to calm the crowd, look
into the grievances, ask workers to choose representatives, and then begin
negotiating with management on behalf of the workers for better conditions
and wages. It is important to note that the local authorities and provincial
trade union quickly take on the role of the workers' representative in
negotiations with management. Often, according to Vietnamese newspaper
reports, they lambast the managers for mistreating workers. The length
of the strike depends on the progress of the negotiations and on whether
workers are willing to accept the terms that management offers. Since
most strikes last only one or two days, this means that in the face of
pro-labour local authorities, management normally quickly concedes
to workers' demands. In a minority of cases, when both workers and
management are adamant, as in the strike at Hue Phong, the strike can
last for a few weeks.

What distresses and frustrates Taiwanese investors is their conviction
that the authorities side with the workers. "They are supposed to come to
mediate, but basically they are here to fight for the workers. It's all one-
sided", complained the Hue Phong director to me in 2006. "The workers
here have better protection than workers in Taiwan!"[20] A Taiwanese
newspaper reported in April 2008:

> Among the Taiwanese business community there is a widely circulated
> rumour that the reason why the strikes are getting bigger and bigger
> is because international foreign organizations are assisting with the

strategies, transferring strike skills. For instance, when the media and riot police arrive, women workers are told to go stand at the frontline to elicit sympathy; or cases of boycotting the legal union and setting up a number of illegal unions, taking turns to bargain, each time bargaining over something different until management gets totally exhausted.[21]

To blame the tactics on international organizations is an entirely unsubstantiated charge. But the article gives a good sense of the Taiwanese managers' exasperation. They cannot conceive that Vietnamese workers can be resourceful and capable of taking on their bosses without outside help.

Taiwanese employers' treatment of workers and their attitudes towards strikes are very different in China. In this, the attitude of the host governments is critical (Chan and Wang 2004). Thus a Taiwanese manager lamented, "We can't use in Vietnam the methods we use in China. Definitely a no go." Why? "Because the mainland Chinese government supports us." While the Vietnamese government does not let the police or factory managers suppress strikers, the Chinese local governments have no qualms in quelling strikes by sending in large numbers of riot police to intimidate workers. The Chinese and Hong Kong press repeatedly describe how workers move out onto the streets, the police arrive, and the atmosphere tenses up. Only occasionally does a strike end peacefully.

During 2008–09, in addition to unpaid wages and wage deductions for dormitory rents and food, workers' protests in Guangdong's Pearl River Delta have had to do with plant closures triggered by the rapid downturn of the global economy. When factory owners absconded, the workers often had not been paid for a few months and lost entitlements as well.[22] Ironically, some of these factories shut down in order to relocate to Vietnam to take advantage of the lower wages there. In most cases, factory management has been breaching the labour law and the workers feel they have the right to take collective action when all other channels are blocked. Normally, some of these workers would have first tried using legal means, through formal complaints to the local authorities and the district trade union, but when unable to get a sympathetic hearing, they turn to drawing public attention to their grievances by escalating collective protest actions. Many of these take the form of workers rushing out of the factory gate, marching in formation to the offices of the local authorities, or staging sit-ins inside or outside factory compounds.[23] A large number of police then appear on the scene to cordon off the strikers and prevent them from marching, driving them back into the factory compound or dispersing the crowds. In the process, violence breaks out and workers get arrested, thrown into police vans, and later charged with disturbing the peace.[24]

Therefore, unlike Vietnamese workers, Chinese workers do not expect the state to be on their side when they explode in fury. It is desperate action taken in full expectation that there is a high chance of a violent reaction by the authorities. The workers calculate that since the factories are legally in the wrong, when the upheaval is over local government officials will use their authority to demand that management abide by the laws — raising wages to the legal minimum required, or reducing excessive overtime, or paying severance compensation. While the outcome is unpredictable, the workers do anticipate the likelihood of violence and suppression. In contrast, when Vietnamese workers embark on a strike, going by the outcome of strikes in the previous few years, they can be confident that they will have state support and that the result will end in their favour. As a result strikes spread quickly, as workers in factories in the vicinity quickly learn to organize their own strikes.

In China, however, suppression by the authorities, including arrests (or driving strike leaders to flee to their hometowns), and allowing management to retaliate against workers after the dust settles through mass layoffs and blacklisting, makes it difficult for activists to form organizing cells.[25]

There have been some anomalous cases where Chinese labour protests resemble Vietnamese ones. The best documented was a series of strikes in 2005 that spread across eighteen factories (sixteen Japanese and two Korean) within three months in the Dalian Development Zone in northeast China (Chen 2010). It engulfed quite a number of factories, indicating that there was some surreptitious organization and coordination. As in the case of Vietnamese workers, these strikers' demands were interest-based — asking for higher wages, better benefits, and a higher overtime premium. Unlike in Vietnam, however, the city authorities and the development zone trade union were hostile towards the strikers. The trade union acted as a government representative. When the strikes spread, the development zone union became somewhat sympathetic to the workers' cause; however, because the city government and Communist Party committee were worried that the strikes might drive away foreign investment, the union only played the role of mediator. Vietnamese authorities appear to be less worried that strikes deter foreign investors, perhaps in the belief that Vietnam has other advantages to offer (Lee 2009).

II.
UNDERLYING FACTORS

How do we account for the differences in the two countries' strike patterns? I have identified a few factors that warrant discussion: first, the relationship between the government and the official trade union; second, the legal regulatory regime; third, the tripartite dispute-resolution institutions; and finally, the legal labour standards set by the government. Of these, the relationship between the government and trade union constitutes the macro political, institutional, and legal parameters within which the other factors play out their differences.

i. Government–Union Relations

Both Vietnam and China are one-party states with corporatist structures. Yet, as described above, there are significant differences in the way in which each state handles strikes. This difference has historical roots. The chapters by Edmund Wehrle and Ben Kerkvliet show that a vibrant trade union movement existed in South Vietnam in the 1960s and 1970s. In China, a genuine trade union had existed in a more distant past, before 1949, and the passage of time means there are no personal memories of this. By 1980 when China began to allow the emergence of capitalist activity, the ACFTU contained only a few elderly officials who had experienced an independent trade union movement.[26] In contrast, the legacy of a militant labour history in South Vietnam is of direct pertinence, especially in this region of Vietnam where a bureaucratic socialist system has never taken root. Some trade unionists' previous experiences likely had an influence on Vietnamese industrial relations policy under *Doi Moi*.

At the Sixth Vietnamese Trade Union Congress in 1988, the party–state was willing to allow the VGCL leeway to operate under the slogan of "renewal, openness and democracy" (Chan and Norlund 1998, p. 184). The trade union structure was decentralized, and the press were allowed to report disagreements between the VGCL and the government over policy issues. This has not been possible in China. The ACFTU has been striving for greater independence from the Chinese party–state, but any differences with the Party and other sectors of the government cannot be aired in public. The public can only construe that differences exist by reading between the lines in the media.

By the early 1990s, both countries had to enact a set of new labour laws to regulate a rapidly changing economic structure which was being challenged by expanding private and FDI sectors. Strikes in the FDI sector were of concern to the authorities in both countries, and as remains the case, the Chinese were apt to use force to suppress strikes. Vietnam's Labour Code and China's Trade Union Law[27] — passed at about the same time in the first half of the 1990s, after intense debates and several dozen drafts — with hindsight laid the foundations of divergence. As a whole these bodies of laws guarantee the VGCL more independence than that given to the ACFTU. The articles regulating collective bargaining in the Vietnam law are far more detailed. According to the Vietnam's Trade Union Law,[28] the functions of the workplace union do not include carrying out work to assist management (Chan and Norlund 1998, p. 185). The Vietnamese laws have prohibitive articles against worker exploitation that are missing in the Chinese laws. The Vietnamese trade union is also given the right to join international organizations and even to accept funding from them. The Chinese trade union law is silent on such a right. On the whole, Vietnamese labour laws are superior to the Chinese.

It is a common belief that developing countries are lax in law enforcement. But comparing Vietnam and China, it does not seem coincidental that Taiwanese investors do not violate the Vietnamese labour laws in the same way they flout the Chinese laws. Prohibitive articles in the Vietnamese law accompanied with penalties exact consequences for violators. One consequence is that the serious problem of unpaid wages in China is not prevalent in Vietnam.

There is also another factor. While in both the VGCL and the ACFTU the top union officials are more pro-labour than the lower levels, in Vietnam this reaches down to the district level; this is not the case in China. As seen earlier, district-level local authorities and unions in Vietnam side with workers during strikes, unlike their counterparts in China. There is a historical reason why district-level governments in the HCMC region are more pro-labour. First, as the political system in both countries loosened up and became more decentralized (this is more significant in China, since Vietnam is only of the size and population of a Chinese province), the behaviour of local governments has had a decided impact on industrial relations. In the greater HCMC region, where land had not been widely collectivized, ownership remains in the private hands of villagers and is inheritable. Provincial and district-level governments, though they have an interest in attracting FDI, do not have a direct stake in renting out land and factory buildings to foreign companies. These local governments are more ready to enforce the law and protect workers' rights than those in China's Pearl River Delta, where under Mao, landownership was transferred to agricultural collectives. Today, in Guangdong Province the agricultural collectives continue to own the land, and they are often coterminous with natural villages; revenues are controlled by the village governments. Almost all agricultural land in the Pearl River Delta region has been turned into industrial zones, and in most areas, land use rights still rest with the collectives, which are actively constructing and renting out factory buildings to foreign investors. Villagers, as a group, have become a rentiér class. The very direct personal gains that can be made from foreign investors using migrant workers from poorer provinces contribute to the villagers' unconscionable disregard for the exploitation of the migrant workers by foreigners (Chan *et al.* 2009, chs. 13–15). The proportion of local villagers to migrant workers can be up to 1 to 100, and no locals need to work at the production lines anymore. There is an unspoken alliance between the local village governments (and the levels of government immediately above them) and FDI enterprises *vis-à-vis* keeping the migrant workers in line.

In both regions, the workplace union branches are weak at the interface between management and labour. But there is a difference. In Vietnam, as is obvious at the ABC Factory, the trade union saw itself as having a separate identity from management even though it did not aggressively represent workers' interests and was too weak to play a role later in negotiating with management, letting the district-level union do this. We also have come across a case in which the trade union of a shoe factory in Vietnam that supplies Nike and other brand-name sport shoe companies is powerful enough to negotiate with management. Because it was able to represent workers' interests, there has been no strike there except for small-scale work stoppages.

In China, the workplace union branches in the Pearl River Delta in the private factories are worse than weak; in the factories where they exist they are an integral part of factory management. Very often a local villager is sent to the factory and given the title of deputy factory manager while simultaneously also holding the title of factory trade union chair. Workers often do not even know of the existence of this virtual union.

Vietnamese workers at the ABC factory have a basic understanding of the importance of a collective agreement. For instance, they insisted that certain demands be written into the contract even though some of those demands were already implemented in practice. In China, when talking to workers and labour NGOs, it was obvious that the concept of collective bargaining is practically unknown in the Pearl River Delta. Though collective bargaining has a legal status, it was only in August 2008 that the ACFTU, with party–state backing, launched a campaign of "collective consultation", urging workplace unions to draw up collective agreements with management. The campaign fired its first shot by targeting China's then more than a hundred Wal-Mart stores (Chan 2007). But close examination of the collective agreement at a Wal-Mart store that was held up as an exemplary model reveals serious procedural irregularities and a collective contract in which staff wages were unlikely to keep abreast of inflation.[29]

ii. The Tripartite Institutional Framework

Countries with long-standing union movements often maintain industrial peace through a well-established tripartite system that involves the state, labour, and employers. Urged by the ILO, both Vietnam and China in the early 2000s set up Tripartite Consultative Committees (TCCs) composed of the state, employers' associations, and the trade union federation. These were established at various levels as platforms for three-party dialogue (Lee 2006*b*). The Vietnamese TCC system is better developed than China's, where employers and labour are beginning to pursue their own goals (Lee 2006*b*).

Vietnam and China both have strong states, weak workplace-level union representation, and well-organized union federations that play a national role. The VGCL in Vietnam, being more independent from the state, can assert its opinions more openly than the ACFTU can in China.[30] In both countries, due to a socialist past, employers' associations are new and not well developed. The Vietnamese Chamber of Commerce and Industries (VCCI) appears to represent its members' interests better in the TCC[31] than does its Chinese counterpart. Perhaps this explains a softer approach taken by foreign investors in their handling of strikes. For instance, in interviews with a large foreign company in Vietnam, it was quite clear that an intensive tripartite dialogue took place in early 2006 when a strike wave broke out. Though the VCCI was weak, employers' interests were represented. The Chinese Enterprise Management Association, by contrast, has not been as well developed, and its representation on China's TCC is weak. A study of the Chinese TCC concludes that, several years after its establishment, its operations still fell far below the standards set by the ILO (Shen and Benson 2008). In contrast, the fact that the VCCI has a role to play in Vietnam helps explain why the ILO office there has successfully exerted some influence in shaping the industrial relations system. As just one example, in April 2010 the ILO office in Vietnam and the Ministry of Labour jointly organized a tripartite conference to discuss draft revisions of the Labour Code and the Trade Union Law.

iii. Legal Procedures Regulating Strikes

After intense debate, a revision to Vietnam's Labour Code (Chapter 14) granted workers the right to strike, laid out in a detailed set of procedures. The Chinese Labour Law does not mention strikes at all, effectively putting this right in limbo. Strikes in China are not legalized nor are they rendered illegal. While critics take China to task for not having recognized the right to strike, it is not mentioned that there are also no provisions prohibiting strikes or defining what constitutes an illegal strike. It remains a grey area to this day. As will be seen, the pros and cons of having or not having a legal regulatory procedure *vis-à-vis* strikes are complex.

To come to grips with this, let us compare the [old] Chapter 14 of the 1994 Vietnamese Labour Code with the Chinese Labour Law of 1994. I will also compare the [new] Chapter 14 of Vietnam's Labour Code with the [old] Chapter 14, pointing out from the workers' vantage point the advantages and disadvantages of the new Chapter. Lastly, I shall compare the new Chapter 14 with China's Law on Mediation and Arbitration of Labour Disputes, passed in December 2007.

The Vietnamese Labour Code's Old Chapter 14 and China's Labour Law

The labour laws passed in 1994 in both countries established institutions and procedures to channel industrial disputes through a three-stage formal proceeding: an enterprise-level conciliation committee, an arbitration committee that is external to the enterprise, and lastly, the court system. In practice, because the workplace unions serving as the representatives of labour on the committees are weak and often are controlled by management, workers do not go to them to resolve grievances. Instead they go directly to the arbitration committee. When dissatisfied with the decision of the committee, workers can appeal to the local court.

An important difference in the two sets of national laws is that the Chinese Labour Law does not contain provisions for collective disputes. When a group of workers who share the same grievances take management to court, their cases tend to be dealt with on an individual basis. This stems from the fact the Chinese law does not recognize nor have any mechanisms or institutions to deal with collective disputes, and by extension does not recognize strikes.

In contrast, the Vietnamese Labour Code makes a distinction between individual and "collective labour disputes" and has separate sections laying down the procedures for dispute resolution (Van Thu Ha 2008, pp. 224–26). Collective disputes are required to go through all three stages. If workers want to go on strike, an application is supposed to be made to the workplace conciliation council first, which can take up to seven days. If the workers are not satisfied with the council's decision, they can go to the arbitration council, which has to make a decision on the case within ten days. If the workers are not satisfied with this decision, they "shall have the right to request the people's court to resolve the matter or to strike" (Article 172). The strike decision shall be made by the executive committee of the workplace trade union after more than half of the employees agree to proceed with the strike. With that vote of approval, the union can notify the labour bureau and the provincial trade union, explaining in writing the case and the day the strike is to take place. Workers who do not go through these steps are prohibited from striking (Articles 173, 174), but the law does not state that such strike actions are illegal. There is no mention of whether or not workers are entitled to payment for the duration of the strike.

The proof of the pudding is in the eating. Despite these pre-strike procedures, none of the known strikes in Vietnam to date has been legal, in that they have not gone through these steps nor have been led by the workplace union. As we have seen, the number of strikes has continued to rise — and these were all wildcat strikes that bypassed the procedures. The Labour Code's Chapter 14 had been ignored.

A revision of Chapter 14 was seen as urgently needed to contain strikes. This time, the Vietnamese government and the VGCL worked closely with the ILO to draw up an amendment. While it is impossible to conclusively say that ILO's advice has had a significant influence on the amended Chapter 14 passed in 2006, many of the key points made in an ILO discussion paper, "Industrial Relations and Dispute Settlement in Vietnam" (Lee 2006), later appeared in the new Chapter 14.[32] These include reforms to the various dispute resolution institutions; distinguishing between disputes over rights and disputes over interests; a "no work, no pay" principle; simplifying and thereby shortening the procedures before a legal strike can take place; compulsory arbitration; and linking collective bargaining agreements (CBA) closely with strike procedures. In the case of wildcat strikes,

> DOLISA officials (or conciliators) would have meetings with workers and employer(s) separately. DOLISA officials (or conciliators) would explain to workers the legal requirements of furthering their interests through negotiation, and the legal consequences if this requirement is not met. DOLISA officials (conciliators) would urge workers to return to work until the procedures of conciliation (and arbitration) would be exhausted. ... The above mode of DOLISA's intervention is a key step to bring the illegal situation of a 'wildcat strike' back to the legal procedure of a third party assisted negotiation (that is conciliation). (Lee 2006a, p. 54)

It was suggested that union and employer representatives from outside the workplace assist in the negotiations.

Subsequently, the ILO office in Hanoi ran an ILO/Vietnam Industrial Relations Project advising and demonstrating to employers and the trade unions how to prevent strikes (Sunoo 2007). The emphasis was on "social dialogue" as a vehicle to maintain industrial peace at normal times, as a way of preempting strikes. But since the strikes have not abated, the social dialogue solution has not been effective.

Vietnam's Labour Law: The Old Chapter 14 and New Chapter 14

The biggest difference in the old and new Chapter 14 is that the new chapter makes a distinction between rights-based collective labour disputes and interest-based collective disputes, as emphasized by the ILO paper. The strike procedures are spelled out in greater detail and are made less laborious.

Collective disputes can now bypass the workplace reconciliation council, which had been management-controlled. Eliminating this first step takes seven days off the procedures. The dispute can be handled right away at the district level by an arbitration body of "full time and part-time members from the labour administration system, union, employers and lawyers' association, or experts in industrial relations in the locality" (Article 170). Similar to some countries such as Australia, collective strike action is not allowed to take place while arbitration is in process.

At this point, a difference is made between rights-based and interest-based disputes. Rights-based disputes are those related to legal violations and are dealt with directly by the chair of the district people's committee. The maximum time given to decide on a resolution is five working days (Article 170*a*). If the workers disagree with the resolution they can begin strike procedures.

Interest-based disputes on the other hand have to be referred to an arbitration committee and will be resolved in accordance to legal compliance. For such disputes related to issues that go beyond the legal minimum such as higher wages, bonuses, work hours, shifts and occupational and safety issues, the maximum time for the arbitration body to arrive at a decision is seven days. The decision then has to be sent to the disputants within two days. The workplace trade union then has to organize a secret ballot. A majority "yes" vote is needed from among the employees of a 300-worker enterprise, and the consent of over 75 per cent of "consulted workers" in enterprises of more than 300 workers is needed before the union's executive branch can put forth workers' demands and notify the employer of the time and place of the impending strike (Article 174*b*). Short of those percentages, the workers cannot legally hold a strike. The notification has to be delivered to the employer, the Department of Labour, Invalids, and Social Affairs (DOLISA), and the provincial VGCL five days prior to the strike date that had been decided by vote (Article 174*b*). If the employer refuses to accept the demands, then the strike can commence.

Since most disputes in Vietnam are largely interest-based rather than purely rights-based (Clarke, *et al*. 2006), shortening the rights-based dispute settlement period by two days does not normally shorten very much the dispute settlement procedure in Vietnam. In fact, in the lengthy debates among the relevant parties during the drafting of the amendment, some participants argued that it was not possible to disaggregate disputes into these two categories (on this, see Ben Kerkvliet's chapter). Some advocates noted that since workers' interest-based demands are unrelated to the law they should be negotiated between labour and management through collective bargaining. Successful bargaining by both parties would eliminate the need for workers to resort to strikes.

While bargaining is in progress, strikes are prohibited. But a comparative study of labour disputes worldwide came to the conclusion that "In actual practice, however, even among those countries which purport to observe either or both of these distinctions, it frequently happens that the demarcation lines between rights and interest disputes, and between individual and collective disputes, tend to overlap, to become unclear, or to vanish entirely" (Benjamin 1979, p. 5). Four experienced trade union officials from Canada, the United States, Australia, and an international union federation similarly have told me that the distinction is quite artificial.

The new Chapter 14 did not work. Since its passage, the number of wildcat strikes has continued to rise. So far as is known, not a single new strike has been classified as legal. We can identify three main reasons why the new amendment has fallen far short of expectations. First, the interest-based dispute settlement procedure is conditional upon on collective bargaining taking place between the workplace union branch and management as a first step. Only when bargaining fails should the case go to the arbitration council. But successful bargaining in turn requires a workplace union that is trusted by the workers as a genuine representative body. But the workplace unions are too weak in Vietnam, and as seen in the ABC case, not trusted by the workers; nor are they respected by management as workers' representatives. Without collective bargaining, the strike procedures are irrelevant. The fact that workers bypass the union to improve their work conditions attests to this failure.

The second reason is the complicated procedure of applying to hold a legal strike. One of the purposes of the amendment was to simplify and shorten the strike procedures so that it would be possible for the workers to take this legal route. But under the revised Chapter 14, even after the majority of the workers have voted to hold a strike, they are required to wait five days before taking any action. This is impractical for strike organizers. Strike leaders can be easily exposed and intimidated, and divide-and-rule tactics will be used by employers to stir up differences and suspicion among workers. Strike leaders do not trust management. That is why all of the strikes are portrayed by the workers as being "spontaneous" and leaderless protests. Only in societies where a mature industrial relations system has developed, where the trade unions are reasonably strong and backed by entrenched workplace branches, can management be trusted to bargain in good faith, and only then do most strikes abide by the legal proceedings. Obviously Taiwanese factory managers with no tradition in engaging in collective bargaining in Taiwan cannot be trusted to await complicated and lengthy pre-strike procedures without using the opportunity to ferret out the strike organizers and to get rid of them. Even in Britain — a country with a mature industrial relations system — most strikes in the twentieth century were wildcat actions (Hyman 1989, pp. 39–46). The third reason is that some of the provisions in the new Chapter 14 further place workers in a disadvantageous position:

- Workers going on strike are no longer entitled to wages and benefits.
- Picketing is now regulated by a prohibitive clause that does not allow strikers to prevent non-strikers from going to work (Article 174dd [1]).
- In the old Chapter 14 there was no definition for an illegal strike, but now Article 173 lists seven conditions under which strikes can be classed as illegal.
- A three-judge committee will decide on the legality of a strike. If the strike is ruled to be illegal, then workers have to go back to work or be disciplined and even charged with criminal offences, and the striking party "shall compensate in accordance to the law". (Art.179 [1]).

The main gain for the workers in the new Chapter is: "For non-unionized establishments, a strike must be organized and led by representatives nominated by workers (hereinafter referred to as workers' representatives). …" (Article 172a). That means that at workplaces which do not have existing unions, workers have a chance to go on a legal strike after choosing their own representatives. However, the same laborious application procedures to engage in a strike apply.

It is unlikely that ordinary workers have read and analyzed the revised Chapter 14. They simply join a strike that they think can help to improve their conditions. As for the small minority of the workers who have studied the new law, why should they bother to take the cumbersome legal route? Why not continue to go on strike spontaneously, as has been the case for the last decade, when the chance of winning has been shown to be high, involving little personal risk? As a result, all strikes in Vietnam have been wildcat, and no worker representatives have emerged who have applied to stage a strike.

Comparing Vietnam's New Chapter 14 with China's Labour
Dispute Conciliation and Arbitration Law

On 1 January 2008 a new Chinese law, the Labour Dispute Conciliation and
Arbitration Law, came into effect. A new law was needed since disputes
skyrocketed from 19,000 in 1994 to 317,000 in 2006, of which 14,000
cases were collective disputes entailing demonstrations or strikes, sometimes
involving violence.[33] Like the prior Labour Law, this new law fails to make
a distinction between individual and collective disputes. Nor does it make a
distinction between rights-based or interest-based protests, or between legal
and illegal industrial actions or strikes. The terms "collective bargaining",
"strike", and "work stoppages" are also absent. China recognized collective
"consultation" as a labour right, but since this new law does not recognize
collective disputes, a collective bargaining precondition is not stipulated.

The only reference to any form of collective dispute is contained in
Article 7, "Where the party in a labour dispute consists of more than 10
labourers, and they have a joint request, they may recommend a representative to participate in mediation, arbitration or litigation activities."
But the procedure for these multi-disputant disputes is the same as for
an individual. As noted, in practice, even when a group of workers with
the same complaint applies for arbitration, they are often dealt with as
individual cases.

This new law tries to rectify many of the problems that had placed
workers at a disadvantage when they used legal proceedings to resolve
their grievances. For instance, previously a worker had to file a complaint
within sixty days from the day of the labour rights infringement. This has
been lengthened to one year in the new law, which is helpful to workers
who need a longer period to seek help to file a case. Now workers no long
have to pay an arbitration fee, which had been a major financial burden
on workers, especially when their cases had to do with unpaid wages. The
maximum period given to an arbitration committee to decide whether to
accept a case is now shortened to five days, and the maximum time for a
ruling is ten days. An arbitration ruling is now compulsory (Article 47),
and because only the employee, not the employer, has the right to a court
appeal (Article 48), a ruling in the workers' favour cannot be overturned
by an employer's appeal to the court or be dragged on and on at court.
Due to all of these changes that are favourable to workers, within half a
year of the law's promulgation there was an explosion of cases lodged at
Shenzhen city's arbitration offices — 23,785 applications, 243 per cent more

than for the same period in 2007, and of these, 22,122 cases were accepted for processing. The arbitration staff was overwhelmed (Ye 2008).[34]

In short, in the past several years both the Vietnamese and Chinese governments have felt that they had to regulate the increasing numbers of strikes by revamping or passing new laws to contain wildcat strikes from spreading. But they have taken different approaches. Vietnam introduced a legalistic, procedural, penal approach. It has always recognized the right to strike but now it also creates a class of illegal strikes. What is interesting is that while workers have refused to play by the rules, neither do the authorities enforce the law. They are not arresting and prosecuting illegal strikers, but instead are bargaining on their behalf with management. By contrast, the Chinese government's method of trying to control the spread of strikes is simply not to recognize collective industrial actions, nor the right to strike, but at the same time China cautiously continues not to make strikes illegal, leaving it as a grey area. It tries to channel all grievances through legal processes and has passed a law to make this easier for individual workers. But because the state does not lay down any procedure for collective actions, when strikes explode, the authorities have tried to suppress them. The contrast between the two countries can be reduced to this: in Vietnam it is a situation of "harsh laws, soft implementation"; in China it is "soft laws, harsh implementation".

iv. Labour Standards: Rights-based vs Interest-based Protests

Earlier it has been pointed out that the distinction between rights-based and interest-based disputes when adjudicating is never particularly clear-cut. Yet in conceptual terms, especially within a comparative framework regarding Vietnam and China, the distinction is useful. As already pointed out, Vietnamese labour protests tend to be interest-based while Chinese protests tend to be rights-based. Vietnamese workers' demands go further than just the minimal legal standards. They want a seniority system and job security. Chinese workers on the other hand tend to seek no more than being paid at least the legal minimum.

In two case studies of strikes described by Chris Chan and Pun Ngai (2009), the workers, similar to those at Stella, rose up due to a sudden drop in wages and increase in the speed of production. Their demands for a wage rise, when converted to yuan per hour, did not go beyond the legal minimum. Because their rights were being violated, and because they had no organized bargaining power, this is all they realistically could ask for.

There are some signs that Chinese stikes may be stepping into a new era — the several cases of the so-called "Honda strikes" that happened in May and June 2010 in which workers at several Honda auto-part plants went on strike demanding a 50 per cent pay rise, a salary structure, and re-election of the workplace union.[35] Though these few strikes were widely covered in the Chinese and international media, they have not spread and became a strike wave. At this stage it is still too early to conclude that Chinese strikes have progresssed from being rights-based to interest-based.

In part, this distinction between labour disputes in the two countries has to do with the labour standards set by the two governments. The better the government's standards, the higher the chance they are of being breached by employers. China's legal regular work hours are set at a 40-hour week; Vietnam's at a 48-hour week. If a Taiwanese employer who operates factories in both countries wants to equalize the work hours he will have to violate the Chinese labour law but not the Vietnamese law.

Similarly in wage setting, Chinese local governments have been adjusting the minimum wage every year based on a formula commensurate with the local cost of living. Thus, an annual increase in the minimum wage normally covers inflation. The Vietnamese government on the other hand did not adjust the minimum wage for a period of six years until 2006, when the increase set for the minimum wage did not make up for the double-digit inflation. Since FDI employers almost always use the minimum wage as workers' basic wage, the wage in Vietnam has been set very low. According to Corpwatch, during the period when the minimum wage remained stagnant, Vietnam's currency dropped almost 15 per cent against the U.S. dollar, and inflation reached 28 per cent (Glantz and Nguyen 2006). To survive the high inflation, Vietnamese workers who staged strikes were struggling for their interests rather than for their legal rights, which had not been infringed upon.

When a minimum wage is low, the necessity for an employer to violate the law also decreases. Perhaps this is where the push for collective bargaining by the Vietnamese local governments (and the ILO as well) comes in, since it is not an issue of pursuing an employer through legal measures to abide by a minimum wage. This is where MOLISA and the VGCL disagree. A Ministry representative in an interview in 2006 indicated this disagreement.[36] He thought the VGCL should try to help workers achieve an acceptable wage through collective bargaining agreements. The

VGCL on the other hand, lobbied for an increase in the minimum legal wage. The VGCL's position was that if the minimum wage was higher, and if employers breached the law in not paying up to the minimum wage or cheated in other ways, then the cases could be dealt with by legal means. The VGCL's responsibility for negotiating with employers on the workers' behalf would be diminished.

The VGCL adopted this stance in the knowledge that the workplace unions are incapable of bargaining. The consequence is what is observed at ABC and elsewhere — Vietnamese workers have to agitate for their demands, and when they do not succeed, they embark on wildcat strikes and let the local governments come in, not to crack down on an employer's violations of a law, but rather to negotiate on behalf of the workers.

III.
THE TRENDS IN INDUSTRIAL RELATIONS PATTERNS

Without effective union representation at the foreign-owned factories, both Vietnamese and Chinese workers rely on the state to help them. They make economic demands on their employers, but make no demands regarding state policy (for instance, they do not demand that the officially set minimum wage be increased) nor political demands (for instance, they do not demand autonomous trade unionism). In both countries, strikes are aimed at appealing to local authorities. In Vietnam the workers go on strike in order to get the local state authorities to negotiate on their behalf. In China, collective actions either take the form of violence at the workplace or street actions such as marching to local government offices asking that pressure be applied to their employers. Vietnamese and Chinese workers remain at the stage of seeking protection from the government, unlike, for instance, Indonesian workers, who hold mass rallies calling on the government to raise the minimum wage. This reflects a difference in the state–worker relationship in the formerly "socialist" states and the developing-nation capitalist states.[37]

But state power in Vietnam and China is exercised differently. The Vietnamese government uses its administrative power to demand interest-based improvements in foreign-owned factories. For instance, during the ABC strikes, government representatives pushed management to set up a seniority-based year-end bonus system and an incremental salary system based on years of service.[38] The government also tries to push brand-name clients to force their suppliers to set up these systems.[39] Since Vietnam emphasizes collective bargaining, this kind of issue ought to have been raised during collective bargaining before strikes erupt.

The Chinese government does not normally resort to direct administrative intervention to get employers to provide a better deal for workers. Instead it enacted a new Contract Law[40] that requires employers to sign open-ended contracts with employees who have already signed two fixed-term contracts and with workers who have had ten years of service (Articles 14 [1] and [3]). This provides such employees with more secure employment. It is up to the employers to abide by the law, and if they do not, it is up to an individual employee to use the law to fight for this legal right through arbitration. This ultimately means more litigation in China, a point that we will return to.

The Vietnamese government for its part uses the law to regulate collective industrial disputes. The elaborate dispute resolution procedures were drawn up to preempt strikes. But this method has not worked. The Chinese government on the other hand has not used any law to regulate strike disputes. The state does, however, resort to a different method of averting strikes — by individualizing all labour disputes and channelling them through the arbitration and court systems, causing a proliferation of litigation cases in China over the past decade.

In turn, this has led to the emergence and proliferation of legal aid clinics, labour NGOs, labour lawyers, and paralegals in the Pearl River Delta. They help individual workers to fight to secure wage arrears and compensation for industrial injuries. Currently there are no fewer than 500 individuals in the Pearl River Delta working professionally as labour-rights protectors, more than 20 among whom have had a significant influence in specific legal areas. There are many more non-professional legal practitioners who began as workers fighting their own personal cases and who, having learned the ropes through self-education, started helping others by becoming what in China today are called "citizens' agents". One who became famous in the past decade-and-a-half has handled 6,000 cases. As these "citizen's agents" become more knowledgeable and skilled in litigation, some workers have been awarded substantial amounts in back pay and in compensation for injuries. In one case, an employer in Shenzhen city was so infuriated that he hired thugs to smash up a legal-aid NGO office and subsequently arranged a vicious street attack on the NGO leader, whose legs were severed with a cleaver. This incident raised great alarm among the labour NGO community in Shenzhen. The rise of litigation and of citizens' agents has catapulted China's industrial relations into a new phase. In response, the Guangdong government has begun to grapple with the question of whether it should attempt to coopt and incorporate the citizens' agents and other labour rights protectors by bringing them under its wing.[41] This initiative potentially places these now-independent advisers on workers' litigation in a vulnerable position, constantly subject to the mercy of the authorities.[42]

The legal aid movement has been instrumental in raising workers' awareness of their labour rights, but the very fact that the movement is framed by the discourse on "rights protection" (*weiquan*; *wei* meaning to protect; *quan* meaning rights) further individualizes labour dispute settlements in a reactive manner. Only when labour rights are being violated, i.e., specifically, when minimal legal rights are being violated, do workers come forth. The Chinese language contains a compound word "*quanyi*" ("*quan*" meaning rights; "*yi*" meaning interests), but when used in China today about labour issues, the word almost exclusively refers to legal rights, not interests.

This narrow focus on legal rights has a delimiting effect on workers' consciousness. Their interests beyond the legal minimum are not protected by law and do not come within the purview of legal aid personnel. Struggling for interests is proactive behaviour that can best be achieved by collective bargaining. But the idea of collective bargaining has not yet penetrated the consciousness of the vast majority of Chinese workers. Due to institutional, legal, political, and social constraints it will be some time before China will develop an industrial relations system in which workers' interests can be voiced and genuinely represented by the ACFTU. Instead, for the time being, China is headed in a direction that is becoming increasingly litigious, interrupted very sporadically by industrial violence. There have been a few known cases of workers trying to demand participatory rights in the moribund workplace-level trade union or, where a union does not exist at a factory, trying to establish their own elected union branch under the ACFTU umbrella. But this is as yet unusual, and there are no signs that the local authorities want to enable workers to have a say in their own union branches or in collective bargaining.

The situation is different among Vietnamese workers, who have developed a knack for organizing strikes and how to strategize and have gained valuable experience in collective solidarity in industrial actions. They have also seen how orderly albeit illegal actions can benefit their cause. As long as the national and local governments and trade union respond by rushing in to do the collective bargaining for them and to help them to negotiate better terms and conditions, they have good reason to resort to militant actions. As a MOLISA official told me, "The system now encourages strikes. Take children, they cry when they want something. If you give it to them they cry more. This is like workers and strikes." In Vietnam a strike pattern has become routinized. But will this last?

A problem facing the workers is that the Vietnamese government is under a lot of pressure from foreign capital. This is most prominently represented by the various chambers of commerce led by the China-based chapter of the American Chamber of Commence, which has been speaking up on behalf of other businesses, including the Taiwanese.[43] The message is that the Vietnamese government needs to be tough on illegal strikes and to strictly enforce Article 176 of Chapter 14. The threatening undertone is that foreign companies will disinvest. The foreign Chambers and their media outlets blame the government for not doing enough about the strikes and for not being able to control inflation, while agreeing that life has been hard for the workers. What the foreigner investors do not mention is that for more than a decade they have gained from a stagnant minimum wage, and that even the recent wage increases have not caught up with inflation. While many of the manufacturers and brand names have been reaping profits, they have made no offers to increase workers' wages.

In light of this, thus far the warnings about disinvesting from Vietnam have been empty threats.

If inflation continues to outpace wage rises and if workers feel their families' livelihoods are being squeezed below their basic needs, will the routinized strike pattern turn more militant and will workers take matters into their own hands to ask for more? Might workers also push the government for a higher legal minimum wage? At higher levels in the system, might the parameters of dialogue shift away from the tripartite institutions started under ILO guidance?

Whatever the scenario, looking back at the experience of the past one-and-half decades in Vietnam and China, cynics have been proven wrong that laws do not matter because they are not enforced. When comparing the two countries, it becomes apparent that the laws have helped set the foundations and frameworks for path-dependency evolution in the two countries' industrial relations patterns.

Notes

I am indebted to Professor Wang Hong-zen of Zhongshan University, Taiwan, who has collaborated with me in a research project titled "Taiwanese Businesses, The Global Production Chain and Corporate Social Responsibility", funded by the Chiang Ching-Kuo Foundation Foreign Scholarly Exchange. I am also indebted to Thuy Thu Pham for her research assistance.

1   Government policy might have changed recently when the police were not sent to suppress the several widely publicized strikes staged by workers in several Honda auto parts supplier plants in Guangdong Province in May and June 2010. At the time of writing it is still unknown whether the authorities will continue to tolerate future strikes.

2   See Ben Kerkvliet's chapter in this volume, Table 6.1.

3   "So vu dinh cong nam 2009 chi bang 30% nam 2008 [Number of Strikes in 2009 being just 30% of 2008]", *Lao Dong*, 5 January 2010, *Lao Dong Online* <http://www.laodong.com.vn/Home/So-vu-dinh-cong-nam-2009-chi-bang-30-nam-2008/20101/169395.laodong> (accessed 8 July 2010).

4   Jiang Huizhen, "Strike Waves in Vietnam: Some Taiwanese Businesses Consider Divesting", *Zhongguo Shibao* [China News], 1 August 2006.

5   See, for instance <http://www.buycar.com.tw/20738> (accessed 21 June 2010).

6   For further reasons why these two regions and Vietnam and China as a whole are worth comparing, see William S. Turley and Brantley Womack, "Asian Socialism's Open Doors: Guangzhou and Ho Chi Minh City", in *Transforming Asian Socialism: China and Vietnam Compared*, edited by Anita Chan, Benedict J. Tria Kerkvliet, and Jonathan Unger (St. Leonards: Allen & Unwin, 1999), pp. 44–73.

7   Liu Jianwqiang, "Workers' Strikes Non-stop Due to Misinterpretation of the New Contract Law", *Zhonngguo Qiyejia* [China Entrepreneur], 14 February 2008.

8   Most of these interviews with management were arranged by Professor Wang Hong-zen and both of us jointly carried out the interviews.

9   Shenzhen Laodong Zhengyi Zhongcai Wang [Shenzhen Industrial Dispute Arbitration Network] <http://www.szlaodong.com/laodongzhengyidiaojiezhongcaifajieshi/> (accessed 15 April 2010).

10   Vietnam Labour Code 23 June 1994 <http://www.ilo.org/dyn/natlex/docs/WEBTEXT/38229/64933/E94VNM01.htm> (accessed 23 June 2010); Vietnam Labour Code 23 June 1994 (as amended 2 April 2002), effective 1 January 2003 <http://www.global-standards.com/Resources/VNLaborCode1994-2002.pdf> (accessed 21 June 2010).

11   The minimum wage was different for other regions: VND790,000 (US$50) for Hai Phong, Ha Long, Da Nang, Nha Trang, Vung Tau, and Can Tho: and VND710,000 (US$45) for other areas.

12   See, for e.g., Die Ming, "Investigation into the Stella Footwear Factory Riot",
     Zhongguo xinwen zhoukan [China's Weekly News]; Zhao Dagong, "Let's
     Talk about the Stella Footwear Factory workers' 'riot'", 26 November 2004;
     Baoxun, <http://www.peacehall.com/news/gb/pubvp/2004/11/200411020111.
     shtml> (accessed 7 July 2010); "The Defense Statements of the Arrested Stella
     Workers", *China Labor Watch*, 23 April 2004 <http://www.chinalaborwatch.
     org/php/web/article.php?article_id=21> (accessed 2 January 2008).

13   Unlike Vietnam, China's minimum wages differ by locality but not by ownership
     type. In other words an official minimum wage set by a local government
     applies to all FDI, SOE or domestic private enterprises.

14   A corporate human resources officer and several MOLISA and VGCL officials
     all thought so when interviewed in 2006 and 2007. They did not rule out the
     possibility that labour activists helped instigate these strikes.

15   "Cong nhan Hue Phong lai dinh cong [Hue Phone workers strike again]",
     VietNamNet <http://www.vietnamnet.vn/xahoi/2008/04/777989/> (accessed
     22 April 2008); "Cong nhan Cong ty Hue Phong tiep tuc dinh cong [Workers
     in Hue Phong companies continued to strike]", Saigon Giai Phong Online
     <http://www.sggp.org.vn/xahoi/2008/4/148922/> (on 24 April 2008).

16   James Hookway, "Inflation Fuels Vietnam Strikes: Workers Demand Hefty
     Pay Increases from Foreign Firms", *Wall Street Journal,* 3 June 2008.

17   For a discussion on how Chinese workers do not comprehend the relationship
     between work hours and wages, see Anita Chan and Kaxton Siu, "Analyzing
     Exploitation: The Mechanisms Underpinning Low Wages and Excessive
     Overtime in Chinese Export Factories", *Critical Asian Studies* 42, no. 2 (June
     2010): 167–90.

18   "Laboring over Workers' Rights", *Beijing Review*, 25 December 2003,
     pp. 46–47.

19   Huang Chuhui, "Guangdong Will Soon Roll out Electronic Monitoring of
     Wage Payment", *Guangzhou Daily*, 14 August 2007, p. 2.

20   Interview conducted in 2006.

21   Ding Wanming, "Strike Grievances: Raise Wages", *Lianhe Bao* [United Daily],
     28 April 2008.

22   Agence France Presse, "Laid-off Factory Workers in China Say Prospects
     Grim", 18 October 2008 <http://afp.google.com/article/ALeqM5iKUyFb1YYI
     wox68VsXJkk3yVkPhQ> (accessed 14 April 2010); *Beijing Times.* "More Job
     Losses in S. China amid Global Financial Crisis", 18 October 2008 <http:
     www.english.sina.com/business/2008/1018/192558.html> (accessed 14 April
     2010).

23   This was precisely what happened in the two strikes described in Chris Chan
     King-Chi and Pun Ngai, "The Making of a New Working Class? A Study of
     Collective Actions of Migrant Workers in South China", *China Quarterly* 198

(June 2009): 287–303. Workers knew they would not get the support of the local government and had to take to the streets, blocking roads, triggering a large police presence resulting in violence and arrests.

24 As the economic downturn deepened in 2009 in the export sector, resulting in larger numbers of factory closures and labour disputes, the local governments temporarily became less inclined to suppressing labour unrest to avoid aggravating tensions.

25 My contacts at grassroots Chinese labour NGOs observed that this is the general situation. It is not easy to find strike activists after a strike has been suppressed.

26 For instance, Jiang Mingdao, former chair of the Shanghai Municipal General Trade Unions, whom I had the opportunity to meet in the early 1990s, had been involved in fighting to get the Shanghai government to index wages against inflation in the 1940s.

27 Trade Union Law of the People's Republic of China — 1992 (Promulgated on 3 April 1992 by the fifth session of the seventh National People's Congress) <http://www.lehmanlaw.com/resource-centre/laws-and-regulations/labor/trade-union-law-of-the-peoples-republic-of-china-1992.html> (accessed 23 June 2010).

28 Law on the Trade Unions, passed by the National Assembly on 30 June 1990, <http://www.congdoanvn.org.vn/english/details.asp?l=1&c=241&c2=241&m=2 26> (accessed 23 June 2010).

29 *China Labor News Translations* (CLNT), "Promising Wal-Mart Chair Resigns over Collective Contract Negotiations", 22 September 2008 <http://www. clntranslations.org/article/34/promising-wal-mart-trade-union-chair-resigns-over-collective-contract-negotiations> (accessed 14 April 2010).

30 For instance, some unionists in Vietnam argue that workplace trade union chairs' salaries should be covered by the union and not the employers, to solidify the workplace union's autonomy. *LookAtVietnam* <www.lookatvietnam. com/2009/03/vietnam-works-for-harmonious-labour-relations.html> (accessed 19 March 2009). In China, where workplace union chairs are also paid by employers, this is not a matter for debate.

31 For example, on the Radio Voice of Vietnam, 12 February 2009.

32 One ILO officer at the Hanoi office in 2006 told me that the Vietnamese government also had its own ideas and did not always take the ILO's suggestions into consideration.

33 Ronald Brown, "China Labour Dispute Resolution", Foundation for Law, Justice and Society, p. 1 <www.fljs.org/uploads/documents/Brown%231%23.pdf>.

34 The great increase in cases may also have been caused by other factors such as the Contract Law (see note 40) that came into effect at the same time.

35 Neil Gough, "Strike Marks a Turning Point for Labour Relations", *South China Morning Post*, 4 June 2010 <http://www.scmp.com/portal/site/SCMP/

menuitem.2af62ecb329d3d7733492d9253a0a0a0/?vgnextoid=3a45ac302
bef8210VgnVCM100000360a0a0aRCRD&ss=China&s=News> (accessed
9 September 2010); Anita Chan, "Labour Unrest and Role of Unions", *China
Daily*, 18 June 2010 <http://www.chinadaily.com.cn/opinion/2010-06/18/
content_9987347.htm>.

[36]   Interview with Nguyen Manh Cuong of MOLISA on 26 January 2006.

[37]   See, for e.g., *Straits Times*, "Minimum Wage Set to be Increased", 26 June
1998.

[38]   Notably, state guidelines require each enterprise to develop its own salary
tables and scale to be filed with the local government department for approval.
Van Thu Ha, "Viet Nam", in *Rights for Two-Thirds of Asia: Asian Labor Law
Review 2008* (Hong Kong: Asia Monitor Resource Centre, 2008), p. 222.

[39]   Information from a human resources manager of a large Taiwanese supplier
corporation. Interview conducted by Wang Hong-zen on 30 November 2006
in Taiwan.

[40]   Contract Law of the People's Republic of China (Adopted and Promulgated
by the Second Session of the Ninth National People's Congress 15 March
1999) <http://www.novexcn.com/contract_law_99.html> (accessed 23 June
2010).

[41]   *China Labor News Translations,* "A New Precedent: Shenzhen Furniture Factory
Worker Wins Two Years Overtime Back Pay", November 2007; "Shenzhen Labor
Activist Attacked", December 2007; "Labor NGOs in Guangdong Province",
January 2008. All available at <http://www.clntranslations.org/archive/>
(accessed 8 July 2010).

[42]   *China Labor News Translations*, "Chinese Labor NGOs and Free Legal Services
Always in a Precarious Situation", January 2010, <http://www.clntranslations.
org/archive/> (accessed 8 July 2010); see also note 25.

[43]   American Chamber of Commerce, "Letter to the Prime Minister re Industrial
Relations in Vietnam, 20 May 2008" <www.amchamvietnam.com/2252>
(accessed 22 October 2008).

References

Agence France Presse. "Laid-off Factory Workers in China Say Prospects Grim",
18 October 2008 <http://afp.google.com/article/ALeqM5iKUyFb1YYIwox68
VsXJkk3yVkPhQ> (accessed 14 April 2010).

American Chamber of Commerce. "Letter to the Prime Minister re Industrial
Relations in Vietnam, 20 May 2008" <http://www.amchamvietnam.com/2252>
(accessed 22 October 2008).

Beijing Review. "Laboring over Workers' Rights", 25 December 2003, pp.
46–47.

Beijing Times. "More Job Losses in S. China amid Global Financial Crisis", 18 October 2008 <http://english.sina.com/business/2008/1018/192558.html> (accessed 14 April 2010).

Benjamin, Aaron. "The Administration of Justice in Labor Law: Arbitration and the Role of the Court". *Comparative Labor Law and Policy Journal* 3 (1979–1980): 1–18.

Brown, Ronald. "China Labour Dispute Resolution", Foundation for Law, Justice and Society, p. 1 <www.fljs.org/uploads/documents/Brown%231%23.pdf>, accessed 23 June 2010).

Chan, Anita, Richard Madsen, and Jonathan Unger. *Chen Village: Revolution to Globalization.* Berkeley: University of California Press, 2009.

Chan, Anita and Irene Norlund. "Vietnamese and Chinese Labor Regimes: On the Road to Divergence". *China Journal* 40 (July 1998): 173–97.

Chan, Anita and Kaxton Siu. "Analyzing Exploitation: The Mechanisms Underpinning Low Wages and Excessive Overtime in Chinese Export Factories". *Critical Asian Studies* 42, no. 2 (June 2010): 167–90.

Chan, Anita and Wang Hongzen. "The Impact of the State on Workers' Conditions: Comparing Taiwanese Factories in China and Vietnam". *Pacific Affairs* 77, no. 4 (Winter 2004): 629–46.

Chan, Anita. "Organizing Wal-Mart in China: Two Steps Forward, One Step Back for China's Unions". *New Labor Forum* 16, no. 2 (2007): 87–96.

Chan, Chris King-Chi and Pun Ngai. "The Making of a New Working Class? A Study of Collective Actions of Migrant Workers in South China". *China Quarterly* 198 (June 2009): 287–303.

Chen Feng. "Trade Unions and the Quadripartite Interactions in Strike Settlement in China". *China Quarterly* 201 (March 2010): 104–24.

China Labor News Translations (CLNT). "Promising Wal-Mart Chair Resigns over Collective Contract Negotiations", 22 September 2008 <http://www.clntranslations.org/article/34/promising-wal-mart-trade-union-chair-resigns-over-collective-contract-negotiations (accessed 14 April 2010).

China Post. "Vietnam Urged to Control Strikes", 23 July 2008 <http://www.chinapost.comtw/print/166766htm> (accessed 23 July 2008).

Clark, Simon. "The Changing Character of Strikes in Vietnam". *Post-Communist Economics* 18, no. 3 (2006): 345–61.

Clark, Simon, Lee Chang-Hee, and Do Quynh Chi. "From Rights to Interests: The Challenge of Industrial Relations in Vietnam". *Journal of Industrial Relations* 49, no. 4 (2006): 545–68.

Contract Law of the People's Republic of China (Adopted and Promulgated by the Second Session of the Ninth National People's Congress March 15, 1999) <http://www.novexcn.com/contract_law_99.html> (accessed 23 June 2010).

Do Quynh Chi. Case Study: Evolution of a New Pattern of Strikes in Vietnam, Hanoi, April 2007, not published.

Fang Qiuxin. "Yuangong jiti shangfang tao gongzi, shengfu juche gongdao poing minfen" [Employees collectively asked for wages, the government adjudicates to quell people's wrath]. *Guangdong laodong bao* [Guangdong Labour], 1 March 1999.

Glantz, Aaron and Ngoc Nguyen. "Happy Meals, Unhappy Workers", *Corpwatch* <http://www.corpwatch.org/print_article.php?id=13358> (accessed 15 March, 2006).

Guangzhou Daily. "Guangdong jiang tuiguang gongzi zhifu dianzi jiankong zhidu" [Guangong will launch an electronic monitoring system over payment of wages], 14 August 2007.

Hookway, James. "Inflation Fuels Vietnam Strikes: Workers Demand Hefty Pay Increases from Foreign Firms". *Wall Street Journal*, 3 June 2008.

Hyman, Richard. *Strikes*. London: Macmillan, 1989.

ILO Press Release. "Vietnam Commits to Strengthening Legal Frameworks for Employer-Worker Negotiations". 1 April 2010 <http://www.ilo.org/asia/info/ public/pr/lang--en/WCMS_125649/index.htm> (accessed 22 June 2010).

Lee Chang-Hee. Industrial Relations and Dispute Settlement in Vietnam. ILO Discussion Paper, June 2006a.

———. "Recent Industrial Relations Developments in China and Viet Nam: The Transformation of Industrial Relations in East Asian Transition Economies". *Journal of Industrial Relations* 4, no. 3 (2006b): 415–29.

Lee, Don. "Multinationals Take a Longer View of Vietnam". *Los Angeles Times*, 11 April 2009.

Radio Voice of Vietnam. "New Model Needed to Ensure Labour Harmony", 12 February 2009 <http://english.vovnews.vn?Utilities?PrintVietn.aspx?ID=99832> (accessed 22 April 2009).

Shen, Jie and John Benson. "Tripartite Consultation in China: A First Step Towards Collective Bargaining". *International Labour Review* 14, nos. 2–3 (2008): 232–48.

Shenzhen Laodong Zhengyi Zhongcai Wang [Shenzhen Industrial Dispute Arbitration Network] <http://www.szlaodong.com/laodongzhengyidiaojiezhongcaifajieshi/> (accessed 15 April 2010).

Straits Times. "Minimum Wage Set to be Increased", 26 June 1998.

Sunoo, Jan Jung-Min. *Understanding and Preventing Strikes in Vietnam*. Hanoi: ILO, 2007.

Turley, William S. and Brantley Womack. "Asian Socialism's Open Doors: Guangzhou and Ho Chi Minh City". In *Transforming Asian Socialism: China and Vietnam Compared,* edited by Anita Chan, Benedict J. Tria Kerkvliet, and Jonathan Unger, pp. 44–73. St. Leonards: Allen & Unwin, 1999.

Van Thu Ha. "Viet Nam". In *Rights for Two-Thirds of Asia: Asian Labor Law Review 2008*, pp. 215–29. Hong Kong: Asia Monitor Resource Centre, 2008.

Wang Hong-zen. "Asian Transnational Corporations and Labor Rights: Vietnamese Trade Unions in Taiwan-invested Companies". *Journal of Business Ethics* 56, no. 1 (2005): 43–53.

Wehrle, Edmund F. *Between a River and a Mountain: The AFL-CIO and the Vietnam War*. Ann Arbor: University of Michigan Press, 2006.

Ye Minghua. "Shenzhen shi shangbangnian laodongzhongcaian bizeng 243%", Chinese Labor Dispute Net, 13 August 2008 <http://www.btophr.com/b_article/19514.html> (accessed 23 October 2008).

8

THE DYNAMICS OF A MULTINATIONAL FACTORY REGIME AND RECENT STRIKES IN VIETNAM

Suhong Chae

"Just as the abandonment of the working class proceeds from the fact of rather than reason for its passivity, so the embrace of social movements often stems from the fact of rather than the reason for their struggles." (Michael Burawoy 1985, p. 9)

In the summer of 2008, Ho Chi Minh City (HCMC) and adjacent Dong Nai Province in south Vietnam were experiencing an unprecedented proliferation of labour conflicts. One trade union leader in HCMC remarked, "this is the most chaotic change in labour–management relations since *Doi Moi*". In the last week of July 2008, at least thirty factories in Dong Nai Province alone were undergoing strikes, while many factories in the industrial zones (IZs) and Export Processing Zones (EPZs) in the greater HCMC area, such as Bien Hoa I, Bien Hoa II, Long Thanh, and Linh Trung, had experienced labour disputes. The strikes were mainly in foreign-invested multinational factories and aimed at commercial or production disruption to protest low wages. Although they were illegal, the strikes were non-violent and peacefully resolved.

To understand the nature of current labour–management conflicts and strikes, this chapter attempts to analyze the process of empowerment and disempowerment of the workers at a micro level in one foreign-invested joint-venture factory. As Hansson (2003, p. 175) postulates, if "conflicts occur outside the formal structure of the partystate and are still dealt with in an ad hoc manner largely depending on the local power configuration where conflicts take place", then we need to explore how that local power is configured.[1] Another question is whether there are consistent structural characteristics behind the "ad hoc manner" in which labour–management conflicts are dealt with.

This study will focus on the history of a factory, SIL,[2] that had been a joint-venture between a private Korean company and a Vietnamese state-owned corporation for sixteen years, and was recently sold to private Vietnamese owners. The factory's early history was marked by a considerable clash of cultures between the Vietnamese workers (who were from the socialist parent factory, May) and the Korean managers, who were accustomed to the tough capitalist discipline of labour-intensive industries in their homeland. Ugly everyday tensions in the factory culminated in a strike, a very rare event in Vietnam in the early 1990s.

In the aftermath of that strike, however, labour–management relations gradually stabilized, and during my first fieldwork period (from fall 1998 to spring 2000), SIL's management had a firm grip over its workforce. Despite worsening working conditions including greater intensity, poorer job security, and stagnant wages, the workers did not attempt to directly challenge the authority of the foreign managers again enough to shake the company's political and economic stability. Stable management–labour relations lasted even through my second fieldwork period in the summer of 2008, despite the wave of strikes then affecting many multinational factories in the surrounding greater HCMC area. Even when SIL's workers discovered that their foreign managers had decided to sell the company in the fall of 2009, there was little resistance. While there were complaints about and anger against the Korean management, the workers simply accepted their fate, however, and did not stage any protests. The workers were were also distracted by their concerns about the impending buyout by the new Vietnamese owners.

This chapter seeks to examine why the workers at SIL did not show any signs of conspicuous resistance in the face of deteriorating work conditions. I will argue that the workers' seemingly mild resistance (or rather passivity) against the foreign management was a product of the social and political processes that had emerged within the factory after a segment of the Vietnamese workers undertook to play a central role in negotiating with the various parties involved: foreign management, the machinery of Vietnamese state (for e.g., power-holders in the socialist parent company and regional trade union leaders), and the factory workers.

This chapter will first explore the history of the particular factory regime that was established at SIL through a modus vivendi established after the initial social, cultural, and political struggles between the new foreign capitalist managers and the former socialist workers. I will then examine the workers' social organizations, cultural activities, and household incomes in the context of the politics of the factory, all of which contributed to the maintenance and reproduction of this labour–management regime. Finally, I will examine the impact of economic conditions on the factory regime, and workers' responses.

By exploring the history of SIL, this chapter seeks to uncover, as in the Burawoy quote which opens this chapter, the "facts" and "reasons" that Vietnamese workers in foreign-invested companies have sometimes been passive and at other times resistant in some multinational factories in Vietnam. In other words, this ethnographic portrait attempts to explain why some foreign-invested factories have been immune to labour conflicts and others have not, given the same macroeconomic circumstances.

THE POLITICS OF PRODUCTION AND THE UNSTABLE FACTORY REGIME

Multinational corporations in Vietnam generally relocate from their home countries to lower their costs and increase their profit margins by taking advantage of cheaper labour. Despite some broad similarities, however, there is no such thing as a typical multinational corporation, or one that is statistically representative from which we can generalize. The political economy of multinational corporations varies widely in terms of the size and type of invested capital, industry and major products, the duration of investment, ownership, location, relationship with local bureaucrats, managerial philosophy, and so on.

While acknowledging such wide variations, in my ten-year acquaintance with foreign-invested factories, I have been struck by what seems to be a consistent theme in foreign managers' accounts. They say, for instance, that there are significant differences between running a factory in their home countries and in Vietnam and that their companies encountered initial difficulties in "disciplining" their Vietnamese workforce, partners, and bureaucrats. Such observations are usually followed by confident assertions of how they were developing or had already developed methods of dealing with these problems.

Their consistently similar stories raise some crucial questions on the particularity of political processes in multinational factories: What difficulties do foreign managers experience in the early stages of running a factory in Vietnam? In other words, what differences do foreign managers experience between their own concepts of work, reward, politics, and ideology and that of their Vietnamese workforce? What kinds of skills and knowledge are necessary to overcome and transform these differences in order to achieve a successful capitalistic discipline? Are there circumstances under which such managerial "know-how" no longer works?

If we are to understand the politics of multinational factories in Vietnam, we need to seek answers to these questions, from the perspective and experiences of both the foreign managers and Vietnamese workers. Interpreting these processes will give us a clue not only as to why certain types of factories have been prone to strikes but also why some factories settle strikes more easily than others. I will first describe and explain what happened in the early history of the multinational textile factory that I have studied for more than ten years.

The Thirteen Month Salary and the "Hot" Christmas Eve Strike

SIL was established as a joint-venture between SI, the Korean parent company, and May, the Vietnamese state-owned enterprise, in August 1992,[3] with the Korean partner holding 70 per cent of the shares and the Vietnamese 30 per cent. The shareholding structure was also reflected in the fact that the management was controlled by the Koreans although both parties agreed to discuss and decide important matters collaboratively. Despite the lack of specific labour legislation for multinational corporations in Vietnam at the time, the Koreans were well aware that they had to have a trade union in this joint-venture with the state-owned company. Hence, despite significantly different views on the role of trade unions, both partners agreed to allow the workers to organize an interim trade union, which would later be transformed into an official trade union.

In March 1993, after an eight-month-long renovation of the existing May factory and after installing the spinning and weaving machines brought in by the Koreans, the factory was ready to begin commercial production. Initially, to save the time and expense of training a new batch of workers, most of the semiskilled and skilled shop floor workers from May were permanently transferred to SIL. On their part, the Korean management brought in approximately forty engineers and shop floor managers to temporarily take charge of machine maintenance and oversee the transferred Vietnamese workforce until production was established.

The factory was thus divided between Korean managers (who imposed discipline) and Vietnamese workers (who were disciplined). A similar hierarchy was also established within the board of directors. Amongst the Vietnamese employees, there was a bifurcation between "core" and "periphery" (or ordinary) workers in May, which was a conspicuous characteristic of socialist factory regimes (Burawoy and Lukacs 1992; Jovitt 1992; Norlund 1995). Around 5–10 per cent of SIL's 650 workers could be classified as having been "core" workers in May. The core workers — party cadres, shift leaders, team leaders, and their relatives — enjoyed, or had the potential to enjoy, some privileges in the socialist factory because of their better "social origin" (*thanh phan xa hoi*),[4] connections, or skills. In contrast, periphery workers, who were mostly semiskilled and unskilled and lacked connections, had been unhappy with the politics of their former socialist factory.

Despite major and minor everyday frictions at SIL, both core and periphery Vietnamese workers initially appeared to be adapting to their new factory life under foreign managers. The periphery workers, in particular, seemed to be more satisfied with the new factory regime because the Korean managers did not recognize the core workers' former privileges. It took only nine months for the simmering tensions between the Vietnamese workers and the Korean managers to explode, however. What finally caused the eruption was friction revolving around the *Tet* bonus, also known as the thirteenth month salary, an established Vietnamese practice for distributing and sharing the annual profits in state-owned companies. Under the centralized socialist system, theoretically, workers had been entitled to compensation either directly by their own companies or indirectly via the redistribution of state wealth after the state-owned companies contributed a certain portion (usually around 15 per cent) of their earnings in tax.

On the one hand, workers had become accustomed to seeing the thirteenth month salary as their legitimate share of the profits, rather than just a reward bestowed by an employer who appropriated their labour. When they found that this was no longer the case under the new owners, the workers were at first perplexed, and then furious. The Korean managers, on the other hand, resented the idea of having to pay a thirteenth month salary and further claimed that they could not afford a bonus since SIL had not made any significant profit in its first year of operation.

The Vietnamese leadership, comprising May's senior managers, executives, and the interim trade union leaders in SIL, had been aware that the workers were seriously dissatisfied, and knew that it could mean trouble, especially at that time of year. As *Tet* drew near, workers desperately needed the addition to their regular salary to buy special food, visit relatives, and for "lucky money" (*ly xi*) to give their children. The Korean management's refusal to give a *Tet* bonus was seen by workers as a challenge to their social ties and to what they held "culturally meaningful" (Thomson 1968, p. 10).

SIL's Korean managers themselves were not unaware of the significance of the Lunar New Year and the practice of giving a bonus, since there was a similar custom at home. They maintained, however, that the Vietnamese workers' demands were based on a fundamentally different logic. They feared that this was a manifestation of socialist thinking that could undermine their capitalist factory regime.

It was a sudden stillness in the normally noisy weaving factory that alerted the Korean managers that something was wrong. The calm before the storm was broken when workers began to gather in front of the two-story main office building. Led by the interim trade union leaders[5] and shop floor managers, they rallied and began to shout slogans such as "*Tet* bonus" and "humane treatment". The protest started at 1 p.m. on 24 December 1993, the day that Vietnamese call *Noel Nong* (Hot Christmas). It continued for a couple of hours until word came through of an emergency meeting of SIL's Korean general manager and the Vietnamese vice-president, as well as high-ranking managers at May and SIL's interim trade union leaders to be held that evening to discuss the disputed issues.

The meeting resulted in a quick end to the crisis. The management agreed to give the workers a *Tet* bonus, equivalent to one month's salary, at least for that year, and to deal seriously with the remaining demands such as the quality of meals, length of breaks, labour discipline, and the form of greetings[6] in future meetings. Although the agreement was only a temporary measure to quickly resolve the accumulated grievances, it was perceived as a positive result by both sides. The hastily granted concessions temporarily appeased the workers' anger and simultaneously avoided reprisals from higher authorities for failure to maintain the peace between foreign investors and Vietnamese workers.

The result was actually a victory for the Koreans: while they had had to compromise by giving in to the workers' demand for a *Tet* bonus, they made it clear that the bonus was not being given as an annual entitlement. The Korean management also triumphed in the sense that it was able to pacify the strike's leaders, who had mostly been core workers in the state-owned parent company May who had felt that they were not being as well treated under the new capitalist factory regime. The core workers were feeling happier, believing that they had demonstrated their power to influence the Korean managers, and hence expected better treatment afterwards.

For the ordinary (periphery) workers, the strike was ground-breaking, as they could hardly have imagined such an overt collective struggle taking place in the state-owned enterprise they previously worked in. Although strikes were neither legal nor illegal at the time, it was an extremely unusual event and attracted the attention of major Vietnamese newspapers such as *Than Nien* (Youth) and *Phu Nhu* (Woman) as well as foreign media such as the BBC.

Clearly, the unprecedented "Hot Christmas Eve" strike imparted lessons to all the participants. Yet most of the primary causes of the strike remained unresolved — except for the partial satisfaction of economic demands from the perspective of "periphery" workers — and were about to develop into more complex politics. Most workers remained deeply frustrated by the fundamental changes in the factory environment and felt that they suffered from unfair and excessive control under their foreign managers.

The Politics of Production and a Nationalistic Backlash

When the workers were transferred from the socialist mother company to the foreign capitalist company, they had been relieved to see similarities between production procedures in their old and new workplaces. They found, however, that work was far more onerous in the new factory. They had experienced the same work intensity in May but there were differences.

In May, they had had to work extra hard during the high season and/ or when there was a sufficient supply of raw materials. In other words, because of the "shortage economy" (Burawoy and Lukacs 1992, p. 18), a characteristic of planned economies, the workers had to engage in "storming production" (Jovitt 1992) but only at certain times of the year. Yet, at May, unlike SIL, they had felt that they had some decision-making autonomy, even during busy periods. Furthermore, they could adjust their working speed collectively under a team leader or a shop floor manager. Under such conditions, since rewards were calculated on a piecework basis, they had sometimes felt that they would prefer to work harder than suffer from a lack of work.

At SIL, they finally had enough regular work but under significantly different conditions. The factory no longer had any problems with obtaining raw materials, a lack of spare parts or mechanical failure but production was at the mercy of fluctuating market demand. But the style and attitude of the new managers was different. Unlike the socialist managers, the Koreans continually supervised the workers, checking the quantity and quality of their ouput. The workers felt that they were now under strict surveillance by managers whose only concern was that they met production standards and quotas. With little room for creativity and autonomy, the workers were experiencing what Harry Braverman (1974) called "the separation of conception and execution in work". Although the division of labour was broadly similar under the old and new factory regimes due to the similar production processes and technology, the concept and exercise of work roles were significantly different. Given the intensified work pace and coercive management practices, the workers felt that they were being continually punished rather than rewarded for their labour.

Under such circumstances, the workers needed mechanisms to air grievances but found themselves in a completely different political realm. As many studies of socialist factories suggest, central appropriation needs distinctive institutional and organizational arrangements within the factory as well as between the factory and the state. The state "as both organizer and owner of production" needs to be "present at the point of production" (Burawoy and Lukacs 1992, p. 32) through a tripartite organizational structure (or quadruple, *Bo Tu,* in the case of Vietnam, since it includes the youth union, *Than Nien*): management, party–state, and factory union functioning as "a two-way transmission belt" (Pravda and Ruble 1986, p. 4) of state policies and information from the shop floor.

SIL had a provisional trade union but its functions and power were radically different from those of the socialist trade union (Jerneck and Nguyen 1996; Norlund 1997). The only way that a worker could convey his or her complaints to the foreign management was by requesting a meeting with SIL's Vietnamese deputy general manager and other administrative staff. However, the Vietnamese manager's role as a supervising partner was limited to being an adviser to the Korean manager.

The Vietnamese workers began expressing their unhappiness in nationalistic terms. This is a well-documented way of channelling class conflict in multinational corporations where the local staff have no other means of airing or resolving their grievances (Kim H. M. 2002; Kim S. K. 1997; Nash and Fernandez-Kelly 1983; Ong 1987). Thus the coercive and obstinate style of SIL's management was attributed to the managers being stereotypically "aggressive, violent and rude" Koreans. The Vietnamese workers generally believed that Korean managers could only communicate with their workers by "yelling (*la*) rather than talking (*noi chuyen*)" on the shop floor because of their innate hot temper. The Korean managers did the same, blaming the Vietnamese national character for their workers being "lazy", "dirty", "irresponsible", having "suspicious" behaviour and attitudes, with a tendency to shirk responsibility by resorting to excuses such as "*khong biet*" (don't know).

In this way, the intensification of labour control in the new capitalist factory produced and reproduced antagonism between the foreign managers, who controlled, and the local workers, who were controlled. Clearly, both the "shouting" Korean managers and the "*khong biet*" Vietnamese workers needed to blame someone for their frustrations. It is also evident that cultural differences provided a reasonable interpretive framework for their troubles and enabled each side to reinforce their national identities by forming a front against "the other".

In retrospect, to understand the essence of the Hot Christmas Eve strike, we need to pay attention to the frustrations caused by the new capitalist factory regime. The workers had been inculcated in a different work environment (in this case, a socialist factory regime) and they had to adapt very quickly to a new one (a capitalist factory regime) with more intense work and stricter controls. They neither knew how to deal with the new situation nor to whom they could express their dissatisfaction. The only way for them to vent their frustrations was by negatively stereotyping others or spontaneously responding to single events. Moreover, they had endured this tough work transition in expectation of higher compensation in the multinational factory; when these expectations turned out to be illusory, they collectively resisted the new factory regime.

The other major factor which enabled them to express their collective frustration during the Hot Christmas Eve strike in 1993 was the existence of a leadership. The core workers from the former socialist factory were able to organize the workers' spontaneous resistance into a strike with the help of their compatriots in higher positions on the shop floor and connections to the socialist parent company. However, the core workers' intention was limited to drawing attention to their ability to exercise power within the new factory regime, power which the foreign managers had hitherto ignored. Once they thought their aim was accomplished, the core workers ended the strike quickly, satisfied that they had the support of higher authorities beyond the factory. They were optimistic that their power would gradually be restored when the trade union was set up. As a result, the strike was settled without really addressing the "ordinary" workers' grievances with the new capitalistic factory regime.

The Dynamics of a Stable Multinational Factory Regime

After the strike, stability was restored relatively quickly and peaceful labour–management relations were maintained. By mid-1994, the company had officially agreed to the establishment of a trade union.

The election for the trade union leaders was neither democratic nor undemocratic. The workers were divided into thirty-two groups corresponding to their respective sections, and selected a total of eighty-five representatives the week before election day. These representatives in turn chose seven executive members among the candidates on election day. The seven executive members then voted for the chairman of the trade union who had a right to choose his or her own staff, including two vice-presidents and an auditor. The democratic part of this process was that the workers were able to discuss their options and grievances and the responsibilities of the interim or incumbent trade union leaders and then choose delegates who could represent their opinions. The undemocratic part of the election was that the twelve candidates for executive membership were pre-selected by the interim (or incumbent) trade union leaders. Although they were required to choose a proportional number of candidates from each section, it was not possible to exclude candidates from certain factions. In addition, the chairman of the trade union had to be recognized by the city trade union, which obviously preferred a Communist Party member who had been inducted in "that same union".

As stipulated in the trade union law, the external city trade union then approved the six elected executive members of the factory trade union. The Korean managers reluctantly signed the agreement, obviously not happy with the composition of the executive committee, who were almost all Communist Party members, and whose chairman, Mr Nguyen,[7] had proved to be a hardliner during the Hot Christmas Eve strike.

Having signed the agreement, the Korean managers now began to find ways to ostracize the executive members of the trade union, incessantly harassing them until they quit. A clerk in the personnel department later described the managers' techniques as the "five tricks": demotion or non-promotion; transfer to an unfamiliar section or assignment; downgrading of work evaluation and hence, a decrease in their monthly bonus; careful monitoring for mistakes that could be used as evidence in a legal dismissal process; and direct inducement of resignation by offering a larger retirement pension. Since none of the "five tricks" violated any specific sections of the Labour Code, it was extremely difficult for the executive to fight back effectively.

Moreover, once management–labour relations had stabilized in the factory after the strike, the trade union leaders were no longer able to attract enough support from their fellow workers to organize any further resistance against managerial manipulations. In the lead-up to and during the strike, the core workers had been able to draw upon their previous influence in May. They were also able to take advantage of SIL's straitened circumstances, which considerably limited the material resources available to the Korean managers to build rapport with the workers. In the post-strike power struggle, however, the core workers lost their support base among the ordinary workers and were outmanouvred by the Korean management.

The company's improved financial circumstances after the first year empowered the foreign managers to facilitate the disintegration of the bloc of old core workers by forming a new core of pro-Korean workers. The political environment outside the factory was not favourable to the old core workers either since the state itself was focused on economic development with the help of foreign capital. The new factory regime thus successfully closed the chapter on the early period of conflict and began a new period of political stability.

The Dynamics of the "Peaceful Years"

With the resolution of the post-strike power struggle, the factory regime entered into an era that both the Korean managers and the trade union leaders called the "peaceful years". Several features contributed to this long period of labour–management stability. First, the company continued to grow and be profitable. Being among the first foreign companies in the textile industry to move to Vietnam gave it a competitive advantage and early entry into the expanding Vietnamese domestic market. With the exception of a brief period during the Asian crisis in 1997, the company prospered, enabling it to have a degree of flexibility to respond to workers' economic demands.

Second, the company also "reduced potential conflict by making and utilizing formal rules and regulations" (Burawoy 1979, 1985; Gordon, Reich and Edward 1982; Litterer 1978) that substantially benefited the Korean management. These rules and regulations allowed management to justify its labour control and disciplinary acts. The managers could now control and discipline the workers more easily by putting troublemakers before the disciplinary committee institutionalized by the collective agreement. Simultaneously, the company tried to improve its image by establishing a comfortable relationship with relevant higher authorities outside the company such as the local government, and local and city trade union officials.

Last but not least, by assigning the role of "middleman" (Bailey 1969, p. 167) to some Vietnamese workers, the company was able to not only try to accommodate the divergent interests of workers and management more efficiently but also have cultural mediators between the Koreans and the Vietnamese. This "middleman" role played by these Vietnamese workers significantly contributed to "soothing and diverting the workers' antagonism" (in the words of one Korean manager) and maintaining the peace in this multinational factory. The middlemen were mainly male, but there were a few female supervisors who worked closely with female workers and mediated in sociocultural areas that could not be covered by the male middlemen. These dynamics turned management control into a less overtly coercive and yet more hegemonic regime with a distinctive, complex power structure. Politics in the factory could be plotted along two intersecting relationship axes (Korean managers and middlemen vs middlemen and peripheral workers) linked within an hierarchical structure (from top to bottom: Korean managers, middlemen, and peripheral workers).

In other words, the Korean managers exercised their hegemony over the factory workforce by controlling the Vietnamese middlemen and supervisors, who in turn controlled the rest of the workers. Hence, the stability of the factory regime pivoted on the role of the Vietnamese middlemen as mediators.

Hui, Kinship, and the Politics of Middlemen

Amongst the workforce itself, there were multistranded relationships based not only on formal work roles but also on informal institutions such as the family, kinship, and the *hui* credit system. Workers' social relations and divisions intersected with other factors such as gender, age/generation, and regional origin. In this section, I will explore, first, how the workers' multifarious social relations were interwoven into and sustained the political structure of the factory, and second, how the workers as self-interested agents used their social ties and networks to manipulate outcomes to their advantage.

Hui are organized voluntarily by workers mainly for financial cushioning against crises. Since a *hui* is an informal credit institution that primarily relies on mutual trust, its social function and cultural meanings are crucial to understanding the workers' lives in the factory. However, the intersections between *hui* members had political consequences since the informal credit unions not only interwove relations between the workers but also simultaneously fostered internal rivalries and antagonisms.

Most of the workers in the factory participated in the credit system and were said to *choi hui* (play *hui*) — or were connected to it in one way or another. In fact, a worker had to be very determined to avoid joining any *hui*, since this could alienate her or him from colleagues in the same section. Workers generally belonged to more than one *hui* at a time.

At SIL each *hui* had around twenty to thirty members, each contributing about VND50,000–200,000 (sometimes up to VND500,000), that is between US$2.50–US$10, every two weeks. *Hui* are organized in a cycle, calculated by the number of members multiplied by the contribution period. If there were thirty members, each contributing once every two weeks (usually on paydays), then the cycle would be sixty weeks. The logic of the *hui* was based on the rule that each member gets to collect all the holdings at one point in the cycle; during the cycle the size of "the pot" therefore increased. Especially, at first — at the beginning of the cycle — the person who asked for the least amount of money (*toi bo*) got what they asked for, and the remainder stayed in the pot. So, for example, if the *hui* collected 30 (members) x US$3, or US$90, in the first collection, the person who received it would very likely be the one who asked for much less than US$90. But he/she had to keep contributing the set biweekly amount of US$3 for the remainder of the cycle. In the process, the *hui* functioned as a way for workers to both save and obtain relatively large sums of money when necessary.

The key factor in the *hui* system was the members' credit and mutual trust. In other words, all the members had to have a guaranteed and constant source of income and the intention of honouring their contributions to the end of a cycle. The necessity of mutual trust among *hui* members provided a space for social interaction, particularly for female workers. Put differently, a worker's close friends were, in most cases, those who worked in the same shift and were in the same *hui*. In sum, the informal *hui* that had developed primarily for economic purposes also significantly contributed to the reinforcement of social ties between workers in the same section. The social ties that were produced and reproduced by the intersecting formal organization of work and the informal organization of *hui* were important for the workers, since their relations and activities were seriously constrained by their demanding work–life conditions.

Ironically, it was also the *hui* that was a source of conflict between workers, often because of a member's financial crisis. Two kinds of financial failure can bankrupt a *hui*: *be hui* and *gat hui*. *Be hui* occurs when the *chu hui* (*hui* organizer) collects the money and runs away. *Gat hui* means that a member fails to continue contributing money after collecting a payout.

Some middlemen tried to take advantage of such fissures and conflicts arising from the *hui*. For example, when there were *hui*-related incidents, the trade union leaders would send *hui* organizers (*chu hui*) a warning by posting a notice to remind workers of the illegality of the credit system as well as loan sharking,[8] largely practised by *hui* organizers. The middlemen might also raise a fund to lend money at no interest to deeply indebted workers and ask the Korean managers to force the loan sharks to write off such debts. Shop floor managers might also begin to firmly refuse some loan sharks' requests to withhold a debtor's salary and allowances. While significantly shrinking some influential loan sharks' activities, such changes, led by some middlemen, indirectly helped other *chu hui*, especially small ones, to expand their business. In short, the power of the middlemen derived both from being embedded in workers' formal and informal social relations and networks, as well as by taking advantage of the fissures and problems arising from these networks.

Another way that the middlemen cultivated ties, power, and influence *vis-à-vis* the ordinary (especially female) workers was to expand their kin relations within the factory. When a senior female clerk in the personnel division tipped me off to the extensive and intricate kin networks in the factory in early 2000, I doubted that even an influential worker could have enough kin members to maintain his or her power in the factory. But as I traced workers' social networks through residential registration documents (*ho so*), resumés, recommendation letters, and interviews, however, I realized that my skepticism was ill founded.

Indeed, most workers had at least one or two family members or relatives in the factory. Some of them even formed large groups, each of which, almost without exception, included an influential middleman. Generally, the size of a family group was proportional to the degree of power and authority that a central figure in the group had within the factory. For example, there were twenty-one kin members in the chairman of the trade union's group. Moreover, a middlemen could expand his power base over non-kin workers in a number of ways. One way was to form a fictitious kinship with workers: a middleman would bestow a great favour by recommending an applicant who was not related to him but to another worker. The new worker who obtained a job through the intervention of this kin group would feel a sense of enormous obligation to the middleman from that group.

In the overall scheme of factory politics, however, I need to emphasize that it was not just the informal social ties and moral obligations to middlemen, and an impregnable hierarchy, that precluded workers from resisting both the collusive domination of powerful middlemen and foreign managers. The ordinary workers themselves seemed to be preoccupied with their own affairs.

Ordinary female workers, for instance, seemed to be more keen to protect themselves from being excessively controlled by some female shop floor managers than to resist the foreign management. Yet while pretending to be apathetic towards factory politics, these female workers would actively seek help from powerful male middlemen and the Korean managers in their everyday struggles against the disliked female supervisors. Such efforts seemed to divert and subvert the ordinary female worker's class antagonism away from the powerful foreign managers and (especially) male middlemen. Hence, the female workers were less likely to engage in a class struggle against management.

Three Realms of Politics in the Hegemonic Factory Regime

This ethnography attempts to locate reasons for patterns of worker resistance and non-resistance or accommodation to the capitalist discipline in the distinctive political structure and the complex politics inside one multinational factory. The distinctive political structure at SIL was created, maintained, and challenged by three different groups of actors interacting with one another through differentiated power, social networks, and cultural meanings. To explicate these complicated political processes, I heuristically distinguish three realms of politics that were interconnected and simultaneously maintained relatively autonomously.

The first political realm was based on the ethnic division between foreign managers and their local workers. In this realm, the foreign managers maintained their superiority over the Vietnamese workers by sustaining clear ethnic and national distinctions between themselves and the workers and by simultaneously inducing workers' consent through hegemonic means.

The second political realm centred on the role of the Vietnamese middlemen. These middlemen maintained and expanded their power by actively mediating between the foreign managers and the Vietnamese workers. Their activities resulted in the reinforcement of the foreign managers' hegemony and accentuated power differences among the foreign managers, the middlemen, and the ordinary workers.

The third realm was gendered, wherein the male-centred political role of the middlemen and the female-centred informal politics of the ordinary workers were interconnected and simultaneously separated through social networks and cultural meanings. In the political realm, the middlemen secured the support of ordinary workers that was necessary for them to empower themselves *vis-à-vis* their own internal politics and the foreign management. Meanwhile, the ordinary workers, especially female migrant workers from northern and central Vietnam, endeavoured to protect themselves in the unequal power structure of the factory regime by taking advantage of their own social networks based on informal institutions such as the informal *hui* and kinship (Chae 2003, pp. 241–42).

The interactions of actors in the three realms of the capitalistic factory regime generated various fissures, conflicts, and collusion between and within factions, groups, and genders, and also produced various kinds of contradictory, ambiguous, and politicized evaluations of their activities among the Vietnamese workers. The real secret of hegemony in the multinational factory regime, as practised by the foreign managers, was in the manipulation of various kinds of social relations that were important to the Vietnamese workers. In turn, the price of domination was particularly high for the ordinary workers, especially for young, female migrant workers.

Economic Conditions and their Impact on Multinational Factory Regimes

If prosperity provides a condition for the stability of a hegemonic political structure, economic difficulties can create a chasm in that structure. Recent economic crises, both worldwide and in Vietnam, have substantially affected the power structures within many multinational factories, including SIL.

The Asian Financial Crisis

Around the end of 1997, many multinational factories in Vietnam were feeling the political impact of the Asian crisis, which had almost paralyzed the Korean economy and in turn exerted a substantial effect on the Vietnamese economy. SIL was no exception.

The crisis amplified the tensions and antagonisms between workers and middlemen in SIL. The parent company (SI) in Korea that had secured most of SIL's profits, was almost bankrupt and subject to a restructuring plan led by a creditor bank. As a result, SIL lost its source of vital financial support. To make things worse, the Vietnamese domestic market in textiles was not only saturated but had considerably shrunk because of the crisis. Losing its competitive advantage, the company had had to continually lower its prices to compete with other textile companies in Vietnam as well as with smuggled Chinese goods.

The company's economic downturn affected the factory's internal social politics revolving around the middlemen in several ways. First, many resources regularly exploited by the middlemen as ways of gaining influence over the workers were no longer available. For example, the company stopped the training program that sent workers recommended by the middlemen such as shift leaders and trade union representatives to a factory in Korea and also temporarily halted recruitment. Second, as the company endeavoured to stay in the black, the company's financial aid and welfare benefits rapidly diminished apace. The trade union leaders had to deal with workers' complaints about a wage freeze and seasonal lay-offs. Finally, as the shop floor managers were pressured to increase productivity, they were required to lay-off workers, and those who remained had to work at an even more intense pace than before. There were more frequent conflicts between shift supervisors and ordinary workers. As tensions between the Vietnamese middlemen and workers heightened, the tacitly collusive tie between the Korean management and the middlemen weakened.

Yet, fortunately, this volatility caused by the financial crisis did not last long. When the economy picked up in 1998, stability was once again restored and lasted for almost another ten years.

Economic Downturn yet Continuing Stability

When I visited SIL in the summer of 2008, the factory regime was still politically stable and the company had not experienced strikes despite the rash of labour disputes in the greater HCMC area. The company's political regime still looked as sound as it had been. However, it seemed obvious that we could not attribute the political stability only to its economic conditions. Company profits had gradually decreased since the end of 1999, chalking up a US$150,000 deficit in the first half of 2008.

Wages at SIL had not increased substantially for the last ten years. As shown in Table 8.1 and Table 8.2, average wages rose only about US$43, from US$85 in 1999 to US$128 in 2008. Workers who received VND1.27 million in 1999 received about VND2 million in 2008.

When I conducted fieldwork in the late 1990s, the average household income of factory workers in HCMC averaged VND1.5–2.5 million (US$100–167) a month, which was a minimum amount neccessary for a household with three to four people to survive (Chae 2003, p. 24; *Saigon Giai Phong*, 16 October 2000). According to the workers I interviewed in the winter of 2008, a household with four people needed around VND4–5 million (US$230–290) at the end of 2007. As the cost of living had substantially risen, workers needed at least VND6 million (US$360) in the second half of 2008 to cover their household expenditure. So, while ten years previously, SIL workers managed to cover half their household expenditure with their wages, in 2008 this was reduced to only a third. Despite their economic hardship, SIL had not shown any signs of upheaval.

TABLE 8.1
Wages at SIL, as of June 1999

Rank	Basic salary (US$)	No. of employees
4B–0	45	0
4B 1–3	46–51	54
4B 4–6	53–57	210
4B 7–9	59–62	178
4B 10–15	63–68	204
4A 1–5	69–71	15
4A 6–10	73–80	3
3A	90–95	5
2B	95–100	3
2A	116 and 127	2
S	220 and 500	2
	85 (average)	674 (total)

TABLE 8.2
Wages at SIL, as of June 2008

Department	No. of Employees	Average salary	
		VND	US$
Office	21	3,395,856	210.92
Electrical	22	3,589,149	222.93
Spinning	337	1,986,528	123.39
Weaving	249	1,931,000	119.94
Water jet	58	1,975,735	122.72
Other	20	2,270,064	141.00
Total	707	2,065,837	128.31

Two factors contributed to the political stability of the factory regime despite the slow rate of wage increase in SIL. First of all, the middlemen had been in the saddle for ten years. Mr. Nguyen had been reelected six times as a secretary of SIL trade union and he had the "know-how" to deal with both Korean managers and Vietnamese workers. He told me that he could maintain "a prolonged rule" because he tried to foster principles such as "harmonious mediation of Korean managers and Vietnamese workers, full knowledge and observance of laws and rules, and active participation in local trade union".

Almost all other middlemen whom I had met ten years before were still working in the factory. They told me that they were too old to move to other labour-intensive factories. Their long-serving presence must have contributed to their ability to control the ordinary workers in the politics of (and in) production. For example, several years ago, they collected considerable amounts of capital cooperatively and began to lend money to ordinary workers through the trade unions so that they could prevent the risk posed by the *hui* system and loan sharking within the factory. Such thoughtful measures consolidated some of the middlemen's positions within the factory regime.

Second, the management and the workers often continued to communicate with each through the middlemen's preemptive mediation, that is, by the middlemen reflecting workers' demands and diffusing grievances. For example, the company raised wages by 20 per cent in February 2008, and in May 2008, decided to raise the VND26,000 (US$2.2) monthly transport allowance per person in response to soaring oil prices. When the oil price jumped again in July 2008, the SIL trade union asked the management for an additional VND2,500 (15 cents) allowance per day, which was under discussion at the time of my visit. In this way, the company quickly responded to workers' demands with the help of the middlemen. As a reward, the company continued to try to take heed of the middlemen's requests and hence guarantee their influence with the workers.

Since the Korean managers and the Vietnamese middlemen had closely cooperated for almost a decade, it appeared easy for them to overcome the temporary economic hardship that the company was facing. Although the company's deteriorating finances obviously worsened working and living conditions as at the time of the Asian financial crisis, the discontent of both foreign managers and Vietnamese workers with each other did not lead to a breakdown in relationships in the form of strikes.

The Recent Economic Crisis and the End of the Multinational Factory Regime

In the summer of 2009, I received the news that *SIL* had been sold off two months before. Although I already knew that the company had been suffering from financial stagnation and a debilitating ownership lawsuit since winter 2007, it was a real shock to me that the multinational factory regime I had studied for more than ten years abruptly ended. When I visited the company that same summer, the name of the company had already been changed from SIL to "Phu".

In the spring of 2007, a Korean company (TEN) renowned for mergers and acquisitions of old factories with valuable real estate had taken over SI. After a year-long legal battle in Vietnam over the ownership of SIL between SI's previous and new owners, the new owner finally took over SIL legally in the spring of 2008. It took only about one year for the new Korean owner to sell SIL again to some private Vietnamese owners. All four Vietnamese owners of Phu are former or current high-ranking managers in May. They first bought the weaving factory in March 2009 and later the spinning factory in May 2009. They bought the SIL factories at the giveaway price of US$700,000. As it turned out, the last owner had been too hasty and the new Vietnamese company, Phu, made a surplus of US$750,000 in its first year of operations alone.

The interesting thing is that there was little conspicuous resistance from the workers and middlemen during the period between the two sales, in this process of abrupt disposal of the entity for which some of them had worked more than fifteen years. The only demands made by the trade union representing the workers was for more severance pay and compensation, as stipulated by the Labour Code. The main reason why they did not express their anxiety in the form of industrial action was that they had found out who the new owners of the company would be and believed that their jobs would be safe under the familiar new (i.e. old) owners. There were some differences in responses to the change between the ordinary and the core workers: ordinary workers worried little about their job security since they believed that there was no reason for the new owners to replace them, which turned out to be correct during the transition.

In contrast, the core workers or middlemen had reasons to worry about their future. It was obvious that the new Vietnamese owners neither needed the middlemen, nor did they intend to allow the sort of influence and power that the middlemen as a group had wielded under the foreign managers. Despite their skills, the middlemen could not protect their own jobs. Some of them, such as the interpreters, saw their role become redundant. The new Vietnamese owners replaced all the office staff, except for a couple of salespersons, with their trusted relatives. The new owners refused to rehire the trade union leaders, including the chairman, since they did not want an experienced trade union leadership in their factory. The new Vietnamese management also selectively rehired individual shop floor managers. The new general manager of Phu said to me that he did not want to work with the shop floor managers who had been "too political" under the previous factory management.

In this way, the multinational factory regime was disassembled and restructured into a new factory regime under Vietnamese ownership. The multinational factory regime that had been established as a joint-venture between a state-owned Vietnamese company and Korean private company finally became a private Vietnamese company. In a sense, this transition reflects the historical tendency of industrial development in Vietnam: initial development by foreign direct investment, accelerated privatization, and the subsequent growth of indigenous industries. It remains to be seen what kind of distinctive socio-political structures will be established in the privatized Vietnamese factory regimes.

CONCLUSION

The labour disputes that proliferated in the summer of 2008 came to a lull temporarily in Vietnam in 2009 due to the global economic crisis and accompanying downturn of the labour market in the greater HCMC area. However, as the world economy has begun to show signs of recovery in 2010, labour disputes have reignited in the area. It is likely that Vietnamese factory workers will continue to demand higher wages as long as their jobs are secure, since they have suffered from a low-wage policy for more than a decade.

Many questions remain about this turmoil of labour disputes, however. Why is it that most Vietnamese workers do not demand more than a wage increase? Why do Vietnamese workers resist nonviolently or peacefully and why do they not attempt to empower themselves collectively so as to effectively resist against (especially foreign) capital? How long will such limited struggles continue? In addition, the question also remains as to the factors contributing to labour disputes and strikes. If the main issue at stake in most labour disputes and strikes is wages, why do some enterprises with better economic conditions experience labour disputes and strikes more often than others with worse economic conditions? Are there other factors that are as important as in the dynamics of labour disputes and strikes?

For a clue to the answers, this chapter described the history of the rise and fall of a multinational factory ethnographically. This study has sought to interprete the characteristics of "the local power configuration where conflicts take place" (Hansson 2003, p. 175) and explored whether there were any structural characteristics in the labour disputes that took place in an "ad hoc manner" (ibid.).

What the early history of SIL demonstrates is that neither economic conditions nor cultural conflicts are always the main reasons for labour disputes in a multinational corporation. SIL experienced an unprecedented strike in its early days because the workers' felt accumulated frustration resulting from the new intensive capitalistic discipline imposed upon them after they were transferred from a socialist state factory regime. While the workers suffered because of the intensified work and greater control, they had almost no channels to air their grievances initially. Under the circumstances, they became furious when they heard that their hard work would not even be compensated by a *Tet* bonus.

What the later history of the same multinational corporation consistently shows is that an efficient and stable political structure is crucial to maintaining "peaceful" labour–management relations. In particular, this ethnography demonstrates that the role of middlemen who can mediate between foreign managers and local workers is very important in a multinational factory regime. This ethnography has explored the complex social relations formed among the agents of political processes and the ways in which these agents utilize fellow workers' cultural networks and practices.

Lastly, it must be remembered that SIL's stable and durable multinational factory regime was finally shaken by economic difficulties. When the multinational company experienced extreme economic hardship, the new general manager employed after the first sale attempted to overcome the predicament by changing the company's political structure. The general manager's misjudged actions led to a decrease in productivity further aggravating the company's economic decline.

My findings imply that workers' economic hardship and ensuing demands are only one factor in the recent labour disputes and strikes in the greater HCMC. To understand the real nature of the labour disputes and strikes, we also need to look at the political processes and the political structures of individual factory regimes. In so doing, we may obtain clues as to why some factories suffer continually from labour disputes and others do not. If we look more closely at the political processes and political structure in a factory regime, it is likely that we will better understand, in Burawoy's formulation, both the "fact" and the "reasons" of the working classes' "passivity" and "struggles".

Notes

[1]   When Hansson (2003) mentions "outside the formal structure of the party-state" and "local power configuration", what she has in mind are mostly the empowerment of local and factory trade unions. In this chapter, I extend the meaning of "local power configuration" to embrace the politics of production in factories.

[2]   The company names SI, SIL, May, and Phu, used for the Korean parent company, the joint-venture company, the Vietnamese parent company, and the new Vietnamese private company described later, respectively, are all pseudonyms.

[3]   Some parts of the history of SIL were published in my article, written in Korean, "A Study of the Political Process in a Multinational Factory in Ho Chi Minh City", *Korean Cultural Anthropology* 40, no. 2 (2003): 143–82.

[4]   Examples of those considered to have good social origins included war veterans, party members, and the working-class poor; in contrast, those who had worked with the former South Vietnamese regime were classified as having a bad social origin.

[5]   The trade union elections had not been held at that stage. The leaders were informally approved by the socialist mother company, *May*, but their leadership still needed to be approved by a formal election. The first trade union was officially established in 1994 as described later in the chapter.

[6]   The Korean managers, used to being shown respect by lower-status employees bowing to higher status ones, found that it upsetting that the Vietnamese workers just "smiled or ignored" them in their presence. Although it had been explained to them that the Vietnamese did not share the Korean and Japanese custom of greeting by bowing down as low as possible — the more respect shown, the deeper the angle — this difference in etiquette continued to be a source of friction between the Korean managers and the Vietnamese workers. Tellingly in Vietnamese culture, according to the workers, a stiff-necked greeting (*cuong co*) is not polite either, but can also signify pride and self-respect, while bowing deeply from the waist (*cuong lung*) or kneeling down (*guc dau*) can indicate subordination and loyalty to those of higher status.

[7]   A pseudonym.

8   The majority of the *hui* in the factory were managed by big *chu hui* who had considerable capital (estimated to be from US$5,000 to US$50,000) and whose primary source of earnings derived from loan sharking. There were basically three different types of loan sharking in the factory. The most direct form of loan sharking was to lend some money to workers. The second form, called *ban tra gop*, was associated with private informal trade in the factory and operated with repayment on an installment plan. The third and most popular method was that a *chu hui* lent money to the members of the *hui* that she or he managed and earned interest via various methods associated with the *hui* activities.

References

Bailey, Frederick George. *Strategems and Spoils: A Social Anthropology of Politics*. New York: Schocken Books, 1969.

Braverman, Harry. *Labor and Monopoly Capital: The Degradation of Work in the Twentieth Century*. New York: Monthly Review Press, 1974.

Burawoy, Michael. *Manufacturing Consent: Changes in the Labor Process under Monopoly Capitalism*. Chicago: University of Chicago Press, 1979.

————. *The Politics of Production: Factory Regimes under Capitalism and Socialism*. London: Verso, 1985.

Burawoy, Michael and Janos Lukacs. *Radiant Past: Ideology and Reality in Hungary's Road to Capitalism*. Chicago: University of Chicago Press, 1992.

Chae, Suhong. "Contemporary Ho Chi Minh City in Numerous Contradictions: Reform Policy, Foreign Capital and the Working Class". In *Wounded Cities: Destruction and Reconstruction in a Globalized World*, edited by Jane Schneider and Ida Susser, pp. 227–48. Oxford and New York: Berg, 2003.

Chan, Anita and Irene Norlund. "Vietnamese and Chinese Labour Regimes: On the Road to Divergence". *China Journal* 40 (1998): 174–97.

Gordon, David, Richard Edwards, and Michael Reich. *Segmented Work, Divided Workers: Historical Transformation of Labor in the United States*. Cambridge: Cambridge University Press, 1982.

Hansson, Eva. "Authoritarian Governance and Labour: The VGCL and Party-State in Economic Renovation". In *Getting Organized in Vietnam: Moving in and around the Socialist State*, edited by Ben J. Tria Kerkvliet, Russell H.K. Heng, and David W.H. Koh, pp. 153–84. Singapore: Institute of Southeast Asian Studies, 2003.

Jerneck, Anne and Nguyen Thanh Ha. "The Role of Enterprise Unions in the Shift from Central Planning to Market Orientation". In *Vietnam in a Changing World*, edited by Irene Norlund, Carolyn L. Gates, and Vu Cao Dam, pp. 159–80. Copenhagen: Nordic Institute of Asian Studies Press, 1996.

Jovitt, Ken. *New World Disorder: The Leninist Extinction*. Berkeley: University of California Press, 1992.

Kerkvliet, Ben J. Tria, Anita Chan, and Jonathan Unger. "Comparing the Chinese and Vietnamese Reforms: An Introduction". In "Transforming Asian Socialism: China and Vietnam Compared". Special issue, *China Journal* 40 (1998): 1–7.

Kerkvliet, Ben J. Tria, Russell H.K. Heng, and David W.H. Koh, eds. *Getting Organized in Vietnam: Moving in and around the Socialist State*. Singapore: Institute of Southeast Asian Studies, 2003.

Kim Hyun Mee. "Power, Media Representation, and Labor Discourse: The Case of Women Workers in South Korea". In *Transforming Gender and Development in East Asia*, edited by Esther N. Chow, pp. 81–104. New York: Routledge, 2002.

Kim Seung-Kyung. *Class Struggle or Family Struggle? The Lives of Women Factory Workers in South Korea*. Cambridge: Cambridge University Press, 1997.

Litterer, Joseph August, ed. *Management: Concepts and Controversies*. Santa Barbara: Wiley, 1978.

Margold, Jane A. "From the Assembly Line to the Front Lines: Filipina Workers in Multinational Factories". Working Paper No. 3, Anthropology Department, Chinese University of Hong Kong, 1995.

Nash, June and Maria P. Fernandez-Kelly, eds. *Women, Men and the International Division of Labor*. Albany: State University of New York Press, 1983.

Norlund, Irene. "Vietnamese Industry in Transition: Changes in the Textile Industry". In *Vietnam in a Changing World*, edited by I. Norland, C. Gates, and Vu Ca Dam, pp. 125–50. Richmond: Curzon Press, 1995.

———. "Democracy and Trade Unions in Vietnam: Riding a Honda in Slow Speed". Paper presented at the 49th meeting of American Association of Asian Studies in Chicago, 1997.

Ong, Aihwa. *Spirits of Resistance and Capitalist Discipline: Factory Women in Malaysia*. Albany: State University of New York Press, 1987.

Pravda, Alex and Blair Ruble, eds. *Trade Unions in Communist States*. Boston: Allen & Unwin, 1986.

Thomson, E.P. *The Making of the English Working Class*. London: Penguin, 1968.

Turtley, William S. and Brantly Womack. "Asian Socialism's Open Doors: Guangzhou and Ho Chi Minh City". In "Transforming Asian Socialism: China and Vietnam Compared". Special issue, *China Journal* 40 (1997): 95–119.

Unger, Jonathan and Anita Chan. "China, Corporatism, and the East Asian Model". *Australian Journal of Chinese Affairs* 33 (1995): 29–53.

9

HOW DOES ENTERPRISE OWNERSHIP MATTER?
Labour Conditions in Fashion and Footwear Factories in Southern Vietnam

Jee Young Kim

In Vietnam foreign-invested enterprises have experienced more strikes than their domestic counterparts. It is thus often claimed that the former have poorer labour conditions than the latter, based on the simple reasoning: the poorer the conditions, the more frequent the strikes. Comparisons between foreign and state enterprises have informed such an argument. Chan and Norlund (1998), for instance, argued that foreign enterprises, especially those funded by Hong Kong, Korean, and Taiwanese investors, are managed in authoritarian ways and often in violation of labour and safety laws. They contrasted them with state-owned enterprises (SOEs) whose socialist underpinnings infused with a paternalistic and collectivist culture help ameliorate the most adverse effects of market pressure on labour conditions in the reform era. According to this view, strikes are caused by labour conditions that are considered to differ depending on the type of enterprise ownership.

Two assumptions underlie this argument: the relative immutability of managerial culture across time and space; and the close relationship between labour conditions and worker resistance. The first assumption is challenged by evidence that firm-level managerial culture changes over time, as suggested by deteriorating conditions in SOEs under transition to a market economy (Whyte 1999). Managerial culture also changes when it crosses national borders, as is indicated by Chan and Wang's (2004) finding that Taiwanese firms in Vietnam have better labour conditions than those in China.

Clarke's (2006) research on strikes in Vietnam casts doubt on the second assumption, that of a strong correlation between labour conditions and strikes. His findings indicate that while in the past workers resorted to strikes largely to fight against abusive treatment and to ensure their legal rights, they now seek to advance their own interests above and beyond legally set minimum conditions and non-abusive treatment. If poor labour conditions per se lead to strikes, the rapid rise in the number of strikes in recent years should mean that legal violations and worker abuse have become more common or more severe. But existing evidence, at least as indicated by strikers' demands, does not support such an assumption (Clarke 2006; Lee 2006). Thus, if a direct causal link between labour conditions and worker resistance is to be questioned, we need to address two issues to better understand the relationship between worker resistance and enterprise ownership type: first, whether enterprises of differing ownership types indeed have different labour conditions; and second, whether they have different internal mechanisms to prevent workers' grievances from turning into collective resistance such as strikes.

This chapter thus seeks to identify in what ways enterprise ownership matters, if at all, by investigating not only labour conditions but also grievance-handling mechanisms on the shop floor. Specifically, it focuses on two aspects of labour conditions, wages and worker abuse, which have been regarded as key causes of strikes. It also examines how enterprise-level trade unions and management handle workers' grievances. By comparing enterprises of different ownership types, this study will help illuminate the relationship between enterprise ownership, labour conditions, and worker resistance.

Data are drawn mainly from in-depth interviews carried out with workers and complemented with a management survey in fashion and footwear factories in the southern industrial centres.[1] The fashion and footwear industries in these areas are well suited to addressing the questions under study. First, these industries have diverse ownership types due to substantial investment from domestic-private and foreign sources. Second, to discern the relationship between enterprise ownership and labour conditions, it is essential to compare enterprises with similar industrial characteristics because labour conditions differ substantially among industries. Third, the fashion and footwear industries have been the focus of several studies on labour conditions in Vietnam (for instance, Norlund 2000; Tran 2005), which allows us to evaluate their arguments in similar industrial contexts. Finally, the geographic scope of this study is particularly pertinent, as strikes in the country have long been concentrated in the fashion and footwear industries in its southern industrial centres.

I begin by describing the characteristics of the factories in the study as well as the data collection procedure. I then present the patterns of remuneration and supervisory abuse inside each factory in turn. Following this, I examine the ways in which workers' grievances are handled inside the factories, paying close attention to the role of the enterprise-level trade union and management. I conclude by discussing the implications of this study.

DATA COLLECTION PROCEDURES AND FACTORY CHARACTERISTICS

The fifty-two factories chosen for this study were sampled from a list of manufacturers of finished shoes, garments, hats/caps, bags, and gloves with at least one hundred employees in Ho Chi Minh City, Binh Duong Province, and Dong Nai Province as of early 2005. I compiled that list by combining thirteen records of enterprises from sources such as domestic and foreign business associations and government agencies and then by verifying the information through phone calls to all the entries in the records. From each city or province, I first selected several districts that had a large concentration of relevant factories to save travelling time. From each of the districts, I chose several factories for worker interviews by categorizing them according to their ownership type, main products (industry), and workforce size.[2] By covering a wide range of factories, the sample allows for meaningful comparison between ownership types.[3]

In-depth interviews with 101 workers (up to 3 workers per factory) were used for this study. All workers were approached and interviewed outside their workplaces without the knowledge of management. They were asked a wide range of open-ended questions about their working conditions, including working hours, wages and benefits, knowledge of relevant labour law, strikes, and their perceptions about the trade union and management. Each interview lasted between 45 and 210 minutes with the median time of one hour. When permitted, interviews were taped and transcribed; otherwise, they were recorded by hand and typed up afterwards.

Table 9.1 shows the type of ownership, main product, and workforce size of the factories in this study. I checked the ownership type by using the aforementioned enterprise list against worker interviews and a management survey carried out the same year. The categories of state-owned, domestic-private, and foreign-invested enterprises are quite straightforward.[4] But what I call "shadow-foreign" requires some explanation.

The shadow-foreign category — known as under-the-counter investment (*dau tu chui*) in the country — is not a formal joint venture between foreign and domestic capital, but in reality is a foreign firm that is registered as a domestic firm under a Vietnamese partner's name. This practice is not uncommon in Vietnam. The precise reason behind this arrangement is likely to vary from case to case, but the most salient seems to be that a lower minimum wage rate applies to domestic enterprises.[5] I classified the enterprises in which workers report that the top manager is not Vietnamese while other sources suggest domestic ownership as shadow-foreign. This decision is based on a confirmed case of a shadow-foreign enterprise in my sample. A Korean investor told me that her factory was run under the name of an SOE whose assets, except the land, she had purchased (M19). One of the two worker interviewees from this factory correctly identified its top manager as non-Vietnamese, even though she said that it belonged to the Vietnamese army (W85). It is possible that a foreign firm is run entirely under Vietnamese management, but it is very unlikely to be the other way round. This example indicates that even though workers may be unaware of the legal status of their company, they do have some sense of who their real employer is. It is thus reasonable to identify shadow-foreign enterprises based on the discrepancy between workers' reports and other sources about the nationality of the top manager.

As both foreign-invested and shadow-foreign enterprises have foreign management in common, I sometimes refer to both as foreign management in contradistinction from state-owned and domestic-private enterprises. Below I present the similarities and differences among the four ownership

TABLE 9.1
Factory Characteristics: Main Product and Workforce Size by Ownership Type
(Unit: number of factories)

Main Product Workforce Size Ownership Type	Main Product			Workforce Size[b]			
	Garment[a]	Footwear	Subtotal	Fewer than 500	500 ~ 999	1,000 ~ 4,999	5,000 or more
State-owned (incl. equitized)	8	2	10	1	4	4	1
Domestic-private	8	1	9	5	3	1	0
Foreign-invested	14	11	25	2	11	7	5
Shadow-foreign	1	7	8	1	2	4	1
Total	31	21	52	9	20	16	7

Notes: [a] This category includes three manufacturers of caps, bags, and gloves.
[b] Workforce size is based on the establishment rather than the entire company (see note 3 for details).

types, focusing on variations in remuneration, supervisory abuse of workers, and internal grievance-handling.

PATTERNS OF REMUNERATION

The reward system is a critical management tool to induce maximum worker efficiency at minimum cost. The factories studied remunerated their workers in different ways as well as at different rates.

Differences in Wage Systems under Domestic and Foreign Management

The piece-rate wage is often regarded as the typical method of payment in the garment and footwear industries. It is highly advantageous to management in that business risks can be more easily transferred from employers to employees, which is achieved by adjusting the piece rates according to fluctuating orders and often downward pressure in product prices offered by buyers. The piece-rate system also helps disguise managerial controls more easily by invoking workers' interest in earning more. Hence, logically, employers should prefer to pay by the piece. But as we shall see, this is not necessarily the case. The most significant difference is observed between domestic and foreign management.

Table 9. 2 demonstrates a stronger preference for the piece-rate wage system by domestic than by foreign management in both formally foreign-invested and shadow-foreign factories. The relationship between enterprise ownership and wage system is presented in Table 9.2 by taking workers, rather than factories, as the unit of analysis, since the method of wage payment differs between jobs within the same factory as well as between factories. In my sample, 82 per cent of the interviewees in SOEs and 94 per cent in domestic-private enterprises, in contrast to 35 per cent in formally foreign-invested enterprises and 27 per cent in shadow-foreign ones, were paid by the piece. Notably, neither the type of product made nor job characteristics fully explain the difference. Even if one takes into consideration only garment workers who are said to receive piece-rate wages, a fairly large difference remains: 90 per cent of those under domestic management ([12 + 15]/30 × 100%) and 54 per cent under foreign management ([11 + 2]/24 × 100%) were pieceworkers. Among fifty-six sewing workers, the most common job category in the fashion and footwear industries, 95 per cent under domestic management, in contrast

TABLE 9.2
Wage System by Factory Ownership Type[a]
(Unit: number of workers, percentage in parentheses)

Ownership Type	All Workers			Garment Workers[b]		
	Piece wage	Fixed wage	Total	Piece wage	Fixed wage	Total
State-owned	14 (82.4)	3 (17.6)	17 (100.0)	12 (85.7)	2 (14.3)	14 (100.0)
Domestic-private	17 (94.4)	1 (5.6)	18 (100.0)	15 (93.8)	1 (6.3)	16 (100.1)
Foreign-invested	17 (34.7)	32 (65.3)	49 (100.0)	11 (50.0)	11 (50.0)	22 (100.0)
Shadow-foreign	4 (26.7)	11 (73.3)	15 (100.0)	2 (100.0)	0 (0.0)	2 (100.0)
Total	52 (52.5)	47 (47.5)	99 (100.0)	40 (74.1)	14 (25.9)	54 (100.0)

Notes: [a] Information on the wage system is unavailable for two workers.
[b] This group does not include the workers who produce caps, bags, or gloves

to 44 per cent under foreign management, were paid by the piece.[6] Clearly domestic management had a stronger preference for the piece-rate system regardless of the product type and job characteristic.

The reason for the difference is unclear. One possible explanation is the characteristic of each factory's specialized product. Some foreign managers whom I interviewed claimed that frequent style changes, small orders, and heavy emphasis on product quality are the main obstacles to adopting the piece-rate system (M2, M8).[7] It is difficult to verify their claim. Of importance, however, is that the wage system has significant implications for supervisory abuse on the shop floor, an issue which I will return to later.

Workers' Earnings

Table 9.3 shows the mean and median as well as the range of workers' average monthly earnings by factory ownership type, which take into account all cash payments including earnings for overtime work. Judging from the mean and median, workers in domestic-private and foreign-invested enterprises earned more than those in state-owned and shadow-foreign enterprises. Interestingly, workers in domestic-private enterprises had the highest earnings despite their lowest legal minimum wage. At the time of data collection in mid-2005, the minimum wage in Vietnam ranged from

TABLE 9.3
Workers' Average Monthly Earnings by Factory Ownership Type, Mid-2005
(Unit: VND)

Ownership Type	N	Mean	Median	Minimum	Maximum
State-owned	15	971,000	1,000,000	700,000	1,250,000
Domestic-private	16	1,036,300	1,000,000	750,000	1,300,000
Foreign-invested	37	1,015,600	1,000,000	730,000	1,500,000
Shadow-foreign	12	985,900	900,000	700,000	1,433,000
Total	80	1,006,900	1,000,000	700,000	1,500,000

Note: Removed from the table are the cases with missing information about monthly earnings (N = 8), the cases in which the monthly earnings did not include overtime earnings (N = 10), and the cases in which the interviewees held low-level supervisory positions such as line leader and line technician (N = 3).

VND290,000 to 626,000: VND487,000 to 626,000 for foreign enterprises in the areas under study (MOLISA 1999) and VND290,000 for domestic private enterprises (Government of Vietnam 2003) and VND449,500 for SOEs in the industries under study (Government of Vietnam 2004).[8]

A host of factors influence workers' earnings. To isolate the effect of factory ownership type, it is necessary to control for relevant characteristics of factories and workers. Table 9.4 presents the result from a regression

TABLE 9.4
Regression Analysis of Workers' Average Monthly Earnings

	Coef.	(S.E.)
Factory Ownership Type		
(Reference) Foreign-invested		
State-owned	–0.062*	(0.034)
Domestic-private	0.055	(0.043)
Shadow-foreign	–0.008	(0.080)
Factory Workforce Size		
(Reference) 5,000 or more		
Fewer than 500	0.043	(0.070)
500 ~ 999	0.015	(0.054)
1,000 ~ 4,999	0.103*	(0.055)
Worker's Employment Duration		
(Reference) 3 years or longer		
Less than 1 year	–0.164**	(0.061)
1 year to less than 3 years	–0.121***	(0.037)
Worker's Job		
(Reference) Non-sewing job		
Sewing job	0.067*	(0.040)
Worker's Sex		
(Reference) Female		
Male	0.073	(0.047)
Constant	13.820***	(0.052)

N = 76; R-squared = 0.320
* $P < 0.10$,   ** $P < 0.05$,   *** $P < 0.01$
Note: [a] The dependent variable is logged.
    [b] The model is estimated by clustering on factories. Robust standard errors are reported.

analysis that holds constant factory workforce size as well as workers' duration of employment, job type, and sex, with the natural logarithm of average monthly earnings as the dependent variable. The workforce size captures the resource capacity of the factories, whereas workers' duration of employment and job type are taken as indicators for their skill levels. Sex accounts for potential sex discrimination in wages.

The positive coefficient indicates higher earnings of the given category of workers than those of the reference category and the negative coefficient indicates the opposite. The table shows that SOE workers earned less than those at foreign-invested enterprises, while those in domestic-private enterprises earned more than either. There was little difference between the workers in foreign-invested and shadow-foreign enterprises. Other things being equal, the best-paying were domestic-private enterprises whose workers earned 5 to 6 per cent more than their counterparts in foreign-invested and shadow-foreign enterprises. And the worst paying were SOEs whose workers earned about 5 to 6 per cent less than did those in foreign-invested and shadow-foreign enterprises but about 11 per cent less than did those in domestic-private enterprises.[9]

One obvious explanation for the differences in earnings is overtime work. It would be ideal to include overtime hours in the statistical analysis. But information on the exact number of monthly overtime hours is quite difficult to obtain through interviews; in many cases workers were unaware of the total number of overtime hours in the month prior to the interview, not to mention the monthly average. This is in part because the seasonality of the industries under study leads to heavy fluctuations in overtime work. In addition, a number of factories did not inform workers of the overtime hours they had worked and some did not even distinguish between regular hours and overtime hours. Qualitative information provided by workers, however, indicates that the large and statistically significant difference between state-owned and domestic-private enterprises results at least in part from the amount of overtime worked. Workers were asked to give details of their working hours, including regular working hours, overtime hours, and Sundays worked. The longest working day was between 12 and 14 hours in ten SOEs, compared to 13 to over 15 hours in nine domestic-private enterprises. SOEs were more likely to limit the number of long working days to three or four times a week than domestic-private enterprises, some of which had long working days for several weeks in a row. During peak seasons, almost all the SOE workers could take two

Sundays off a month but some workers in domestic-private enterprises could not take any Sundays off. Extreme cases of excessive working hours were found in domestic-private enterprises. One example was an ironing worker who alternated, day and night, eight hours of work and eight hours of rest without any Sundays off. Notably, she had worked in an SOE but had quit due to its low and unstable wage (W88).

Conventional wisdom has it that SOEs have better conditions and are more law-abiding. Consistent with such a view is that SOE workers had less excessive overtime. An exclusive focus on their shorter overtime hours, however, hides the fact that, in practice, SOEs are not that much different from other ownership types. Most SOE workers still had overtime hours that well exceeded the legal limit and their shorter overall working hours resulted in lower average earnings. When wages as well as working hours are taken into account, it is at best misleading to conclude that SOE workers are better off than those in other enterprises.

To sum up, a comparison of remuneration patterns reveals that workers in domestic-private enterprises earned the most and those in SOEs the least. This was related to the fact that the latter did less overtime work. To draw a conservative conclusion, the more hours worked, the higher the earnings. The type of enterprise ownership does not have much impact on workers' earnings, apart from the hours worked.

DISCIPLINARY IMPLICATIONS OF INCENTIVE PAYMENTS

Vietnam's Labour Code explicitly prohibits fines.[10] At the same time, the minimum wage, set at very low rates, has failed to serve as a meaningful guarantee for subsistence. As maximizing incentive payments is crucial to workers' own survival, the strings attached to them and fines can have similar effects in controlling their work behaviour.

One may think that factories under the piece-rate system are less likely to use the bonus system to control workers' behaviour. After all, you earn as much as you work, as was often mentioned by the pieceworkers interviewed. In reality, however, those factories still employed an array of bonuses that constituted a large proportion of workers' earnings, which have huge disciplinary implications.

An in-depth investigation of the wage structure in enterprises of different ownership types is beyond the scope of this study. But the most elaborate incentive system is found in SOEs. One example is a fully state-owned garment factory that had both individual and group performance bonuses. The individual or 'ABC' bonus was determined by productivity (monthly piece earnings), adherence to factory rules, defect rates, and absenteeism. Each member of a 45-person sewing line was evaluated every month on the ABC scale. The bonus ranged from VND100,000 to 200,000. A piece-rate worker who received VND800,000 to 1,000,000 a month in this factory would receive a performance bonus amounting to 11 to 22 per cent of her monthly earning if an average of VND900,000 is assumed (W1). The group performance bonus was based on productivity competition between production lines, a "socialist" practice that is alive in some SOEs. The top three lines in the competition won the prize of VND200,000 to 500,000. Each winning line retained the money in its collective fund, to which each of its members also had to contribute VND5,000 every month. The fund was used not only for the welfare of its members, such as to pay for visits to sick colleagues, the year-end party, and *Tet* gifts; it was also used as a tool for lateral control to ensure that workers on the entire line fulfilled their collective responsibilities, such as compensating for products lost on the line (W2). This type of wage structure makes workers bear responsibility not merely for their own behaviour but also for that of their peers on the same line, intensifying top-down pressures to raise productivity.

That both fines and incentive payments impose similar control over workers can be illustrated by the attendance bonus system. Factories often make a distinction between missing work with and without prior permission and reduce the bonus accordingly. In the case of an SOE, missing a day without permission would cost a footwear worker over 10 per cent of her monthly earning of VND850,000 to 900,000 — a day's wage, the VND50,000 monthly seniority bonus, half of the VND50,000 monthly attendance bonus, and part of the annual bonus that was determined by attendance records (W11). Recall that the median monthly income of the workers interviewed was VND1,000,000 (see Table 9.3). Only with full attendance could this footwear worker earn an amount close to, though still less than, the median level. The same applies to the 100 per cent state-owned garment factory discussed earlier, which paid VND100,000 to 200,000 as an ABC bonus. If workers missed work without permission, they would lose up to VND200,000 in monthly income — i.e., 20 per cent of the median income (W2). It should be noted that being absent from work without permission is closely tied to the fact that it is not easy to obtain leave, especially when factories need workers to meet deadlines.

The annual bonus often referred to as the thirteenth-month salary is yet another tool used by management. The piece-rate wage played a crucial role in tightening the linkage between the bonus and workers' performance. SOEs generally paid an annual bonus equivalent to an average monthly piece-rate earning. Among the nine SOEs with relevant information available, two enterprises determined the bonus amount based on attendance and performance records, six paid the equivalent of the average monthly piece-rate earning with or without some additional bonus, and one, a fixed amount that was tied to length of employment. Eight out of nine state-owned factories tied the annual bonus to workers' productivity and/or work behaviour. On the other hand, among the eight domestic-private factories, the practice varied. One enterprise did not pay an annual bonus. One paid an equivalent of the average monthly piece-rate earning. The remaining six all attached strings to the annual bonus, such as performance and attendance requirements. In short, all domestic-private enterprises that paid an annual bonus aligned it closely with workers' productivity and/or work behaviour.

In contrast, thirteen out of twenty foreign-invested factories paid a bonus equivalent to the one-month base wage without conditions, and a few added some amount to the one-month base wage on the basis of performance and attendance records. Four factories deducted money from the annual bonus of the one-month base wage for poor attendance records. One factory determined the annual bonus based entirely on attendance, the amount of which was higher than a one-month wage if a worker did not miss work. And two factories paid much less than the monthly base wage. About a half of the foreign-invested enterprises paid a fixed annual bonus, regardless of workers' productivity and behaviour. A similar pattern is also observed for four shadow-foreign factories with relevant information available: they all paid a fixed amount without linking it to workers' performance.

In sum, both state-owned and domestic-private enterprises linked workers' wages more tightly to performance than foreign-invested and shadow-foreign enterprises. This is best illustrated by the rules by which each enterprise type determines the annual bonus. As will be discussed below, the reward system has had some effect on disguising managerial controls over workers, explaining in part the difference in supervisory abuse of workers among ownership types.

ABUSIVE TREATMENT OF WORKERS

Managerial controls require people to discipline workers during the labour process. This task falls to the supervisory staff on production lines. There is often friction between the supervisory staff and line workers, which sometimes results in worker abuse. To examine the degree of abusive treatment of workers, supervisory abuse is operationalized as "verbal, emotional, or physical abuse by a supervisor that occurs more than just rarely" (Hodson *et al.* 2006, p. 391). Workers were asked to describe their supervisors' treatment rather than to rate the extent of supervisory abuse. By taking into account all relevant comments from worker interviewees, the level of supervisory abuse is subsequently quantified on a scale of 1 to 5 in ascending order; 1 indicating a very low level of abuse, 2 moderately low, 3 neither low nor high, 4 moderately high, and 5 very high.[11]

As in the case of earnings, enterprise ownership type is not likely to be the sole determinant of supervisory abuse. It is thus important to isolate the effect of ownership type from those of the other relevant factors. I conducted a regression analysis by including the wage system, workers' duration of employment, and factory workforce size. Forms of wage system are likely to influence supervisory abuse, since the piece-rate system may be just as effective as visible and oral control in pressuring workers to speed up by tightly linking productivity to earnings. Workers' own comments also indicate that duration of employment is correlated with abusive treatment. A garment worker reported, for instance, that his line leader swears at new hires when they make defects but not at workers with long service (W74). Finally, factory workforce size is taken into consideration, since one study found that the larger the workplace, the higher the level of supervisory abuse of workers because abusive supervisors are more able to hide behind the protection of anonymity in large workplaces (Hodson *et al.* 2006). Although in my sample such behaviour was usually visible and audible to other workers on the shop floor, workforce size is included in the model to explore what effect it has on supervisory abuse.

Table 9.5 presents the result from the regression analysis. Recall that the dependent variable of supervisory abuse is coded such that the more the abuse, the higher the score. The coefficients in the table indicate the difference between the reference and the comparison category: a positive coefficient means more abuse, and a negative coefficient, less abuse, respectively, in each of the comparison categories than the reference category.

TABLE 9.5
Regression Analysis of Supervisory Abuse

	Coef.	(S.E.)
Factory Ownership Type		
(Reference) Foreign-invested		
State-owned	−0.135	(0.384)
Domestic-private	−0.819*	(0.421)
Shadow-foreign	0.438	(0.480)
Form of Wage System		
(Reference) Time-based fixed wage		
Piece-rate wage	−0.494	(0.365)
Interviewee's Employment Duration		
(Reference) 3 years or longer		
Less than 1 year	−0.112	(0.320)
1 year to less than 3 years	−0.534**	(0.254)
Workforce Size		
(Reference) 5,000 or more		
Fewer than 500	−1.277**	(0.501)
500 ~ 999	−0.900**	(0.422)
1,000 ~ 4,999	−0.790*	(0.411)
Constant	4.129***	(0.335)

N = 97; R-squared = 0.368
* $P < 0.10$, ** $P < 0.05$, *** $P < 0.01$
Note: The model is estimated by clustering on factories. Robust standard errors are reported.

The abuse score of domestic-private enterprises is 0.819 point lower than that of foreign-invested ones, and the difference is statistically significant. On the other hand, the abuse score of shadow-foreign enterprises is 0.438 point higher than that of foreign-invested enterprises. Notably, there is only a very small and statistically insignificant difference between state-owned and foreign-invested enterprises: the former have an abuse score 0.135 point lower than the latter. Other things being equal, then, supervisory abuse was the highest in shadow-foreign factories and the lowest in domestic-private enterprises, with state-owned and foreign-invested enterprises falling in between.

Supervisory abuse is also partly attributable to the wage system. As is expected, pieceworkers reported less abuse than did those paid by time rate. The difference was 0.494 point, though statistically insignificant. Another model without the wage system factored in (not shown here) results in larger differences among enterprise ownership types. This indicates that a part of the difference in worker abuse among ownership types in fact stems from the difference in the wage system. In other words, monetary controls over workers through the piece-rate wage predominant in domestic enterprises partly substituted for the verbal and physical controls in foreign enterprises.

The effects of workers' duration of employment and factory workforce size on supervisory abuse merit brief comment. The lowest level of abuse is found in workers with one to three years of service and the highest level in those with over three years of service, with those with less than a year's service falling in the middle. It is rather puzzling that the highest level of abuse is found in workers who have worked for the longest period. But that finding may have to do with the fact that during interviews, workers described interpersonal relations and the atmosphere on the shop floor as well as their own experiences, all of which are taken into account in determining the level of abuse. The higher abuse score observed for workers with longer service is at least partly attributable to the fact that they had more to say about workplace conflicts.[12] The effect of factory workforce size on supervisory abuse is clear-cut: large factories were more abusive than small factories. The abuse score of the smallest factories with fewer than 500 workers was 1.277 point lower than that of the largest factories with 5,000 or more workers. This finding is consistent with Hodson *et al.*'s (2006). But the highly visible and audible nature of abusive behaviour that this study captures suggests the need for a different interpretation. Factory workforce size seems to indicate the degree of bureaucratic inflexibility, which transmits and intensifies production pressures down the factory hierarchy with the most adverse consequences on those on the lowest rung.

The regression result compares the average level of abuse among ownership types. A further insight can thus be gained by inspecting its distribution pattern. As Table 9.6 shows, moderately low or middle levels of abuse are mostly observed in SOEs, and only very low or moderately low levels in domestic-private enterprises. On the other hand, a highly polarized pattern between low and high levels of abuse is found in foreign-invested

TABLE 9.6
Supervisory Abuse by Factory Ownership Type
(Unit: number of workers, percentage in parentheses)

	Level of Supervisory Abuse					
Ownership Type	*Very low*	*Moderately low*	*Neither high nor low*	*Moderately high*	*Very high*	*Total*
State-owned	1 (5.9)	9 (52.9)	5 (29.4)	1 (5.9)	1 (5.9)	17 (100.0)
Domestic-private	8 (47.1)	9 (52.9)	0 (0.0)	0 (0.0)	0 (0.0)	17 (100.0)
Foreign-invested	8 (16.3)	12 (24.5)	8 (16.3)	14 (28.6)	7 (14.3)	49 (100.0)
Shadow-foreign	1 (7.1)	3 (21.4)	2 (14.3)	6 (42.9)	2 (14.3)	14 (100.0)
Total	18 (18.6)	33 (34.0)	15 (15.5)	21 (21.7)	10 (10.3)	97 (100.1)

enterprises, whereas the pattern is clearly skewed toward the abusive end in shadow-foreign enterprises.

Overall, the average level of supervisory abuse is broadly consistent with the view that domestic management treats its workers better than foreign management. However, the differences among four types of enterprise ownership are not consistent with existing interpretations about worker abuse. The higher level of worker abuse in SOEs than in domestic-private enterprises belies the received wisdom that socialist institutions and practices mitigate against abusive treatment of workers in SOEs. It is instead more consistent with the aforementioned observation that SOEs' elaborate incentive schemes control its workers more tightly and thus have more severe disciplinary consequences. As for enterprises under foreign management, two findings are worth underscoring. The illicit type of foreign investment — shadow-foreign enterprises — is more abusive toward workers. Furthermore, there is a highly polarized pattern of worker abuse among formally foreign-invested enterprises in ways that cannot be predicted from the influence of national-level managerial culture, a factor that is argued to directly influence worker abuse.[13] One of the mediating factors is likely to be the reward pattern discussed earlier. Another is likely to be the mechanism for limiting the potential for supervisory abuse, an issue that we will explore below.

THE ROLE OF THE ENTERPRISE TRADE UNION

The enterprise union in Vietnam has been often considered ineffective in protecting workers' interests and ameliorating workplace conflicts. However, SOEs' unions have been regarded as different. According to Clarke (2006, p. 348), for instance,

> the labour force in SOEs is more tightly monitored by the 'group of four' (Director, Communist Party cell, trade union and Youth League) than is the labour force in non-state enterprises, so that discontent is more easily identified and mollified or snuffed out.... The trade union is also probably more effective at monitoring management observance of the labour law and worker discontent in SOEs.

Similarly, Chan and Norlund (1998, p. 191) argued that the "collectivist ethos and corporatist structure" help ensure better labour conditions in SOEs. By contrast, the union is seen to play little role in foreign enterprises. In his study of Taiwanese firms in Vietnam, for example, Wang (2005) found that their unions served cosmetic purposes largely in the interests of management. It can be expected then that the union's role should be most pronounced in SOEs, especially in handling workers' grievances.

Little has been studied about actual union activities at the enterprise level, let alone the differences among ownership types (see Clarke *et al.* 2007). Based on comments from workers, the union activities can be categorized into four types: welfare, entertainment, personnel and production-related, and grievance-handling.[14] There were unions in forty-eight of the fifty-two factories under study.[15] Ten of the forty-eight unions had no activities, existing only in name. Among those that were somewhat active, the predominant focus was on welfare, such as visits to sick workers, monetary contributions to weddings and funerals, and the provision of gifts on special occasions like *Tet*. As Table 9.7 shows, over 70 per cent of the unions (34/48) carried out some welfare activities, which typically involved collecting dues and distributing funds for designated purposes.

TABLE 9.7

Activities of the Enterprise-Level Trade Union by Factory Ownership Type
(Unit: number of factories)

| Ownership Type | No union | Union | Union Activities^a | | | | | Total |
			Welfare^b	Entertainment^c	Personnel/Production	Grievance handling^d	No union activity	
State-owned	0	10	5	5	2	7	1	10
Domestic-private	2	7	3	0	0	0	4	9
Foreign-invested	0	25	21	6	1	7	4	25
Shadow-foreign	2	6	5	1	0	0	1	8
Total	4	48	34	12	3	14	10	52

Notes: ^a When at least one worker in each factory mentioned the given union activity, the factory union is considered to take up that activity.

^b Examples of welfare functions are financial contributions to weddings and funerals and visits to sick workers.

^c Examples of entertainment activities are picnics and concerts and singing contests which specifically involved the union according to the interviewed workers. Entertainment activities that did not involve the union are excluded.

^d Grievance handling includes the cases in which the union collected workers' opinions and addressed workers' grievances.

Interestingly, the union's welfare function was more salient under foreign management than under domestic management; it was carried out by half of the unions in SOEs but by over 80 per cent in foreign-invested firms.

Unions also organized entertainment: typically, picnics, parties, singing and essay contests, and in a few cases, concerts involving professional singers. Entertainment functions run by unions were found in half of the SOE unions, in a quarter of foreign-invested enterprises but were rare in domestic-private and shadow-foreign enterprises. But the union-run entertainment activities do not render SOEs different from the other ownership types; a large number of factories had similar events without the union involvement. Take the company picnic, the most common union-organized event, as an example. Workers had company picnics in 80 per cent of SOEs (8/10), 78 per cent of domestic-private enterprises (7/9), 68 per cent of foreign-invested enterprises (17/25), and 63 per cent of shadow-foreign enterprises (5/8).[16] Some picnics were organized by the unions and others by management. SOEs were more likely to devolve the task to the union.

The personnel and production-related function was central to the state-socialist union model under central planning, and it is said to persist in SOEs in the reform era (Clarke *et al.* 2007, p. 553). As shown in Table 9.7, however, only three unions (two state-owned and one foreign-invested enterprise) assumed personnel and production-related roles, such as launching campaigns to raise productivity and industrial hygiene standards and administering medical insurance. In sum, the union functions in welfare, entertainment, and personnel and production reveal little evidence that union activities are the main areas of differentiation among enterprise ownership types, though unions in state-owned and foreign-invested enterprises were more actively engaged.

What is in fact different about SOE unions, however, is their role in handling workers' grievances. Table 9.7 shows the degree of unions' grievance-handling role by enterprise ownership type. When asked what activities the union carried out in their factories, at least one worker in 70 per cent of SOEs (7/10) and 28 per cent of foreign-invested enterprises (7/25), but in none of the domestic-private and shadow-foreign enterprises, indicated that the unions handled their grievances. This picture is consistent with the view that unions in SOEs help mollify workers' discontent.[17]

Closer inspection of how SOE unions deal with workers' grievances reveals an interesting pattern. The activities and effectiveness of a union could differ in factories belonging to the same SOE. For example, a worker reported that her plant's union was much weaker than that of another plant in the same SOE, commenting that only the latter organized campaigns to collect workers' opinions, even though both plants were located right next to each other (W69). Similar plant-level differences were also indicated by workers in another SOE. Two workers — from a garment and a footwear factory on the same premises — assessed their respective plant-level unions very differently. According to the garment worker, the union stood on the workers' side and helped redress "rightful" complaints (W3). According to the footwear worker, on the other hand, "the union only exists in form to allow [management] to claim that it meets the legal requirement on paper" that every enterprise must have a union (W4). The reason behind the plant-level difference is unclear but one possible explanation is the personality of the chairperson because "[o]nce it has been established, the workplace trade union is left largely to its own devices" (Clarke *et al.* 2007, p. 557). This view indicates that structural factors such as collectivist culture and socialist institutional arrangements might not be as important as have been posited in determining the effectiveness of trade unions.

Clarke (2006) argued that the fundamental cause of the proliferation of strikes in Vietnam is the failure of unions to represent workers' interests through collective bargaining.[18] However, the findings of this study indicate that unions may be able to reduce the chance of workers' collective resistance by assuaging their dissatisfaction without recourse to collective bargaining.

MANAGERIAL RESPONSIVENESS TO WORKER GRIEVANCES

The trade union is only one of the channels through which workers' grievances were handled. When asked how they cope with grievances at work, workers reported there were other channels, which also reveals differences in managerial responsiveness.

> "If we're not happy about the piece rate, we go to the line leader. She will then meet with the council of directors. If we're not happy about the line leader, we write a letter, collect signatures from our fellow line members, and send it right away [to the office]. There is a grievance deposit box" (W52).

"I will talk to the foreman or write a letter and put it in the grievance deposit box" (W90).

"We can write a letter to the Taiwanese general director. They [management] will review [it] and give us an answer. ... Every few months the Taiwanese general director also calls a meeting directly with workers. If a worker in a line is unhappy about something, she can raise that issue and they will review and resolve it" (W9).

"If we're not satisfied, those of us that are bold will raise [our] voices and those afraid remain silent" (W17).

"We just talk to one another and never voice grievances [to management]. We could send a letter; there is a grievance deposit box there. But few people [do so]" (W34).

"I leave them in my heart" (W99).

To examine workers' perceptions of managerial responsiveness, their comments about how management handled their grievances were coded into a five-point scale of responsiveness, with 1 for a very low level, 2 moderately low, 3 neither low nor high, 4 moderately high, and 5 very high. Workers were asked a series of questions that included whether they and their colleagues had ever raised complaints in the factory, in what ways they did so, and what the result was. The coding took into consideration all relevant comments.

Table 9.8 presents the result of a regression analysis that takes into account factory workforce size and workers' duration of employment. Workforce size is included in the model to control for the degree of bureaucratic inflexibility that is likely to be more common in large factories. Workers' duration of employment is also included, since those with shorter service probably had fewer chances to observe management's reaction to their voices, which would have been taken as neutral responses in the coding process.[19]

Table 9.8 demonstrates large differences in managerial responsiveness among ownership types. SOE management was regarded as the most responsive by their workers with nearly one point higher on the scale than that of foreign-invested enterprises. Domestic-private enterprises also received a higher score than did foreign-invested enterprises, although the difference is not statistically significant. Shadow-foreign enterprises had the lowest score, nearly one point lower than the foreign-invested enterprises.

TABLE 9.8
Regression Analysis of Managerial Responsiveness

	Coef.	S.E.
Factory Ownership Type		
(Reference) Foreign-invested		
State-owned	0.984***	(0.265)
Domestic-private	0.473	(0.481)
Shadow-foreign	−0.957**	(0.389)
Workforce Size		
(Reference) 5,000 or more		
Fewer than 500	0.501	(0.650)
500 ~ 999	0.509	(0.546)
1,000 ~ 4,999	0.227	(0.540)
Interviewee's Employment Duration		
(Reference) 3 years or longer		
Less than 1 year	−0.387	(0.326)
1 year to less than 3 years	−0.202	(0.281)
Constant	2.694***	(0.628)

N = 91; R-squared = 0.244
** P < 0.05,   *** P < 0.01
Note: The model is estimated by clustering on factories. Robust standard errors are reported.

Overall, domestic management was more responsive to workers than foreign management.

A further insight can be gained by investigating the distribution of the scores. Table 9.9 reveals that 88 per cent of SOE workers, and 60 per cent of their counterparts in domestic-private enterprises, perceived their management to be moderately or very responsive. The respective figures for foreign-invested and shadow-foreign enterprises are 41 per cent and 8 per cent. But what is not revealed in the regression analysis is the high degree of polarization within the category of foreign-invested enterprises: 41 per cent of their workers felt management to be responsive and 47 per cent not responsive.

Enterprises from Hong Kong, Korea, and Taiwan have been often lumped together for their authoritarian management culture without due

TABLE 9. 9

Managerial Responsiveness by Factory Ownership Type

(Unit: number of workers, percentage in parentheses)

	Level of Managerial Responsiveness					
Ownership Type	Very low	Moderately low	Neither high nor low	Moderately high	Very high	Total
State-owned	0 (0)	0 (0)	2 (11.8)	12 (70.6)	3 (17.7)	17 (100.1)
Domestic-private	0 (0)	5 (33.3)	1 (6.7)	5 (33.3)	4 (26.7)	15 (100.0)
Foreign-invested	5 (10.6)	17 (36.2)	6 (12.8)	9 (19.2)	10 (21.3)	47 (100.1)
Shadow-foreign	4 (33.3)	6 (50.0)	1 (8.3)	0 (0)	1 (8.3)	12 (99.9)
Total	9 (9.9)	28 (30.8)	10 (11.0)	26 (28.6)	18 (19.8)	91 (100.1)

consideration of their enterprise-level differences (see Chan and Norlund 1998, pp. 181–82; Whyte 1999). If that approach is correct, the level of managerial responsiveness in foreign-invested enterprises should have been polarized between those from Hong Kong, Korea, and Taiwan on the one hand and those from other countries on the other. My sample had forty-one workers in the first group and six workers in the latter who had French, Japanese, and Thai general directors. When the responsiveness score was compared between the two groups, the latter indeed had a higher score, as is consistent with the received wisdom. Importantly, however, large variations are found within the first group: 37 per cent of the workers perceived their management to be moderately or very responsive and 51 per cent the opposite. This pattern again suggests the need to unpack overarching concepts such as managerial culture to better understand enterprise-level differences.

Overall, domestic management paid more attention to workers' grievances. Timely managerial handling of workers' discontent is likely to help avert strikes. Hence, the reason why foreign enterprises have experienced more strikes than their domestic counterparts lies partly in their different degree of managerial responsiveness to workers' grievances.

CONCLUSION

Workers who were interviewed for this study often said that factories were more similar than different: "It's the same everywhere (*O dau cung the*)". There is some truth to this perception. In domestic-private enterprises, workers were able to earn more money under the least abusive environment, but only by putting in extremely long hours. In SOEs where management and union paid most attention to their grievances, workers earned less, albeit with shorter work hours than in domestic-private enterprises. In foreign-invested enterprises, if fortunate, workers ended up with less abusive supervisors, unions that heeded their grievances, and more responsive management, while earning more income than in SOEs though less than in domestic-private enterprises. If they were not so lucky, however, workers had to face abusive supervisors and unresponsive management. Workers in shadow-foreign enterprises earned a little more than in SOEs but they had to tolerate the most abusive supervisors and most uncaring management. Indeed workers' comments that there are more similarities than differences between the various factories stems precisely from the fact that no enterprise type was consistently better or worse across the spectrum of labour conditions in terms of wages, working hours, supervisory abuse of workers, and managerial responsiveness.

Existing studies often assume that ownership type indicates something fundamental about the nature of an enterprise. Hence, in SOEs, state control over means of production is assumed to bring better benefits to workers than private ownership because the socialist institutional legacy is posited to limit the arbitrary exercise of managerial power and hence limit supervisory abuse. This study, however, has found that other things being equal, workers' earnings were the lowest in SOEs, though this was in part caused by shorter work hours. SOEs also had higher levels of supervisory abuse than domestic-private enterprises despite their unions' stronger role in handling workers' grievances and a more responsive management. The popular belief that state control and socialist institutions are beneficial to workers is not consistent with this pattern of supervisory abuse. As I noted earlier, the way incentive payments are structured to exert control over work behaviour is likely to be an important part of the explanation.

Foreign enterprises are different from domestic enterprises. Enterprises from Hong Kong, Korea, and Taiwan have been regarded as abusive toward workers due to their authoritarian management culture (Whyte 1999). This study has found some evidence in support of this view, especially in terms of supervisory abuse and managerial responsiveness. However, focusing on authoritarian management culture as an overarching explanation for labour conditions overlooks a great deal of variation within the category of foreign enterprises. The most obvious is the difference between formally foreign-invested and shadow-foreign enterprises: the latter were substantially worse in almost all aspects of labour conditions. Less salient, but still significant, is the difference within the category of foreign-invested enterprises. Even among those from the countries with a history of authoritarian management practices, quite a few had rather caring management and unions that attended to workers' grievances. Little has been known about the factors that produce these differences. Future research that compares foreign enterprises with a similar origin can illuminate those differences by closely examining internal organizational practices such as incentive systems.

The findings of this study suggest the need to revisit the proposition that worse labour conditions provoke more resistance. As discussed earlier, a part of the difference in strikes between foreign and domestic enterprises is attributable to the internal buffering mechanisms that can lower the chance of workers' discontent developing into collective resistance — a stronger grievance-handling role of state-enterprise unions and higher managerial responsiveness in both domestic-private and SOEs.[20] But this study stops at identifying the degree of union and managerial attention without investigating how effective those internal mechanisms have been in actually resolving workers' complaints. Addressing the latter question is crucial to understanding more fully the relationship between enterprise ownership, labour conditions, and worker resistance.

Notes

[1] As part of a larger research project, I also conducted a management survey of 124 factories in 2005, which includes about half of the factories selected for the worker interviews. Managers' comments are noted by the letter M and the numeric code assigned to each interviewee. Workers' comments are

similarly indicated by the letter W followed by the respective numeric code. For details about data collection procedure, interview questions, and a full list of interviewees, see Kim (2007).

2   It is not a random sample, however, as I chose to oversample both foreign and state-owned enterprises to draw meaningful conclusions about differences among ownership types. As domestic private enterprises form the bulk of this sector, followed by foreign-invested and state enterprises in that order, random sampling would have resulted in too few foreign and state enterprises. The sample also includes more garment than footwear factories because of the preponderance of the former.

3   The unit of analysis is the establishment, instead of the company as a whole, which counts all plants on the same premises as a single factory as long as they belong to the same enterprise. This decision is based on prior factory visits, which revealed that factories belonging to the same enterprise had different labour conditions depending on their locations. There is one exception, however. I separately counted two factories belonging to the same SOE that are located next to each other, since one is a footwear factory and the other a garment factory.

4   Of ten state-owned factories that are covered, three had 100 per cent state ownership according to the information from the management survey. As for the SOEs that completed or were in the process of equitization (*co phan hoa*) at the time of the interview, information about the degree of state ownership control is available only for two cases with 51 per cent and 30 per cent state ownership, respectively. Legally speaking, the second case was no longer an SOE. Nevertheless, I lumped all equitized enterprises under the SOE category rather than treating them as domestic-private enterprises for two reasons. First, equitization occurred mostly in the early 2000s, close to the time of worker interviews. It is reasonable to assume that management culture does not change within a short period, especially in light of the fact that equitization did not result in radical change in top management, according to some interviewed factory managers. Second, the sample has only a small number of equitized enterprises, so it is not realistic to treat them as a separate ownership category.

5   Another likely reason is the perception of tighter government control over foreign enterprises. I had an opportunity to observe how that perception may influence decision-making, while accompanying a Korean investor who was looking to rent a domestically owned factory to set up his own garment company. The Vietnamese owner claimed, "When Koreans run a company, there may be a conflict with the local government. They [the latter] send people to ask something about workers and labour laws, etc. But for Vietnamese companies, they don't do that as much." He then said that using the existing

business registration of a domestic company was one option, though it would require higher rents (personal observation, 19 October 2004). The factory owner would clearly benefit from the higher rental income but he would also have to take on a greater risk if the new investor were to have financial troubles such as unpaid debts and wage arrears.

6   Among thirty-eight footwear factory workers, four-fifths under domestic management (80 per cent) were paid by the piece in contrast to five of thirty-three workers under foreign management (15 per cent). Although footwear factory workers' high concentration in foreign-managed enterprises does not make the comparison too meaningful, the pattern is consistent with that observed for the garment industry.

7   Under the piece-rate system, workers have every incentive to produce the largest number of products without due consideration to product quality.

8   The minimum wage for SOEs is based on the government-issued wage scale that SOEs in different industries are required to follow. There is some uncertainty about the precise minimum wage for SOEs, however, since different jobs had different minimum wage rates (Government of Vietnam 2004).

9   This calculation is based on the analysis that takes foreign-invested, shadow-foreign, and domestic-private enterprises as the reference category in three separate models that are not shown here. To take an example, an 11 per cent difference in earnings between domestic-private enterprises and SOEs is based on the coefficient of -0.116 for SOEs in the model that takes the former as the reference category. Exponentiating the coefficient results in a ratio of 1 to 0.890 between domestic-private and state-owned enterprises, that is, a difference of 11 per cent. In other words, if workers in domestic-private enterprises earned VND1,00,000, their counterparts in SOEs earned VND890,000 on average, when other things are held constant.

10   This is stipulated in Article 60.2 in the 2002 Amendment of the Labour Code (Socialist Republic of Vietnam 2002).

11   Two Vietnamese native speakers coded workers' comments on the five-point scale. Relevant comments were centred around four interview questions:

1. What happens if you make defective items?
2. What happens if you do not fulfil the output quota?
3. How do the Vietnamese supervisors treat workers?
4. How do the foreign supervisors or managers, if there are any, treat workers?

12   Another explanation may have to do with the managerial tactic of "changing blood" (*thay mau*): that is, replacement of long-term workers with new hires to reduce labour costs. A few workers with over three years of service in my sample in fact reported some pressures to quit and high levels of supervisory abuse (W79, W80).

Jee Young Kim

13   One may argue that the polarization in foreign-invested enterprises results from their country of origin. When the abuse score is compared between foreign-invested enterprises from Hong Kong, Korea, and Taiwan and those from other countries (France, Japan and Thailand), the former have a higher score than the latter on average but importantly they still retain large variations in the abuse score, albeit skewed toward the more abusive end than the latter.

14   I classified their activities on the basis of whether at least one worker in each of the factories mentioned them.

15   When workers said they did not know if there was a union, the case is treated as having no union. Interview questions include not just what activities the union carried out but also whether the companies had specific activities such as picnics. When workers mentioned that the union was involved in organizing picnics even though union-organized entertainment events were not specified when they were asked about union activities, I categorize the picnics as a union activity.

16   Factories where the most recent picnic took place more than three years prior to the interview are considered not to have them. There was one such case in my sample.

17   The evidence from my sample is not entirely consistent, however. When asked about how they dealt with grievances at work and whether there were offices or enterprise personnel in charge of handling their grievances, at least one worker in 40 per cent of SOEs (4/10) and 48 per cent of foreign-invested enterprises (12/25), but in none of domestic-private and shadow-foreign factories, mentioned the union. Therefore, workers' answers about the union's grievance-handling role were different depending on interview questions. As workers in 40 per cent of SOEs (4/10) and 20 per cent of foreign-invested enterprises (5/25) gave consistent answers about the union's involvement to both questions on union activities and grievance handling in the factories, however, it can be concluded on balance that SOE unions were more active in dealing with workers' discontent than their counterparts in foreign-invested enterprises.

18   Clarke *et al.* (2007, pp. 557–8) identified isolated cases of collective bargaining. Among several cases of collective bargaining, they noted that the bargaining process was substantive, involving real negotiation and compromise between the union and management with workers' input in the process, in domestic-private and joint-venture enterprises, while the bargaining process was formalistic in SOEs. On the other hand, they found no meaningful collective bargaining and collective agreement in wholly foreign-owned enterprises. Among the 48 unions in my sample, however, the only union which had active collective bargaining, which resulted in higher wages and bonuses, is found in a 100-per cent Japanese-owned enterprise. One of the two worker interviewees from

this enterprise described her trade union as "strong but not dead" (W18) and the other was one of the very few workers with a clear understanding of collective bargaining agreements (W19).

[19] When workers' comments did not include any information on managerial responsiveness, the cases were removed from the analysis, however.

[20] The flip side of this question is what factors increase the chance of worker resistance. Previous studies emphasize workers' capacity to organize themselves (Tran 2005) and their perceived chance of a successful outcome (Clarke 2006; Lee 2006). The latter may in turn be associated with enterprise ownership if workers in foreign enterprises are more likely to expect the state to support them when they go on strike than their counterparts in domestic enterprises (Wang 2005).

References

Chan, Anita and Irene Norlund. "Vietnamese and Chinese Labour Regimes: On the Road to Divergence". *China Journal* 40 (July 1998): 173–97.

Chan, Anita and Wang Hong-zen. "The Impact of the State on Workers' Conditions: Comparing Taiwanese Factories in China and Vietnam". *Pacific Affairs* 77, no. 4 (2004): 629–46.

Clarke, Simon. "The Changing Character of Strikes in Vietnam". *Post-Communist Economies* 18, no. 3 (2006): 345–61.

Clarke, Simon, Lee Chang-Hee, and Do Quynh Chi. "From Rights to Interests: The Challenge of Industrial Relations in Vietnam". *Journal of Industrial Relations* 49, no. 4 (2007): 545–68.

Government of Vietnam. Decree No. 3 of 15 January 2003 Concerning the Adjustment of the Wage Rate and Social Insurance Benefits, and the Renovation of the Regulatory Structure for Wages. 2003.

———. Decree No. 205 of 14 December 2004 Stipulating Wage Tables, Wage Scales and Allowances for State Enterprises. 2004.

Hodson, Randy, Vincent J. Roscigno, and Steven H. Lopez. "Chaos and Abuse of Power: Workplace Bullying in Organizational and Interactional Context". *Work and Occupations* 33, no. 4 (2006): 382–416.

Kim Jee Young. "Governance Beyond Borders: Anti-Sweatshop Regulation in Vietnam's Fashion and Footwear Industries". Ph.D. dissertation, Department of Sociology, Harvard University, 2007.

Lee Chang-Hee. *Industrial Relations and Dispute Settlements in Vietnam*. ILO Discussion Paper. Hanoi: ILO Office in Vietnam, 2006.

Ministry of Labour, Invalids, and Social Affairs (MOLISA). Decision No. 708 of 15 June 1999 by the Minister of Labour, Invalids and Social Affairs on the Minimum Wage of Workers in Enterprises with Foreign Investment Capital. Hanoi, 1999.

Norlund, Irene. "Survey of Working, Living and Trade Union Conditions in Foreign and Private Companies in Ho Chi Minh City and Da Nang. Textile, Garments and Shoe Industries in Vietnam". Final Report, Project between the Vietnam General Confederation of Labour and the Norwegian Confederation of Trade Unions. Copenhagen: Nordic Institute of Asian Studies, 2000.

Socialist Republic of Vietnam. The Labour Code of the Socialist Republic of Vietnam (as Amended in 2002). Hanoi: Nha Xuat Ban Chinh Tri Quoc Gia, 2002.

Tran, Angie Ngoc. "Sewing for the Global Economy: Thread of Resistance in Vietnamese Textile and Garment Industries". In *Critical Globalization Studies*, edited by W. Robinson and R. Appelbaum, pp. 379–92. New York and London: Routledge, 2005.

Wang Hong-zen. "Asian Transnational Corporations and Labor Rights: Vietnamese Trade Unions in Taiwan-Invested Companies". *Journal of Business Ethics* 56, no. 1 (2005): 45–53.

Whyte, Martin King. "The Changing Role of Workers". In *The Paradox of China's Post-Mao Reforms*, edited by Merle Goldman and Roderick MacFarquhar, pp. 173–96. Cambridge, Mass.: Harvard University Press, 1999.

10

EXPLOITATIVE RECRUITMENT PROCESSES AND WORKING CONDITIONS OF VIETNAMESE MIGRANT WORKERS IN TAIWAN

Hong-zen Wang and Danièle Bélanger

In the past two decades, the rapidly industrializing Asian region has witnessed highly mobile intraregional labour flows. A key feature of this phenomenon is the critical role that intermediary actors play at all stages of the labour migration process. Governments sign bilateral agreements on the export and import of low-skilled and unskilled labour and delegate the job of organizing the migration of workers to recruitment and placement actors. This profit-making system that recruits, trains, transports, and places workers in distant foreign workplaces is often referred to as the migration industry. Highlighting the centrality of intermediaries in labour migration, John Salt and Jeremy Stein (1997) describes the industry as "migration as a business".

Since the early 1990s, this migration industry has seen unprecedented growth due to the rapid increase in contract migrant labourers moving between the economically developing and developed countries of Asia

(Hugo 2004; Skeldon 2000). Japan and the so-called "tiger economies" of East Asia — Taiwan, South Korea, Hong Kong, and Singapore — have opened their doors to increasing numbers of temporary migrant workers from the Philippines, Indonesia, Thailand, Vietnam, Bangladesh, and China. Despite their centrality and importance in Asian labour migration, those involved in the migration industry have been little studied, partly due to the difficulty of separating legal from illegal activities and the obstacles associated with a thorough investigation of such activities (Hugo 2004). Nonetheless, intermediary actors and their relationships with states and workers are an extremely important influence on migrant lives, working conditions, and income; any serious attempt to understand migration needs to pay attention to the role of these actors and the relationships among them.

In this chapter, we document and discuss the complexities of international labour export and import using the Vietnam–Taiwan dyad as a case study: Vietnam being the sending country, and Taiwan, the recipient. This system is complex, involving placement and recruitment intermediaries, state officials, and workers who rarely have a full understanding of the entire system in which they are all embedded and participate in. This system constitutes an elaborate network in which players have differential levels of power and gain unequal benefits. Moreover, as foreign nationals, the workers caught in this system are in a vulnerable position, easily exploited by employers due to their lack of citizenship in the recipient nation.

Using interview data collected in Vietnam and Taiwan between 2003 and 2007 from a sample of migrant workers and their family members, private and state intermediaries, government officials, Taiwanese employers, representatives of recruitment and placement agencies, and workers attending migrant training schools, we document how, through various mechanisms, workers' labour finances a profit-oriented system in which intermediaries and other recruiting agents (including governments through taxes and other ancillary fees) reap significant benefits. Most of the workers interviewed were put in dependent and vulnerable positions with respect to their employers and the host government authorities. Many failed to improve their economic situation by "exporting" their labour, or could only do so if they toiled for a pittance for very long hours under poor working conditions. We contend that any policies designed to help these labour migrants to improve their conditions need to pay greater attention to this intermediary layers of actors in the migration process.

INTERNATIONAL LABOUR MIGRATION IN
ASIA AND TAIWAN

While the majority of Asian migrant workers went to the oil-rich countries of the Middle East in the 1980s, the trend shifted in the early 1990s, with an increasing number moving for work within Asia, a transition considered to be one of the most significant shifts in world migration destinations since the 1970s (IOM 2005). During the second half of the 1990s, an estimated 2.6 million Asian workers migrated for contract work overseas every year (ILO 2004, p. 12). Low-skilled and unskilled workers constitute the largest share of such intraregional migrants. These migrants work in factories, on construction sites, households, farms, fisheries, or in services (Piper 2004), and have a powerful social impact on both sending and receiving nations. The widely researched case of Filipino migrant workers is emblematic of the importance of the phenomenon: with 7 million workers abroad (nearly 10 per cent of the population), transnational activities between the Philippines and numerous recipient countries have illustrated how transnational families, activities, and activism are transforming societies (Parrenas 2001).

Demographic transformations partly explain the current Asian migration flows of temporary guest workers. Rapidly declining fertility and ageing populations in some Asian economies contribute to the need for guest workers. Higher levels of education in recipient nations also leave employment gaps in the 3D (dirty, demanding, and dangerous) sectors in which foreign workers are employed. Migration within Asia has also increased due to the integration of labour markets as part of globalization (Gills 2002). For those living in the less economically developed nations of the region, seeking work elsewhere is attractive since it is associated with higher wages.

In the Asian migratory regime, Taiwan is a labour-importing country and officially began imported foreign labour in 1991. Table 10.1 shows the number of migrant workers from different Southeast Asian countries employed in the two main target sectors — manufacturing and social services — as of 2009. Taiwan needs unskilled labourers for construction and factory work that has not been outsourced to other countries. Workers from Thailand, the Philippines, and Vietnam keep wages low in Taiwan, allowing Taiwan-made products to compete in the global market. In addition. Taiwan's ageing population has seen a surge in demand for cheap unskilled carers. In 1988 the percentage of the population aged over 65 was

TABLE 10.1
Migrant Workers in Taiwan, by Occupation and Gender
(October 2009)

Country of Origin	Total no. of Workers	Industrial workers			Welfare workers[a]		
		Total no. industrial	% of Country Total	% Female	Total no. in Welfare	% of Country Total	% Female
Total	347,618	173,583	49.93	13.83	174,035	50.07	49.54
Indonesia	137,501	17,806	12.95	1.57	119,695	87.05	86.42
Malaysia	10	10	100	0	0	0	0
Philippines	70,537	48,028	68.09	34.48	22,509	31.91	31.28
Thailand	61,611	60,284	97.85	13.54	1,327	2.15	1.81
Vietnam	77,957	47,455	60.87	17.02	30,502	39.13	38.72
Mongolia	2	0	0	0	2	100	100

Notes: [a] This includes domestic helpers and aged care workers.
Source: Employment and Vocational Training Agency (EVTA), "97nian waiji laogong yunyong ji guanli diaocha" [Survey on the use and management of migrant workers, 2008]), Table 3, <http://www.evta.gov.tw/files/61/97年外勞提要分析(上網)2.doc> (accessed 10 December 2009).

only 5.7 per cent, while in 2007 it had increased to 10.2 per cent (MOI 2009). The traditional practice of caring for elders within the family is no longer sustainable due to industrialization and the high rates of female participation in the labour market. A lack of institutional facilities for the elderly exacerbates the demand for home-based care. The solution to the care crisis has been the supply of cheap Asian female domestic workers.

Vietnam has been a major source of foreign labour for Taiwan since 2000. At the end of October 2009, there were 77,957 Vietnamese workers in Taiwan, or 22.4 per cent of the foreign workforce in Taiwan (see Table 10.1). Of these Vietnamese migrant workers, 55.7 per cent were female, about 60 per cent of whom worked in private homes taking care of the elderly or doing domestic work, while the remainder worked in factories, fisheries, and farming. Initial contracts are for two years with permitted extensions of up to six years.

In January 2005, however, Taiwan closed its doors to hiring domestic workers from Vietnam; the reason given was that there was a high incidence of "runaway" Vietnamese domestic workers who had entered the illegal, hidden job market. As a result, since then, a majority of Vietnamese (about 61 per cent, see Table 10.1) have been employed in the manufacturing sector. Nevertheless, while Taiwan needs guest workers to fill gaps in its labour force, it does not want them to become long-term residents, let alone citizens. Guest workers are temporary sojourners with very limited rights and the entire system is designed to avoid settlement and integration (Tseng 2004, p. 32), resulting in an exploitative migrant labour regime.

VIETNAM'S EXPORT LABOUR POLICY

Vietnam's entry into the regional labour migration circuit began after several decades of tight state control over the internal and international mobility of Vietnamese citizens was lifted. Before the collapse of the East European socialist bloc and the erosion of alliances between the former USSR and other communist countries, however, Vietnam had sent migrant workers to the Council for Mutual Assistance (Comecon) countries (Hardy 2002). Vietnamese were sent to work in other Comecon countries in lieu of loan repayments and earned very meagre incomes, if anything at all. This legacy meant that northern Vietnam already had a labour-exporting infrastructure in place when it entered the Asian labour markets in the early 1990s, largely in the form of state-owned labour-export agencies (*cong ty xuat khau lao dong*). Over 400,000 migrant workers were sent to various countries in Asia between 1995 and 2005 (MOLISA 2006), most of them low-skilled and unskilled workers from rural areas. The export of labour is now part of Vietnam's official development policy, based on the assumption that migrants will acquire new skills and send remittances home. The leading labour-export destinations are Taiwan, Malaysia, Japan, and South Korea, with 90 per cent of migrant workers working in these four countries in 2005.

Although the Communist Party of Vietnam (CPV) still dominates the national economy, there are many powerful and influential groups pursuing their own interests (see Beresford 1997; Gainsborough 2002; Kerkvliet 2001). One Taiwanese intermediary agent who runs a business in Vietnam explained:

> At the beginning, the Ministry of Labour, Invalids and Social Affairs of Vietnam (MOLISA) only allowed 15 state-owned labour-exporting companies. All of them were state-owned enterprises belonging to MOLISA, but seeing that MOLISA was making money, other ministries also wanted to take part in the business of exporting labour. Because other ministries were also involved in exporting procedures, such as providing workers' physical checkups, and criminal record checks, etc., the Ministry of Health and the Ministry of Education also wanted to run labour-exporting companies. From November 1999 to November 2002, because different departments did not cooperate with each other, labour-exporting procedures could not be successfully organized in Vietnam. This caused a shortage of Vietnamese labour in Taiwan. The major cause of the problem is that each of these ministries or departments fought with the higher-level government for their right to have their own labour-exporting companies. After this period of haggling, in 2003, there were at least 158 state-owned labour-exporting companies.

In short, the government has had to open up the labour-export industry to all other ministries and departments, which has led to competition among them for a share, resulting in chaos. State-owned enterprises (SOEs) do not actually go to rural areas to recruit workers and depend on local governments and private recruiters. Since the industry is not officially open to private enterpreneurs, SOEs subcontract their labour export licences and make a profit. Indeed various powerful groups compete to profit from the migrant labour business.

FIELDWORK AND DATA

Our analysis relies on data collected by Wang in 2003, 2005, and 2006 and by Bélanger from 2005 to 2007. The project involved qualitative in-depth interviews with former migrant workers and their family members, high-ranking MOLISA officials, officials at the district and commune levels, officials from Vietnamese and Taiwanese recruitment and training agencies, trainers, and individual subcontractors or intermediaries. Government officials were interviewed in Hanoi, while migrant workers and lower-ranking bureaucrats were interviewed in three rural communes of a neighbouring province.

In total, we interviewed seventy-five Vietnamese who had worked as migrant workers in Taiwan and had returned to their home communities in Vietnam, and twenty-nine other informants. An additional fifteen Vietnamese migrant workers were interviewed in Taiwan. The majority of interviews were conducted in Vietnam because interviewing foreign workers in Taiwan, where many of them have very limited freedom to meet and interact with strangers, tends to be difficult. Domestic workers are typically confined to their employers' homes, and factory workers generally reside in dormitories where they have little or no free time and limited opportunities to interact outside the factory. Nonetheless, we managed to conduct fifteeen interviews in Taiwan through personal networks and through an NGO offering counselling, emergency shelter, and legal aid to migrant workers facing difficulties (mostly illegal salary deductions but also abuse and trafficking). The interview guidelines included questions on how individuals became migrant workers (how they were recruited) and how much money they paid before leaving and to whom the money was paid (most interviewees had kept receipts detailing how much they paid for each service through the process and showed these receipts to the researchers during the interview).

We also collected data on their pre-departure training experiences in Vietnam and their working lives in Taiwan. Workers who had escaped and entered the illegal system were not hesitant about sharing their stories, since they felt they had had legitimate reasons to "run away" (usually because of mistreatment by employers, not being paid, or not having enough overtime work to pay back their brokerage fee), and now they had nothing to lose. At worst they would be deported home. Throughout the interviews, it was obvious that the workers themselves were aware of some risks inherent in going to work in another country, but they had accepted this in the hope of being among the successful ones.

Some workers succeeded in saving enough money to bring back home (the largest sum in our sample being US$7,000 after three years), while about 30 per cent of them returned before the end of their contracts due to difficulties with working conditions, work relations, or the inability to adapt to living away from their families. Among our interviewees, the average stay was eighteen months, although initial contracts were for two years, with the possibility of extending to three years; following this first contract, they could go back to Taiwan for another three-year period on a second contract.[1] Two of the migrants we interviewed had been victims of trafficking and had dealt with what they called "fake agencies" (*cong ty ma*) that they could no longer trace after their return.

MIGRATION POLICY IN VIETNAM AND TAIWAN

The Taiwan government uses labour importing as a tool of "foreign labour diplomacy" to gain favour with certain neighbouring countries. It decides on which countries can send guest workers to work in Taiwan.[2] If anything negative happens between Taiwan and one of its labour-supplying countries, Taiwan could immediately freeze labour importation from that country. For example, in 1999, after the foreign ministry of the Philippines publicly rejected a visa to Lee Teng-hui, the former president of Taiwan, the Taiwan Council for Labour Affairs immediately announced a freeze on the import of workers from the Philippines.[3] When the Chair of the Council for Labour Affairs applied for a visa to go to Thailand to attend a conference on Thai migrant labour in 2004, she received only a tourist visa instead of the usual courtesy visa given to high-ranking officials, because the host country had given in to a protest over the visit by China. The Taiwan government immediately applied a "soft freeze" of labour imports from Thailand to express its unhappiness.[4]

To deploy its "foreign labour diplomacy" fully, Taiwan's Council for Labour Affairs deals with this issue bilaterally, that is, through "country to country" discussions. With Vietnam, it negotiates labour import quotas and recruiting procedures with MOLISA. There are two official recruitment avenues for importing Vietnamese labour to Taiwan: first, through an intermediary company that holds a licence from the Taiwanese government to hire Vietnamese workers and second, through direct hire by employers (see Figure 9.1). In Vietnam, all labour-exporting is managed by the Department of Overseas Labour Management. Those allowed to export labour are mainly state-owned intermediary companies, and in order to work abroad, workers must register with a labour-exporting SOE. Hence, Vietnamese public enterprises (ostensibly not-for-profit) recruit workers in Vietnam, and intermediary agencies in Taiwan (officially for-profit) mediate between workers and employers to facilitate the recruitment and placement process.

For the Taiwanese employers, direct hire is not feasible for several reasons. First, they have no idea where to find suitable workers. Second, employers usually want workers immediately after they submit their hiring request. But Vietnam requires the worker to possess a special skills certificate after at least 60 days of training in a training centre. This requirement makes it impossible for employers in Taiwan to hire workers immediately.

FIGURE 10.1
Recruitment Process in Taiwan and Vietnam

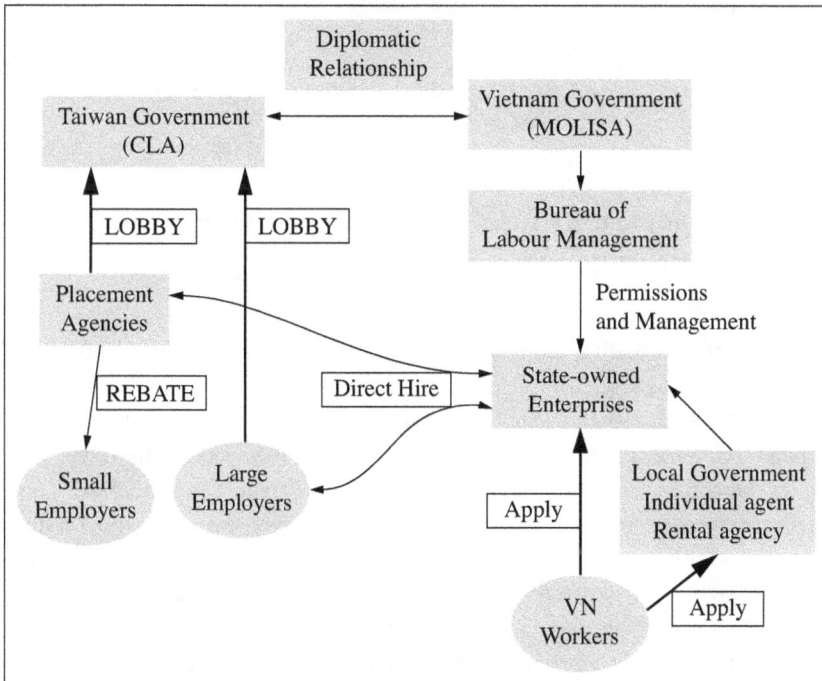

If they use an intermediary company, then everything will be handled for them. Intermediary companies know where to find workers in Vietnam and have a ready pool of workers at their training centres available on demand. Finally, the application procedures are very complicated, and employers prefer to pay fees to an intermediary rather than get involved. As a result, most employers hire migrant workers through an intermediary (see Table 10. 2).

TABLE 10.2
Channels through which Taiwanese Factories Hire Migrant Workers (percentage of total, June 2009)

	Direct Hire	Recruitment agency	Hired from other employers	Other sources
Total	0.6	99.0	4.9	0.1
Manufacturing	0.5	99.0	4.8	0.1
Construction	1.9	97.4	6.6	–

Notes: An employer has multiple ways of recruiting migrant workers, hence the colums total more than 100 per cent across.
Source: EVTA, "97nian waiji laogong yunyong ji guanli diaocha" [Survey on the use and management of migrant workers, 2008], Table 14, <http://www.evta.gov.tw/files/61/97年外勞提要分析(上網)2.doc> (accessed on 10 December 2009).

RECRUITMENT AND PLACEMENT IN THE VIETNAM–TAIWAN LABOUR MIGRATION PROCESS

As shown in Figure 9.1, in Vietnam, the system is officially run entirely by SOEs, but, in reality, many private and semi-private agents are involved — as businesses engaged in recruiting, training, and sending migrant workers abroad. Our data indicates that most workers from rural areas do not deal directly with the recruitment agencies; instead, they go through various agents who are in contact with the agencies. Private intermediaries are thus at the centre of the recruitment process in Vietnam, working for the agencies which receive orders for workers from Taiwan. Contrary to what the Vietnamese press often suggests, it is not only in Taiwan that workers are charged exorbitant fees and extra charges; in Vietnam too, the business of recruiting migrant workers is booming and generating substantial profits for some. Because the entire system is poorly regulated and decentralized, some free agents can easily take advantage of the situation and deceive eager peasants who wish to go abroad.

In the data we collected from various actors involved in the migration process, we identified three types of unofficial actors within Vietnam: private individual Vietnamese recruiters, Vietnamese local governments, and Taiwanese or Vietnamese private recruitment companies outsourcing a licence from a Vietnamese labour-exporting SOE.

Private individual recruiters hire workers on behalf of a labour-export company or another individual recruiter. Most workers we interviewed were hired by an individual recruiter whom they met in their community. The involvement of these individuals partly resulted from the difficulty that the state-owned intermediary companies (located in large cities) faced in finding suitable candidates in the countryside. Although some state-owned labour-export agencies do send recruiters to enlist workers in the countryside directly, this is rare; few recruiters from the city are able to, or want to, enter rural communities for this purpose. Private recruiters are thus engaged to approach workers on behalf of company recruiters. In some instances, there can be a chain of several private recruiters before reaching the one who has direct contact with the labour-export agency. Needless to say, this increases the costs to workers, who are unaware of the number of layers they have to get through before reaching the actual recruiting agency.

In some cases that we encountered in our fieldwork, the private individual recruiters are themselves former employees of labour-exporting SOEs. Drawing on their extensive network and connections, they can now make more money working privately; some individuals work both for themselves as well as for a labour recruitment company. In our research, private individual recruiters could be local (recruiting in the home community) or non-local (recruiting in other communities) actors.

Following initial contact with a private recruiter, it was not uncommon for workers to wait six to twelve months before being sent to a training centre in Hanoi. Throughout the process, the recruiter periodically asks the candidates for more money to keep up the "paperwork" relating to their registration as migrant workers. Both private and company-hired recruiters receive a "per head" payment from the recruitment agency. In Table 10.4 we see that private recruiters average a profit of US$400 to US$500 per worker. Recruiters who are employed by the recruitment agency or company receive between US$100 to US$200 per worker.

Labour-exporting SOEs work with local governments by sending official memos to provincial (*tinh*) and district (*huyen*) level authorities to disseminate recruiting information via the district people's committees. The process is described by the manager of a labour-exporting SOE:

> Usually Vietnamese intermediary companies send an official recruiting announcement to local governments. After they receive the announcement, local governments disseminate the information by broadcasts or posters to inform that all workers can get registered at the local government. Once they have a certain number of registered potential workers, our company sends someone there to select workers.

Through such cooperation, local governments have an opportunity to be involved in the recruitment process and to make a profit by charging workers intermediary fees for introducing them to the labour-export agency. Unlike private individual recruiters, local governments have direct links with the labour-exporting SOEs. Often, children or relatives of local government officials who wish to work overseas are able to go through this route. Despite the role of personal networks in this type of recruitment, the fees paid by workers recruited in this manner are not necessarily less than those going through private recruiters.

Some of our informants worked for companies that were entirely private. These agencies — run by either Vietnamese or Taiwanese — operated by "borrowing" the licence of a Vietnamese SOE for a fixed fee, depending on the duration of the arrangement. On the surface, these labour-export agencies appeared to be state enterprises, but, in fact, they were entirely privately run for-profit by charging intermediary fees directly to workers. Based on the testimonies of some former employees of these pseudo-SOEs, there appears to be no mechanism in place to monitor adherence to export-labour laws or treatment of migrant workers (including fees charged) by these agencies. The subcontracting of migrant worker recruitment and training is advantageous for SOEs, which do not have to do all the work themselves, yet can still collect fees from workers. A Taiwanese businessman who runs one such intermediary company in Vietnam said in an interview that:

> Labour-exporting company A does not have a licence to recruit workers in Vietnam; it rents a licence from a Vietnamese SOE. Here, there are many Taiwanese businesspeople that cooperate with Vietnamese SOEs. Not all SOEs can get orders from Taiwan; therefore, they go through these people who have their connections with Taiwanese intermediary

companies. They provide operating channels for Vietnamese SOEs to export workers to Taiwan. Some of these Taiwanese companies are the branch of their mother companies in Taiwan, while others are independent private labour-exporting companies. They either recruit workers in the name of state-owned companies or get orders from factories or intermediary companies in Taiwan and pass on the orders to Vietnamese labour-exporting SOEs.

In this system, two layers make a profit: the SOE that leases its licence (approximately US$200 per worker, Table 10.4) and the private company that operates under the name of the SOE (approximately US$825 to US$950 per worker, Table 10.4). Such licence renting seems common due in part to the lack of coordination between recruiting orders from Taiwan and state-owned recruitment agencies in Vietnam. This void leaves room for the development of an intermediary layer of key actors who reap a profit.

The placement process in Taiwan is market-based, involving only two major players — employers and recruitment companies. In contrast to the Vietnamese recruitment system that is officially state-run, the Taiwanese system is entirely private and operates for profit. The Taiwanese government only grants licences. Many intermediaries compete for employers' orders in the migrant workers' market in Taiwan. To be qualified to apply to the Taiwanese government to hire migrant workers, Taiwanese employers need to belong to one of the following categories: enterprises with a large amount of investment, have major public construction projects, or are private employers who require care for a seriously disabled family member. The government decides who is qualified to hire foreign labour and who is granted a licence to serve as an intermediary. In the Taiwanese political context, people who have connections with legislators or government administrative departments can get a licence more easily.

Taiwanese placement agencies collaborate with recruitment agencies located in Vietnam when they win a bid for placing workers. This collaboration may take three different forms:

- Taiwanese placement agencies place orders with Vietnamese companies who recruit workers, train them, then send them to Taiwan. These Vietnamese companies are also responsible for providing services to workers while in Taiwan.
- Some Taiwanese placement agencies get orders and establish a training centre in Vietnam, but ask a Vietnamese company to recruit the workers for them.

- Taiwanese companies take care of the entire labour-exporting process. They get recruitment orders in Taiwan, rent a licence in Vietnam, find Vietnamese workers, and train them. In this case, the Vietnamese SOE that rents the licence to the Taiwanese company charges a fixed amount per worker.

Different operating models generate different modes of fee distribution among actors; for example, a Taiwanese company that takes care of all facets of the labour-exporting process will also take most of the profit. Regardless of the players involved in the recruitment–placement process, Taiwanese placement agencies that receive orders from employers hold more bargaining power and Vietnamese companies have no choice but to cooperate with them. This contentious issue shows the asymmetrical power relations between Taiwanese companies (recruitment and placement) and Vietnamese companies (recruitment).

In the labour-importing market, employers are in a stronger position *vis-à-vis* the placement agency because the agencies have to pay employers fees in order to get the orders (Tsai and Chen 1997). According to Cai Qifang, a legislator who used to hire foreign workers for his enterprise in Taiwan, many placement agencies came to his company to compete for orders and offer kickbacks.[5] All these kickbacks would eventually be paid by migrant workers through various fees and salary deductions (the average amount of kickback per worker is US$800 to US$1,000, see Table 10.4). The various deals contracted between employers and placement agencies explain part of the variation in salary deductions taken from workers' wages.

The guest-worker scheme enables profit-pursuing intermediary organizations to recruit new migrant workers in a continual cycle (through short contracts and high rates of early returns) in order to maximize profit. Many practices uncovered through our research are not in line with the legal responsibilities of intermediary agencies towards workers. For instance, agencies are supposed to help workers change employers if the employer can no longer provide adequate work (for example, due to a factory closure or production interruption) but most workers are simply sent back to Vietnam when this happens. By terminating existing contracts and importing new workers, intermediary agencies maximize their profits, since they make the most money from a worker during his or her first year of employment.

AUTHORIZED FEES, UNAUTHORIZED CHARGES, AND THE DISTRIBUTION OF PROFIT

Going to work abroad is never "free" for migrant workers. All our informants had to borrow money to pay pre-departure fees and charges or downpayments. In addition, workers have large portions of their salaries deducted in the first year to pay taxes in Taiwan, and other fees not covered by the downpayments. We first provide a breakdown of the authorized fees paid by workers based on government publications and interviews in Table 10.3. Utilizing our interview data, we then assess the "other charges" paid by workers in Table 10.4. "Other charges" may be unauthorized but not necessarily illegal because they are not referred to in the laws or regulations. These estimates, although based on a small sample, explain why most migrant workers do not have any net income in their first year abroad. We found that the only migrants who earned a net income during their first year in Taiwan were those who had a large amount of overtime work.

It is noteworthy that not a single domestic worker had any net income in the first year of her contract. Two models of recruitment charges are used: the downpayment model charges about US$6,300 paid before departure, in which case less money is deducted from one's salary when working in Taiwan. A second one is the salary deductions model. About US$1,800 is paid before departure, but more money will then be deducted from the salary. The charges paid by both groups of workers we interviewed (factory workers and domestic workers) did not vary a great deal, however, although factory workers tended to pay in advance and domestic workers tended to pay in the form of salary deductions.

The charges that Vietnamese guest workers must pay in their first year as stipulated by the Taiwanese and Vietnamese governments are shown in Table 10.3. Officially, guest workers in Taiwan receive a minimum wage which totals an annual income of US$5,760, regardless of their work sector.[6] In their first year in Taiwan, however, Vietnamese workers must pay income tax, fees for two physical checkups, placement agency service fees, residence application fees, insurance, and dormitory rent, all of which are deducted from their salary — a total of up to NT$91,680 (US$2,715). Workers must also pay fees in Vietnam for pre-departure physical checkups and training, criminal record checks, passports and visas, and their airline tickets and departure tax. In addition, each worker must pay the annual

TABLE 10.3
Taiwan and Vietnam governments' regulations on charges to migrant workers (first year of a work contract only)

Items	Regulated cost in local currencies	Regulated cost in US$
Regulated charges in Vietnam[a]		
Health check	VND500,000–600,000	31.84–38.22
Pre-departure training	VND1,050,000 per month for up to three months	66.88–200.64
No criminal certificate	VND100,000	6.37
Passport	VND200,000	12.74
Visa to Taiwan	US$66/normal[a]	66.00
Airfare (average cost)	VND4,850,000	300.00–318.47
Airport departure tax	US$14.00	14.00
1st year government income tax before departure	NT$15,840	480.00
Subtotal		977.83–1,136.44
Regulated charges in Taiwan[b]		
Income tax (6%) deducted from salary every month	NT$11,400	345.36
Labour & health insurance	NT$4,680	78.54
Service fee charged by Taiwanese placement agency	NT$21,600	654.54
Health check (twice in Year)	NT$5,000	151.51
Residence application fee	NT$1,000	
Accommodation and food	NT$30,000 to 48,000	901.01–1,454.50
Subtotal	*73,680 to 91,680*	*2161.26–2714.75*
Total authorized charges in Year 1		US$3,139 ~ 3,851
Total minimum wage in Year 1		US$5,760.00
Theoretical annual net wage to worker		US$1,909.00 to US$2,621.00

Notes: [a]US$99.00 for express issue.

ᵇExchange rate: US$1: VND15,700: NT$33 (2006).
ᶜIncome tax depends on how long a foreigner stays in Taiwan during a calendar year (January 1st to December 31st). For those who stay for less than 183 days in the calendar year, the income tax equals 20 per cent of Taxable Total Income, while those who stay more than 183 days, the income tax equals 6 per cent of the Taxable Total Income as deducted of the Non-Taxable Amount, the Standard Deduction Amount, and the Wage/Salary Deduction Amount. Here we use the second condition, i.e., only 6 per cent of Taxable Total Income. Charges are lower for year 2 and 3 and thus net income tends to increase over time.
Sources: Bureau of Overseas Employment, "Dang ky hop dong va xac nhan ban cam ket cho lao dong di lam viec tai Dai Loan", So 148/QLLDNN-TTLD, 31/01/2005. Cited from Bureau of Overseas Employment (2005), "Gioi thieu van ban", in Viec Lam Ngoai Nuoc, pp. 18–19; Employment and Vocational Training Agency (EVTA), "Foreign Worker's Affidavit Regarding Expenses Incurred for Entry into The Republic of China to Work and the Wage/Salary", <http://wwwold.evta.gov.tw/download/affidavit-2.doc> (accessed 31 July 2007).

income tax of US$480 for the first year to the Vietnamese government *before* their departure. The total amount paid to the Vietnamese government is between US$977 and US$1,136. The combined authorized charges by the Taiwanese and Vietnamese governments are up to US$3,851 per worker in the first year. If we subtract this amount from a pre-tax income of US$5,760, the net annual income for year one should be about US$1,909 (US$5,760–$3,851). As mentioned, among our interviewees, however, only the few who worked a lot of overtime managed to be left with any net income during their first year.

Table 10.4 provides the approximate breakdown of fees paid to different players in the system. We collected the data from workers' payslips provided by their employers in Taiwan and from receipts of other payments that workers had kept (including various pre-departure expenses). Based on detailed testimonials from various players, we estimated that migrant workers paid approximately anything from US$6,124 to $7,461, of which 40 per cent stays in Vietnam and 60 per cent goes to Taiwan.

In Vietnam, because the recruitment process is decentralized, complex, and competitive, the distribution of profit among different players varies. If an SOE recruits and trains workers, then the workers need to pay to obtain certificates and documents necessary for leaving the country. The company can then appropriate about 30 per cent of the total amount generated by one worker through payments and labour in the first year of the contract, however. State-owned companies rarely have the capability and resources to perform all the required tasks; therefore, as has been described, they work with licence-renting companies, individual agents, and local governments. The profit distribution depends on the cooperation model. Most individual agents receive about US$200 per worker from recruitment companies for introducing workers. Licence-renting companies have to pay US$200 per worker to the SOE, and, subsequently, make a profit by charging the worker fees for training, document preparation, ticket booking, etc., which amounts to approximately 14 per cent of the worker's total income in the first year of employment.

In Taiwan, where most of the profit accrues (60 per cent), distribution also differs depending on the type of collaboration between the various intermediaries. In cases where guest workers are employed by small companies, the employer receives about 25 per cent of the money. Employers can make a total of US$1,500 to US$1,650 per worker for the first year if they charge US$70 monthly in accommodation fees and receive between US$667 and US$1,000 in kickbacks from the intermediary company. Approximately 9 per cent of the money is stipulated by the Taiwanese government for physical examinations, income tax, labour insurance, etc. Another 26 per cent is taken by the Taiwanese intermediary company for officially stipulated fees, service fees, and payment on the migrant worker's debt to the company. The Taiwanese intermediary company's profit will be greater if it also rents a licence in Vietnam and runs the recruitment and training. As a licence-renting company, it will receive 14 per cent of the total amount. The portion of this amount paid by the migrant worker can be as high as 40 per cent. If they recruit workers directly, large companies, such as the Kaohsiung Mass Rapid Transit Company, can acquire 50 per cent of the total fees paid by migrant workers in the first year.

So if we combine the authorized fees and the "other charges", workers are required to pay an average of US$6,124 to $7,461 in the first year. But their salaries in the first year only amounted to about US$5,760 (not including overtime income). Typically, it takes about 15 months for a guest worker to recoup these expenses before she/he can start earning money. One representative from a large placement agency in Taiwan whom we interviewed estimated that workers placed through his company stayed in Taiwan for an average of 17 months, while our data shows an average duration of 18.4 months per stay, which is very close. Failing

TABLE 10.4
Profit Appropriated by Different Players per Worker in the
Recruitment System

Private Vietnamese local recruiter in Vietnam	US$400 to $500
Individual agent in Vietnam working for recruitment agency	US$100 to $200
SOE in Vietnam	US$200
Recruitment agency in Vietnam	US$660 to $760
Taiwanese placement agency	US$825 to $950
Kickback to Taiwanese employer	US$800 to $1,000
Total profit extracted from one migrant worker	US$2,985 to $3,610

Source: All fees listed in this table are averages calculated from amounts obtained in the interview data and from documents provided by interviewees (salary sheets and receipts).

to make much income in the first year was a bitter disappointment for all workers, who were greatly concerned about how their families could pay back the monthly interest on their loans (about 1.0 per cent to 1.2 per cent per month for bank loans or 1.2 per cent to 1.5 per cent for private loans). This system often puts pressure on workers to "run away" in the hope of earning money in the illegal work sector. Some return home prematurely, afraid of being caught in this system by staying too long. Early returnees are promptly replaced by new migrants who, in turn, provide high returns to intermediaries who prefer a high turnover rate of migrants.

What are the conditions that sustain this system? How have workers and their labour become commodified to the extent that they have to work for more than a year before earning any income? And what is the effect of this system on a migrant worker's conditions in Taiwan? As we argue below, the combined effects of the Vietnamese political system, the Taiwanese guest-worker scheme, and the regulation prohibiting workers from changing employers allow such a system to continue.

POOR LABOUR CONDITIONS IN TAIWAN

One reason why migrant workers are totally under the control of their employers is that Taiwan's guest-worker scheme does not allow workers to change employers. Article 59 of the newly revised Employment Law stipulates that guest workers can change employers with the approval of the central administrative department only in the following situations:

- the employer or person being cared for dies, or emigrates;
- a ship is detained, sinks, or cannot operate;
- the employer terminates the contract, closes the factory, halts production, or does not pay workers according to the contract; or
- for other reasons not caused by the guest worker.

Such regulations are very strictly enforced, and disputes generally end up in an early forced return for the worker. Although the law allows for mediation when there is a labour dispute, the process is time consuming and the guest workers involved has to work for another employer during the process.

The essentially bonded labour situation makes it difficult for migrant workers to fight against poor working conditions. Migrant workers are usually expected to work very long hours, are paid lower wages, and tolerate harsh discipline in the factories where they work.[7] The Labour Standard Law has a provision which protects migrant workers by ensuring that they are paid a minimum wage and restricting the maximum number of hours they must work. Despite that, they work about 226 hours per month on average, according to government statistics (see Table 10.5 below). This violates Article 32, which regulates maximum overtime hours in a month to a maximum of 46 hours for male workers and 32 hours for female workers. According to a survey done by Chan and Wang[8] on labour conditions for local migrant workers in Vietnam and China, the Vietnamese worked only 204 hours a month, while the Chinese worked 213 hours in factories. Even though Taiwan has a much more developed economy, foreign workers there work much longer than domestic migrant workers in China and Vietnam.

Even when working hours seem to conform to labour codes, the labour intensity is another problem. According to the Labor Standard Law, the employer can arrange a total overtime of forty-six hours over a certain period to meet high season demand. For example, the employer can ask workers to work forty hours of overtime in a week — sixteen hours every day for seven days—followed by no overtime work in the next three weeks. One Vietnamese female migrant worker in a large electronics company in Kaohsiung said, "Can you imagine that it has been many days

I have not seen the sun? During the past three days I worked thirty-two hours, i.e., worked for sixteen hours, went to bed for eight hours, and then worked for another sixteen hours. In that month I had seventeen days of overtime work."

To facilitate such long working hours, migrant workers in Taiwan, like their counterparts in China, are placed in dormitories so that they can be easily controlled by their employers. According to official survey data, 99 per cent of migrant workers live in dormitories provided by employers (EVTA 2009). Employers report that migrant workers want to earn more money so they like working overtime. Living in the dormitories eliminates the need to commute and enables them to work even longer hours. Migrant workers are in debt for the first 18 months abroad, so they must work overtime to pay back what they owe. In reality, they cannot refuse overtime work because employers can easily dismiss them and send them back home. One female interviewee reported bitterly that she was dismissed and sent back home to Vietnam at the end of her three-month probation period in Taiwan because she told her supervisor that she could not work overtime due to health problems. One company instituted the following rule regarding overtime work: "Workers have to ask permission from management three days in advance if they want a leave of absence for personal reasons. In principle the company will agree, but, if not approved due to workload,

TABLE 10.5
Working Hours of Migrant Workers in Taiwan's Factories
(June 2008; hours per month)

	Total	Normal	Overtime hours
Total	225.6	178.3	47.3
Manufacturing	225.4	178.2	47.2
Construction	230.8	180.9	49.9

Note: This survey was conducted by the Bureau of Employment and Vocational Training in 2008 to understand the use of migrant workers by Taiwanese employers. It was a general survey by mailing questionnaires, and it collected responses from 6,983 companies and 7,235 families.

Source: EVTA (2009) 97nian waiji laogong yunyong ji guanli diaocha [Survey on the use of foreign labourers and management of migrant workers, 2008], Table 3 <http://www.evta.gov.tw/files/61/97年外勞提要分析(上網)2.doc> (accessed on 10 December 2009).

workers still have to come to work." Another regulation states that "those who ask for leave without permission for three successive days will be repatriated home."

Although they are paid the legal minimum wage, migrant workers face discrimination in the workplace due to their lack of citizenship. Migrant workers must work the night shift, which no Taiwanese workers will do. They do not receive better pay for the night shift; however, they get one free meal and a "nutrition allowance" of US$2 per day. In contrast, Taiwanese workers receive a "food allowance" of US$85 every month. Migrant workers do not receive any of the benefits that are provided to Taiwanese workers: such as a one-month salary bonus for the Lunar New Year, a seniority bonus, a half-month salary bonus during the Dragon Boat and Mid Autumn festivals, and a stock option bonus.

There is no law prohibiting migrant workers from becoming members of the trade union, but in practice they are not allowed to join. If migrant workers have grievances, most of them turn to the recruitment company for help. Taiwanese factories rely heavily on recruitment companies to communicate with migrant workers, and sometimes to manage the dormitories (Nguyen 2008). Migrant workers have US$90 deducted from their pay every month to live in very poor conditions in the dormitories. A small room without air conditioning can house ten workers. One interviewee described her dormitory:

> Every room accommodates ten persons. Summer is very hot, as hot as a stove. The space is very limited, and the air is hot and humid. Our room is next to the main road, and it is very noisy. The sun comes through the glass window, and it is so hot that we have to put newspaper over it, so the room is normally dark. Everyone works at night shift, so now (11:00 am) everyone is sleeping. We worry very much about water. Sometimes the water is very dirty. We have to buy mineral water to brush our teeth. The management has come to check the water quality from time to time, but it never improves.

If migrant workers cannot stand the unbearable working conditions, normally they just escape from their employers and try to find new jobs through personal networks. However, the Taiwanese government has very strict methods to prevent "runaway foreign workers", and it is quite "efficient" at finding any workers who manage to run away. In the past fifteen years, over a million migrant workers have entered Taiwan to work, but a great majority of them have also left Taiwan before their contract expired. Of the total number of migrant workers, only about 2 per cent have overstayed and still remain in Taiwan (Tseng and Wang 2011). The government works diligently to prevent migrant workers from running away and punishes any offenders harshly. According to the regulation (Article 56 of the Employment Law), workers who "run away" from their employers for more than three days are considered illegal migrants. When caught by the police, they are immediately incarcerated and then repatriated (allowed under the Article 34 of the Immigration Law). Unlike Taiwanese citizens, escapees or "runaway" workers have no right of appeal, even if they left because of serious abuse or intolerable working conditions. The treatment of migrant workers illustrates important inconsistencies in Taiwan's policies and laws, which forbid arrest and detention without any legal procedures or right of appeal (Li 2003).

CONCLUSION

In summary, the international labour migration system between Vietnam and Taiwan that we examine in this chapter has the following characteristics. First, intermediaries are unavoidably embedded in a complex and transnational meso-level set of institutions. Second, the commodification of the migration process makes migration a costly path for migrant workers. The profit-oriented migration industry often leads to the debt-bondage of workers caught in a vicious cycle, having to pay back a large debt rather than accumulating capital. Third, migration and work policies that prevent the creation of a competitive market for the employment of migrant workers create a worker-employer bondage that prohibits workers' mobility within the receiving nation. This servitude disempowers workers and worsens their conditions.

Due to the structural characteristics of the transnational labour migration institutions, the so-called "intermediary problem" and the "runaway migrant worker problem" in Taiwan remain unsolved. Such problems cannot be attributed only to the greed of intermediaries and cruelty of employers. The domestic political economy in both Vietnam and Taiwan, the legitimization of the guest-worker scheme, and Taiwanese regulations that reduce workers to becoming bonded labourers all combine to produce this exploitative international labour migration regime. Aspects of the political economy of both Vietnam and Taiwan lead to a continual loop of migrant worker exploitation. Given such an institutional setting, many players maximize their profit at different stages of the migratory process. Meanwhile, the income of individual migrant workers is siphoned off by others.

We believe that in order to understand the labour migration process embedded in both the internal and international political economy, we should study this issue from the perspective of transnational organizations. Previous studies of Asian migration have rarely looked at the issue from a transnational organizational perspective, and we hope that our study helps to fill this gap. We also propose that the institutional approach and national political economic contexts influence the operation of the intermediary organizations, which contribute to the exploitative labour migration regime. If governments can better regulate intermediary agencies, and grant migrant workers the right to change jobs in the recipient countries, workers will be able to enjoy some freedom, a more balanced power relationship with their employers, and be less easily victims of labour abuses.

If we aim to improve the working conditions of migrant workers, it is critical that the institutional links between state and intermediary agencies be redesigned. To alleviate the collusive repression of employers and intermediary agencies, the best policy strategy to address the current situation in Taiwan is to allow migrant workers to freely change employers and work in Taiwan on a long-term basis. In Vietnam itself, where the issue of "labour export" is considered politically sensitive, the experiences of workers with recruitment and fee payments have to be told to uncover the privatization of labour export as a profit-making enterprise.

Notes

1   The revision of Article 52 of the Employment Law in June 2007, which came into effect on 13 July 2007, allows blue-collar migrants to stay and work in Taiwan for up to nine years.
2   Chen Ju, "Zhijie pingu kaiqi laozi huhui zhilu" [Direct hire opens a door for capital-labour mutual benefits] <http//www.e-agent.com.tw/main-diction.php> (accessed 8 January 2006).
3   *Central Daily News*, "Feilubin zhengfu bixu gaixuan yiche" [Philippines government should change its policy], Editorial, 4 August 1999.
4   *Commercial Times Daily*, "Pingyi lingjia jingji de wailao zhengce" [Regarding foreign labour policy and economic policy], Editorial, 12 December 2004.
5   Cai Qifang, "Wailao shi yizhi bei bole haojicengpi de niu" [Foreign workers are like oxen sold many times], *Taiwan Ribao* [Taiwan Daily News], 30 August 2005.

[6]   In July 2007, the Taiwan government raised the monthly minimum wage to
      NT$17,642 (about US$534).
[7]   Lan Pei-Chia, *Global Cinderellas: Migrant Domestics and Newly Rich
      Employers in Taiwan* (Durham: Duke University Press, 2006) documents
      working conditions for domestic helpers in Taiwan in detail.
[8]   Anita Chan and Hong-zen Wang, unpublished survey data.

References

Beresford, Melanie. "Vietnam: The Transition from Central Planning". In *The
    Political Economy of South-East Asia: An Introduction*, edited by Garry
    Rodan, Kevin Hewison and Richard Robinson, pp. 179–204. Melbourne:
    Oxford University Press, 1997.
Cai Qifang. "Wailao shi yizhi bei bole haojicengpi de niu" [Foreign workers are
    like oxen sold many times]. *Taiwan Ribao* [Taiwan Daily News], 30 August
    2005.
Central Daily News. "Feilubin zhengfu bixu gaixuan yiche" [Philippines government
    should change its policy], Editorial, 4 August 1999.
Chen Ju. "Zhijie pingu kaiqi laozi huhui zhilu" [Direct hire opens a door for
    capital-labour mutual benefits] <http//www.e-agent.com.tw/main-diction.php>
    (accessed 8 January 2006).
Commercial Times Daily. "Pingyi lingjia jingji de wailao zhengce" [Regarding
    foreign labour policy and economic policy], Editorial, 12 December 2004.
Educational and Vocational Training Administration (EVTA). Council for Labour
    Affairs. "Appendix 1: 16 Appeals from Thai Workers and Responses from the
    Employer". *Gaoxiong jieyun Tailao renquan chacha zhuanan xiaozu diaocha
    baogao* [Report on Kaohsiung MRT Thai workers' human rights] <http://www.
    evta.gov.tw/labor/accou.> (accessed 30 December 2005).
———. "97nian waiji laogong yunyong ji guanli diaocha" [Survey on the use
    and management of migrant workers, 2008], Table 3 <http://www.evta.gov.
    tw/files/61/97年外勞提要分析(上網)2.doc> (accessed 10 December 2009).
Gainsborough, M. "Political Change in Vietnam: In Search of the Middle-Class
    Challenge to the State". *Asian Survey* 42, no. 5 (2002): 694–707.
Gills, D.-S. "Introduction: Neoliberal Economic Globalisation and Women in Asia".
    In *Women and Work in Globalising Asia*, edited by D.-S. Gills and Nicola
    Piper, pp. 1–12. London: Routledge, 2002.
Hardy, Andrew. "From a Floating World: Emigration to Europe from Post-war
    Vietnam". *Asian and Pacific Migration Journal* 11, no. 4 (2002): 463–84.
Hugo, G. "Asia on the Move: Research Challenges for Population geography".
    International Journal of Population Geography 2, no. 2 (1996): 95–118.
———. "International Migration in the Asia-Pacific Region: Emerging Trends
    and Issues". In *International Migration: Prospects and Policies in a Global*

Market, edited by D.S. Massey and J.E. Taylor, pp. 77–103. Oxford: Oxford University Press, 2004.

International Labour Organization (ILO). "Towards a Fair Deal for Migrant Workers in the Global Economy". Report VI for the International Labour Conference, 92nd Session. Geneva: ILO, 2004.

International Organization for Migration (IOM). *World Migration 2005: Costs and Benefits of International Migration*. Geneva: IOM, 2005.

Kerkvliet, B.J. Tria. "An Approach for Analysing State-Society Relations in Vietnam". *Sojourn: Journal of Social Issues in Southeast Asia* 16, no. 2 (2001): 238–78.

Lan Pei-Chia. 2006. *Global Cinderellas: Migrant Domestics and Newly Rich Employers in Taiwan*. Durham: Duke University Press.

Li Z. "*Yimin zhidu yu waiguoren renquan wenti zuotanhui zhuanti taolun*" [Roundtable discussion on migratory regime and foreigners' human rights]. *Taiwan Bentu Faxue Zazhi* [Taiwan Local Law Magazine] 48 (2003): 51–65.

Ministry of Interior Affairs (MOI). "Selected Demographic Data in Taiwan, 1975–2007" <http://www.ris.gov.tw/ch4/static/st20-12.xls> (accessed 7 July 2009).

Nguyen Hong Nhung. "Sushe shi gongren bifenggang haishi qiye kongzhihuan?" [Are dormitories worker's shelters or a part of capitalist control?]. Master's thesis, Graduate Institute of Southeast Asian Studies, National Chi Nan University, Puli, 2008.

Parrenas, R. S. *Servants of Globalization: Women, Migration and Domestic Work*. Stanford: Stanford University Press, 2001.

Piper, N. "Rights of Foreign Workers and the Politics of Migration in South-East and East Asia". *International Migration* 42, no. 5 (2004): 71–97.

Salt, John and Jeremy Stein. "Migration as a Business: The Case of Trafficking". *International Migration* 35, no. 4 (1997): 467–94.

Skeldon, R. "Trends in International Migration in the Asian and Pacific Region". *International Social Science Journal* 165 (2000): 369–82.

Tsai, M. and C. Chen. "Guojia, wailao zhengce yu shichang shijian: jingji shehuixue de fenxi" [State, foreign worker policy and market practices: An approach from economic sociology]. *Taiwan Shehui Yanjiu Jikan* [Taiwan: A Radical Social Science Quarterly] 27 (1997): 69–95.

Tseng, Yen-fen. "Yinjin waiji laogong de guozu zhengzhi" [Nationalist policy on importing foreign workers]. *Taiwan Shehui Xuekan* [Taiwan Journal of Sociology] 32 (2004): 1–58.

Tseng, Yen-fen and Hong-zen Wang. Governing Migrant Workers at a Distance: Managing the Temporary Status of Guestworkers in Taiwan. International Migration.

INDEX